Speaking Infinities

JEWISH CULTURE AND CONTEXTS

Published in association with
the Herbert D. Katz Center for Advanced Judaic Studies
of the University of Pennsylvania

Series Editors: Shaul Magid, Francesca Trivellato, Steven Weitzman

A complete list of books in the series
is available from the publisher.

SPEAKING INFINITIES

God and Language
in the Teachings of
Rabbi Dov Ber of Mezritsh

Ariel Evan Mayse

PENN

UNIVERSITY OF PENNSYLVANIA PRESS

PHILADELPHIA

Published by
University of Pennsylvania Press
Philadelphia, Pennsylvania 19104-4112
www.upenn.edu/pennpress

Printed in the United States of America on acid-free paper
1 3 5 7 9 10 8 6 4 2

Library of Congress Cataloging-in-Publication Data

Names: Mayse, Ariel Evan, author.
Title: Speaking infinities : God and language in the teachings of Rabbi Dov
    Ber of Mezritsh / Ariel Evan Mayse.
Other titles: Jewish culture and contexts.
Description: 1st edition. | Philadelphia : University of Pennsylvania Press,
    [2020] | Series: Jewish culture and contexts | Includes bibliographical
    references and index.
Identifiers: LCCN 2019049767 | ISBN 9780812252187 (hardcover)
Subjects: LCSH: Dov Baer, of Mezhirech, –1772. | Hasidism. | Language
    and langauges—Religious aspects—Judaism. | Mysticism—Judaism.
Classification: LCC BM198.2 .M395 2020 | DDC 296.7/12—dc23
LC record available at https://lccn.loc.gov/2019049767

For Adina,
with eternal love
unfolding across the
infinite journey of our words

Contemplate your voice and thoughts. Come to realize that they are nothing but divine vitality and spirit.

—Rabbi Shlomo of Lutsk

Heavy silence will crouch like a bull
on all the words.
And it will be as hard for me to part
from the names of things
as from the things themselves.

—Zelda Schneurson Mishkovsky

Contents

Preface

Dov Ber of Mezritsh is a figure shrouded in mystery. Although he is widely regarded as one of the most important and creative Jewish thinkers of the eighteenth century, his theology is exceptionally difficult and complex. Scholars and historians of religion have long attempted to make sense of his laconic homilies and penetrate his obtuse mystical symbolism. They have struggled to piece together his biography and better understand his place in the development of Hasidism. Indeed, interest in Dov Ber extends far beyond the walls of the academy. A wide range of Jewish seekers, thinkers, and philosophers have turned to Dov Ber's sophisticated devotional teachings as holding the seeds for a renewal of contemporary Jewish life. Present-day Hasidic leaders have been captivated by his mysterious teachings, seeing them as a remedy for a religious movement that has lost much of its spiritual momentum. His writings and indeed his outsize religious personality have had an enormous impact on the most important renewal movement of Jewish modernity.

This book argues that Dov Ber's reflections on the nature of language and the power of human speech rest at the heart of his allure. Abraham Joshua Heschel, a modern Jewish mystic who drank deeply from the wellsprings of Hasidism, argued that restoring the power and dignity of language was the key to human flourishing after the unspeakable tragedies of the twentieth century. "The renewal of man," claimed Heschel, "involves a renewal of language."[1] The noted philosopher Charles Taylor has suggested that the experience of modernity demands that we "return to, while reexamining, Aristotle's definition of the human being as 'Zwon echon logon'."[2] Reclaiming our identity as "speaking beings," individuals for whom the word is constitutive as well as communicative, is a crucial step in reckoning with the nature of what it can mean to be human.

Dov Ber's theory of language gives contemporary readers an opportunity to grasp the power of words as that which makes us human. He holds a vision of God as dwelling in the heart and mind of the mystic, embodied in the faculty of language and expressed through our words. Language tears away the veil that divides the mystic from God, but it accomplishes something more. Dov Ber's teachings are attentive to a sublime kind of intentional interiority, portraying the inner religious journey as a quest to unite human language with the ineffable echoes of divine silence. The language of our worship, argues Dov Ber, may break the chains of silence that shackle the Divine, giving life to the word and speaking God into being.

The present book was written with several different audiences in mind. For scholars interested in the development of Jewish mysticism—and Jewish thought and theology more generally—*Speaking Infinities* offers a novel interpretation of the vital religious thinker at the helm of early Hasidism. I am also seeking to reach a broader scholarly audience. To do so I have tried to make the difficult concepts at the core of Dov Ber's kabbalistic theology accessible to all those who wish to ponder the enduring enigma of the relationship of mind, language, and the life of the spirit. These are the motifs that undergird this book and guide its narrative. I hope that *Speaking Infinities* will hold much for those invested in the questions of language and what it means to be human in a world in which words have been devalued to the absurd.

Speaking Infinities grew forth from my experiences as a teacher in a wide variety of academic and religious settings. I struggle to make the often-recondite concepts of Jewish mysticism accessible to a diverse range of students engaged in the life of the mind. Teaching these Jewish sources as a humanist requires me to step beyond the boundaries of Jewish thought, showing students that mystical texts both ancient and modern may speak to the deepest questions of existential meaning. Humanities faculty are tasked with creating a space for the moral, ethical, and spiritual reflection that is a critical component of the quest for self-formation at the heart of liberal education. Embracing this role is, I believe, all the more important at research universities without divinity schools. We must help our students cultivate reverence for the immense power of language and reflect on the abyss that rises up when the word is misused.

Like all teachers, I struggle with the limits of language as a finite medium of communication. My time in the classroom is sown with frequent pauses, allowing students to gaze beyond the surface in an effort to consider the pulsing heart of the text. Together we enter the quiet liminal zone of interpretation, an echo chamber that surrounds its words as white spaces upon the page. But, like Dov Ber, my refusal to sink into permanent silence represents an embrace of the quest to share of my inner world with my students. Choosing speech over silence links us to other human beings, forming an intimate conduit of communication between masters and disciples, parents and children, and experts and novices. These words serve as vessels, channels through which the possessions of one human mind and soul are shared with others. In spending the past decade with the teaching of Dov Ber, writing about his life and thought has become a kind of spiritual practice. In what follows, I have attempted to share something of that with the readers of this book.

A Note on Transliteration and Style

Biblical passages are based on the New Jewish Publication Society 1999 translation, though in many cases I have adapted it to reflect the Maggid's understanding of the verse. The spelling of Hasidic figures and place-names accords with that of *The YIVO Encyclopedia of Jews in Eastern Europe*, ed. Gershon D. Hundert (New Haven: Yale University Press, 2008), and the Slavic spelling is also given when a location is mentioned for the first time.

Introduction

Opening Words

God emerges from silence through the pathways of language. All divine revelation, from creation to the theophany at Sinai, originates in a preverbal inner realm that gradually unfolds. The cosmos was formed through the divine word, perhaps even through the Torah itself. God's creative utterances continue to inhere in the cosmos, animating all existence and causing the world to shimmer with divine linguistic power. This process took on a different form at Sinai, as God's endless wisdom became cloaked in the mantle of words. Summoned by the prophet Moses from the reservoir of infinite silence, the Torah became a garment of letters for this boundless divine life-force. Rather than one-time events whose significance is relegated to historical memory, these processes continue as God—and God's language—is reborn through the power of human speech.

These bold reflections on the religious significance of language are found in the sermons of Rabbi Dov Ber Friedman of Mezritsh (1704–1772). Enshrined in Jewish memory simply as "the Maggid" (preacher), Dov Ber played a critical role in the formation of Hasidism—a movement of mystical renewal that became one of the most important and successful forces in modern Jewish life.[1] His homilies offer an original approach to the place of words in mystical experience, exploring a wide range of philosophical and devotional issues connected to language. It is commonly assumed in the study of religion that mystical illumination is necessarily beyond language. The homilies of Dov Ber demonstrate otherwise. His sermons portray words as a divine gift, referring to the faculty of language as nothing less than an aspect of God dwelling within the human being. God's presence in the cosmos, revealed with particular intensity in the heart and mind of the mystic, is manifest through the power of sacred speech.

Dov Ber's innovative theory of language is the singular key to unpacking his abstract mystical theology, which is complex, elliptical, and riven with tension and contradiction. This theme is also critical for understanding his teachings on the devotional life and religious practice. Sacred study, claims the Maggid, reenacts the intimate encounter between God and Israel at Sinai. The study of Torah becomes linked to the prelinguistic realm of divine thought, ushering a flood of creative inspiration. Because God's wisdom is continuously contracted into the words of Scripture, this revelatory act of divine self-limitation enables one to pierce the mantle of language and reclaim the sacred vitality within its letters. And, drawing a parallel between God and the human teacher, Dov Ber suggests that ineffable wisdom flows through the preacher's words—and, in particular, through his parables— into the mind of the disciple. The task of the discerning student, claims the Maggid, is to reverse the process of revelation by reaching inward to the ideational core concealed in his teacher's words.

The student's quest into the sacred language of the text is mirrored by the internal journey of the worshipper in prayer. Communion with God, taught Dov Ber, is attained as the worshipper articulates the words of prayer with concentration, arousing the divine vitality hidden within the letters of the liturgy. In such moments of uplift, the divine "word" speaks through the worshipper, revealing once more that human language may come to embody the divine quality of sacred speech. Accessing the sacred quality requires the worshipper to trace language back to its original divine source, stripping away all attachment to the physical world and entering the state of Nothing (*ayin*). This encounter with God's infinity and the resulting overflow of blessing leads the worshipper back to the spoken word. Language, argues Dov Ber, is never abandoned in the quest to stand in God's presence.

The Maggid's sophisticated theory of language is rooted in medieval Jewish mysticism, a vast literature that bears the influence of Neoplatonic and Islamic philosophies of language as well. Dov Ber follows the position of the Kabbalists, who describe Hebrew as a divine tongue holding unlimited cosmic secrets. But his theory of language goes deeper yet, since he suggests that *all* human speech may become filled with divine life-force and power. The gift of language may be abused, of course; speech does not automatically become a vessel for God's vitality. Vapid conversations are nothing more than husks, empty words devoid of holy energy. But, argues Dov Ber, the worshipper's contemplative awareness of the divine root of language may sanctify even ordinary conversations. The Maggid's homilies suggest that all languages—even their mundane forms—become redeemed when returned to their divine source.

This vision of language and the critical *novum* of all human speech as sacred was shaped by Dov Ber's encounters with Yisra'el ben Eliezer of Mezhbizh (d. 1760). The Ba'al Shem Tov (Master of the Good Name), or the BeSHT, as he was commonly known, eventually came to be viewed as the paterfamilias of Hasidism. His teachings put forward a vision of radical divine immanence, emphasizing joy in worship and the centrality of prayer. The BeSHT's teachings reserve a special place for the power of religious language. He describes the words of prayer, study, and even ordinary speech as vessels for God's presence. Letters—especially those of spoken words—effect healing by drawing spiritual vitality into the cosmos.[2]

I shall argue, however, that in many respects Dov Ber was the true founder of Hasidism and the foremost innovator of its early theology. He was a creative, independent, mystical thinker whose originality cannot be reduced to a "disciple" of the BeSHT. Dov Ber's introspective and contemplative religious path was markedly different from the approach suggested in the teachings of the BeSHT.[3] Taking the latter's notion of God's immanence as a kind of linguistic vitality echoing in the cosmos, Dov Ber developed a theory of language in which all human tongues have the potential to become sacred. This notion, intimated in the BeSHT's theology, is fully realized in the Maggid and further expanded in the many works of his disciples.

This understanding of the place of language in the life of the spirit provides an alternative to the common portrait of mystical uplift as beyond words. The Maggid's vision of sacred speech as the potential of all language also overturns a second assumption shared by many historians and sociologists of religion: a fundamental and insoluble dichotomy between the sacred and the mundane. Émile Durkheim, for example, argued that "the division of the world into two comprehensive domains, one sacred, the other profane, is the hallmark of religious thought."[4] This totalizing and hierarchical categorization of religious life—including language—remains a regnant assumption, though it has been critiqued in recent years.[5]

In their *Ritual and its Consequences*, Adam Seligman and his coauthors have offered a paradigm on religious praxis and language that will help us illuminate the complexity of the Maggid's theory. They argued that "ritual

is something that is happening to some extent all the time, in the most seemingly common, mundane aspects of our lives."[6] Ritual therefore "teaches us to
live within and between different boundaries rather than seeking to absolu-
tize them."[7] Their book extends ritual theory to the domains of architecture,
music, and literature. Their arguments can—and should—be extended to
conceptions of religious language as well. The notion of a universal division
between the holy and mundane realms, however, has hardly disappeared
from contemporary scholarship.[8] The idea of a *lingua sacra* is indeed common
to many religious traditions—including Judaism—but the Maggid's depiction of human speech as a manifestation of God's language brooks no such
essential distinction and demands a different approach to the interface of sacred and mundane.[9]

The sanctity of human language in giving voice to divine silence depends
not on the singular quality of a particular tongue but on the contemplative
attunement of the speaker.[10] It was Martin Buber who first claimed Hasidism as unique among religious teaching in its insistence on breaking down
this distinction, claiming all of human life as potentially embraced by the
realm of the sacred. The Maggid's theory of sacred speech, reaching beyond
the sacralization of Hebrew into the realm of all verbal expression, is a key
element in this path of expanding the boundaries of the holy.

Dov Ber's theory of language is also characterized by contradictions. He
was not a systematic philosopher; attempts to interpret his homilies as a
coherent corpus will obscure the flexibility of his religious symbolism by
glossing over contradictions and pressures. His claim that all languages—
not just Hebrew—may become divine is a significant break with the tradition of thought within Jewish mysticism called Kabbalah, but it is not
consistent throughout the entire corpus of teachings attributed to him. Dov
Ber's works, like the kabbalistic theology to which they were heir, was
dominated by a kind of ethnocentrism in which "Israel" and "humanity" are
constantly conflated.[11] In his teachings, the holy power of words may be awakened only by the Jewish people, though this does not seem to him to negate
the possibility that all languages may become sacred.[12]

Another sustained tension characterizes Dov Ber's teachings, a paradox
that emerges from the very core of his theological project: God is immanently present and, in a sense, radically hidden and perhaps even absent.[13]
The Maggid's intricate philosophy rests on a formulation regarding the relationship between *yesh* (being) and *ayin* (Nothing), concepts inherited from
medieval Kabbalah and reworked by the Maggid into a unique metaphysics.[14]

Ayin, the divine Naught, is described as a pool of limitless potential beyond even the emanated structures of the Godhead itself. *Yesh*, on the other hand, is the existence of a world made possible by God's "diminishment" or "contraction" (*tsimtsum*) of this infinite and wordless light. The Maggid's theology describes *yesh* and *ayin* as mutually dependent rather than two stages in a linear process. The cosmos is suffused with a pool of unified potential, a silent divine language of Naught that echoes within all things.[15] Just as the spoken word is animated by thought and the meaning that it conceals, the physical world—and the human being within it—thus gives expression to God's otherwise unknowable and unexpressed word.

One might imagine that a human being should be wordless before this Naught, but the Maggid's teachings offer an alternative. His descriptions of the unfolding of God often evoke the stirring images of a parent and child, or a teacher with a student. Such personal and highly anthropomorphic images of God seem to unravel the Maggid's abstract theology of the divine Naught rather than advancing it.[16] But they do not. Rather, one sees here a tension between wordlessness and language that can be found in other faiths. Islamic and Christian literatures are filled with what is often called "apophatic" or negative theology, a theory that posits that God may be described or known only through negation rather than positive attribution.[17] "By not speaking, not desiring, and not thinking, one arrives at the true and perfect mystical silence," said the seventeenth-century priest Miguel de Molinos, "wherein God speaks with the soul, communicates himself to her, and in the abyss of her own depth, teaches her the most perfect and exalted wisdom."[18] Such teachings assert that language must be avoided because the Divine, ineffable and imponderable, may be known only through tranquil waters of soulful silence.[19]

This theological and devotional path, also described as the *via negativa*, reached its zenith in Jewish literature in the works of Moses Maimonides (1135–1204). "We are dazzled by His beauty," wrote Maimonides, "and He is hidden from us because of the intensity with which He becomes manifest, just as the sun is hidden to eyes that are too weak to apprehend it. . . . Silence with regard to You is praise."[20] The Maggid, like almost all Jewish thinkers after the thirteenth century, wrote in the shadow of negative theology and its various kabbalistic reformulations. But Dov Ber's sophisticated theology of language, linked to the symbolic vocabulary of earlier Jewish mysticism, offers a powerful vision of the renewal of God's word through the transformation of human language.[21]

Dov Ber's teachings illustrate a phenomenon that Michael Sells has called the "performative intensity" of mystical texts. This rhetorical turn allows language to fold inward, thus bridging the gulf between God's transcendence and human experience. Sells argues that "real contradictions occur when language engages the ineffable transcendent, but these contradictions are not illogical."[22] Words enable a worshipper to embrace the paradox of God's simultaneous presence and absence, allowing for a synergy that transcends the dichotomy between the two states of being. "There is an infinite regress," says Sells, "in which every referent recedes beyond the name that would designate it. Language becomes indefinite and open-ended. No closure is reached. Each saying demands a further unsaying."[23] This tack of using language to overcome its own shortcomings is meant to spark an experience in the reader—or the listener. It evokes "an event that is—in its movement beyond the structures of self and other, subject and object—structurally analogous to the event of mystical union."[24] Mystical theology spins words into a gossamer of paradox and power, gesturing outward without forcing the worshipper to compromise his foothold in the world of language or in the ineffable beyond.

The rhetorical impact and linguistic wizardry of the Maggid's homilies were noted by one of the early visitors to his school in the town of Mezritsh. Less concerned with abstract cosmology than most medieval Jewish mystics, the Maggid's teachings on creation and revelation describe the ways in which these processes are paralleled by—and manifest within—the inner religious life of the individual. To illustrate his points, the Maggid often employs parables and examples drawn from the realm of human experience. This desire to ground the implications of his theology in the terms of religious devotion is one of the defining characteristics of Hasidic teachings.

Something more is at stake in the Maggid's theory of language as spanning between the human and the Divine. The Maggid's teachings attempt to maintain a transcendent idea of God even as the homilies constantly underscore the presence of divine vitality in the cosmos and in human words.[25] His abstract God is neither the austere Prime Mover of Jewish rationalists nor the divine watchmaker of the philosophical deists, but a God born of language that represents a remarkable departure from the doctrines of the medieval Kabbalists. Offering language as a bridge between the polar extremes of divine absence and presence, Dov Ber describes words as linking God's silent transcendence with the sacred immanence manifest in words.[26]

The quest to draw these two realms together, claimed Dov Ber, rests pon the fulcrum of human speech.

History and the Languages of God

Early twentieth-century studies of mysticism tended to emphasize contemplative silence as the highest rung of the religious quest. The works of William James, Evelyn Underhill, and Rudolf Otto, among many others, pointed toward something that they described as a universal spiritual experience, a common core beyond the realm of language that is shared across faith traditions.[27] William Ralph Inge, a prominent Anglican priest and an influential professor of divinity, claimed that "the phase of thought or feeling which we call Mysticism has its origin in that which is the raw material of all religion, and perhaps of all philosophy and art as well, namely, that dim consciousness of the beyond, which is part of our nature as human beings."[28] The wordless heart of mystical religion, goes the argument, is essentially the same across all traditions. Silent and timeless experiences of divine transcendence are only later translated into the specifics of language by individual worshippers.

These philosophers and scholars were looking to find something that transcended institutional religion in their time. They sought a universal spiritual current that might remain untouched by the host of threats posed by modernity—biblical criticism, historical scholarship, growing secularism—intellectual challenges that appeared to be unraveling the tradition before their eyes.[29] This attempt to identify an essential core of all mystical traditions sparked critiques from a wide variety of scholars and philosophers of religion.[30] But the notion of wordless silence as the height of mystical experience exerted a powerful influence on twentieth-century Jewish theologians and philosophers as well.

The famed Martin Buber (1878–1965), who spent over five decades bringing the spiritual riches of Hasidism to a non-Hasidic readership, was one of these scholars.[31] In his 1909 book, *Ecstatic Confessions*, Buber writes that "what is experienced in ecstasy (if one may really speak of a 'what') is the unity of the I. . . . One is removed from the commotion, removed into the most silent, speechless heavenly kingdom—removed even from language."[32] A similar approach to the limits of language appears in Buber's later dialogical writings. In his *I and Thou* (1923), for example, he claims that "only

silence toward the Thou, the silence of all tongues . . . leaves the Thou free
and stands together with it in reserve where the spirit does not manifest itself but is."[33] He frequently emphasized the power of spoken language to
unite individuals in true and earnest dialogue, but Buber continued to emphasize silence as critical to such encounters and as a key part of his existential theology.[34]

Gershom Scholem (1897–1982), a younger colleague of Buber's and the
founder of the academic study of Kabbalah, sought to chart a very different
narrative regarding the place of language in Jewish thought.[35] Scholem
wanted to distinguish Jewish mysticism from all the other kinds of mystical
religion, and he quickly seized on the kabbalistic theory of language in order to do so. He argued that the Kabbalists met their God through the portal of words, retreating only rarely into claims of ineffability.[36] Electrified by
issues of language, he set out to write his dissertation about this subject.
Scholem ultimately chose to write on a more constrained topic—a critical
edition and translation of an early kabbalistic book—but investigating the
place of language in Jewish mysticism became the work of his life across the
next six decades.[37]

Scholem's insistence on the linguistic nature of Kabbalah vis-à-vis all
other mysticisms, offered in response to Buber and the other universalizing
scholars, was already put forward in Scholem's landmark *Major Trends in Jewish Mysticism*.[38] Noting that although the Kabbalists shared the common
mystical complaint regarding "the utter inadequacy of words," he argued that
Jewish mystics are distinguished by their "metaphysically positive attitude
towards language as God's own instrument."[39] For medieval Jewish mystics,
Scholem claimed, the encounter with God happens within—and through—
the words of the Torah, understood by the Kabbalists as a tapestry of divine
names filled with sacred light.[40] Other Jewish mystics stepped into the divine presence through the words of prayer, which formed the structure of a
contemplative inner quest toward the upper reaches of the Godhead. In the
eyes of these medieval mystics, language—and particularly Hebrew—
represented far more than a conventional means of communication. Human
words were described as a repercussive echo of divine revelation, a powerful
force emanating from God's most sacred name and linked to it evermore.

"Language is the essence of the universe," said Scholem. His fullest and
most direct remarks offered on this subject appeared in a two-part essay.[41]
These were delivered first as lectures at the Eranos conference in 1970, where,
as Joseph Dan has argued, Scholem explored "the position of Jewish mysticism

within the wider framework of the humanities" together with scholars like Henri Corbin and Mircea Eliade.[42] In this essay, a tour de force of erudition and insight, Scholem argues that the medieval Kabbalists embraced

> the conception that creation and revelation are both principally and essentially auto-representations of God himself, in which, as a consequence and in accordance with the infinite nature of the divinity, certain instants of the divine are introduced, which can only be communicated in terms of symbols in the finite and determined realm of all that is created . . . [and] the further conception that language is the essence of the universe. . . .
>
> The language of God, which is crystallized in the name of God and, in the last analysis, in the one single name itself, which is its center, is the basis of all spoken language, in which it is reflected and symbolically manifest.[43]

Scholem suggests that the mysterious divine language described by Kabbalists is one without grammar, possessive of a symbolic quality that allows it "to communicate something which goes way beyond the sphere which allows for expression and formation."[44] This sacred godly tongue is essentially a translation of the ineffable divine name (Y-H-V-H, known as the Tetragrammaton), recast in language through creation and revelation. But it is more than that: this divine language is the root of "spoken language" and thus the origin of all human speech.

Such ruminations on the linguistic theory of Kabbalah did not emerge ex nihilo. Scholem was a close friend of the Jewish philosopher and literary critic Walter Benjamin (1892–1940). Scholem's reading of Kabbalah and its theology was shaped by Benjamin's "On Language as Such and on the Language of Man." Though published posthumously, the essay was written in 1916 and shown to Scholem not long thereafter. The young Scholem, already interested in issues of language, was swiftly enraptured. In the conclusion of Benjamin's essay, we read: "The whole of nature, too, is imbued with a nameless, unspoken language, the residue of the creative word of God, which is preserved in man as the cognizing name and above man as the judgement suspended over him. The language of nature is comparable to a secret password that each sentry passes to the next in his own language, but the meaning of the password is the sentry's language itself. All higher language is a translation of lower ones, until in ultimate clarity the word of God unfolds, which is the unity of this movement made up of language."[45] Human language evokes the infinite language of being, drawing on its power and translating this vital divine tongue into names. God's utterances continue to resonate in the world, though, as Benjamin notes, "the word of God has not remained creative; it has become in one part receptive, even if receptive to language."[46] Nature and the cosmos are constituted by this ineffable language, one that is given articulation through the partnership of human speech. All human tongues—"so many translations, so many languages"[47]—are partial renderings of this infinite speech rooted in God's essence; human languages are grounded in the divine name, which animates words and yet dwells ever beyond them.

Scholem's writings on the linguistic theory of Kabbalah should be seen as an attempt to use this paradigm to interpret the literature of medieval Jewish mysticism. It is therefore quite striking that Scholem refused to apply this way of thinking about mysticism and language to his studies of eighteenth-century Hasidism. He was deeply ambivalent about Hasidic theology, often downplaying its creativity. "This burst of mystical energy was unproductive of new religious *ideas*," claimed Scholem, "to say nothing of new theories of mystical knowledge."[48] The sole innovations of Hasidism, in his view, lay in its new form of social leadership and its ability to translate kabbalistic symbols into a vocabulary for internal psychological processes.

It was passive renunciation and the quest for meditative silence that Scholem identified as the heart of Dov Ber's spiritual path. Followed closely by his student Joseph Weiss, Scholem suggested that the Maggid portrayed *devekut* (communion with God) as total self-effacement and contemplative quiet.[49] Although Scholem and Weiss were hesitant to draw comparisons between Hasidism and the mystical literatures of Christianity and Islam, their reading of Hasidism was guided by visions of wordless *ekstasis* and self-annihilation in these traditions. Scholem vocally rejected Buber's existentialist reading of Hasidism and his reading of Jewish mysticism in general, but on this point, it seems that Scholem was himself deeply influenced by Buber's interpretation of the mystic quest as a journey toward wordless silence.[50]

The work of Rivka Schatz-Uffenheimer, the first and only scholar to devote an academic monograph to Dov Ber and his school, reiterates this thesis in greater depth.[51] Her 1968 *Hasidism as Mysticism* (*Ha-Hasidut ke-Mistikah*), which began as a doctoral dissertation written under Scholem's watchful eye, explores Hasidism as a mystical phenomenon akin to early modern Christian quietism. Though Schatz-Uffenheimer admits to certain differences that distinguish early Hasidism from other mysticisms, her book portrays the Maggid's teachings on wordless rapture as largely similar to those of the Christian quietists. "Total silence," she claims, "accompanies the peak of the ecstatic state."[52] Describing Dov Ber's approach to worship, Schatz-Uffenheimer argues: "Man continues to recite the prayers until an awesome stillness descends upon him, and his thought ceases to function in particular. . . . In the word-play of the Hasidim: 'the I (ani) becomes Nought (ayin)': a condition of utter annulment is established in the 'flash of an eye,' tantamount to the state of nothingness sought by the mystic."[53] This attempt to identify self-annihilation and contemplative silence as the cornerstones of the Maggid's theology is clearly indebted to conceptions of mysticism from the early twentieth century. And, in attempting to prove her case, Schatz-Uffenheimer fundamentally misconstrued the Maggid's positive theory of language and his bold embrace of the revelatory capacity of human and divine words.[54]

Critical reevaluations of Scholem's and Schatz-Uffenheimer's approach to the school of the Maggid have appeared in recent decades. Moshe Idel, Seth Brody, and Ron Margolin have argued that the worshipper's empowered return to the world—rather than passive renunciation—is the ultimate goal of Dov Ber's religious journey.[55] Mendel Piekarz rejected Scholem's and Schatz-Uffenheimer's uniform definition of devekut as mystical "annulment" in all early Hasidic sources. By contrast, he suggests that the term was used by Hasidic thinkers like Dov Ber to describe a broad spectrum of religious experiences with varying degrees of intensity.[56] Examining Dov Ber's contemplative path, Haviva Pedaya has insightfully demonstrated that the Maggid's introspective journey does not necessarily demand the full transcendence of speech.[57]

It is true that the Maggid refers to a realm of creativity and inspiration that lies beyond language. It is into this region that the mystic journeys in his contemplative prayer, tracing spoken words back to their roots in the mind, and then the ineffable beyond. Schatz-Uffenheimer was undoubtedly correct in highlighting the Maggid's distrust of the physical realm.[58] But for all his pietistic distaste for pleasure, Dov Ber's embrace of words as a divine gift was absolute and unequivocal. This distinction between the Maggid's positive attitude toward language and his deep ambivalence about the material realm is absolutely critical, and it is one that has been vastly underappreciated in scholarship thus far.[59]

The realm of quiet contemplation, however, is restricted by its silence. Flashes of inspiration, human as well as divine, are but fleeting sparks until these insights are revealed through the structures of speech. Dov Ber argues that the unfolding journeys of human cognition and speech are firmly intertwined with the divine processes of revelation. The Maggid's teachings describe the human consciousness as rooted in God's infinite wisdom (*hokhmah*), a flow of divine energy that infuses the physical world with vitality. The mystic must venture into the ineffable realm, moving beyond his personal identity and transcending the self.

The purpose of this journey lies not in the mystic's permanent absorption into God's wisdom but in the return to the community and this-worldly service. God's revelation through language, claimed Dov Ber, is a reciprocal process. Words and letters, which represent a divine gift, must be restored to their godly source through human efforts.[60] The task of the worshipper is to draw vitality into the words of prayer and study, coming to know God's presence through contemplating the unfolding divine language of the cosmos and the sacred power hidden in the words of Scripture. Doing so, claims Dov Ber, returns human language to its divine source and unfetters God from the isolation of silence.

I argue here that Schatz-Uffenheimer and Scholem have, in many respects, missed the key to the Maggid's theory of language and thus to his theological project. Setting this right will highlight his take on the imbrication of human and divine speech, shedding new light on religious teachings of Hasidism, the linguistic theories of modern and medieval Jewish mysticism, and the place of language in mystical religion more broadly. The present book takes the insights of Scholem's thesis about the linguistic theory of Kabbalah and applies them to the theologian at the heart of early Hasidism. Dov Ber recast language as a mode of continuously summoning forth the Divine from the bonds of ineffable silence. In contrast to the dialectical emergence of human language from God's ineffable name, described at length by Scholem, the Maggid saw divine language as being renewed through sacred speech as God and the worshipper are joined in human speech.

Radiating Outward

The influential theory of language shared by Scholem and Benjamin was deeply shaped by the writings of Johann Georg Hamann (1730–1788), a

German philosopher and Christian Kabbalist whose life directly overlapped with that of the Maggid.[61] His works were deeply concerned with issues of language both human and divine, and reveal an interesting convergence of mysticism and modern philosophy.[62] Fiercely critical of rationalist approaches to language, Hamann's thinking on this subject differed significantly from many prominent comparative linguists, philosophers, and philologists of the eighteenth century.[63] His influential "Aesthetica in Nuce: A Rhapsody in Cabbalistic Prose" (1762) argues for the existence of a divine language that is constituent of being:

> Speak, that I may see you!—This wish was fulfilled by creation, which is a speech to creatures through creatures; for day unto day utters speech, and night unto night shows knowledge. Its watchword traverses every clime to the end of the world, and its voice can be heard in every dialect. The fault may lie where it will (outside or in us). . . .
>
> To speak is to translate—from an angelic language into a human language, that is, to translate thoughts into words.[64]

God's immanent word is broadcast through creation, for all of nature conceals a hidden echo of the divine language.[65] Poetry, argued Hamann, is the most elevated form of language, a tongue closest to the divine source from which all human speech emerges. This interweaving of divine and human language, of God's word as interpreted and translated into human speech, is key. "Everything divine, however, is also human," writes Hamann in another essay on language. "This *communicatio* of divine and human *idiomatum* is a fundamental law and the master-key of all our knowledge and of the whole visible economy."[66] The idea of "communication of attributes" (*communicatio idiomatum*) was long used by Christian theologians to explain the singular interchange of human and divine properties within the figure of Jesus. But Hamann surprises in invoking the term in referring to the totality of human language as a translation of God's ineffable speech.

The implications of this theory of language for the study of Hasidism, one of the most important Jewish movements of the past three hundred years, has remained a story yet untold. Dov Ber of Mezritsh and Johann Georg Hamann were separated by a vast gulf of geography, culture, and religion. Though Hamann's essay was published some ten years before Dov Ber's death, their teachings on the imbrication of divine and human language were obviously unknown to one another. Yet these two creative religious thinkers lived in the same century, nurtured by many of the same medieval mystical traditions. Hamann's description of God's language of creation mirrors the Maggid's homilies about the divine word reverberating in the cosmos and becoming translated into human speech. Scholem's linguistic interpretation of medieval Kabbalah was drawn from his conversations with Benjamin, and both were shaped by their discovery of Hamann.

My goal here is not to put forward a comparative work. We have noted the dangers of interpreting the Maggid's teachings through the broadly construed lens of mysticism. And yet, as the example of Hamann drives home, the broader context is important. To what extent may we situate a figure such as the Maggid in a discourse with which he was totally unfamiliar? How might we go about this task without effacing the unique elements of Dov Ber's legacy?

Here are paths I might have taken. One way to go about this is to search for resonances that span intellectual traditions, exploring similarities between the Maggid's teachings and those of other religious thinkers without looking for direct historical influence. Such affinities are indeed readily apparent. Schatz-Uffenheimer's comparison of Dov Ber to the Christian quietists was deeply problematic, but it was not entirely off the mark. Another instructive comparison may be found in the early *recogimiento* movement and the emphasis on mystical prayer among the sixteenth-century Spanish Franciscans.[67]

Conceptual links between Dov Ber's theology and medieval Islamic thinking on language as a mediating force between God and man are particularly striking. Hasidic and Kabbalistic theories could easily be linked to Islamic thought on everything from the divinity of language, to the differences—and similarities—between human and divine language, to the preexistence of the Qur'an and the idea of a primordial Scripture cloaked in language through revelation.[68] There is a fascinating comparison waiting to be drawn between the Maggid's conception of divine wisdom (*hokhmah*) and the cosmology and contemplative systems of certain strains of Tibetan Buddhism.[69] Exploring such correspondences are beyond the scope of the present work, but there is another very important book to be written on the subject.

There are problems, however, with these paths. Recent approaches to comparative study of religion tend to emphasize discontinuity rather than "*the recollection of similarity*" that was generally favored in the past.[70] The distinctions that emerge from the focused, restrained, and contextualized comparison of religious thinkers are often more telling and instructive than their points of similarity.[71] In considering this point, we might compare the Maggid's theology to the following fragment of a sermon by Meister Eckhart, the thirteenth-century Mendicant preacher: "In the soul's essence there is no activity, for the powers she works emanate from the ground of being. Yet in that ground is the silent 'middle': here is nothing but rest and celebration for this birth, this act, that God the Father may speak his word there, for this is by nature receptive to nothing save the divine essence, without mediation. Here God enters the soul with his all, not merely with a part, God enters her the ground of the soul."[72] A similar paradox of God's silence, though rarely posed as such, is there at the heart of the Maggid's homilies. Rather than Eckhart's description of sinking into the Naught or the wordless "ground" (*Grund*) of the soul, for Dov Ber the rift between the human and divine realms must be bridged through language. The worshipper traces his words back to their divine root, coming to see that human speech is *the* revelatory garment for God's unfolding wisdom.

My choice has been to explore the Maggid's theory of language by interrogating his philosophy on its own terms. This mode of scholarship will, I believe, disclose the similarities between his thinking and that of other religious thinkers without occluding the distinctions. As Elliot Wolfson has put it, "Delving deeply into the ground of one tradition opens paths to explore others."[73] Some of these forays are found in the footnotes of the present book. I hope that attentive readers will see how Dov Ber's teachings can inform and enrich the study of other religious traditions.

What we find as a result of this focused exploration is that the Maggid's vision presents a contrast—quite stark, at times—to the Western philosophical tradition and modern language theory. Dov Ber's approach differs fundamentally, for example, from that of analytical philosophy of language, a discourse that pulls toward empirical questions of mind and reality, of propositional logic, of sense and nonsense, of truth claims and their veracity. Such issues are a far cry from the issues at the heart of Dov Ber's sermons. He was an associative exegete, a preacher, and a religious leader who was concerned with theological, homiletical, and experiential dimensions of language.

Of course, there are resonances between Dov Ber's theology and modern philosophies of language. The Maggid's frequent deconstruction of biblical words or verses, breaking them into smaller units and penetrating

through their semantic meaning, bears a certain resemblance to the interpretive mode of critical theory.[74] Dov Ber's teachings on kabbalistic *mythos*
share something in common with the theory of mythic language and symbolic forms advanced by Ernst Cassirer (1874–1954). More immediately, the
Maggid's description of students unpacking the words of a teacher in order
to discover their ineffable core evokes the hermeneutical theory of Friedrich
Schleiermacher (1768–1834). "Hermeneutics and rhetoric are intimately related," he claimed, "in that every act of understanding is the reverse side of
an act of speaking, and one must grasp the thinking that underlies a given
statement."[75] The Maggid was another teacher for whom issues of exegesis
and communication were critical to philosophy of language. Schleiermacher,
another German theologian and philosopher whose career overlapped with
Dov Ber's, provides yet another portal through which to place the Maggid
in dialogue with modern language theory.

Such resonances—and contrasts—remind us that Dov Ber was a religious thinker who flourished on the threshold of modernity, a theologian
whose life overlapped with the careers of Moses Mendelssohn, Immanuel
Kant, and Ludwig van Beethoven. The eighteenth century was a time of great
foment in terms of thinking about language in particular. Developments in
philology, philosophy, and comparative linguistics led to new theories regarding the nature and origins of language and the interface between different tongues.[76] This shift came in the wake of a radical transformation in
the attitude toward language, as religious medieval paradigms of language,
regnant for hundreds of years, were beginning to change.[77] Unchained from
its divine moorings, language was increasingly seen as a construct of mankind rather than a divine creation. Particular languages were valorized because
of their antiquity and elegance, or their capacity to convey sublime philosophical ideas, but not because of their sacred origins.

Returning to the Maggid's historical context, the ideas of the Enlightenment and the Jewish Haskalah reached the Jews of Congress Poland and
the Russian Empire only in the nineteenth century.[78] The elite scholars of
Vilna or Brody may have been acquainted with some of these philosophical
developments, but there is no evidence suggesting that they were known to
the Maggid. Any contact his younger students may have had with the Haskalah took place after the Maggid's death. As an insular Jewish thinker from
a small shtetl, Dov Ber lived and taught in an intellectual framework where
medieval and even premedieval certainties remained untouched by the challenge of nascent modernity. The Maggid's adopted home of Mezritsh was

entirely different from the cosmopolitan Vilna inhabited by Eliyahu ben Shlomo (known as the Ga'on or "Genius"). This unflagging critic of Hasidism lived in a veritable "epicenter" of Jewish learning and intellectual life.[79] Mezritsh was, by all accounts, a small and relatively unimpressive town, one unlikely to be pierced by the lance of secularism or reform.

Irreligiosity among the youth was by no means unknown even in the small cities of eastern Europe in the 1700s.[80] Some of these young seekers and rebels ended up in the Maggid's court, attracted by his theological daring and his exegetical craft. Solomon Maimon, one of the Maggid's eighteenth-century listeners, attested that "each of us felt the part of the sermon dealing with his verse contained something referring directly to his own pressing personal concerns. Naturally, we were amazed."[81] There is, of course, no reason to suggest any influence of the Western philosophical tradition on Dov Ber's thought—or vice versa. But I am arguing that the Maggid's teachings should be interpreted as part of a broader intellectual landscape and the new conceptions of language emerging in the eighteenth century.[82]

Hasidism is a product of the eastern European milieu in which it was born. The social and cultural placement of early Hasidism—the physical proximity to non-Jews, the daily contacts between Jews and non-Jews, the relative lack of persecution in the Polish-Lithuanian Commonwealth—is important for this discussion.[83] But many of the Jews in these lands spoke the local Slavic vernacular, as well as Yiddish, with Hebrew limited to the learned elites. This social and economic integration, albeit a limited one, may have played an implicit role in their expansive view of sacred speech.[84] As a movement of a spiritual renewal that took root in the small sub-Carpathian villages of eastern Europe, Hasidism and its spiritual vision represent a different instantiation of Jewish modernity emerging concurrently with the projects of Mendelssohn and Eliyahu of Vilna.

The pressing questions that spurred Dov Ber's theological quest were not born ex nihilo in the eighteenth century, nor have they lost their relevance to modern thinking about language. Issues of holiness and words, of the limits of the mind and the gift of language, of the imbricated expressions of divine and human speech—these are enduring struggles of the spirit. In gesturing toward how one might place Dov Ber's teachings in a realm of philosophical and religious discourse other than his own, I aim to show that the Maggid's teachings provide contemporary readers with a case study through which to consider the marbled intersection of philosophy of language and the study of Jewish mysticism. The Maggid's theology turns spoken words, inner experience, and contemplative union with God into allies rather than enemies. Though often cast as perennial opposites, the Maggid's teachings on language and mystical devotion offer a compelling alternative to the commonly held assumption of incompatibility.

A Life and Its Echoes

The present book begins with an exploration of Dov Ber's life, such as it may be known to us. The Maggid's biography must be gleaned from scattered anecdotes, legends, and occasional historical sources, as we know frustratingly little about his career. This lack of information forces us to distinguish between the historical personage of Dov Ber of Mezritsh, about whom very few verifiable details remain, and the figure that emerges from the composite array of textual and oral traditions that have shaped the memory of the Maggid and his legacy. Drawing on these different sources will demonstrate the ways in which the image—or images—of the Maggid has been set into the crown of Hasidism.

Such biographical lacunae are further complicated by the fact that the Maggid was a preacher, a teacher of living communities, who left almost nothing behind him in the way of religious writings. Hasidim emerged from, and spread within, what was essentially an oral culture.[85] Its earliest leaders generally did not choose to put their homilies into writing, and their sermons were transcribed by disciples. As these homilies were set into writing and eventually printed, the teachings were translated from Yiddish into Hebrew. These transpositions further complicate the usability of Hasidic homilies, including those of the Maggid, for contemporary scholarship.

The earliest layers of Hasidic literature, however, have preserved a remarkably rich array of the Maggid's teachings captured by his disciples. These textual artifacts include printed homilies, *regimen vitae* (conduct literature), unpublished manuscripts, and a wealth of traditions quoted in the works of Dov Ber's students. Each of these corpora greets the scholar with unique features and challenges. The published collections of the Maggid's homilies, starting with *Maggid Devarav le-Ya'akov* (1781), feature most prominently in this book, but I draw on the full spectrum of teachings attributed to the Maggid in seeking to tease forth his theory of language. Without assuming the existence of a single authoritative text of any one sermon, and without attempting to reconstruct Maggid's *ipsissima verba*, I explore the diversity of these traditions while tracking their consistency.

Dov Ber was a daring theologian, the founder of a central Hasidic school, and a leader whose teachings guided the emergence of a socioreligious movement that shaped the course of Jewish modernity. He occupies a venerated place in the self-understanding of almost all Hasidic communities from the eighteenth century to the present day. These groups have cultivated different images of this early Hasidic leader, preserving—and recasting—his life and sermons in divergent ways. The process of internal Hasidic canonization began in the years immediately following his death, as Dov Ber's different students carried forward his memory and teachings and reinterpreted them in a variety of ways.

The book and its exploration of the Maggid's theology conclude not far from where they began, examining Dov Ber's claim that redemption is the reawakening of sacred speech. Like an enormous mountain that can be moved only one stone at a time, this complete transformation of language must be accomplished through the work of individuals rather than by the efforts of a single leader in one fell swoop. Each person is faced with a unique task, renewing God's word by sanctifying human speech and unpacking the echoes of infinity from its words and letters. This vision of uplifting language as undertaken by the members of a community rather than an individual *tsaddik* may well reflect the early emergence of Hasidism from among Dov Ber's many different disciples.

Despite the relatively closed nature of his theological discourse, universal themes emerge from Dov Ber's life and his theory of language. The tale of the Maggid's life is the story of an introspective mystic, painfully shy and utterly confident in equal measures. Wary of the company of others and alert to the boundaries of language, the Maggid was a religious intellectual for whom God is revealed through the innermost reaches of the mind and heart. But Dov Ber was pulled toward a life of public teaching and leadership.

He became "the Maggid" only when a circle of disciples had come to see him as their spiritual guide, clustering around his charismatic religious presence and describing him as a master whose words united heaven and earth. As a preacher at the heart of this community, Dov Ber struggled with language and its limits in attempting to convey his intricate theology, and, perhaps, his own religious experiences. Rather than admitting defeat, sinking into claims of ineffability or allowing himself to remain in private contemplative silence, the Maggid embraced the quality of human speech as a vehicle for divine revelation.

The careful reader of this book will find a critique of Scholem's theology of language alongside his and Schatz-Uffenheimer's reading of early Hasidism. In a 1926 letter to Franz Rosenzweig on the nature of modern Hebrew, Scholem suggested the scarcely tamped-down religious nature of the language would explode once more. "After invoking the ancient names day after day, we will no longer be able to hold off their power," writes Scholem. "We have awakened them, and they shall appear, for we have summoned them up with awesome power."[86] Despite the intentions of secular Zionism, thought Scholem, the Hebrew language could not be permanently released from its sacred associations. Such anxieties continued in Scholem's *Diogenes* essays, but in these later works he is keen to express God's absence from language and the "silence of tradition": "This, then, is the great crisis of language in which we find ourselves. We are no longer able to grasp the last summit of that mystery that once dwelt in it. The fact that language can be spoken is, in the opinion of the Kabbalists, owed to the name, which is present in language. What value and worth language will be—the language from which God will have withdrawn—is the question which must be posed by those who still believe that they can hear the echo of the vanished word of the creation in the immanence in the world."[87] For Scholem, as for Benjamin and Hamann, "only the poets presumably have the answer" to this hollowing-out of language. God has withdrawn from language, claimed Scholem, and the sacred resonance is no longer accessible to its modern speakers.

The Maggid of Mezritsh, a voice from the eighteenth century, offers a very different perspective on the "crisis of language." He represents the world that still existed prior to the desacralization of language, but I hope to demonstrate that his theory has much to share with those who strive for a postmodern resacralization of speech. Dead words fill our lives, from social media to empty—though dangerous—political rhetoric, but we have forgotten the capacity of language to become an echo chamber in which sacred reverberations linger. Dov Ber describes the cosmos as illuminated by God's word, an immanence that is directly linked to the human faculty for speech as a sublime melody of language both human and divine. This language of creation is renewed through human action, claims Dov Ber, as God is expressed and reborn through the power of our speech.

PART I

Foundations

Chapter 1

The Life of the Maggid

With you people, the Hasidim are one thing, and the teacher
and the teachings are another. That is why you need written
texts. We, our teacher, and the teachings were all truly one.
We had no need for written texts.

—The Wolper Rebbe, disciple of the Maggid

The experiences of the group are reflected in the activities of
the individual; they stimulate him and help fashion the forms
of this creativity. The trail-blazer leaves his imprint on his age
and on future ages, but his age leaves its imprint on him as
well.

—Isadore Twersky

First Encounters

The Jews of eastern Europe were well acquainted with holy men and mystical
pietists. Some of these figures retreated from the world, fleeing into ascetic
solitude or withdrawing from society in order to form small mystical fellowships. Others were popular faith-healers reputed for their shamanistic
skills, including clairvoyance or miracle working. Such professional *ba'alei
shem*, or "masters of the Name," represented an important element of eastern
European Jewish society. They wrote amulets based on divine names, used
incantations to cure the sick, and performed similar magical feats. Certain
ba'alei shem also developed expertise in herbal healing, and some knew bits
and pieces of early modern medicine.[1]

The eighteenth-century movement of renewal known as Hasidism emerged from the teachings of the BeSHT. Scholars debate the extent to which this enigmatic and creative mystic may rightly be described as the "founder" of Hasidism, as there is no evidence that he set out to establish a new religious movement within Judaism.[2] The BeSHT lived in Podolia (present-day Ukraine) near the Carpathian Mountains, but we know very little about his life that does not come from internal Hasidic sources. Legends tell of humble beginnings; perhaps he worked as a slaughterer, and a schoolteacher's apprentice. These jobs were evidently followed by a period of prolonged solitude, and, in the 1730s, the BeSHT began to share a new type of religious life that foregrounded the values of joy and ecstatic prayer. Although tax records reveal that he was employed as a resident Kabbalist by the Mezhbizh community, the BeSHT's legacy in Hasidic memory has been shaped primarily by his impact as a religious teacher and spiritual guide rather his legacy as a *ba'al shem*.[3]

Dov Ber of Mezritsh is commonly portrayed in Hasidic sources as the foremost student of this famed religious leader. Scholars have disproven the once-regnant narrative in which the Maggid inherited some centralized position of leadership of Hasidism after the BeSHT's death.[4] Hasidism grew forth out of small circles of spiritual teachers and their disciples, all loosely connected to the figure of the BeSHT, and these groups had yet to develop a sense of coherent identity by the time of the Maggid's rise to power in the 1760s. The different Hasidic communities that eventually emerged were linked by their allegiance to the memory of the BeSHT—and to the Maggid, with few exceptions—but these groups remained without any united or centralized leadership.

It is clear that the Maggid and his theology were transformed by encountering the BeSHT. Getting at the nature of their relationship, however, is particularly difficult. The notion of the Maggid succeeding the BeSHT as the leader of early Hasidism is hopelessly anachronistic. The commonly accepted model of an intimate, sustained relationship of master and disciple will not do either. Their interactions were likely very few in number, and they seem to have met only toward the end of their lives.

Evidence for this is found in the fact that Dov Ber's homilies rarely quote the BeSHT directly. Nor do the Maggid's sermons invoke his teacher's name as a source of authority, setting his homilies apart from those of other early Hasidic thinkers. Rather than inheriting a corpus of specific teachings, what the Maggid absorbed from the BeSHT is best described, I believe, as an ethos, a sensibility, or an approach to the religious life. Dov Ber took this legacy and developed it further, reshaping and reinterpreting key aspects of the BeSHT's teaching in light of his own religious personality and philosophy. The Maggid also combined the new spiritual orientation with a new social structure. In many crucial respects Dov Ber's center in Mezritsh was the model for what became the Hasidic *hoyf*, or "court"—a physical and communal structure defined by rituals and choreography that remains the most important Hasidic institution into the present day.[5]

Dov Ber must therefore be considered one of the foremost architects of the emergent socioreligious movement that developed into Hasidism. The Maggid's role in the formation of Hasidism is much like Paul's place in the inception of early Christianity. Like Dov Ber of Mezritsh, Paul was just one of a number of important leaders loosely connected to a charismatic spiritual teacher. Yet he was distinguished by his vision and the compelling power of his rhetoric, and, although by no means the sole founder of the early church, Paul had a critical hand in giving shape to the movement that coalesced around the legacy and memory of Jesus of Nazareth.[6]

This chapter explores the arc of the Maggid's life. Investigating this legacy will bring us to consider the intersection of discipleship and language. Dov Ber's homilies describe the bond between master and student—or students—as rooted in the transformative power of words. Language functions as a vehicle of instruction, but the Maggid argues that teachers do more: they reveal God's presence in human speech. Thus do they awaken their disciples to a cosmos that is saturated with sacred divine letters. The significance of language and the place of words in spiritual pedagogy was the subject of much reflection in medieval Jewish mysticism. It was also among the key tenets received from the BeSHT, though, as we shall see, Dov Ber expanded and rebuilt these ideas into a unique theory of language.

The Maggid, like the BeSHT, evidently preferred the oral word in spiritual education. Dov Ber did not chose to—or, perhaps, chose *not* to—put his own ideas into writing. Textual witnesses of the Maggid's homilies were transcribed, edited, and translated by disciples. The absence of written teachings from Dov Ber himself compounds the scarcity of details concerning his life. These lacunae complicate our attempt to paint an intellectual portrait of this early Hasidic leader. We must piece together internal Hasidic sources and stories, and the paucity of reliable texts about the Maggid's biography will require us to cast our net rather widely. The earliest layers of Hasidic hagiography are dotted with stories about Dov Ber, but such tales cannot support even a rudimentary sacred biography.[7] We will therefore turn to stories recounted in his disciples' books and to the oral traditions passed down and eventually published by his descendants.[8] With due caution, we will also draw on the more recent collections from a later phase in the development of the Hasidic story.[9]

Like Talmudic legends, Islamic hagiography, and Christian sacred histories, Hasidic traditions must be used with care. Many tales bear obvious elements of imagination, exaggeration, and fantasy, especially as they were collected and retold by modern thinkers in the late nineteenth and early twentieth centuries.[10] But hagiographical traditions have been an important part of Hasidic culture and religious life since the eighteenth century. These stories cannot be relied on for historical information, but the tales shed some light on how Hasidic tradition has preserved, interpreted, and, at times, reconstructed the image of its early leaders.[11] The stories, together with homilies, reveal how the figure of the Maggid and his religious teachings have been seared into the memory of Hasidism.

One of Dov Ber's sermons describes the Hasidic leader as a *tsiyyun* or *siman*, a "reference point" or "semantic marker," gesturing toward the infinite beyond. Like a spoken word that alludes to the untold mysteries of the mind, the Maggid suggests that sacred individuals and religious teachers reach into the limitless pool of creative vitality and translate this silent potential into concrete language. A similar veil looms across the Maggid's factual biography. The historical Dov Ber of Mezritsh is elusive, inhabiting a realm of shadowy eternity that is forever out of reach. A formidable image (or images) of the Maggid and his theological legacy, however, emerges from these varied hagiographical traditions and from the remarkable number of teachings preserved in his name.

Beginnings and Early Life

Dov Ber Friedman was born in approximately 1704 in Lokatsh (Pol. Lokacze, Ukr. Lokachi), a small town near the city of Rovno (Ukr. Rivne). There are no indications that he descended from an established rabbinic family or scholarly line,[12] though Dov Ber was well educated and must have studied Kabbalah in addition to the Talmud and legal codes.[13] He evidently made his living as a *melammed*, a "teacher of children." Dov Ber worked for a time in Torchin (Pol. Torczyn) to the east of Lokatsh, perhaps after having married the daughter of one of its residents, and followed the common custom of moving near his in-laws. In eastern Europe, the position of *melammed* lacked both prestige and ample remuneration, and traditions describe the destitution of Dov Ber's family in these years.[14] The Maggid's later homilies on the religious significance of poverty may have been born of this experience from his young married life.[15]

Dov Ber moved to the nearby city of Mezritsh (Pol. Międzyrzecz; mod. Ukr. Mezhyrichi) at some point in the early 1760s, perhaps after a short tenure in the town of Rovno.[16] He was employed as the *maggid* (preacher) in Mezritsh, serving the same function in the neighboring town of Korets (Pol. Korzec). The position of *maggid* (pl. *maggidim*) was an important one in eastern Europe, though it was considerably less prominent than that of the official town *rav* (rabbi). *Maggidim*, both itinerant and stationary, represented a social class of second-tier intellectuals, standing somewhere between the masses and the scholarly rabbinic elites.[17] The title *maggid meisharim* was generally conferred on one who had been appointed as the preacher of a particular community, but it is worth noting that, to my knowledge, no stories depict Dov Ber delivering a sermon before a large public audience in a communal synagogue.

Eighteenth-century Mezritsh was home to an elite *beit midrash* (study-house) for learned scholars that included a number of Kabbalists, but Dov Ber does not appear to have been counted among its members.[18] This *beit midrash* was one of many similar institutions sprinkled throughout towns and cities of central and eastern Europe. The disastrous collapse of the movement that surrounded the seventeenth-century Shabbatai Tsevi, a kabbalistic maverick with messianic pretensions, had left many Jews suspicious of mystical religion. In central Europe bans were issued against the dissemination of Kabbalah in an attempt to restrict its knowledge to small circles of elites. Numerous elite *kloyzen* (also "study-houses") were established so that scholars could study mystical texts in a sequestered environment.[19] But in eastern Europe, a region whose culture had long been infused with mystical pietism and magical practices, the roots of popular kabbalistic ideas and rituals were deeply entrenched. In these communities, folk practices blended with rituals adapted from those of the Safed Kabbalists.[20] In these lands Kabbalah remained an integral part of popular practice as well as elite religion into the eighteenth century.[21]

Dov Ber came of age as a traditional eastern European Kabbalist, an ascetic mystic and perhaps a visionary but not a popular healer or a

wonder-working *ba'al shem*. The Maggid's early devotional life evidently focused on study and penitence, and his later sermons and hagiographical traditions continue to espouse a religious ethos defined by a deep fear of sin. This
ethos was similar to—but not identical with—the attitudes of eighteenth-
century moralistic literature produced by eastern Europe Jews.[22] It was only
after many long years in this mode of worship that Dov Ber came to be associated with the BeSHT.

The BeSHT was wary of the dangers of religious guilt and the psychological and physical damage wrought by penitential practices.[23] His teachings
emphasized that one must be ever mindful of the divine vitality in all aspects
of the cosmos, often described as sparks of holiness or divine letters trapped
within the corporeal world. Freeing these sparks is one of the ultimate goals
of religious service, delivering the fallen *shekhinah* (the divine presence, often
depicted as female) from current exile. For this reason, one may serve God
through all "ordinary" physical deeds, such as eating, drinking, and dancing,
as well as by performing the commandments. Dov Ber's encounter with the
BeSHT and the latter's relatively world-affirming mystical theology changed
the Maggid significantly, but the ascetic impulse remained part of Dov Ber's
spiritual path long after their meeting.[24]

The Maggid and the Ba'al Shem Tov

Dov Ber must have encountered the BeSHT for the first time in the
1750s. We know very little about the circumstances or frequency of their interactions, and literary evidence suggests that they met only a few times.[25]
One of the earliest texts to reflect on their connection is the introduction to
Maggid Devarav le-Ya'akov (1781), the first printed compendium of Dov Ber's
sermons. Shlomo of Lutsk, the book's editor and the author of this introduction, was a relative of Dov Ber as well as a devoted disciple. He had much
to gain from asserting a unique connection between the BeSHT and the
Maggid. It is thus noteworthy that Shlomo's presentation is a far cry from
the overwrought descriptions of Dov Ber's "succeeding" the BeSHT as the
leader of Hasidism found in later hagiography:

> One time I heard [the following] from his [i.e., the Maggid's] holy
> mouth: he studied the language of the birds and the palm trees,
> and so forth, with the BeSHT. He learned the secrets of the holy

names and unifications (*yihudim*),[26] and studied the book *Ma'ayan ha-Hokhmah* with him as well.

He taught him the explanation of each word. He [the Maggid] showed me the letters and script of the angels *Sefer Razi'el [ha-Malakh]*, saying that [the BeSHT] had taught him all this.[27]

The Maggid, claims Shlomo of Lutsk, received a set of miraculous skills from the BeSHT. This included direct knowledge of the angelic alphabet and how to decode the language of nature. The ability to grasp the "language of the birds and the palm trees" crops up in rabbinic and mystical literatures, where the skill is associated with figures like Shimon bar Yohai and Yitshak Luria. Attributing such knowledge to the Maggid—and the BeSHT—situates them in a long line of venerated mystical leaders.[28]

Sefer Razi'el ha-Malakh and *Ma'ayan ha-Hokhmah* typify the sort of literature that the BeSHT and the Maggid may well have studied together. The former integrates reflections on the power of language in *merkavah* traditions, Rhineland Pietism, and pre-Lurianic mysticism, combining them with the texts for various amulets and incantations commonly found in medieval Kabbalah.[29] Several works called *Ma'ayan ha-Hokhmah* were known in eighteenth-century Poland, all of which were much concerned with issues of language, creation, and revelation. Some of these works include meditations on God's sacred name that are said to induce knowledge of the languages of nature.[30] Neither of these books can be described as a mainstay of the classical kabbalistic canon. Blending the magical, theological, and experiential elements of religion, these works are precisely the sort of books that would have been cherished by eastern European *ba'alei shem*.[31]

Shlomo of Lutsk's introduction also claims that Dov Ber learned certain angelic names from the BeSHT, which would enable him to predict the future and to prevent calamties slated to befall the Jewish people. When Shlomo asks the Maggid why he, unlike the BeSHT, did not put this arcane knowledge to practical use, Dov Ber offers a cryptic reply: "To do this, one must perform certain unifications (*yihudim*)."[32] Are we to understand the Maggid's apparent reticence may have stemmed from humility or an outright lack of confidence?

More likely it reflects a turn away from the more magical approach of the BeSHT. The Maggid's homilies struggle with the notion of changing God's will through prayer, but neither his sermons nor the hagiographical stories about his life refer to the predictive, apotropaic, or otherwise magical qualities of angelic names. *Sefer Raziel ha-Malakh* and *Ma'ayan ha-Hokhmah* are almost never mentioned in the Maggid's homilies.[33] The reticence to build a reputation on miracles or to invoke these magical works may indicate that the Maggid was distancing himself—consciously or unconsciously—from the class of the *ba'al shem* without depreciating their skills or subverting his revered teacher.[34] The Maggid was an introverted, contemplative mystic driven by a set of theological and social concerns quite different from that of the expansive and extroverted BeSHT.[35]

A wealth of later literary and oral legends attempted to fill in the striking gaps regarding the relationship between the Maggid and the BeSHT, reconstructing the bond between these two masters in the decades after their deaths.[36] Among these, the tales of Dov Ber's first encounter with the BeSHT preserved in *Keter Shem Tov* (1794) and *Shivhei ha-BeSHT* (1814) stand out because of their early date as well as their influence on later Hasidic tradition. Both accounts refer to the Maggid's initial meeting with the BeSHT as a kind of life-altering conversion to a different way of approaching religious life.[37] The dissimilarities between the tales, however, are quite telling, as are the many questions that they leave unaddressed.[38]

The tale of their meeting presented in *Keter Shem Tov* describes the Maggid as an accomplished Talmudic and kabbalistic scholar. Hearing of the BeSHT's reputation for efficacious prayer, the Maggid decides to visit him and judge the master's spiritual prowess for himself. Dov Ber is astonished when he is greeted by strange behavior and offhand remarks rather than a deep spiritual teaching. He decides to return home, but before he departs, the Maggid is summoned to meet with the BeSHT:

> The Baal Shem Tov asked the Maggid, "Can you learn?" He replied, "Yes." The Baal Shem Tov said, "Yes, I've heard you can learn." He then asked, "Do you know something of the wisdom of the Kabbalah (*hokhmat ha-kabbalah*). "Yes," the Maggid replied. . . .
>
> So the Baal Shem Tov showed him a certain passage in *Ets Hayyim*.[39] The Maggid said, "Let me take the book and examine it for a while in order to really grasp it." Then he told the Baal Shem Tov the plain-sense meaning (*peshat*) of the passage. The Baal Shem Tov said, "You don't know anything." He kept studying, telling the Baal Shem Tov, "My explanation is correct. If you

know a different explanation, please tell me and we'll see with whom the truth is found." The Baal Shem Tov replied, "Stand up," and he did so. The names of several angels were included in this passage, and, as soon as he recited it, the entire house was filled with light and a fire surrounded them. They actually witnessed the angels that were being mentioned. The Baal Shem Tov told the Maggid, "Your explanation was correct, but your study was without any soul."[40]

The Maggid is described as a learned scholar who reads kabbalistic sources with ease. But the tale depicts Dov Ber as lacking the BeSHT's skill for conjuring up a mystical experience through reading texts. The Maggid's interpretation of the source was apparently sound, but his exegesis is portrayed as purely cerebral, lacking heart and meaning. This was the spiritual deficiency that the BeSHT sought to correct. The story in *Keter Shem Tov* describes this moment of illuminated reading as fundamentally transformative, for the Maggid remains in Mezhbizh and absorbs "great and deep wisdoms" (*hokhmot gedolot ve-'amukot*) that he carried with him upon returning to Mezritsh.

The parallel account of this meeting presented in *Shivhei ha-BeSHT* is patterned on the earlier story in *Keter Shem Tov*, but the early nineteenth-century witness includes a few critical differences.[41] It portrays Dov Ber as weakened by his self-imposed penitential regimen, journeying to Mezhbizh to seek the BeSHT's well-known healing powers. The Maggid is once again greeted with bizarre behavior, but the author of *Shivhei ha-BeSHT* informs the reader that the BeSHT has actually been waiting for Dov Ber to come to visit him. As the sorely disappointed Maggid prepares to depart, he is summoned to meet with the BeSHT and asked to read aloud from a work of medieval Kabbalah. The BeSHT is unsatisfied with the Maggid's interpretation, and as he begins to recite the text himself, the room is filled with a terrifying splendor of "lights and torches" like those that accompanied God's revelation at Sinai. The awestruck Maggid remains in Mezhbizh to study with his newfound master, but, as Dov Ber readies to depart, the BeSHT begs him for a blessing.

The tales preserved in *Keter Shem Tov* and *Shivhei ha-BeSHT* agree in depicting Dov Ber as a mature intellectual and scholar before he met the BeSHT. Neither refers to the Maggid's other teachers, emphasizing the special connection between these two individuals.[42] The two accounts also concur in describing the Maggid's conversion after witnessing the BeSHT present a startling new method of reading mystical texts. Early Hasidic teachings generally favor oral speech over the written word, but the flights of mystical exegesis foregrounded in this tale embody the complicated hybridity of Hasidic culture.[43]

In his landmark study of the oral scaffoldings that surround many religious writings, William Graham writes: "A sacred text can be read laboriously in silent study, chanted or sung in unthinking repetition, copied or illuminated in loving devotion, imaginatively depicted in art or drama, solemnly processed in ritual pageantry, or devoutly touched in hope of luck and blessing."[44] These tales of the BeSHT and the Maggid illustrate the mutual dependence of written and oral culture among some eighteenth- and nineteenth-century Jews. The Hasidic stories describe how a sacred text may be turned into an oral gesture when it is recited aloud. The result is a revelatory theophany, an intimate mode of performative interpretation born of the direct encounter of master and disciple.

Though perhaps intimated in the story in *Keter Shem Tov*, the depiction of the Maggid as destined to inherit the BeSHT's mantle of leadership is clear in the tale in *Shivhei ha-BeSHT*.[45] This argument of succession reflects the overall thrust of *Shivhei ha-BeSHT*, an early nineteenth-century attempt to construct a sacred history of Hasidism and its intellectual origins. Most later Hasidic hagiography continues this narrative of inheritance, though tales from various groups do so in very different ways. The stories of the Ruzhin dynasty, a Hasidic community founded by Dov Ber's great-grandson Yisra'el of Ruzhin (1796–1850), highlight the Maggid's singularity by minimizing his connection to the BeSHT.[46] Other hagiographical traditions take the opposite tack, accentuating the Maggid's fealty in bringing his own students to visit the BeSHT.[47]

We noted that this notion of linear succession, once treated as historical fact, has been disproven in recent decades.[48] Historical evidence suggests that the Maggid was one of many individuals in the loose-knit circle around the BeSHT. Several of these figures attracted their own disciples and operated as Hasidic leaders independent of Dov Ber's influence.[49] Individuals who had been connected to the BeSHT did not, by and large, become students of Dov Ber after the former's death in 1760.[50] Stories about the BeSHT's disciples vying to assume his position are undoubtedly anachronistic, although the profound differences in personality and spiritual ethos found in the hagiography may indeed be grounded in historical reality.

Dov Ber was not the sole inheritor of the BeSHT's legacy, or even the closest disciple of the paterfamilias of Hasidism. The encounter between the two was clearly a determinative moment in Dov Ber's life, but it is note-worthy that the Maggid's sermons rarely invoke the BeSHT or his teachings by name.[51] Direct references may have been included in the original oral forms of Dov Ber's sermons, mentions that were lost as the homilies were put into writing. But the Maggid, who likely interacted with the BeSHT only a handful of times, probably did not possess a large body of specific teachings heard directly from the BeSHT.[52]

The Maggid's teachings make no significant attempt to ground his own ideas in the BeSHT's teachings in order to prove their authenticity or demonstrate authority.[53] Whereas the writings of Ya'akov Yosef of Polnoye (d. 1783), another important disciple of the BeSHT, sought to *preserve* his master's teachings by quoting them at length, the Maggid's homilies may rightly be described as offering a new stage in the theological development and sophistication of the BeSHT's approach to the spiritual quest. Dov Ber's sermons integrate key elements of the BeSHT's theology, including a radical conception of divine immanence, intense commitment to prayer, the importance of joy, and, above all, the centrality of words in the devotional life. But, as we shall see, Dov Ber recast the BeSHT's ideas about human and divine speech into an original and sophisticated theory of language.

The Maggid's Circle and Early Hasidism

Dov Ber's fame and reputation increased between 1760 and 1772, during which time he lived in the towns of Mezritsh, Rovno, and Hanipoli. Along with his duties as an official *maggid*, Dov Ber was occasionally called on to intervene in communal matters.[54] The Maggid established himself as the leader of a loosely-knit circle of disciples, an array of charismatic figures and intellectual talents in their own right who went on to become the leaders of early Hasidism. Indeed, the Hasidic movement was built around the memory of the Maggid by personalities from among Dov Ber's immediate circle of disciples. But the contours and dynamics of the group surrounding the Maggid are vexingly opaque.[55] We do not know, for example, the number of disciples connected to the Maggid, how long each of these students stayed in Mezritsh, or how they related to one another during his lifetime.[56]

There is a rather rich description of the Maggid's center in the autobiography of Solomon Maimon (1754–1800).[57] Together with the brief references to the Maggid's circle in early anti-Hasidic bans (see below), and the occasional mention of gatherings or anecdotes in the works of Dov Ber's disciples, Maimon's description of his short visit to Mezritsh in his youth remains one of the most valuable sources regarding the Maggid's life in the 1760s. These heavily edited reminiscences were first published in German in 1792–1794, intending to present eastern European Judaism to a western audience. But scholars have vetted Maimon's account of Dov Ber's court by comparing his version of the Maggid's teachings to others preserved in Dov Ber's name. And Maimon's remarks on Hasidic ideology—including panentheism, devotion founded in joy, the quest for self-transcendence, and cultivation of feeling (rather than logical philosophy or rational knowledge)—were particularly astute.[58]

Maimon visited Dov Ber at some point in the late 1760s, perhaps staying for as long as several weeks. His interest was piqued by secondhand knowledge of Dov Ber's teachings, conveyed to him by a wandering disciple. Maimon claims, "I couldn't help but admire the high quality of these thoughts, and was impressed with the ingenious exegesis supporting them."[59] The entrancing homily led him to journey to an unspecified master "B—" residing in the town of "M—," surely none other than Dov Ber of Mezritsh himself. Denied a private audience,[60] Maimon was invited to attend the leader's Shabbat table and assured that he would find personal spiritual meaning in "the most exalted teachings directly from his mouth" during his public address:

> I arrived on the Sabbath for the festive meal and found that a
> large number of important men from all the region had gathered
> for the occasion. The great man finally appeared, cutting an
> impressive figure, dressed as he was in a white Atlas robe. Even
> his shoes and his tobacco container were white (among Kabbalists
> white is the color of grace). He gave each one of the arrivals a
> *Schalam*; that is, the great man greeted each of them.
>
> We sat down to eat, and a solemn silence reigned during the
> meal. After we had finished, the leader sang a celebratory, spiritu-
> ally uplifting melody. He held his hand in front of his forehead for
> a few moments, then began to call: "Z. from H.! M. from R.!
> S.M. from N.!"—the names and places of residence of all the new

arrivals, something that astonished us more than a little. Each
one of us was asked to recite a verse from the Holy Scripture. We
did this. Thereupon, the leader began to give a sermon, taking
the verses we had recited as the text. Even though they were
completely unconnected verses from different books of the Holy
Scripture, he linked them together with such artistry that they
seemed to form a single whole. Even more extraordinary was that
each of us felt the part of the sermon dealing with his verse
contained something referring directly to his own pressing
personal concerns. Naturally, we were amazed.[61]

The young Maimon—probably in his teens—was greatly impressed by the
Maggid's charismatic presence as well as the philosophical depth of his sermon. He eventually grew disenchanted with Hasidism, but the experience
in Mezritsh evidently left a significant and lasting impression on Maimon.
This impact is visible throughout his *Autobiography*, often in surprising ways.
He frequently uses parables to great effect in his book, drawing on the style
of Hasidic homilies in addition to a medieval philosophical convention.[62] His
observation that Hasidic sermons emerge from exegetical improvisation
rather than carefully planned sermons is quite insightful. Maimon even rep-
licates the Maggid's style of interpretive extemporizing in a later dialogue
with Enlightenment figures in Berlin, revealing a way in which the Maggid's
style swiftly influenced Jewish discourse outside of Hasidic circles.[63]

His short account offers historians critical grist for thinking about the
Maggid's center in Mezritsh as a precursor of the Hasidic court, which
emerged as a highly structured institution in the late eighteenth and early
nineteenth centuries.[64] The Maggid's practices, such as the public sermon
around a ritualized meal on Shabbat, may well have served as a model for
the courts founded by some of his immediate disciples. Dov Ber set himself
up as a leader to whom others journeyed, a departure from the model attributed to his own teacher. Most legends describe the BeSHT as a peripa-
tetic spiritual master, though historical records show that he was employed
by the community in Mezhbizh. This hagiographical image of the BeSHT
as a wanderer seems to be confirmed by the wide variety of disciples throughout Volhynia whose lives he touched.[65]

The shift to a stationary model of religious leadership may have been
precipitated by the fact that Dov Ber held an official appointment as *maggid meisharim* or communal preacher in the towns of Mezritsh and Korets.

If we are to believe the common hagiographical detail of his infirmity of the leg, the shift to a stationary mode of leadership may also have been a practical concession to his difficulty with walking. The choice to remain in Mezritsh had significant social and ideological results that changed the course of Hasidism. Dov Ber's visitors experienced a kind of scholarly and spiritual performance, a tightly controlled display fusing theological reflection with theatrical ceremony. Maimon's testimony reveals that this homiletical exhibition impressed many of those who called at the Maggid's door.

Maimon's work also suggests that Dov Ber delivered his homily before a random assortment of visitors rather than an exclusive group of scholars who were already well known to him.[66] In addition to these public sermons, we may presume that other modes of personal instruction were made available to the Maggid's closest disciples. The physical structure of later Hasidic courts often reflected what might be called concentric circles of membership or affiliation; the leader received the community at large and studied with more advanced disciples in different spaces.[67]

Why might this range of visitors and students have been drawn to Mezritsh? Some talented intellects, many of whom went on to attain prestigious rabbinic posts, may have been attracted by the power of the Maggid's theology. As was the young Maimon, such figures may have been "impressed with the ingenious exegesis" driving forward Dov Ber's exegetical wizardry. But these scholars are only part of the story. A well-known Hasidic tale portrays a student traveling to Mezritsh simply to observe how the master tied his shoes, suggesting that this individual was enthralled by the Maggid's charismatic presence rather than his scholarly reputation.[68]

Another tradition recalls that the young Shneur Zalman of Liady (1745–1812), evidently a budding scholar of some repute, gravitated toward the Mezritsh circle because of Dov Ber's passionate approach to fiery prayer rather than his Talmudic acumen.[69] Only a few tales portray the Maggid as dazzling newcomers with his clairvoyance.[70] Dov Ber seems to have achieved renown among his disciples mostly as a scholar, a gifted homilist, and as a mystical pietist rather than a faith healer or clairvoyant seer.[71] We do not have many tales of simple people coming to the Maggid—as they had to the BeSHT—in search of blessings or healing. That lack is significant, for the Maggid himself could hardly be called a popularizer.

Relatively little is known about the time these visitors-cum-students spent in Mezritsh. We do not know how long they tarried with the Maggid, nor do we know which books or religious exercises were the focal point of their studies. Considerable attention must have been given over to the rituals of Sabbath and other holidays, particularly since these were likely the times in which people visited Dov Ber. Some may have come to Mezritsh with the expectation of studying with the Maggid consistently. The model of the *yeshivah* came rather late to the Hasidic world, and it is unlikely that the Maggid's center functioned primarily as an academy for improving textual scholarship.[72]

The large volume of early Hasidic manuscripts does reveal that several of Dov Ber's disciples were transcribing huge numbers of teachings; he must have addressed his followers frequently. The highly varied corpus of written sources transcribed in Dov Ber's name may represent private classes, instructions given to a core group of students, and public sermons delivered before a broader community. Many of these creative homilies present spiritualized interpretations of passages from the Talmud, the curricular heart of the academies of learning in central and eastern Europe.[73] Only a small number of teachings appear to be sustained discourses on aspects of Lurianic Kabbalah. The sophistication and intricacy of these homilies make them worthy of note, and they reveal the depth of Dov Ber's engagement with kabbalistic traditions, but they are uncharacteristic of the Maggid's corpus as a whole.[74]

Bracketing the question of curriculum, a few internal sources by his disciples shed some light on their time in Mezritsh. The following excerpt from a letter by Avraham of Kalisk (1741–1810), for example, describes the circle's studies with Dov Ber as follows: "When I and my colleagues heard just one word of the Maggid of Mezritsh, we would be satisfied with that one utterance for a long while—if we had come only to hear a single word, it would have been enough for us. We kept guard over [the teaching] with holiness and purity, until a second word was forthcoming, as it says, 'when you find honey, eat what you need, lest [you become filled with it and vomit it forth]' (Prov. 25:16)."[75] Avraham's words paint a vivid picture of Dov Ber's disciples studying together with assiduous focus, slowly moving from one matter to another only after a significant period of consideration. This letter was written at least two decades after Avraham's tenure in Mezritsh. It was penned in response to the publication of a theological treatise by his colleague Shneur Zalman of Liady, an event that Avraham of Kalisk saw as the untoward outpouring and popularization of kabbalistic secrets that were best restricted to the elites. This context reveals a polemic edge in the passage cited above, but Avraham's description of studying with the Maggid is fully consistent with Dov Ber's descriptions of sacred study as an exercise in sustained contemplative attunement.

These traditions leave us with the mysterious figure of the Maggid standing at the heart of the loosely defined circle in Mezritsh. His life and homilies represent a critical moment, an intermediary stage in the emergence of the Hasidic notion of *tsaddik*. The idea of the "righteous person" or "holy man" as a communal leader was one of the most important social and theological innovations of the Hasidic movement.[76] Drawing on a range of earlier models, the Hasidic master fused the aspects of the biblical priest, prophet, and the king, as well as kabbalistic notions of the *tsaddik* and, in some cases, the eastern European institution of the *rav*.[77] Dov Ber's sermons refer to the *tsaddik* as a powerful individual whose worship and words are capable of transforming the cosmos. Rarely does the Maggid describe this figure as a communal leader surrounded by disciples, or as one who "descends" into the masses in order to raise ordinary people to a higher spiritual level.[78]

How should we account for the discrepancy between Dov Ber's foregrounded role in the emergence of Hasidism on the one hand, and his depictions of the *tsaddik* as a private, inwardly driven mystic on the other? There may have been a marked disconnect between the Maggid's teachings on the nature of the *tsaddik* and the leadership institutions that emerged in his lifetime.[79] But Dov Ber's sermons on the power of the *tsaddik* must have had a self-referential dimension, fusing reflexive murmurings with theoretical meditations on the nature of the kabbalistic holy man. This doubling of language may indeed have been clear to the members of his circle. Perhaps, as Arthur Green has suggested, the tension reveals that the naturally retreating Maggid was hesitatingly drawn into his position as a communal leader in Mezritsh.[80]

There is another perspective on this question that must be considered. The holy man of Dov Ber's homilies may not preside over a fully developed Hasidic community, but a significant number of his sermons do refer to the *tsaddik* as a teacher surrounded by a flock of students. These disciples, claims the Maggid, force the master to emerge from the comforts of contemplative silence. Such sermons depict the *tsaddik*'s struggle to overcome the limitations of language, translating the expansive vistas of his mind into concrete words that must be unpacked by his disciples. This combination of spiritual teacher and communal leader in the *tsaddik*, embodied in the figure of Dov

Ber as well as in the ideational content of his sermons, became a defining characteristic of almost all later Hasidic leaders.[81]

Dov Ber's Final Years and the Legacy of the Maggid

Conflict was fated to play a major role in the last two years of the Maggid's life. Dov Ber relocated from Mezritsh to Rovno between 1770 and 1772,[82] and, during this time, the scholarly elites of White Russia and Lithuania were growing more vocal in their opposition to early Hasidic leaders and practices.[83] The Maggid's students had spread his teachings into White Russia and Lithuania as well as Podolia and Volhynia. In 1772, the conflict with the opponents of Hasidism, who eventually coalesced into a bloc called *mithnaggedim* (opponents) broke out in earnest with the publication of a *herem*, or "writ of excommunication," in the towns of Brody, Vilna, and Shklov. These decrees were followed by caustic anti-Hasidic pamphlets and the public burning of Hasidic manuscripts.[84]

Though accusations of theological infractions were not entirely absent, these polemics suggest that Lithuanian scholars were incensed more by the social improprieties of some of Dov Ber's students than by their theology.[85] Such flashpoints include the formation of their own prayer quorums, changing the times of worship, adopting new regulations for ritual slaughter, unbecoming and boisterous movements during worship, and acting disrespectfully toward scholars of Torah. A few of these documents refer to the Hasidim collectively as Mezritsher, obviously alluding to their connection to the Maggid, but it is worth noting that Dov Ber's name rarely comes up in these polemics. When he does appear in broadsides, the Maggid is mentioned briefly and without any of the vehemence marshaled against other early Hasidic leaders.[86] The authors of the anti-Hasidic writings may have been reticent to ridicule Dov Ber directly, perhaps seeing him as a reputable scholar or Kabbalist.[87]

Lack of direct textual evidence makes it difficult to determine the Maggid's reaction to the growing opposition by the Lithuanian elites. Nothing in the immediate corpus of teachings attributed to Dov Ber seems to be a direct reaction to them, although in several homilies—perhaps late ones—the Maggid counsels silence as the correct response to accusations from one's detractors. But Dov Ber may have attempted to prevent his students from inciting the wrath of the Lithuanian scholars.[88] A public letter written by

his student Shneur Zalman of Liady, who emerged as one of the most important Hasidic leaders of the late eighteenth and early nineteenth century,
describes a gathering of the Maggid's disciples in Rovne in summer 1772 in
response to the writ of excommunication. Shneur Zalman claims that the
Maggid rebuked his disciple Avraham of Kalisk for outrageous public dis-
plays of enthusiasm in 1770, including deprecating the study of Torah and
performing cartwheels in the public square.[89]

This letter must be read with a critical eye. It was written in 1805 amid
a fiery controversy between Shneur Zalman and Avraham of Kalisk.[90] Both
economic and theological issues were at stake in this conflict, which hinged
on the question of which leader's spiritual path was more authentic to the
legacy of the Maggid. This context, however, does not make the letter's mention of a meeting necessarily inauthentic, and it seems unlikely the idea was
made up out of whole cloth. The epistle was an open letter addressed to the
Hasidic community, referring to the Rovno gathering in 1772 as an event
that was "publicly known." Shneur Zalman described a similar meeting in
an earlier letter from circa 1778:

> These [anti-Hasidic] tracts were sent throughout the communi-
> ties of the Diaspora. It would not be believed, were I to tell of the
> great humiliations and afflictions suffered by the famous *tsaddikim*
> of Volhynia. They were unable to remain in their homes, and they
> sought refuge beneath the wings of our great master, of blessed
> memory, in the holy community of Rovno.
>
> [They held] a meeting of counsel, inquiring what to do.
> There were many ways to proceed, to thwart and disrupt their
> thoughts [i.e., the malevolent intentions of the *mithnaggedim*]; to
> write things about them that are bitter many times over, in the
> language of truth that endures forever, publishing them and
> sending them throughout [the lands of] Jacob. And there were
> other paths as well.
>
> But our great master chose to take no action against them,
> because the power of Israel lies entirely in their words, to cry out to
> God and to disrupt their wicked thoughts and prevent their hands
> from doing anything. Just as he interpreted it for us, so it was.[91]

Shneur Zalman depicts the Maggid's students, downtrodden and pursued,
as fleeing to their teacher in order to escape the wrath of their accusers. He

claims that they were ready to turn the tables on their opponents by circulating broadsides of their own, but the Maggid enjoined them to take no
action other than prayer. Such supplications, claimed Dov Ber, are the only
way to inspire divine intercession and thus ensure defense of his disciples.
Salvation is found in the language of prayer rather than polemics; words,
not deeds, deliver them from the hands of the *mithnaggedim*. We shall see
that this emphasis on the redemptive qualities of language is reflected
throughout the Maggid's sermons.[92]

Dov Ber relocated from Rovno to the small town of Hanipoli (Pol.
Annopol) in the last months of his life.[93] Very little is known about the
reasons behind this move or the final period of the Maggid's biography. The
Maggid had been infirm and physically weak for many years, and his illness
appears to have intensified considerably in this period.[94] Dov Ber died on
December 15, 1772, and he was buried in Hanipoli. His close disciple Meshullam Zusya Weisblum, a native of that city, was interred next to him nearly
three decades later.[95]

The Hebrew date of the Maggid's death—the 19th of Kislev—came to
be celebrated in Hasidic communities. Hasidic legends embellish the circumstances of his death. One particularly interesting tale describes Dov Ber's
coffin moving of its own accord, refusing to rest until his disciples cried out
that such a miracle would transform the whole world into followers of
Hasidism.[96] This story is obviously a bit of late hagiography, but it does
mirror the Maggid's reticent attitude toward miracles. The tale may also
reflect Dov Ber's misgivings, or at least ambivalence, about turning the spiritual ethos forged by the fellowship in Mezritsh into a mass movement.[97]

The Maggid's influence on later generations of Hasidism was shaped by
his family as well as his students. Hasidic tradition remembers the Maggid
and his wife as having had only one child, a son born circa 1730 after many
years of infertility. Avraham, named for the Maggid's father, is often called
"the Angel" (*ha-malakh*) because of his ascetic leanings. Legends describe
his intense introspection and piety as having been even more extreme than
Dov Ber himself.[98] Avraham served as the *maggid* in Fastov (Ukr. Fastiv),
perhaps struggling to inhabit a public role despite his brooding contemplative piety.[99]

Dov Ber's saintly child outlived him by just a few years. Avraham died
at a young age in late 1776. His first wife predeceased him, but Avraham's
second wife, Gittel, the daughter of a prominent Talmudic scholar, survived
her husband for many long years.[100] Hasidic lore glowingly refers to her

wisdom, describing Gittel as witnessing visions of Dov Ber and her deceased husband.[101] She never remarried, and although the account of her life in *Shivhei ha-BeSHT* concludes with a rosy ending, Gittel was evidently financially bereft and died after moving to the land of Israel.[102]

Avraham is rightly counted among the Maggid's students whose teachings bear the imprint of his father's legacy.[103] His homilies are conceptually and terminologically similar to those of Dov Ber, including the focus on the contemplative quality of the intellect, the quest to experience the divine Naught (*ayin*), and the necessity of total abstention from the physical realm.[104] Of particular note is Avraham's consistent focus on issues of language. Like his father, he frequently refers to the practice of raising up speech to its source, linking spoken words to their origin in the worshipper's mind and ultimately to the font of language streaming forth from the Godhead itself.[105] Avraham denounces the allure of silence despite his ascetic bent, arguing that God created the cosmos in order to reveal the divine presence through the medium of human speech.[106]

Inherited dynasties had not yet emerged on the scene of Hasidic history by the 1770s. Dov Ber's son neither fashioned himself as leader after his father's death nor took a prominent role in the spread or emergence of Hasidism.[107] This decision to remain a small-town *maggid* rather than a leader among Dov Ber's disciples may reflect Avraham's personal theology as well as his retreating personality. Amplifying his father's teachings on the subject, Avraham's homilies portray the *tsaddik* as a private mystic who turns inward and journeys into the deepest realms of the devotional mind.[108]

Hasidic communities were founded by some of the Maggid's later descendants. Avraham's son Shalom Shakhna of Prohobist (Ukr. Pohrebyshche), who died in 1802, left behind him a six-year-old son named Yisra'el. This young man went on to establish one of the most important and powerful Hasidic dynasties in the city of Ruzhin, and then Sadagora. Yisra'el was a controversial but charismatic leader, and his claims to authority and legitimacy were, at least in part, based on being the great-grandson of the Maggid.[109] His own descendants, who established themselves as *tsaddikim* in Sadagora, Chortkov, and Boyan, remain a very important part of the present-day Hasidic landscape.

The theological and social legacy of the Maggid was primarily carried forward by his many disciples. In fact, several of these students—including Aharon of Karlin (1736–1772),[110] Menahem Mendel of Vitebsk (ca. 1730–1788), and Avraham of Kalisk—seem to have operated as independent leaders and teachers of smaller communities during their master's lifetime. This fact, argues Ada Rapoport-Albert, further demonstrates that neither the BeSHT nor Dov Ber should be described as the leader of united Hasidic movement.[111]

Hasidism as such was born in the last quarter of the eighteenth century, as the ideology and new social structures began to crystalize through the efforts of the Maggid's students, and as increasingly public conflict with the *mithnaggedim* forced the Maggid's disciples to articulate their theology as their identity as a distinct social group began to cohere. This makes it tempting to dismiss the notion of a Mezritsh "circle," even as a relatively unstructured community, as an anachronistic projection.[112] Rapoport-Albert has claimed that individual disciples traveled to study with the Maggid for variable periods of time, departing Mezritsh without maintaining close ties—either with the Maggid himself, or with the other scholars and students with whom they may have come into contact. Her argument is grounded largely in textual silence, based on the small number of witnesses to communication between Dov Ber and his students and among the disciples themselves.

It is possible, however, to refer to a decentralized group of scholars as a flourishing religious movement even though it lacks centralized leadership.[113] Numerous references to one another in the later published works of Dov Ber's students offer some evidence of an emerging "circle" of disciples,[114] as do the many letters they exchanged[115] and the relatively early hagiographical traditions in which the Maggid's students interact with one another.[116] This is also true of the figures mentioned in the anti-Hasidic bans starting in 1772, writings that gesture toward a loose-knit group of people associated with this circle.[117] Important familial connections were also forged between Dov Ber's disciples as well. In addition to marriages between their children, we should note that the Maggid's own grandson was raised by several of his former disciples.[118]

Attempting to identify a stable or cohesive circle of well-defined disciples is to misunderstand the links that held the Mezritsh group together. Theirs was a shared theological project of renewal, one that emerged from their own religious personalities and creativity and the legacy of the Maggid.[119] The homilies and teachings of Dov Ber's students bear the unmistakable influence of the Maggid's theology, even when not directly citing a specific tradition from their teacher.[120] The disciples may not have kept up "any links by regular correspondence" with the Maggid, but the charismatic image of their teacher and his theology were imprinted on their careers and spiritual paths.

By the mid-1760s Dov Ber had emerged as one of the most powerful voices in the chorus of those branching from the BeSHT's spiritual ethos. The core group of some dozen disciples, including a wide range of extraordinary and talented students, built Hasidism in the decades after the Maggid's death. The spread of these disciples did not reflect a conscious decision, either as a consensus or from single centralized authority, to turn Hasidism into a popular or mass movement. Dov Ber did not send out his disciples to carve up the territory of eastern Europe and champion the banner of Hasidism, nor can he be described as the architect at the head of this transformation. This transition from elite circle to mass movement was an organic process, a development driven by spiritual excitement and born aloft by the religious personalities of the leaders.

The expansion of Hasidism from small groups into larger communities, both during the Maggid's lifetime and after his death, was swift though not instantaneous. It took on distinct forms in White Russia, Ukraine, and regions that are now Poland. Some of Dov Ber's particularly learned disciples traveled far in order to secure official positions as the rabbis of prominent towns and cities; these included Shmuel Shmelke Horowitz in Nikolsburg (1726–1778), Pinhas Horowitz in Frankfurt am Main (1731–1805), and Levi Yitshak in Ryczywół, Pinsk, and Barditshev (ca. 1740–1809). Other students, like Shlomo of Lutsk, remained in the area of Mezritsh and Korets long after the Maggid's death. Still others, like Shneur Zalman of Liady and Menahem Mendel of Vitebsk, went on to found Hasidic fellowships in or near their places of origin.[121] The very different attempts of these disciples to adapt, recast, and translate Dov Ber's spiritual message grew into the multifaceted religious movement that exerted a powerful force on Jewish modernity.

Chapter 2

Sacred Words

God cannot remain silent in a language in which He has been
evoked thousands of time to return to life.

—Gershom Scholem

Contemplate your voice and thoughts, coming to realize that
they are nothing but divine vitality and spirit. Each derives
from its root and source on high. . . . It is so with regard to the
World of Speech, the origin of language for all speaking
creatures. Indeed, [this sacred linguistic vitality] extends to all
other creatures, for the Holy One's words are in all things.

—Shlomo of Lutsk

Holy Languages

The religion of Israel, from most ancient times, has been famous for its reverence for sacred speech. This understanding of language is rooted in the opening chapter of Genesis, which describes the creation of the world through a series of divine commands. This narrative lends itself to an interpretation of God forming the cosmos through the divine word, a mythos that became foundational to many rabbinic and medieval readings of creation. The biblical emphasis on aural and linguistic experience over visions of the Divine is noteworthy as well.[1] This legacy, surfacing also in the Neoplatonic formulation of John 1:1–5, carried through into the Talmudic tradition and later kabbalistic streams.[2] Teachings on the power of language inform rabbinic understandings of creation and revelation, as well as devotional practices like study and prayer. The Talmudic sages' emphasis on the word of God as manifest in sacred Scripture was key to their claims of religious authority. Yet the rabbinic approach to the project of interpretation bespeaks a kind of verbal intellectuality, a love of the Divine manifest in exegesis and the depths of sacred language.[3]

New approaches to language emerged within the Islamic orbit, when medieval Jewish thinkers encountered the sophisticated theological and programmatic reflections of the Greco-Arabic tradition.[4] Medieval Jews were confronted by polemics over language, forcing them to respond to the manner in which Islamic scholars extolled Arabic for its divine origins as well as its unparalleled aesthetic beauty. These debates reached their peak in medieval Iberia and its swirling eddy of cultural, spiritual, and philosophical currents. Islamic and Christian Iberia was also home to a flourishing and increasingly prominent community, or communities, of Kabbalists—a phase of Jewish mysticism that began with a small group of twelfth- and thirteenth-century Provençal scholars whose teachings eventually spread west into Iberia.

Confronting the austere and transcendent God described in the works of rationalist philosophers, the writings of the medieval Jewish mystics developed a rich theology in which language flows from the sacred essence of God's name.[5] Human words, and indeed the very being of the cosmos of itself, are described as sustained echoes of the divine language that surges forth from the ineffable Tetragrammaton. Deeply influenced by apophatic tendencies of Neoplatonism, these medieval mystics grappled with the question of to what extent God may be known by the human mind or described in words.[6] The early Kabbalists were also steeped in a school of thought that attributes a uniquely sacred quality to Hebrew.[7] This intellectual thrust, visible also in the prekabbalistic works of the Iberian philosopher and poet Judah Halevi (ca. 1075–1141), extends the rabbinic conception of Hebrew as the "Holy Tongue" (*leshon ha-kodesh*) by linking it to the revelatory and creative properties of God's most sacred name.

Though wary of the limits of language and its possible misuses, Jewish mystics rarely lapse into unabashed claims that God's infinitude and essence can be adequately represented only through silence. Medieval Kabbalists affirmed the power of words in religious life and theology, developing a wide range of contemplative practices linked to the words of the liturgy and the variety of divine appellatives.[8] These thinkers, like mystics across many different religious traditions, often deployed language in creative or paradoxical ways in order to overcome its limitations.[9] Early Kabbalists also sought to transcend the boundaries of words by developing a vast reservoir of symbolic language. This rich matrix of associations and symbols, inspired by biblical verses, rabbinic teachings, and subsequent mystical interpretations, has been elaborated and refined over the years. At the heart of this system are the *sefirot* (sing. *sefirah*)—a series of emanations bridging the gap between the abstract, unknowable Divine and its immanent presence in this world—which became the conceptual anchors to which the vast array of symbols adheres. The flexibility and richness of these symbols afford the Kabbalists a mode of speaking about divine matters that extends beyond the literal meaning of words.[10]

The symbolic language of Jewish mysticism began to take on a recognizable and relatively stable form in the *Bahir*, which circulated in late twelfth- or early thirteenth-century Provence.[11] It reached new heights in the Zohar, the crown jewel of medieval Jewish mysticism, and the development of this expansive symbolic language—together with more specific theories of language—continued unabated. But the symbolic vocabulary of medieval Kabbalah, and the accompanying "intentions" (*kavvanot*) or "unifications" of the *sefirot* and names of God (*yihudim*), also grew increasingly complicated and abstruse across the years.[12] This was particularly true in the wake of the Safed renaissance of the sixteenth century and its spread across the next 150 years. By the dawn of Hasidism in the eighteenth century, some religious thinkers had come to see that the kabbalistic visions of language had largely come to pieces under the weight of their own convoluted intricacy. Hasidic teachings on the devotional power of all human language should be seen as emerging in the wake of this collapse.

The Hasidic Word

Dov Ber's teachings on sacred speech draw on a vast array of sources from earlier Jewish literature, including traditional rabbinic texts and the full range of Jewish mystical literature, from *Sefer Yetsirah* to the Zohar and the writings of Safed Kabbalah.[13] Aspects of the Maggid's homilies share particular resonances with the works of Avraham Abulafia, a thirteenth-century mystical maverick who developed an array of techniques—from cleaving to the letters and their permutations to contemplating various divine names—to spark a prophetic experience.[14] The unique spiritual qualities of Hebrew, the only divine language and the source of all others, were the foundation of his enterprise. This understanding of Hebrew as the only *lingua sacra*, shared among all medieval Kabbalists, makes the Maggid's extension of holiness to all speech all the more striking.

Along with Abulafian language mysticism and the corpus of Lurianic writings produced by Hayyim Vital (1542–1620), the Maggid was also inspired by the other kabbalistic thinkers of Safed, including Moshe Cordovero (1522–1570), who describes the letters as "vessels" (*kelim*), "palaces" (*heikhalot*), and a "habitation" (*makhon*) for *ruhaniyyut*, or "spiritual vitality."[15] More broadly, Cordovero devoted an entire section of his magnum opus, *Pardes Rimmonim*, to explicating the meaning of each of the Hebrew letters.[16] The Maggid was also indebted to the writings of the late sixteenth-century Yisra'el Sarug (fl. 1590–1610). His version of the Lurianic doctrine, which was prominent in eastern Europe, refers to the emanated "garment" (*levush*) of creation as composed of letters.[17]

The Maggid's approach to theology and religious life was shaped by his readings of medieval Kabbalah. His theory of language was fundamentally transformed by his encounter with the BeSHT's conception of God's immanence in human speech. Describing words and letters as vessels filled with near-infinite divine vitality, the BeSHT portrayed the cosmos as saturated with a godly life-force composed of the twenty-two Hebrew letters.[18] God spoke the world into being, and this sacred divine language continues to animate the fabric of existence. Such descriptions of the power of language, particularly its spoken form, abound in the BeSHT's teachings.

One of the most important sources addressing this subject is the BeSHT's letter to his brother-in-law Gershon Kitover, a Pietist and scholar then living in the land of Israel.[19] This epistle, which asserted notable influence on later Hasidism, reports an "ascent of the soul" during which the BeSHT rose into the heavens and met the Messiah.[20] There among the celestial palaces he claims to have become acquainted with a new body of sacred wisdom, including certain charms and holy names that he is forbidden to reveal. However, the BeSHT also notes that the Messiah is promised to arrive "when your wellsprings overflow outward . . . and when all can perform the unifications (*yihudim*) and ascents as you do." Explaining the contours of this duty, the BeSHT offers the following instruction to his brother-in-law:

> While you are praying and studying, aim to achieve a unification
> (*yihud*) through each and every utterance that crosses your lips. In

each word and every letter there are worlds, souls and divinity (*'olamot, nefashot ve-elohut*) that rise and connect, becoming linked to each other. Afterward the letters come together to form a word, and are truly unified in their divinity. You should join your soul to them in every one of these aspects.

Then all the worlds will form a single unity. They will then rise up and produce immeasurable joy and delight [in the heavens]. If you consider the joy of a bride and groom in our diminished and material realm, [you will get some sense] of how much greater it is in this exalted sphere.[21]

The vocalized words of prayer and study, claims the BeSHT, must be accompanied by the correct meditations. Seeing human speech—composed of words and letters—as expressing God's life-force, the worshipper achieves uplift through the union of his soul with the divine vitality that dwells within the language. The BeSHT illustrates this technique by highlighting the potency of worship and study, but he simultaneously extends the vision by noting that such intentions must be performed together with "each and every utterance that crosses your lips." All speech, it seems, may—or must—contain "worlds, souls and divinity." The precise meaning of this triad is without clear literary precedent, but it suggests that the spoken word may enfold cosmos, self, and divinity into a single linguistic expression of devotion.[22]

Scholars have identified a wealth of shamanic or "talismanic" traditions in the BeSHT's teachings on language. Stories of miraculous cures or magical elements in the BeSHT's approach to words are unsurprising, of course, given his reputation as a *ba'al shem*.[23] But these traditions coexist alongside experiential descriptions of the worshipper or scholar encountering God through tapping into the divine core of spoken words. Such a moment of spiritual illumination is found in the following sermon by the BeSHT's grandson, Moshe Hayim Efrayim of Sudilkov:

"Make a light source for the 'ark' (*teivah*)" (Gen. 6:16). My grandfather [the BeSHT] interpreted "ark" (*teivah*) as "word"[24] . . . and he interpreted "make a light source in the ark" to mean "see to it that you illuminate the word that you articulate."[25] He commented on this at great length.

Scripture is saying that if you sometimes notice that the light is hidden, and cannot be seen at all, and you do not know what to do in order to open the word and remove the occlusion so that the light is revealed, the verse explains, "the opening of the word" (ibid.)—open the word so that it is not closed and sealed, as in, "I was silent, speechless" (Ps. 39:3).[26]

Just as one's vision of divine immanence in the cosmos may be diminished at times, the sacred life-force concealed in the letters is not necessarily self-obvious. The BeSHT's advice, amplified in his grandson's interpretation, is to throw "open" the words of prayer by unveiling their sacred hidden light as they are spoken aloud:

> "Put [the entrance to the ark] at its side" (Gen. 6:16). If you seek it, you will find "an entrance" to the word "at its side," meaning that surely there is light in the very same darkness.[27] It is simply hidden.
> "Make lower, second and third levels for it" (Gen. 6:17). This should be explained according to what I heard from my grand-father: there are worlds, souls and divinity in each and every word. The "ark" is alluding to this, since "ark" means "word." "Lower" means worlds, which is the lowest level. "Second" refers to the souls, and "third" (shelishim) means divinity, as in "and leaders (shalishim) over them all" (Ex. 14:7), for He rules and directs all. "Make" all of these, meaning that the words that you speak should be with this intention and with perfect faith that each word holds "lower, second and third levels," which are the worlds, souls, and divinity. Understand this.[28]

The power of once-dim words may be rekindled, because God's vitality is hidden within them just as in all elements of the cosmos. This text also presents the notion that language includes "worlds, souls, and divinity," which may be aroused and united through the worshipper's contemplation. The spoken word is thus transformed into a lustrous vessel for God's immanent presence, sheltering—and uncovering—the Divine just as the biblical ark delivered Noah from the deluge.

Such teachings emphasize that language may serve as a vehicle for divine revelation, but words do not automatically disclose their sacred properties. "One connects to God through the letters of Torah and of prayer," summarizes Ya'akov Yosef of Polnoye in the name of his teacher the BeSHT.

"One must attach his mind and innermost vitality (*penimiyyuto*) to the inner spiritual vitality in the letters. This is how to understand, 'Let Him kiss me with the kisses of His mouth' (Song 1:2)—it is connection of Soul to soul."[29] The divine vitality in the letters enables a moment of intimate communion between God and the worshipper, but only if the latter's contemplative awareness has aroused the innermost divinity dwelling within the spoken word.[30]

A significant number of traditions attributed to the BeSHT, including the epistle to Gershon Kitover, may be interpreted as intimating that *all* human speech possesses a divine quality.[31] Some of the BeSHT's homilies quite clearly extend the devotional power of language beyond the words of prayer or study, claiming that certain *yihudim* are meant to accompany words spoken in the marketplace or the ordinary conversations between two human beings.

This point is made with succinct clarity in the following tradition, a teaching representative of many others found in early Hasidic literature: "From the holy mouth of the BeSHT, I heard the following explanation about the Sages' teaching 'the ordinary conversations of scholars require study'[32]: the essential perfection of each and every *tsaddik* is that he does not break his connection with God for even a single moment. In all words, even when the leader converses with ordinary people about mundane matters, he sees to it that he maintains his connection [to the Divine]."[33] All language is composed of the same fundaments—that is, the same twenty-two letters of the Hebrew alphabet—regardless of its context. Each word includes an element of the Divine when it is combined with the proper attunement. Ordinary conversations between two spiritual comrades may thus be transformed into a holy encounter in which the words are as filled with divinity as those of prayer or sacred study. Descriptions such as the following appear in a wealth of Hasidic sermons from the movement's infancy: "I heard from my teacher [the BeSHT] that there are unifications (*yihudim*)[34] in spoken words, whether it is the speech of Torah and worship or that shared with a friend in the marketplace. One should connect to him and raise him up, each according to his rung. Some are accomplished through sacred speech (*dibbur bi-kedushah*) and others through mundane speech (*dibbur hol*), which is [also] composed of the twenty-two letters of the Hebrew alphabet."[35] Collectively these traditions on the potential holiness of mundane words represent one of the key innovations of Hasidism vis-à-vis the earlier kabbalistic tradition. Even speaking about mundane matters does not necessarily interfere with the ultimate goal of attaining *devekut* ("communion" or even "union" with God); even banal or ordinary words may serve as vehicles for God's presence.

When taken as a whole, however, the BeSHT's legacy does not undo the critical distinction between sacred speech and mundane language. Other homilies suggest that different modalities of language effect divine union at various degrees of intimacy and elevation.[36] This includes the coarse—but not inappropriate—works spoken by mongers and merchants, as well as the deep spiritual conversation shared between two companions. But a wealth of traditions from the BeSHT refer to the performance of religious speech as bringing about a moment of communion between the various elements of the Godhead. The power of language ultimately extends to all of its various forms and instantiations, but many—perhaps most—traditions from the BeSHT preserve the distinction between religious language and ordinary speech.

The BeSHT has rightly been described as an extroverted mystical type focused primarily on the aural elements of sacred language.[37] His homilies do include a contemplative element, apparent in traditions such as the following statement by Ya'akov Yosef of Polnoye: "I heard this quite clearly (*mefurash*) from the mouth of my teacher [the BeSHT]: 'A person is entirely present in the place that his mind resides.'"[38] This short teaching and the many others like it emphasize that a worshipper's thoughts are more determinative than the place of his physical body. Although he highlights speech as a vessel of revelation, the BeSHT notes that spoken language can express only a tiny fraction of the mind's infinite potential. For this reason one's thoughts must never be allowed to drift away from the presence of God.[39] Such traditions regarding contemplation add another important dimension to the BeSHT's accounting of sacred language, acting as a bridge between teachings on spoken language and those regarding the infinite power of the human mind.

The Sources of Language and Human Speech

Dov Ber constructed his theory of language on the BeSHT's notion of divine immanence in human words.[40] Turning to questions of language in nearly every homily, the Maggid's sermons interrogate many of the fundamental issues that have beleaguered and excited religious thinkers and philosophers across the centuries: What is the nature of language? Where does it come from? Is language naturally divine, or is it purely conventional?

What are the fundaments of language? What is the relationship between thought and words? Is there something—a realm of cognition or experience— beyond language? Like many eastern European Jews of his time, he was little concerned with issues of grammar, philology, or comparative linguistics, areas of interest that became more important in the decades after his death. But the BeSHT's presentation of the divinity of language captured Dov Ber's heart and mind. His devotional and theological project, marbled with sophisticated philosophical murmurs and reflections, explores the power of the word and its importance for the inner life.[41]

The Maggid understood the process of redeeming language by "raising it up" to its source in the Divine to be the crux of religious service and key to cultivating a life of contemplative holiness. Similar turns of phrase about returning sacred fragments or holy sparks to their divine origin are common in Hasidic literature.[42] One reads of "lifting up" the sparks to their source in the Godhead, or "raising up" the strict judgments (*dinim*) to the place of rebirth or mercy.[43] Such a formulation of uplifting speech, redolent of the medieval kabbalistic traditions to which Dov Ber was heir, seems rather opaque to the modern reader.

What does the Maggid really mean? Can language truly be "returned" to God without annihilating it, thereby essentially undoing the project of creation? This question returns us to the debate between Gershom Scholem and Martin Buber regarding whether Hasidism's approach to the physical should be seen as world-affirming or world-denying.[44] The Maggid's teachings on the power of language, I shall argue, offer a fresh vantage point from which to reconsider the contours of this debate between Scholem and Buber. Rather than negating the power of words or retreating into meditative silence, the Maggid argues that the process of elevating words to their divine source requires a full and unreserved embrace of language. God formed the cosmos through a series of creative utterances that continue to saturate the fabric of existence with sacred life-force. Moreover, all acts of revelation— divine, but also human—are driven by the urge to break forth from silence and cast one's wisdom into words.

Our discussion of Dov Ber's theory of language begins with an insight connected to the philosophical question regarding the origins of words: Is language a conventional system of signs, the meaning of which has been agreed on by a certain community or group, or does language possess inherent or natural meaning?[45] The Maggid follows the position of the Kabbalists, who, as we have seen, uniformly describe Hebrew as a divine tongue in which words connect fundamentally to their referents, and which holds untold cosmic secrets. But Dov Ber's theory of language goes deeper yet, since he claims that human speech is studded with divine vitality and power. The worshipper's words express God's own speech, and, as we shall see, this understanding hinges on the essential nature of language rather than the singular quality of a particular tongue.

The conception of the human as the "speaking being" is commonly found in Jewish thought under the influence of Aristotle, but for the Maggid it goes beyond such definitions. The ability to give life to the word, says Dov Ber, is a sacred faculty given to humanity by the divine breath that continuously animates the body and soul.[46] One's every utterance is filled with God's power because the name Y-H-V-H is, by necessity, "garbed in every word and expression."[47] We should not overlook the paradox in depicting the ineffable divine name, no longer pronounced as it is written, as the source of all language. Y-H-V-H is often interpreted in Jewish mystical sources as referring to God's capacity to bring existence into being (*mehaveh et ha-kol*).[48] Rooting language in this name draws a parallel between the unfolding of the cosmos through God's word and the surging, sacred power that animates language both human and divine.

The Maggid identifies human language as emerging from what he calls the "World of Speech" (*'olam ha-dibbur*).[49] His theory links *'olam ha-dibbur* to *malkhut*, the tenth of the *sefirot* that is associated with *shekhinah* (the divine presence). This connection anchors human speech in *shekhinah*, which animates the cosmos:

> A *tsaddik* who worships through the [divine power of the] letters becomes connected to the supernal wisdom (*hokhmah*).[50] . . . He enters the gateway of Naught (*ayin*), concentrating on the fact (*ma'aleh 'al libo*) that, were it not for the power of God in him, he would be nothing at all.
>
> That being the case, all [that he is and does] derives from God's power. Human speech is the divine World of Speech, through which the world was created. The World of Speech proceeds from [God's] wisdom. This is the source of pleasure and delight that God receives from the worlds.
>
> Even now, the worshipper should speak only for the sake of divine pleasure, thus returning the letters to their ultimate source in *hokhmah*.[51]

An individual at prayer must strive to link human language to its divine counterpart, coming to realize that the World of Speech is the source of all his words. This union of the worshipper's speech with its divine root causes God to delight, sparking an intensified moment of empowerment as worshipper encounters the divine presence that is spoken into being through his words.[52] This connection can only be effected, however, if the one praying is cognizant of being filled with God's word as the source of his language.

The human being must therefore worship God solely through the sacred quality of language with which he has been infused. Yearning to return to its holy source, *shekhinah* or the indwelling aspect of the Divine is offered back to God through acts of human devotion. This ecosystem of breath, a constant recycling of sacred energy, is made possible through the intertwining of language that is both human and divine. The Maggid seems unthreatened by the paradoxical implications of this idea. He lovingly describes God as engaging in an act of self-worship accomplished through human speech:

> "Your God is a priest."[53] This means that we serve God only through the power that He has given. [Our] thought and speech are the World of Thought and the World of Speech. Therefore, we serve Him because of Him. This is [the meaning of] "Your God is a priest"—He worships Himself, as it were, through Himself [i.e., through the divine speech which God grants to man]. . . .
>
> A person must consider himself nothing (*ayin*), for the Holy One does not come to dwell within, becoming embodied in him, if he considers himself something (*yesh*). God is infinite (*ein sof*) and cannot be held by any vessel.[54]

Self-transcendence is the key to unlocking the spiritual power of language. A worshipper who considers himself to be "something," seeing his language as an autonomous faculty, is nothing more than a finite container incapable of receiving the divine presence. Through breaking down the walls of the ego, however, one is transformed into a vessel capable of holding the infinite Divine. This allows the worshipper to embody the quality of divine speech, turning his words into an expression of God's sacred language.

The Maggid's descriptions of becoming emptied of the self recall Ibn Arabi's account of the mystic quest as polishing the mirror of the soul. Dov

Ber's teachings also evoke notions of kenosis in Christian mystics like Meister Eckhart and John of the Cross.[55] According to the Maggid, however, this process requires neither a posture of nonaction nor a retreat into pure silence. In fact, he argues precisely the opposite: the words of a person who has cultivated this degree of inwardness and awareness quite literally become vehicles of theophany, brooding resurgences of the divine language of creation.[56] Such unity of God and the human being through the power of language elicits tremendous joy, for the worshipper's delight in sacred service mirrors—and causes—delight in the Divine.[57] God's awakening is born in the stirrings of the heart and expressed through the power of human words.[58]

This technique of attaching one's speech to God through negating the private interests of the self is a defining characteristic of the *tsaddik*. The wicked, in contrast, revel in what they perceive as their independent capacity for language: "'A slanderer separates himself from the lord' (*mafrid aluf*; Prov. 16:28), that is, he separates himself from the Master (*alufo*) of the world. He separates his speech from the World of Speech, and his thoughts from the World of Thought."[59] Ignorance of the divine presence manifest in human words sets the sinful apart from the righteous, for such denial opens a chasm between the individual and God. In another homily, the Maggid draws this distinction in even stronger terms:

> The *tsaddikim* could create a world if they wished to do so.[60] "The heavens were created by the word of Y-H-V-H" (Ps. 33:6), and it is written "and He breathed into him the soul of life [and man became a living soul]" (Gen. 2:7), which is rendered by the Targum as "a speaking being."
>
> One cannot refer to parts when speaking of God, for God is endless (*ein sof*). One cannot describe the Infinite as blowing only His speech into his nostrils. Therefore, [all of God's essence] was included in this speech.[61]

Aristotle defined speech as a uniquely human characteristic, a notion that is reflected in the Targum or Aramaic translation, and Dov Ber seems to have in mind Nahmanides' comment on Genesis 2:7: "One who blows into the nose of another, does so from his very essence."[62] But the Maggid has added what appears to be a highly original interpretation. The divine word, and God's vitality within it, was breathed into Adam and thus invested within human beings for perpetuity. Rather than a social construct or a conventional agreement, the deepest stratum of what becomes language is the capacity for sacred speech with which humanity has been imbued: "This is why *tsaddikim* can create a world, if they so desired. The speech of the *tsaddik* is totally pure, with no separating veil [to alienate it from the divine realm]. Unlike the [words of the] slanderer, who separates himself from the Master, the *tsaddik's* speech is intimately connected (*medubbak u-mekushar*) to its source. It is just like God's speech, from which heaven and earth were created."[63] The *tsaddik* is mindful of the fact that the capacity for speech is a divine gift, one that a human being is imbued with by God. This intimate and enduring connection between divine and human words may be severed through inattention, but, when nurtured, it is manifest through the creative quality of the *tsaddik's* speech.

Rooting this mythos of the power of words in the primordial creation story suggests that it is, in theory, accessible to all worshippers rather than the exclusive purview of the religious elites. The same divine vitality dwells within each person; all individuals have the same potential to cultivate sacred speech that emerges directly from *'olam ha-dibbur*.[64] Realizing this power is a matter of contemplative choice, and the righteous and wicked are thusly characterized by their differing relationship to language. The unvirtuous slanderers assert the independence of their language, whereas *tsaddikim* embrace the divine potential within the human word. Surrendering their linguistic autonomy, however, allows *tsaddikim* to become creative beings capable of imitating God through their illuminated speech.

The Boundaries of Sacred Speech

The Maggid's description of the worshipper's capacity for language as an embodiment of the divine word raises several critical questions: Does it apply to ordinary words? Does it hold true of all languages, or is it a unique feature of Hebrew? Is it a capacity shared by all people? The term *leshon ha-kodesh* (the holy language) is strikingly rare in the Maggid's teachings on language, particularly when considered against the backdrop of earlier kabbalistic sources in which Hebrew is consistently lauded for its unique power, beauty, and its essential divinity. Dov Ber's references to the Jewish people and the power of their words often depict an essential relationship between Israel and the Hebrew language. Such homilies, however, are complemented by sermons intimating that humanity possesses the divine word.

The Hebrew Bible makes no forthright claim regarding the uniqueness of Hebrew either as a divine language or as one with particular cultural significance.[65] This attitude shifted in the Second Temple period as Hebrew, closely associated with the Temple and with the Torah, was reconceived as possessing singular religious and national meaning.[66] The pseudepigraphal book of Jubilees describes Hebrew as the "revealed language" and the "language of creation,"[67] but the term *leshon ha-kodesh* as such appears first in a Qumran text in reference to primordial language preserved only by Abraham and his descendants.[68]

The designation of Hebrew as Holy Tongue is found sporadically in classical rabbinic literature, in legal contexts as well as legendary musings.[69] The Jerusalem Talmud, for example, records a debate regarding the original language mentioned in Genesis 11:1. One opinion claims that all seventy languages were known before the Tower of Babel, suggesting that people could understand one another because all were multilingual. But another sage identifies this pre-Babel tongue as that of "the singular One of the world, the sacred tongue (*yehido shel 'olam, leshon ha-kodesh*)."[70] A later rabbinic midrash weaves these themes together in a claim that while Hebrew was the original language, the subsequent division into the seventy languages became a part of the cosmic hierarchy along with the seventy nations.[71] Another midrashic work describes a return to Hebrew as part of the messianic redemption, interpreting the "pure speech" mentioned in Zephaniah 3:9 as a reference to the primordial language.[72] These rabbinic sources of late antiquity, however, offer neither a theory of language nor a sustained explanation of the singularity of Hebrew.

The short but influential *Sefer Yetsirah*, an early work that had a great impact on later Jewish mysticism, further developed the idea of creation through language implied by the Hebrew Bible.[73] *Sefer Yetsirah* describes God's formation of the universe by means of the "thirty-two pathways of wisdom," namely, the ten *sefirot* and the twenty-two letters of the Hebrew alphabet. This work thus introduces the term *sefirot* into the Jewish lexicon for the first time. In this context, however, they refer to something very different from the complex web of symbols they will represent in medieval Kabbalah. Here the *sefirot* are simply the numerical (*mispar*) elements used by God to fashion the world. It is interesting to note that *Sefer Yetsirah* does not examine the shapes of the letters nor their numerical values, techniques that were central in later Jewish mysticism.[74] This work does not assign a special status to Hebrew or designate it a "holy tongue" vis-à-vis other languages, though election of Hebrew is implied by the narrative of creation through twenty-two letters. Its preoccupation with the creative power of the letters was this work's greatest contribution to the Jewish mystical tradition.[75]

Medieval Jews in Islamic lands were called to respond to the glorification of Arabic, especially that of the Qur'an, for its divine origins as well as its unparalleled aesthetic quality.[76] Though most Jewish philosophers reserved a special status for *leshon ha-kodesh*, they fiercely disagreed regarding which qualities—if any—render Hebrew uniquely sacred. The Andalusian philosopher Judah Halevi, for example, drew a distinction between conventional human languages and the divine language of Hebrew, reserved by the Jews for sacred purposes. Hebrew is the language of creation and revelation, said Halevi, and only the words of God's beautiful and eloquent tongue are particularly appropriate to their objects of reference.[77]

Halevi's writings on Hebrew may be fruitfully contrasted with those of Maimonides, who famously—and controversially—argued that all languages, including *leshon ha-kodesh*, are conventional.[78] This includes Hebrew, defined as "holy" primarily because of its lack of obscenities and its potential ethical characteristics. This rationalist claim sparked the ire of Kabbalists such as the thirteenth-century Nahmanides, who were firmly committed to the divine nature of Hebrew.[79] These medieval mystics saw language as rooted in the unfolding of being, and as the primary medium through which the rift between the human and divine realms could be bridged.[80]

When viewed against this historical backdrop, it is quite startling that Dov Ber's homilies refer to the distinctive qualities of Hebrew in only a few instances. The Maggid points out that each of the proverbial "seventy languages" possesses words for all living things, and thus wonders why the midrash describes Adam's naming of the animals as a miraculous feat beyond even the angels.[81] Dov Ber explains that the Hebrew word for any beast— indeed, any noun—is its essential name in the heavenly realm; all other ways of referring to the object are simply conventional.[82] Adam was graced with the wisdom to discern each animal's true divine root in the worlds above, thus grasping the letters from which its vitality derives.

The Maggid elsewhere suggests that each word of the Hebrew language has a root in the worlds above, playing on the double meaning of the term *shoresh*.[83] In grammatical terms a *shoresh* refers to the letters (usually three) that are the basic structure of most Hebrew words. However, in kabbalistic literature the term *shoresh* denotes an object's or person's place of origin in the Godhead. Words may therefore be broken down into their essential root letters, which are grounded in the formless realm of the divine mind, and may then be effectively recreated. This linguistic flexibility inherent in the Hebrew language is the secret to biblical exegesis, for the meaning of all biblical verses to be dramatically reinterpreted.[84]

In a surprising number of homilies, however, the Maggid argues that all languages, and indeed all peoples, are rooted in the letters of the Torah. This suggests that Hebrew—the language of Scripture—is the source of all other languages.[85] That Hebrew is somehow the source of all other tongues need not define them as holy, of course. A particular language may still be unique even if all speech is—or can become—sacred. But the Maggid seems to suggest something that extends beyond medieval Jewish pictures of the tree of languages with Hebrew as the trunk: the Hebrew letters are foundation stones or building blocks of all human language, and therefore all speech includes and is animated by a sacred spark of this divine tongue.

The singularity of Hebrew may have been assumed in his insular eastern European Jewish community, but I suspect there is another reason for the Maggid's reserve regarding the primacy of *leshon ha-kodesh*: exalting one particular language, even Hebrew, at the expense of all others would contradict Dov Ber's claim that all speech may be an expression of God's word (*'olam ha-dibbur*). Constantly foregrounding the singularity of Hebrew would have undercut one of the pillars of his theory of language: that *all* human language, not just Hebrew or the specific words of religious liturgy or rituals, may become holy. This is a point that Dov Ber asserts with great vehemence while, as we shall see, still allowing it to remain fraught with ambiguity.

In the introduction to this book, we noted that the idea of a *lingua sacra* is found in religious traditions and cultures across the world. This notion of a holy tongue is often interpreted as linked to a dualistic vision in which the sacred is defined in contradistinction to the mundane or profane realms.[86] The Maggid's panentheistic theology, however, allows for no such gulf between the holy and the ordinary realms. Though he lauds the study of Torah and worship, Dov Ber's homilies make it clear that the proper intention will transform ordinary language into holy speech.

No fundamental distinction may be drawn between sacred and mundane words, argues the Maggid, because all human language is composed of the same fundamental elements. In one sermon, we read, "What is the difference between the letters of idle chatter and the letters of Torah? The difference is that the letters of idle speech are held captive [in the *kelippot*], and the Holy One wants them to be redeemed."[87] God longs for the human worshipper to uplift the fallen divine language, which has become "trapped" in the mundane realm when used to express a debased or untoward idea.

Dov Ber imagines these fallen letters as crying out from the snares of ordinary speech, yearning to return to their divine origin. The worshipper's task is to free these words by restoring them on high, "raising up the letters and drawing divinity (*elohut*) into them."[88] Taking a Lurianic image of lifting up the sparks and giving it a linguistic twist,[89] the Maggid claims that returning all language to its godly source is the ultimate aim of one's religious life:

> The ultimate goal of [sacred] service is to raise up the holy sparks
> that have fallen into brokenness. [This includes] all words
> and thoughts, which are all letters. If they come from idle chatter,
> they are letters of brokenness. Everything must be lifted up to its
> root. This is why someone who has an idle conversation trans-
> gresses a positive commandment,[90] and must take immediate
> action in order to raise it to its source. This is the meaning of,
> "Even the ordinary conversations of the sages require study"
> [i.e., idle speech must be followed by a positive deed].[91]
>
> And this is the meaning of, "The land will be full of the
> awareness of '*et*' Y-H-V-H" (Isa. 11:9). "*Et*" represents the letters
> from *aleph* to *tav*. These are the letters of speech and thought.
> "Awareness" (*de'ah*) refers to connection.[92]

The world is filled with the letters of God's language, sparks trapped in the physical realm when the vessels of creation shattered and released their light.[93] Idle conversations hinder the redemption of this fractured language from its exile. Therefore, one who forgets himself and chatters frivolously—even a scholar—must rectify the mistake by focusing on his words and contemplating their divine origin. The Maggid's citation of the Talmudic maxim "Even the ordinary conversations of the sages require study" is surprising, for he seems to be suggesting that a scholar's mundane conversations are no better than idle speech. The "study" they require is none other than the positive action that must follow all forms of debased speech.[94]

The worshipper who has cultivated "awareness" (*da'at*) of the sacred divine language that inheres in the cosmos, however, links his words to the fallen letters of creation and thus raises them up to their root.[95] Such a person, whose mind is trained on God, develops the power to infuse all ordinary conversations with the spirit of the Divine.[96] And such individuals, claims the Maggid, have the additional responsibility of lifting up the coarse or banal words spoken by others:

> This is how the Maggid explained [the mishnah]: "and their
> opposite (ve-hillufeihem) is true for the boor (golem)."[97] What
> emerges from his holy words is thus: the enlightened one must
> raise up whatever he sees and hears from another. Even [if] one
> person is speaking to another about material things and so forth,
> [his speech] must be raised up to the Creator. He must transform
> (la-hahlif) that which was originally an earthly combination [of
> letters] into a spiritual one. This cannot be accomplished unless
> he raises them to divine wisdom (hokhmah), the primordial point,
> the letter yod, which is formless matter (golem). From that point
> he can draw forth [new potential], making whatever letter he
> wishes or any combination required for the service.[98]

The "enlightened individual" (maskil) is charged with raising up all human conversations, even if he is simply the listener. He does so by absorbing the letters of speech, bringing them into his contemplative mind and returning them to the source from which all language flows. This infinite pool deep within the worshipper's mind is associated with the sefirah hokhmah and with yod, the initial letter of the name Y-H-V-H. There, in this realm of unformed wisdom, language is present only in the most inchoate of forms. Therefore, claims Dov Ber, the contemplative listener must reach into this inner reservoir. He enters the meeting place of God and the human being in the human mind, and brings forth new permutations that transform ordinary words into a spiritual language of redemption.

Does the Maggid recommend that such a person seek out opportunities to uplift conversations with ordinary people? Is one simply expected to do so when confronted with a situation in which he cannot avoid such a banal verbal exchange? Several of Dov Ber's sermons do suggest that the practice of raising up ordinary words is intended to prescribe religious behavior. Certain elite individuals, he implies, should look for fallen language in need of restoration:

> "Behold, they may gather together, but nothing is devoid of Me"
> (Isa. 54:15).[99] A person connected to the tsaddik, watching him

serve God by sitting and learning, will sometimes [encounter] the *tsaddik* speaking idle words.

This is like a parable about the king's son who walks among the villagers to search out the treasure held by one of them. He must dress up like a villager, so that they will not recognize him as the king's son. [Thus they will] reveal all of their secrets to him, [such as] the location of the treasure.

So does the *tsaddik* speak with God. He is attached to the Divine, connecting his words to God. He is referred to as an emissary of the Holy One, who goes out to find the divine attributes (*middot*).[100]

A *tsaddik's* disciples will see their leader behave in a variety of ways, including telling humorous and banal anecdotes or stories.[101] His inner contemplation amid this ordinary speech is invisible to outside observers, and even the *tsaddik's* own students will be astonished by discussion of such trite matters. This mundane language is only a facade, however, because the *tsaddik's* seemingly ordinary words contain divine vitality as well. In fact, the illumination of his speech is unrecognizable precisely because it is too intense for those around him:

This is the meaning of, "Behold, they may gather together" (*hen gor yagur*)—when he is out of his element (*be-gerut*) and speaking idle words, then "there is nothing devoid of me"—there are some people who believe that the Holy One is not found here. But this is because the brightness is too great, as they said about a light so strong that it overwhelms one's sight.[102] It cannot be perceived because its light is revealed to such a degree that the mind cannot grasp it. . . .

In truth, He created them, even if the fact that He is embodied [within them] is not clear. . . . This is [the true meaning of] "nothing is devoid of Me"—no thing exists without Me.[103]

The *tsaddik* is connected to God even when conversing with ordinary people or speaking of mundane matters. The Maggid presents this uplifted speech as an ideal to be actively pursued, rather than a necessary compromise. The worshipper, argues Dov Ber, must leave the intimate safety of his personal communion with the Divine in order to raise up the holy sparks hidden in ordinary speech.

The aim of this journey into the divine core of mundane speech, whether voluntary or involuntary, is to raise up the fallen letters and restore their link to the divine root.[104] There is danger, claims the Maggid, in attaching oneself to ordinary people and lower forms of spiritual language. The *tsaddik* must take care not to lose sight of the holy sparks hidden within mundane language; only thus will he prevent himself from becoming ensnared in the "husks" that surround them.[105]

In this homily, the Maggid draws a clear parallel between God's immanence in the cosmos and the divine vitality at the heart of language. This rare embrace of corporeality is rather striking, given that so many of Dov Ber's sermons evince a pronounced distrust of serving God through ordinary deeds. This skepticism was an expression of his pietistic and ascetic nature, an attitude not fully effaced by his encounter with the BeSHT. On the subject of redeeming ordinary language in all of its various forms, the Maggid's teachings are emphatically and unreservedly positive. But the close-knit association between divine immanence and the potentially sacred core of all words in texts like this suggests that the Maggid's affirmative stance, though inconsistent, was linked to his theory of language as the indwelling of God. We may now interrogate this fraught issue, which cuts across Dov Ber's oeuvre, in greater detail.

Serving God in a World Full of Letters

Dov Ber's sermons describe the cosmos as continuously sustained by God's creative word. In many teachings, this vision rests on his exegesis of the opening chapter of Genesis, but he also draws on the ancient rabbinic and kabbalistic traditions regarding the world being created through the letters of Torah.[106] The Maggid frequently illustrates the immanent presence of divine language in the cosmos with the watchword "the power of the Maker within the made" (*ko'ah ha-po'el ba-nif'al*). Dov Ber cites the phrase as if it were drawn from ancient sources; however, although it is commonly cited in later Hasidic sources, its provenance remains ambiguous.[107] Like the holy kernel that animates even ordinary speech, the vital power of God's creative utterances must be uplifted from the physical world and returned to its source.

The Maggid's relationship to raising up these divine letters found in the corporeal world is quite complicated.[108] Some homilies claim that worshipping God by means of ordinary actions, such as eating or drinking, is a critical element of religious devotion.[109] The Israelites were exiled to Egypt, suggests Dov Ber, in order to raise up the fallen sparks trapped there.[110] Elsewhere he notes that words of Torah spoken at table will raise the coarse act of eating to a sacred level; the letters trapped in the food long to be consumed by a holy person.[111] In one surprising teaching the Maggid even refers to liberating the sacred linguistic energy in food as a mode of "studying" Torah.

In other teachings, however, the Maggid's tone is quite circumspect regarding the possibility of serving God through ordinary physical deeds. His descriptions of the danger inherent in this sort of service far exceed his cautious, yet inclusive, approach to uplifting banal conversations. A *tsaddik* must eat only enough to survive, he claims, for any gross or extraneous eating is a cardinal sin. And since the true essence of food is the divine letters within, one must look past its physical shell and consider only the sacred vitality.[112] Fasting and other such techniques aimed at shattering one's longing for worldly pleasures have an important place in the Maggid's teachings.

Dov Ber's admonitions regarding disciplined asceticism underscore the need to eliminate all lust or desire for the physical world, but they do not necessarily demand that one sever any connection with the physical.[113] One may serve God through eating or drinking together with the classical commandments, provided that this service is unencumbered by ulterior motivations. The Maggid's cosmos is, after all, animated by the divine word that longs to be reconnected to its godly origin. The following homily, presented among the teachings by Menahem Nahum of Chernobil, is emblematic of his master's approach to the earthly realm:

> My teacher often referred to this as "mundane matters conducted in a purely holy manner."[114] Even acts that appear to be mundane should be carried out in a pure and holy way, since there is Torah in everything. In eating, for example, how much Torah and how many paths [of service] are to be found, [beginning with] washing one's hands. So too in matters of business.
>
> My master said that the lifeblood of these things lies in the Torah and laws that are to be found within them. God and Torah are one, so that everything has some relationship to Torah, even the lowliest creature.[115]

All physical deeds are opportunities to serve God, says the Maggid, because the corporeal world is filled with Torah. An individual whose behavior accords with Jewish law may therefore come to worship God through his every action. This is possible not simply because of the worshipper's unwavering allegiance to following the divine fiat, but because his engagement with the physical will arouse the inner vitality of all things. All activities may be sanctified as one becomes attuned to the fact that everything reveals the power of the Maker.

Dov Ber gives the examples of ritual handwashing before partaking of bread and the rules governing commerce, but makes it clear that the power of Torah dwells within *all* creation. Furthermore, since Scripture is itself a garment of words cloaking the ineffable Divine, God's linguistic vitality inheres in all things as well.[116] Involvement with physicality does not necessarily degrade one's spiritual life, although other traditions have the Maggid describing it as a lesser order of religious service.[117] The worshipper is tasked with raising up these letters, transcending the search for self-gratification and performing even the most ordinary deeds with contemplative attunement. Such service, intimates the Maggid, has a critical role to play in bringing about redemption.[118]

The Maggid's sustained ambivalence about raising up God's language from the physical world is visible in a lengthy homily describing two kinds of *tsaddikim*. The first type of figure is adored by God because of his positive engagement with sacred letters of the physical world. He lifts up the sparks and connects the external dimension of the cosmos to the divine vitality within. Such a person earns God's affection by returning these aspects of the divine word to their original source in heaven and healing the divine fracture.

The second type of *tsaddik*, by contrast, draws near to God without raising up these fallen letters. His proximity to the Divine is simple and inherent, unconnected to being involved with the corporeal. Dov Ber compares these two without declaring which of them is greater, perhaps telegraphing some of his own ambivalence on the subject, and the Maggid illustrates their simultaneous value with an example plucked from the realm of human experience: "There are two sorts of love. A father may love the actions of his wise child, taking pride in his offspring's clever deeds or the wise words the child speaks. The other sort of parental love is more essential; anything the child says finds favor with the parent, because of this love."[119] The first kind of *tsaddik* uplifts the earthly realm by connecting it to the heavens, whereas the second is graced with an innate connection to God. Yet, despite the attractive simplicity of the second *tsaddik*, only the deeds of the first can restore the fallen letters of Torah from the physical realm and thus bring the world one step closer to redemption.

Dov Ber often refers to the letters as a metaphor for the indwelling divine vitality, a framing that is largely synonymous with the mythos of the sacred sparks inherited from Lurianic Kabbalah.[120] However, a significant number of traditions suggest that Dov Ber invokes this image in a more literal sense, emphasizing that the worshipper must encounter the holy word that sustains the cosmos. Shlomo of Lutsk, setting forth Dov Ber's thinking on this subject, preserves the following explanation:

> It may seem that this world is visible to the eyes, and the spiritual world and its pleasures cannot be seen. . . . But the physicality of each thing is only a vessel and a boundary that defines its appearance, taste and smell. The spirit [inside it] is the vitality of the Creator, drawn into and bounded by this physical thing. It is the letters and the holy words of the Divine, for these letters are spiritual, sweet and full of wondrous taste and smell. . . .
>
> The words of the Holy One inhere in all things, as it is written, "the heavens were made by the word of Y-H-V-H" (Ps. 33:6). They are the names of each thing, like "bread" (*lehem*) and "water" (*mayyim*), and so forth. This is the vitality and the taste, and the smell, and the appearance of each word (*dibbur*). The vitality is drawn forth according to the letters and combinations of words of each thing. . . . Each thing is created and emanated from the blessed One's vitality, and therefore everything must be uplifted to its Source by means of eating and drinking, through the deeds of God's sacred people with great attachment to the holy Creator. Even impure things and forbidden foods, and all prohibited things, which are dark and lacking, have a little vitality. These are uplifted through keeping the negative commandments. . . .
>
> Everything is the illumination, divinity and vitality of the blessed Creator. . . . "It is like the silkworm whose garment is both a part of it and upon it,"[121] as it says in the Zohar.[122]

The divine word is the spiritual life-force of all created things; these letters imbue physical objects such as food or drink with taste, smell, and even their appearance. Sensitivity to the immanence of God's utterances is, for the Maggid, the meaning of the psalmist's confession "I have placed Y-H-V-H before me always" (Ps. 16:8). Everything in the earthly realm, from physical objects to human language, is a manifestation of God's language.

While the particular letters with which all elements of the world are imbued are not themselves visible, these words are translated through the appearance, smell, and taste of each thing. Positive engagement with these corporeal phenomena has everything to do with the indwelling of God's word in the human form. As Elliot Wolfson has so felicitously argued, "The textual panorama of medieval kabbalah, the site of the incarnational insight is the onto-graphic inscripting of flesh into word and the consequent conversion of the carnal body into the ethereal, luminous body, finally transposed into the *literal* body that is the letter, hyper- literally, the name that is the Torah."[123] One's sensual perception and experience of the physical world lead him to an awareness of the letters within the cosmos, an engagement that is crucial for returning the letters to their source in God. The worshipper's senses translate his experience of an object back into the underlying divine letters, an act of reverse translation through which one encounters God's immanent presence manifest in the language of the cosmos.[124]

Concluding Remarks

We have seen that the Maggid seems to expand the concept of sacred language to include all conversations, provided that such speech is accompanied by the correct contemplative thought. He refers to worship through physical actions—such as eating and drinking—as uplifting the sacred letters, raising the fallen divine language out of the corporeal mire and restoring it to its root. Dov Ber's teachings on this subject, however, are thick with ambiguity and tension. Let us pause for a moment in order to reflect on the philosophical implications of this development as it pertains to the Maggid's theory of language.

Echoing the teachings of the BeSHT, many of Dov Ber's homilies emphasize that no worshipper can remain in a constant state of intensified *devekut*. Such consistency, argues the Maggid, would be neither psychologically sustainable nor even desirable.[125] It is precisely those subtle fluctuations of the spiritual life, of drawing near to the Divine and then retreating, that bring pleasure to both man and God. These soulful peregrinations preserve one's individual identity from becoming extinguished before the Divine. Though perhaps ultimately an illusion, this constructed vision of the self is critical to the Maggid's theology. Only an individual, a speaking being in whom the divine world has become embodied, may accomplish the religious goal of returning all language to God.

The Maggid's sermons put forward a spiritual path in which the worshipper maintains his intimate connection with God to greater and lesser degrees of intensity. Sustained communion with the Divine is possible, argues the Maggid, because human beings are continuously immersed in divine language, which animates human speech as well as the cosmos. That all words may be raised up to God, including the sacred letters within the physical world, opens new vistas of experience beyond the strict confines of formal religious obligations. The words that surround the worshipper from all sides and those that fill him from within, including the "letters of thought" (otiyyot ha-mahashavah) that govern the structures of the mind, derive from the language of Torah and from the sacred utterances from which the world was hewn. The letters of Scripture and the language of the world are thus two different—but interconnected—garments of the Divine. One who contemplates these letters, or uses them in constructing his thoughts, draws God's presence into his mind.[126] Other worshippers reach into the depths of the Divine by engaging with the sacred language reverberating in the physical world, uplifting God's word through eating, drinking, and other seemingly mundane actions.

A brief foray into the writings of Moses Mendelssohn, one of the Maggid's contemporaries, will bring the *novum* of Dov Ber's theory into relief. In the 1783 *Or li-Netivah*, the introduction to *Netivot ha-Shalom*—the Hebrew commentary and German translation of the Pentateuch—Mendelssohn gives a definition of the Holy Tongue as the language of revelation and prophecy.[127] This understanding of *leshon ha-kodesh* as the bridge between God and humanity places it squarely within the sacred realm, but even so Mendelssohn argues that Hebrew is also distinguished for its aesthetic and melodic quality. "This alone suffices [to establish its] advantage, superiority, and glory over all other languages," he writes, "so as to confer on it the name 'sacred tongue.'"[128] He also notes that the Holy Tongue is exalted for its qualities related to logic and cognition: "Hebrew is unique among other languages known to us; none of those [other] languages have as much precision in aligning the conjunction and disjunction of words with the connection and differentiation of ideas, such that the ways of the language correspond in this sense with the ways of the mind and its thoughts, and external speech is perfectly arranged and aligned with internal speech."[129] Mendelssohn saw logic and language as being firmly intertwined. Following the ancient and medieval philosophers, he drew a distinction between "external speech" (the physical sounds of language) and "inner speech" (the verbal but not-yet-audibly expressed language of thought). As Edward Breuer and David Sorkin have demonstrated, Mendelssohn clearly believed that "it is only through language or speech that thought takes shape, develops fully, and becomes communicable."[130] The finer one's language of inner thought, the more beautiful and crystalline one's verbal elocution will become. In this sense Hebrew triumphs over all other human languages, even if, as Mendelssohn suggests, if it is essentially a conventional language.

The Maggid's theory of divine speech as inclusive of all human language represents a remarkable departure from the philosophies of language in medieval kabbalistic thinking. The uniqueness of Hebrew is implied by a few homilies, and suggested more overtly in others, but the Maggid's homilies generally expand the notion of holy language far beyond the confines of a particular *lingua sacra*.[131] The Maggid lived in a multilingual culture in which a sacred, liturgical, and literary language existed together with the robust vernacular of Yiddish.[132] The mutual interdependence of these two deeply Jewish languages in Hasidism runs quite deep, and the Maggid's expansive definition of sacred speech was surely enabled, at least in part, by the fact that the letters of Yiddish are the same as those of the Hebrew alphabet.[133]

In premodern eastern Europe, languages and alphabets were divided by religious community, and the Maggid's sermons evince the deep love for the Hebrew letters inherited from his kabbalistic forebearers. Nowhere does he explicitly attribute such significance to the Slavic languages in the marketplace or the countryside around him. But the Maggid's philosophical position regarding the sacred potential of all human language is an amazing break with the kabbalistic tradition, even if he and his students were unaware of this radical change.[134] Unthreatened by the findings of modern language theory or attempts to introduce linguistic reform to Jewish communal or liturgical life, the Maggid's bold teachings on the holiness of all speech offer an alternative to the oft-cited paradigmatic division between holy and mundane. Dov Ber's theory broaches a notion of sacred language as a universal human phenomenon that is continuously animated by the divine word.

Chapter 3

From Speech to Silence

By any measures of liberation and empowerment, language is
not just a creation of humanity, it *is* humanity. Language . . .
is the substance of intelligent thought. It recounts episodes of
the past and those imaginable into the future—among which
choices made constitute decision and we call free will. The mind
assembles experiences and constructs stories from them. It never
pauses. It evolves continuously. As old stories fade with time,
new ones are laid upon them. At the highest level of creativity,
all human beings talk and sing and they tell stories.

—Edward O. Wilson

The Elements of Language

The Maggid's theology describes human speech as charting the very course
of God's own self-disclosure. This movement from divine silence into sacred
word is the heart of Dov Ber's teachings on creation and revelation. Both
divine and human language, claims the Maggid, emerge from within the
hidden depths of the preconscious and pass through the contemplative
mind on their way to becoming articulated speech. The Maggid refers to
these initial phases of preverbal speech as *hokhmah* (wisdom) and *binah*
(understanding), also called *mahashavah* (thought). After passing through
the structures of cognition, this creative font of vital energy is vocalized
through sound and then expressed in the particular structures of spoken
language—be it God's sacred letters of the Torah, or the words of worship
and study.

Much of the Maggid's oeuvre may be seen as reflection on the wonders of this revelatory disclosure, a process in which the human and divine realms are inscrutably intertwined. His meditations on this subject clearly build on a foundation inherited from the Zohar, which describes divine speech as surging forth from the realm of ineffable silence and entering words through the matrix of the *sefirot*.[1] Dov Ber's contribution to this insight lies in his understanding of human and divine language as ever-imbricated and coterminous forms of revelation. The term *medabber*, which defines the human as a "speaking being" in medieval philosophy and Kabbalah, is taken seriously but fundamentally reinterpreted by Dov Ber. It is the fact and process of speech that casts humanity in the divine image, for God's presence in the cosmos is renewed—and reborn—through the evocative power of human language.

These broader philosophical reflections have been noted in previous chapters and are explored in greater depth throughout this book. Doing this fully demands that we first examine the Maggid's presentation of the particular elements of speech and cognition.[2] The arc of language is one in which the contemplation of words is presented as the core of spiritual life, a journey that leads the worshipper to connect spoken words with the power emerging from the deepest seat of human consciousness. Before moving to an analysis of his teachings on cognition or contemplative intellection, we begin with the building blocks of language as he conceived them.

These fundaments are letters, or, more precisely, the twenty-two consonants of the Hebrew alphabet. All language, says Dov Ber, is constructed from these sounds.[3] The Hebrew term *ot* (letter) refers to both a phonetic sound and a written sign, and although the Maggid primarily refers to letters as an aural phenomenon, his focus on the power of language is by no means exclusively applied to the spoken word. He refers to the letters as "vessels" (*kelim*),[4] because when integrated into specific patterns and "combinations" (*tserufim*), these units support the semantic load of meaning with which the speaker has imbued them.[5] But the Maggid also describes the letters as vessels because of their capacity to hold sacred vitality, revealing God's primordial wisdom as it is translated into the cosmos.[6]

It is worth noting in brief that this dimension of the Maggid's theory has much in common with the phenomenon of the "conduit metaphor" explored by Michael J. Reddy.[7] Taking English as a case study, he argued that one's understanding of language is formed in very basic ways by the semantics of his or her native language. English refers to communication as the compression of meaning into words that is unpacked or recovered by the listener.

This vision of words as "conduits" for meaning, claims Reddy, informs the way English speakers think about the idea of language more broadly. He notes that words may also become a source of strife, if the speaker and listener disagree over the meaning of a word or phrase. For Dov Ber, by contrast, the metaphor of letters as vessels exhibits the greatest potential revelatory power of language. Words disclose an infinite God that is otherwise restricted in silence, and the letters of human speech are conduits for ideas that originate far beyond the shores of language.

The consonant letters of Hebrew are meaningless—even lifeless— without the vowel points (*nekudot*) or cantillation notes (*te'amim*) that shape their pronunciation and articulation.[8] Strictly speaking, the cantillation notes represent a system of punctuation and musical notation that guide the reader, but the Maggid interprets them as referring to a melodic quality of language hovering beyond the literal definition of a word. These notes, associated with the *sefirah hokhmah*, represent the hidden reservoir of wisdom concealed in a letter or word.[9] The *ta'am* is the meaning of the word, but it is also much more. Homiletically interpreting the tripartite homonym of *ta'am* ("taste," "reason," and "meaning"), the Maggid describes the *te'amim* as the very essence of language.[10] The vowels likewise enliven the letters of speech and show a reader how to articulate ambiguous words.[11]

As with the *te'amim*, the Maggid invokes the vowels as a symbol representing the ideational core or essential semantic "point" contained within the linguistic vessels.[12] Together the vowels and the melodic quality control language by shaping the meaning of words and guiding the manner in which they are articulated and interpreted.[13] In fact, in several teachings the Maggid describes them as "delivering" the letters from their inanimate stasis. Desiccated speech is saved from semantic torpor by the melodious qualities of words and the infinite field of wisdom that is their lifeblood, a linguistic moment that mirrors—and perhaps causes—the redemption of the indwelling divine presence (*shekhinah*) from its cosmic exile.

All letters are formed by means of one of the "five places of articulation" (*hamishah motsa'ot ha-peh*) or physical regions of speech: throat, lips, teeth, tongue, and palate.[14] The five positions of the mouth are identified with the second *heh* of Y-H-V-H (the letter has the numerical value of five), also long associated with *shekhinah*.[15] The spoken letters are combined in order to form words, and the Maggid generally refers to the result of this as *dibbur*, or the realm of articulated speech. At times the Maggid uses *dibbur* to describe humanity's capacity for spoken language, invested within humanity by the Divine, but the term may also refer to specific words or particular utterances (in the plural, *dibburim*). Classical Kabbalah also associates *dibbur* with *malkhut* and *shekhinah*, and, for the Maggid, this link means that language serves as the manifestation of God's presence in the cosmos as well as the access point through which the contemplative begins the journey through the *sefirot* to the *Ein Sof* or the infinite Divine.[16]

Written and Spoken Words

The teachings of the Hasidic masters generally privilege spoken language over written words. This characterization largely holds true for the Maggid's homilies, though there are a few notable exceptions. One teaching attributed to Dov Ber identifies "writing down the secrets of Torah" as a technique for attaining *devekut*.[17] This tradition may represent an interpolation of one of Dov Ber's disciples, in whose time it had become more commonplace to write down Hasidic homilies. But "isolation from other human beings" (*hitbodedut mi-benei adam*), a practice well attested in the Maggid's teachings and *regimen vitae*, appears on this same list. This may reflect that fact that writing is often a solitary occupation.[18] Given his deeply inward contemplative approach and his frequent comments about the necessity of solitude, it might seem conceivable—even likely—for Dov Ber to laud the spiritual power of writing. The Maggid refers to the World of Speech countless times in his descriptions of the continuum of human and divine language, but never suggests that a godly quality called the "World of Writing" becomes embodied in a worshipper.[19] That Dov Ber does not do so reveals something about the complexity of his religious personality.

Written forms of language are by no means ignored in the Maggid's teachings. Haviva Pedaya has argued that Dov Ber's approach to language is primarily visual, which she contrasts with the BeSHT's focus on the significance of oral sounds.[20] The Maggid's sermons do include reflections on the mystical importance of the letters' shapes. Certain descriptions of the contemplative process through which one penetrates into the heart of a word, whether in prayer or ordinary conversation, do indeed highlight the visual component of language:

> One must place all of his thought into the power of the words
> that he is speaking, until he sees the lights of the words sparking

against one another (*mitnotsetsim zeh be-zeh*). Many lights are born in them.

This is the meaning of, "A light is sown for the righteous, and joy for the upright of heart" (Ps. 97:11). The lights of the letters are divine chambers into which the [world of] Emanation is drawn.[21] One must divest the soul from the physical body, so that the soul can be clothed in the thoughts he is speaking.[22]

The letters of speech, claims Dov Ber, are vessels that conceal a quality of divine vitality that is experienced in the form of light. Like a flint struck against a rock, new illumination is kindled as the letters and words come into creative friction with one another. The collective effect of the Maggid's image is synesthetic. The Maggid is referring to the apparition of light within spoken language, one in which the vocalized words give rise to a spiritual vision.

A remarkable passage found in *Darkhei Tsedek*, a collection of early Hasidic *regimen vitae*, outlines a contemplative practice in which the written, oral and intellective aspects of language are brought together:

> One can contemplate the letters that he is physically speaking, drawing them in his mind as they are written in Hebrew script (*ketav ashurit*). Through thinking of the shape of the holy letters in this way, the letters are uplifted.
>
> This was also revealed by the teacher [the Maggid] of my master [R. Elimelekh of Lizhensk], may his light continue to shine. This [contemplation] takes much practice. For example, when one says, "give me" (*gib mir*) to his friend, he should imagine them before him in a Hebrew script (*ketav ashurit*).[23]

This tradition offers a concrete description of a meditative technique, a relatively rare phenomenon in the corpus attributed to the Maggid. The worshipper is directed to imagine the forms of the Hebrew letters within his mind as he speaks a word aloud, thus blending the oral and written forms of language in a single contemplative moment. A surprising element of this important teaching also confirms our suspicion that the Maggid extends his contemplative approach to language beyond Hebrew. The example of spoken language to be imagined in a classic Hebrew font is actually a phrase in Yiddish!

The Maggid's teachings frequently ascribe rich symbolic meaning to the shapes of the letters, using their form to articulate a theological point.[24] On this subject, the Maggid's commitment to the singularity of Hebrew—or perhaps better, to Jewish languages—is quite pronounced; nowhere in his corpus do we find significance attributed to the written forms of other languages. One example of this mode of exegesis is recalled in a sermon of Levi Yitshak of Barditshev, one of Dov Ber's foremost disciples:

> God created the world through the Torah; the world was created with twenty-two letters. The shapes of the letters have significance, as is mentioned in *Sefer ha-Temunah*[25] and the Lurianic writings. The holy luminary the Ba'al Shem Tov revealed the [meaning of] the shapes of the letters.
>
> I heard the following from my master, the holy luminary Dov Berish: there are reasons for the shape of the letters, which are supernal lights. *Yod* represents *tsimtsum* [i.e., the primordial withdrawal of God's light], the letter *vav* is expansion, the letter *shin* refers to the three columns [of the *sefirot*], and the letter *aleph* has a point above and a point below.
>
> Now although there is no up or down in the worlds above, in the realm of the mind and the angels, nor is there any boundary that would allow us to refer to "spreading out," my teacher [the Maggid] said that when the worlds and the supernal lights clothe themselves in the human body and take on corporeal garb, the lights of the mind are visible in a concrete form like the image of the letters (*ke-dimayyon ha-otiyyot*). The focusing (*tsimtsum*) of the wisdom [of a teacher] in the way that it is contracted into the mind of a student is like the shape of the *yod*, and the *vav* is the image of spreading out [in the disciple's mind], and so forth for all of them. Thus have I received from my teacher.[26]

The language used by God in creating the world included the written forms of the Hebrew letters.[27] These shapes, claims Dov Ber, are also reflected in the intellectual and spiritual processes of the human mind. As in other elements of the Maggid's theology, the association of kabbalistic symbols with inner processes should not be misconstrued as negating or superseding their mystical connotations. The Maggid has internalized the symbols of written language, but the visual encounter with the letters is an integral part of the spiritual experience, even as they are simultaneously interpreted as alluding to cosmic dynamics within the Divine.

Elsewhere Dov Ber uses the image of writing a Hebrew letter as a meta-phor for human deeds that become filled with spiritual vitality.[28] Like the expanse of white on a blank piece of paper, the life-force within a person is diffuse and unbounded. The worshipper's vitality must be poured into a con-crete religious action, which provides a boundary for this inward energy. The same is true for a letter, whose external contours restrict the black ink poured into its midst. The scribe's black ink creates a negative white space within the boundaries of the letter; although this space existed previously, it becomes distinct only as the form is drawn around it.[29] The same is true for all human actions, which focus the worshipper's life-force by directing it into a specific vessel. Like the letters on a page, both deeds and words pro-vide the inner inspiration with a medium of concrete expression.

Such homilies and stories suggest that the Maggid did indeed ascribe significance to certain forms of written language together with spoken words. But the emphasis of his devotional theory undoubtedly rests on the aural qualities of language rather than its written elements. Dov Ber claims that all human speech is animated by *kol* (voice), a basic vocalized sound that nec-essarily inheres in all words but may also be expressed without them.[30] *Kol* is abstract and unformed in comparison to clearly defined words; it consists of nothing more than a physical sound that cannot be understood by an-other until being shaped through specific words and letters:

> *Kol* is unformed (*golmi*); it is simply a voice. *Dibbur* reveals, for it is the detail that explains the general [i.e., the abstract].
>
> Now if, for example, *kol* were not joined to *dibbur*, the *dibbur* would never become audible. But if there was no *dibbur*, [the *kol*] would remain unformed and impossible to understand.[31]

Voice and speech are thus, according to Dov Ber, mutually dependent. Ar-ticulated words, *dibbur*, cannot be expressed without the energy of *kol*, but the inchoate and potential meaning of *kol* is only revealed as it is shaped into clearly defined letters and words.[32] For the Maggid, as in classical Kabbalah, *kol* represents the *sefirah tif'eret* and the *vav* of the name Y-H-V-H.[33] Thus uniting *kol* and *dibbur* effects a simultaneous unification on planes both cos-mic and personal. It brings together the letters *vav* and *heh* of the sacred name, and it unites *tif'eret* with *shekhinah* (the masculine and feminine ele-ments of the Godhead). Drawing *kol* into *dibbur* unites the two concrete properties of speech within the worshipper himself, and the speaker is called on to unite his spoken words with the physical sensation of the sound as it is reverberating within his body.[34]

The primary goal of divine service, says the Maggid, is properly aligning the stream of language from the deepest realms of the mind with the spoken utterance. This is accomplished through uniting a second dyad found throughout the Maggid's homilies: *'olam ha-dibbur* (the World of Speech) and *'olam ha-mahashavah* (the World of Thought).[35] This symbolic pair plays a critical role in the Maggid's theory of language. It does not, however, appear as such in the teachings of the BeSHT, and for this reason *olam ha-dibbur* and *'olam ha-mahashavah* afford an excellent window into Dov Ber's development and expansion of his master's teachings.[36]

The latter is associated with the *sefirah binah* (lit. "understanding"), a deeper cognitive element of language that animates both *dibbur* and *kol*.[37] The Maggid often underscores that there can be no speech acts without thought.[38] This means that spoken language generally expresses an idea that first appears in the mind, but the Maggid also intends it as a prescriptive instruction: the worshipper must constantly seek to unite the World of Speech and the World of Thought in every utterance.[39] *'Olam ha-dibbur* and *'olam ha-mahashavah* are linked as the oral elements of language are aligned with the realm of cognition and contemplation within the speaker's mind.

The unification of *'olam ha-dibbur* and *'olam ha-mahashavah*, claims Dov Ber, is rather different than that of *kol* and *dibbur*, both in terms of kabbalistic symbolism and the religious experience it entails. Whereas connecting *kol* and *dibbur* brings together masculine and feminine elements of God, linking the letters *vav* and *heh* of Y-H-V-H, both *binah* and *shekhinah* represent the divine feminine. *Binah* represents the divine mother, the source of the lower seven *sefirot*, and *shekhinah* the feminine divine presence that has been exiled within the fractured world. *Shekhinah* must be repaired so that its bond with *binah* can be restored, creating a balance between these two feminine elements. This union also brings together the first *heh* (*binah*) with the second *heh* of Y-H-V-H, the sacred name that is the root of all human and divine language.[40]

The Languages of Thought

Dov Ber's mystical homilies on the relationship between thought and language broach, albeit implicitly, critical questions that are familiar to any student of the philosophy of language: How are thoughts translated into spoken language? Do ideas first emerge without words, which are only necessary to facilitate interpersonal communication, or is cognition itself determined by the structures of language? And do all processes of cognition take place in words, or are some aspects of intellection and contemplation beyond language? These questions shall concern us for much of the remainder of this chapter.[41]

The Maggid refers to the "letters of thought" (*otiyyot ha-mahashavah*), which appear first in the *sefirah binah*.[42] Cognition and intellection are purely internal processes, which the Maggid describes as taking place within the "heart,"[43] but the letters to be disclosed later as speech are born deep within the mind: "It is known that all twenty-two letters and the five places of articulation[44] exist in thought, which is the root of all the letters. One cannot speak anything aloud without thinking of it first. If he does bring forth a word without any thought, it will lack understanding, wisdom and intelligence. Thus, thought is the root of all the worlds, which were revealed through speech."[45] The letters of cognition drive forward all spoken language, giving it meaning, vitality, and structure.[46] The Maggid suggests that even words spoken without forethought must have been concealed within the mind; otherwise they could not have been articulated.[47] This claim that spoken words simply express linguistic formations that were already present in the mind appears with some variation across the Maggid's corpus: "This is a great principle: every word, before it is aroused from thought by the five positions of the mouth, must exist in his thought beforehand. It is truly hidden there, since one can only speak the words that were there in his mind first. Everything that a person thinks in his mind happens by means of letter combinations."[48] The mind, says Dov Ber, includes the seeds of spoken language in the form of letters. Articulated words simply express something that had already arisen in thought through the concrete medium of speech.[49] In a few rare instances the Maggid even describes the letters of thought as a kind of inward speech (*dibbur penimi*), which he distinguishes—rather opaquely—from articulated oral language.[50]

Mahashavah or *binah*, the realm of active cognition, is the wellspring or source from which all articulated speech flows forth.[51] The fact that both the World of Speech and the World of Thought are defined by letters and language allows them to be united.[52] But how then does the language of the mind differ from spoken words? The Maggid often reiterates that the mind is tremendously powerful and dynamic, flexing against the boundaries of time and accomplishing even astounding feats in a single moment.[53] One may grasp an idea quickly with the intellect, but the Sisyphean task of finding the correct verbal formulation may take a great deal longer.

The Maggid also describes *binah* as the seat of mystical contemplation, for *devekut* is achieved by keeping one's thoughts constantly trained on God rather than the temptations of the world.[54] Such a mind is transformed into a dwelling place for God, as the divine presence is drawn into the structures of one's thoughts.[55] This happens when one thinks of something positive, but it is just as true if he contemplates negative and destructive things.[56] Invoking an idea found in the teachings of the BeSHT, the Maggid explains that one's entire being is present wherever his mind is focused, even if his physical body is elsewhere.[57] All lesser, debased thoughts or emotions must be traced back to their ultimate source in the World of Thought.[58] By doing so, pride or lust, for example, may be transformed into positive traits such as human dignity and love of God. Such letters of thoughts are like the holy sparks trapped in the "husks" (*kelippot*) during the cosmic "shattering of the vessels" (*shevirat ha-kelim*); they must be uplifted and repaired through the process of contemplation.[59]

Active intellection, what we might call "conscious thought," transpires in a dynamic region of the mind that is characterized by flexibility and a nearly inexhaustible font of contemplative power. But *binah* is also restricted by the structures of language, for there all thoughts are conceived by means of finite letters that form recognizable words and linguistic patterns. Throughout the Maggid's homilies we find ample references to a fertile realm called *hokhmah* ("wisdom"), the source of the energy that flows into the Worlds of Thought and Speech.[60] Articulated speech is the final result of a long process that originates in *hokhmah*, but, as we shall see, the limits of language gesture beyond even this creative pool of potential vitality.[61]

The unfolding of language as a mighty river that gushes forth from the well of *hokhmah* is mirrored, however, by a contemplative journey that stretches in the opposite direction. In the act of worship, study, or even finely attuned conversation, one links *dibbur* with *kol* and trains the mind on *binah*, thus uniting the *sefirot* of *malkhut*, *tif'eret*, and *binah*. This accomplished, one may then reach into the depths of *hokhmah* and dip into the font of language itself.[62] At this rung, the presence of words or even letters is ambiguous as best, and in these discussions of *hokhmah*—and beyond—the Maggid's relationship to the power of the word is most fraught with tension.

The Boundaries of Language

The Maggid's positive approach to language is grounded in his understanding of letters and words as vessels that reveal God's infinite being. The limitations of speech do not pose an intractable impediment for the worshipper or the spiritual educator. As Dov Ber constantly reiterates, sublime insights may—and must—be communicated through the medium of language. But a few of his homilies refer to the power of contemplative silence, an insight he must have gleaned from his own religious experience. Such sermons gesture toward a kind of religious service that transpires beyond the normative frameworks of language.[63] One particularly evocative formulation refers to the worshipper stretching toward a vista "above the letters, in which everything is spirit," perhaps suggesting that one arrives at rapturous quiet in the heights of spiritual experience.[64] *Pace* Scholem and Schatz-Uffenheimer, however, these few teachings reveal only part of a very complex story. The Maggid's spiritual path culminates not with wordless contemplation, but with the empowered reclamation of sacred speech that reveals the hidden mysteries of the divine and the innermost pathways of the human mind.

The *sefirah hokhmah*, argues Dov Ber, represents a highly abstract plane of contemplation that stretches beyond even the letters of thought.[65] The power of *hokhmah* animates and dwells within all letters—including those that serve as the fundaments of cognition. But the source of this ever-flowing current is unrestricted by the limited vessels, the letters and words into which the divine vitality eventually flows.[66] In *hokhmah*, everything exists in the graceful unity of unformed potential, without differentiation or distinction. Although the life-force may be translated into cognitive and spoken language, the purest forms of *hokhmah* cannot be fully articulated in words. For this reason, it provides worshippers with an access point to a divine realm past ordinary processes of intellection.[67]

There is, it seems, a further stage even beyond the rung of *hokhmah*. On more than one occasion Dov Ber makes reference to a specific region of the mind that he calls *kadmut ha-sekhel*,[68] perhaps best translated as the "pre-intellect" or the "preconscious mind." This site is described in the Maggid's sermons as a bubbling fountain of inspiration and a rushing river from which ideas and vitality constantly flow forth. This theory of *kadmut ha-sekhel* (alt. *kidmat ha-sekhel*) is among Dov Ber's most original ideas, and a prime example of the manner in which the Maggid blends the language of the *sefirot* together with descriptions of spiritual processes of intellection and the inner workings of the human psyche.[69]

New interpretations of Torah, claims Dov Ber, and other forms of religious inspiration represent one of the lower rungs of prophecy, a kind of spontaneous outpouring of soulful knowledge from the root of language.[70] This same effervescent dynamism means that *kadmut ha-sekhel* is beyond one's conscious understanding.[71] It can be reached only through divestment from physical pleasures and unmooring the contemplative faculty from self-awareness. But achieving *kadmut ha-sekhel* does not, as we shall see, require the worshipper to permanently relinquish the sacred power of language.

The importance of the Maggid's sermons on *kadmut ha-sekhel* for our discussion of language is readily apparent. In one homily, we read:

> Even *hokhmah* is called a garment and an attribute (*middah*) of the
> *Ein Sof.* . . . The difference between *hokhmah* and the other
> attributes (*middot*) is that since they are bound by time, they
> cannot receive and give at the same moment. This is not true of
> *hokhmah*, which is the primeval matter (*homer ha-rishon*) that
> [continuously] loses its form and dons [another one]. It never stays
> the same. Without cessation, it constantly gives [vitality] to what
> is below it and receives from that which is above it, like the
> instantaneous blink of an eye.[72] This cannot be grasped (*ein
> yekholim la-'amod 'alav*).
>
> For example, the letters of thought [i.e., *binah*] flow without
> interruption from *kadmut ha-sekhel*, meaning *hokhmah*. Different
> letters stream forth from *kadmut ha-sekhel* at each moment, as
> they are stripped [of their form] and passed on to [the realm of]
> thought. [*Kadmut ha-sekhel*] is then embodied in other [letters],
> giving them to thought [as well]. [*Hokhmah*] itself cannot be
> grasped.[73]

The Maggid associates *kadmut ha-sekhel* with *hokhmah*, the region of the mind that is characterized by constant motion and dynamic change. This teaching is a good example of the way in which the Maggid uses the vocabulary of the *sefirot* to describe the processes of the human mind as well as those of the Godhead.

Kadmut ha-sekhel is a reservoir from which the individual letters of thought flow into *binah* and join together, but *hokhmah*'s own energy cannot remain static for even a moment. It would be unnecessarily simplistic, however, to assume that *hokhmah* is utterly beyond language. *Kadmut ha-sekhel* is home to letters as well, which are being constantly tossed about in the eddies of the mind. *Hokhmah* thus seems to function as a liminal or intermediary stage between an entirely superlinguistic realm, perhaps the *sefirah keter,* and the relatively concrete world of *binah*.[74]

This homily brings up a fascinating subtlety in the Maggid's theology of language. The letters themselves seem to exist in some form in *kadmut ha-sekhel,* but *hokhmah* is also described as a concentrated and undifferentiated form of energy that takes on real structure only as it enters *binah*. *Kadmut ha-sekhel* is the origin of the letters, and the Maggid refers to them as an ever-changing linguistic "garment" for the vitality of *hokhmah*. The dynamic realm of *kadmut ha-sekhel* is thus the reservoir of unformed potential for all specific language, and it is the source from which the energy that animates words and letters flows into the mind and voice, eventually becoming articulated in the specifics of spoken language.[75]

The notion of *kadmut ha-sekhel* is linked to Dov Ber's understanding of the nature of prophecy qua revelation, a flow of divine vitality that extends to the mind of the receiver and therein becomes cloaked in language.[76] The association between the *tsaddik* and the prophet is not uncommon in early Hasidic thought, appearing in the polemics against the BeSHT as well.[77] Opposition may have forced Hasidism to downplay this element of its teaching, but traces of the *tsaddik*-cum-prophet remain visible in Hasidic literature. While the Maggid was less concerned with the cultivation of prophecy (*nevu'ah*) or the Holy Spirit (*ruah ha-kodesh*) than many earlier medieval Jewish philosophers and mystics, his teachings on this subject cast important light on the question of language and *kadmut ha-sekhel*.[78] "Today, in the time of exile," the Maggid famously taught, "it is easier to attain the Holy Spirit than in the time of the Temple."[79]

The justification offered for this assertion is fascinating. In former days when God dwelt in the Temple, only certain elect individuals had permission to approach the Divine. Such intimacy was granted only to a select few, requiring lengthy preparation and careful orchestration of ritual. But in the present day, says the Maggid, God is "on the road" (*ba-derekh*), and all who seek may come into the divine presence: "When a person links their mind (*mehashev be-dekevut*) to the Blessed One, He alights upon [the worshipper] immediately and dwells with him."[80] The sacred power of the contemplative mind offers an open channel for connecting to the Divine, far more accessible than the one-time temporal locus of the Temple.

The prophetic experience, taught the Maggid, skirts the boundaries between linguistic experience and an encounter with God that emerges from inexpressible depths of the human mind:

> If one speaks with attachment to the world above—without any "strange" thought [i.e., distraction]—and a thought comes to him as a prophecy (*nevi'ut*), then certainly it shall be so!
> This thought comes [to the worshipper] because of the decrees made on high regarding that matter. At times, one may hear a voice speaking, because he has connected the voice of his prayer and the voice of his Torah to the supernal Voice. It may sound like a voice speaking about the future.[81]

Elsewhere, the Maggid suggests that God sends an array of "letters" equally to all prophets, but that they are unformed and highly elastic.[82] This offers a rather large degree of creative freedom to the prophet, since it is up to the individual to decide how these letters are to be manifest. He is connected to the divine mind, and can then consciously rearrange the inchoate message of the letters as he sees fit. Another tradition, however, offers a different accounting of prophetic creativity:

> It was truly within [the prophet's] power to transform the prophecy from one of anger to compassion when formulating the prophecy (*be-dabro leshon ha-nevu'ah*). This does not mean that the prophet actually changed the words, God forbid, that he heard from the Holy One. Rather, the matter depended on the prophet's melody (*niggun*); [the meaning of the prophecy followed] the melody in which he conveyed the prophecy to Israel. . . . [83]
> This is the meaning of, "The Lord God has given me learned language" (*leshon limmudim*, Isa. 50:4). That is, the prophecy is in his [the prophet's] language by means of the melody and the cantillation notes.[84]

The prophet is not permitted to change the words of a given prophecy. He can, however, transform the divine message it conveys by altering its melody. The cantillation notes (te'amim), the melodic quality that gives meaning (ta'am) to the prophetic revelation, rest in human hands. The structure or semantic content of the prophecy remains static, but through tapping into the *hokhmah*—the infinite potential meaning illustrated by the cantillation notes—the prophet may indeed alter or even overturn the original fiat. This bold interpretive strategy goes beyond just rearranging the letters. The *tsaddik*, suggests Dov Ber, has free rein to transform the meaning of a prophecy by reaching into the musical heart of language and remaking the message as he sees fit.[85]

Our discussion of *kadmut ha-sekhel* and the prelinguistic realm of human consciousness—beyond the ken of rational understanding but within the threshold of experience—leads us to the role of silence in the Maggid's spiritual path. A small number of homilies underscore the value of quiet in the contemplative life.[86] In some cases, this silence is presented as the response of a stunned and overwhelmed worshipper to the majesty of the Divine. What use are words, the Maggid asks, when encountering a God that surrounds and fills all the worlds?[87] A very few homilies depict silent contemplation taking one beyond even the realm achieved when contemplating the letters: "'Silence is a fence for wisdom. . . .'[88] 'A fence for wisdom' means a boundary. When one is silent, he does not arrive at *hokhmah* or *binah*, for he arrives at a level that is even higher than *hokhmah*. He receives something that is above him. When he is giving, he cannot receive, since that which is busy giving forth cannot absorb at the same time.[89] This is the meaning of 'silence is a fence for wisdom.' When the mind rises above, it ascends farther and farther to its very root, and the mind is strengthened."[90] Wordlessness creates contemplative space because a teacher engaged in verbal communication cannot be simultaneously alert to the murmurings of the inner mind. Ze'ev Wolf of Zhitomir, a contemplative among Dov Ber's students, recalls a tradition affirming this point:

"Extol Y-H-V-H with me" (Ps. 34:4). His [King David's] attribute was *malkhut*, the World of Speech. The Maggid used to say that whenever a person is consumed with bringing forth a word, his mind is not free to think about anything, since that which is busy giving forth cannot absorb.[91] King David alluded to this, teaching the holy people Israel to "extol Y-H-V-H," referring to the World of Thought—make it great and expand it.

But how can you broaden the World of Thought? "With me,"
meaning "with my [i.e., King David's] attribute. I represent the
World of Speech, as it exists when one refrains from speaking out
loud." By means of this [internalizing of speech], the World of
Thought is expanded and empowered.[92]

The Maggid's homilies often portray an ideal in which thought and speech
exist in seamlessly imbricated continuity. This sermon, however, suggests
that the worshipper or teacher must enter a quiet state in order to allow his
mind to soar. One's focal power and his faculty for speech must be directed
inward, thereby uniting *malkhut* with *binah* and rising beyond them both.
The result is a meditative journey, an interior quest in which no linguistic
energy is expended externally.[93] We should remember, however, that the
Maggid embraces language as the structure of thought and medium of cognition; this means that abstaining from verbal speech is a far cry from transcending words or letters entirely.

Teachings such as these are complemented by a short biographical
anecdote in the work of Yisra'el of Kozhenits, another one of Dov Ber's prominent disciples. In this story, the Maggid's theory of language seems to reflect
his own experience as a communal teacher: "We received [the following] from
our teacher and master [the Maggid]: Sometimes the *tsaddik* is connected to
the upper worlds in his mind. He cannot open his mouth to share a teaching (*halakhah*) with them, descending to them by stepping down from his
level. Therefore, they must prepare the way and open the channel [of com-
munication] with things like their questions."[94] At times, the *tsaddik*'s contemplative rapture will prevent him from speaking to the community
surrounding him. This may include even his closest disciples. His students'
words, however, can penetrate this web of meditative silence. They are tasked
with drawing their teacher from this wordless state of communion, forcing
him to take part with their questions and thus returning him to the domain of verbal language.

Might this tradition about a spiritual master who is totally engrossed in
his own meditation bespeak the Maggid's ambivalence regarding his public
leadership? Could it perhaps reveal something about the complexities of engaging with an intimate group of elite disciples? The Maggid remained an
introspective mystic even after having met the BeSHT, and the growing pressures of his role as a teacher and leader may have conflicted with some of his
religious instincts.[95]

Solitude, for the Maggid, prevents one from becoming distracted from the primary aim of uniting his inner world through meditative speech.[96] This private goal is best accomplished beyond the chatter of others. Dov Ber also underscores the value of secluded quiet because some religious experiences may transpire—even if momentarily—outside the frameworks of ordinary language:

> One connecting himself [to the Divine] should begin with the World of Action (*'olam ha-'asiyyah*). He must then ascend in his mind, higher and higher, and then higher still, until he arrives at the world of the angels (*ofanim*), and then at the world of creation (*'olam ha-beriyyah*), until he senses in his mind (*yargish be-mahshavto*) that in thought he has ascended all the way to the World of Emanation (*'olam ha-atsilut*). This is what the Zohar calls thought without any deed.[97]
>
> One must be careful not to fall from this exalted thought of the highest worlds, descending below. He must resolve with all of his might to remain above in his thoughts, as it is written, "Be not like a senseless horse or mule whose movement must be curbed by bit and bridle" (Ps. 32:9).[98] He must make a barrier, so as not to fall. When he is connected to such a great degree, he will be strong no matter what comes up in his thoughts. He is connected to the blessed One, and knows that He is the source of all. . . .
>
> Just as a person walks from room to room, one should walk through the worlds above in his mind. Nobody else may be in the house when he wishes to connect, since even the chirping birds can negate [his attempt]. The very thoughts of another [worshipper] disrupt it.[99]

This meditative exercise does not culminate with a direct visionary encounter with an image of the Divine. Indeed, nothing of the sort is to be found in the Maggid's corpus. The fact that the homily makes no mention of letters or language, however, is quite remarkable. The mode of service that leads the worshipper to the depths of contemplative silence is one of sustained visualization rather than linguistic meditation.

The Maggid's descriptions of visual contemplation (called *histaklut*) offer another perspective on his understanding of the limits of language.

This issue, which threads together the issues of spoken words with visual images, returns us to the ancient rabbinic trope of Israel seeing at Sinai that which was ordinarily heard.[100] Dov Ber generally invokes the term *histaklut* in reference to the mystical power of gazing on a physical object, thus connecting it to its root in the Divine through the mind of the worshipper. *Histaklut* links *hokhmah* and the physical world, enabling the mystic to work miracles through connecting an object's letters to their infinite source.[101]

But the power of contemplative gazing extends beyond the magical, for Dov Ber claims that such visioning can spark an immediate experience of self-less transcendence in the mind of the beholder.[102] Several of his homilies link *histaklut* to elements of language, noting that the image of the object on which one is gazing is internally reconstructed through the letters of thought and thus linked to the infinite pool of *hokhmah* that dwells in the inner world of the mystic.[103] *Histaklut*, thus construed, opens a channel through which the font of *hokhmah* courses into the physical word. This vitality emerges from an ultimate source beyond all language and is linked to the cosmos through the gaze of the worshipper. And yet, it is only through words—through the letters of thought and speech—that this divine life-force comes to inhere in the world.

The Power of the Word

The realm of *hokhmah*, or *kadmut ha-sekhel*, is to some degree unrestrained by the confines of words and letters, and a number of the Maggid's homilies describe a contemplative realm beyond even cognitive language. But the primary thrust of the Maggid's teachings consistently underscores the enormous spiritual power of human words. Meditative quiet remains but a temporary stage in the arc of the worshipper's spiritual journey leading into the depths of the mind and back. The quest to attain silent, prelinguistic realms of the mind is never elevated to the ultimate goal of religious service, for, without words and letters, such new inspiration and illumination cannot reach the cosmos. The Maggid's embrace of language extends to his approach to pedagogy as well, averring that language is a necessary tool for communication. The riches of the intellect—as well as the depths of one's mystical experience—cannot be revealed to another human being without recourse to the structures of articulated speech.[104]

Silence may allow the worshipper to reach for the highest rungs. But recourse to wordless contemplation also threatens to leave the cosmos devoid of God's vitality. The world was created in order to fulfill a divine need, says the Maggid, and therefore it cannot be abandoned or even permanently transcended:

> The *mussaf* prayer on Shabbat includes *keter*.[105] We raise the World of Speech up to the World of Thought. There the illumination is so great that no distinctions are visible. But according to this, no vitality would remain in this lower world. This world exists because of a divine need,[106] for there can be no king without a people. Therefore, we immediately recite, "Where is the place of His glory." "Where" (*ayeh*) refers to the three initial *sefirot*, where there are no divisions. Then we say, "From His place may He turn in compassion," to bestow his goodness here, since there can be no king without a people. . . .
>
> The life-force of all things comes from the World of Speech, meaning the letters. Now the letters long to connect to their source. It is their vitality. But when some change is required, then the letters of speech are lifted up beyond the attributes (*middot*). [The one praying] falls silent and cannot speak until the transformation has been accomplished. Then song may be recited once more.[107]

Wordless quiet is a crucial stage in this process, though it is only a transient moment in the service of returning the language to God. Raising up the letters through the various cognitive worlds, and thus reinfusing them with sacred life-force, is immediately followed by drawing them back down—our summoning them forth—so that the influx of divine vitality may be revealed in the world.[108] Fundamental transformation, of the world and of the self, can be accomplished only by raising the letters of speech back to their source. The experience of returning them to this prelinguistic world (called *keter*) is so powerful that the contemplative is stunned into silence. But the worshipper must then return to the liturgical melody after this change, now offering a radiant song infused with new divine vitality.

We have noted that, according to the Maggid, the various stages of language refer to the *sefirot* of *hokhmah, binah, tif'eret,* and *malkhut* as they correspond to the letters of Y-H-V-H. This sacred name imbues human language with its fundamentally sacral quality because it is, claims Dov Ber, "necessarily garbed in every word and expression."[109] God's holy name is understood to be the source of all language, but mapping the *sefirot* onto this appellation and then applying both to the emergence of language suggests that the worshipper's process of drawing thoughts into speech unites and completes the divine name:

> It is known that the four worlds are [as follows]: The Root of
> Thought (*shoresh ha-mahashavah*), Thought (*mahashavah*), Voice
> and Speech. And it is known that the blessed One fills all the
> worlds, and surrounds all the worlds; no place is devoid of Him.
> Therefore, one can speak all words, even those that are not words
> of Torah, since it is known that these [seemingly mundane]
> utterances are [also] the World of Speech.
>
> However, a person who pays no mind to this, thinking that
> God is above in heaven and he is on earth, is not permitted to
> speak many words, because he cannot restore them . . . this is the
> meaning of the verse, "For God is in heaven and you are on earth;
> that is why your words should be few" (Eccl. 5:1)—if you think
> that this is true, you should speak but a little.[110]

The four realms of language and cognition, here given as varying slightly from the schema drawn above, are associated with the primary *sefirot* in the Maggid's theological system as well as the letters of God's sacred name. This correspondence between the parts of speech, the unfolding of the Godhead, the structures of the cosmos, and the ineffable divine name is deeply repercussive. Human speech embodies the divine word, and the worshipper's language—*all* language—aligns the *sefirot* and draws vitality from *hokhmah* into *shekhinah* or *malkhut*. This process of eliciting the flow of blessing is coterminous with the phases of cognition within the worshipper's mind.

Speech begins with a flash of inspiration, maturing into a structured thought that is eventually given voice and articulated in words. These stages exactly parallel the expansion of the Divine from ineffable silence into the cosmos. One who fails to realize that language is animated by the divine power should remain quiet, for fracture and discord are the result of the speech of a person who believes that God is purely transcendent and disconnected from human words. But for those who have cultivated a deeper awareness of these spiritual and cognitive movements, language unites the indwelling of

God within the human form with the divine expanse that infuses the cosmos with being.

Language is a divine gift, one that demands great responsibility and commands human action.[111] Connecting the different elements of speech and thought unites the *sefirot* and transforms both the divine realms and the one who is speaking:

> One should consider that the World of Speech, which speaks
> through him, is such a great world. All the worlds were created
> with it, as it is taught, "'when they were created' (*be-hibaram*,
> Gen. 2:4)—with the five positions of the mouth" (*be-heh baram*).[112]
> Through this, one may consider the grandeur (*tif'arto*) of God.
> All the vitality of the worlds comes from speech, and speech is the
> world of awe (*yir'ah*).[113] *Shekhinah*, as it were, becomes focused and
> dwells in the words of his mouth, as it is taught in *Sefer Yetsirah*,
> "[the letters] have been imbued within the mouth."[114]
> If this is true of speech, how much more so is it the case for
> the World of Thought, and the other sublime lights that have no
> limit and cannot be grasped (*ein sof ve-heker*). As one begins to
> think, he should say in his heart that the World of Speech has
> been contracted into the mind and dwells[115] within the aspects of
> *hokhmah* and *binah*. It is fitting to have awe before such a great
> world, and not pray for one's physical needs. He should consider
> that he is an aspect of God above (*helek elohah mima'al*). . . .
> This is what it means to pray with no ulterior motivation
> (*lishmah*)—for the sake (*le-shem*) of speech [i.e., *heh*], since speech
> desires to connect to thought. When one thinks with love and
> awe, voice (*kol*) and speech delight in one another. *Hokhmah*
> watches this and derives pleasure, like a father who derives
> pleasure from his child. Thought yearns to come into the voice, so
> that it may also come into speech.[116]

Human thought and speech embody the *sefirot*, bringing the elements of the Godhead into communion through sacred deeds and words. But this passage offers far more than a recondite kabbalistic guide to uniting the *sefirot*, as it describes a powerful religious experience as well. The contemplative approach to language begins with the awareness that one's speech is divine, imbued within humanity from the earliest moments of creation. This leads him to consider God's splendor, and then to realize that if the immanent divine presence is found in all spoken words, it must also be true that one's intellectual and contemplative faculties are God's attributes embodied within man. This consciousness precipitates an overwhelming sense of wonder, but the awe does not render the contemplative speechless. Indeed, awareness that he is an element of the Divine changes one's relationship to speech, but it does not force him into silence.

Human beings have a religious duty to engage with and redeem language, but the Maggid daringly suggests that God shares a similar responsibility. This need is willingly accepted by the Divine out of love rather than being intrinsic to the nature of God's being, but this in no way diminishes the immediacy of the demand to transform language:

> It is known that speech is called the attribute of *malkhut* [i.e., "kingship"]. The reason for this is that the servants of the king can only obey his speech, since they cannot apprehend his thought, and [his] speech [in turn] listens to [his] thought. . . .
>
> The King Himself has no need for speech. For the sake of the recipients [of his beneficence], it was necessary to contract Himself into a voice (*kol*), and then into speech. But everything is utter oneness; all is the King alone, only the vessels are differentiated. . . . But if the King had a wise servant, who could understand his thought, certainly [this servant] would need to obey his thought.[117]

God is compelled, as it were, to speak and become confined by the matrices of language for the sake of humanity. It is only through these many stages of divine self-limitation that worshippers come to grasp the King's desires, for, without speech, the cosmos echoes with the silence of the divine will.[118] Dov Ber seems to raise a fascinating possibility that certain discerning individuals may go beyond the divine word, but we should mention a more conservative formulation of this idea recorded in the Maggid's name by Levi Yitshak of Barditshev: human beings have been denied permission to enter into the mind of the Divine, and, therefore, they must listen to and serve God according to the word.[119]

The Maggid reiterates that "everything is utter oneness; all is the King alone," even after the King's thought is contracted into the vessels of language and born in words. Letters and speech hold a finite amount of divine wisdom, thereby mediating the revelation and preventing it from overwhelming the receiver. But the distinction between the different vessels, the particulars of speech, and being, is a matter of appearance rather than essence. In true Hasidic fashion, says the Maggid, everything remains God even after the processes of *tsimtsum* and divine limitation. This is true of the cosmos and the realm of the *sefirot*, but the Maggid applies it to the worshipper's mind and speech as well. Human language affords an opportunity to overcome the limitations of the world defined by particularity and multiplicity, through revealing the ineffable. All words, although they appear separate, unite the speaker with the infinite Divine as they are raised up and returned to their root in God.[120]

Letters and Ladders

Ludwig Wittgenstein (1889–1951) was perhaps the most important analytical philosopher of the twentieth century. His skeptical vision of language, an approach that is particularly visible in the early period of his career, has been the subject of much comment.[121] Rather than juxtaposing the Maggid's teachings on the boundaries of speech and cognition to those of Christian mystics, as per Schatz-Uffenheimer, I believe that Dov Ber's *novum* is brought into relief when compared to the terse, evocative writings of this Austrian-born philosopher.

The famed ending of Wittgenstein's *Tractatus Logico-Philosophicus*, the only book published in his lifetime, reads as follows:

> My propositions are elucidatory in this way: he who understands
> me finally recognizes them as senseless, when he has climbed out
> through them, on them, over them. (He must, so to speak, throw
> away the ladder, after he has climbed up on it.)
>
> He must surmount these propositions; then he sees the world
> rightly.
>
> Whereof one cannot speak, thereof one must be silent.[122]

This cryptic passage at the conclusion of Wittgenstein's early magnum opus is generally taken to describe the philosopher's brush against the limits of language. In doing so, the philosopher moves beyond words and enters a realm of non-sense that is utterly indescribable. Marjorie Perloff has noted that, according to Wittgenstein, one who successfully climbs this ladder arrives at the "commonsense recognition that there are metaphysical and ethical aporias that no discussion, explication, rationale, or well-constructed argument can fully rationalize—even for oneself."[123] Confronting such irresolvable mysteries demands the philosopher step outside the systems of language, rising above even the most succinct and precise philosophical statements.

This image of the ladder, first ascended and then ultimately transcended, may be intended as a reference to the *Tractatus* itself. "My work consists of two parts," wrote Wittgenstein, "the one presented here plus all that I have *not* written. And it is precisely this second part that is the important point."[124] When one has reached the pinnacle of his philosophical quest, stepping into the domain of things that are truly "important," language buckles under the inscrutable paradox and the ladder of logical propositions must be cast away. Such critical reflection, says Wittgenstein, is possible only in silence.

The Maggid's teachings, by contrast, offer a very different perspective on the contemplative's encounter with the ineffable. Rather than the rungs of philosophical language, Dov Ber's mystic climbs the ladder of words and letters in an inward journey toward the infinite pool of divine wisdom concealed in his heart and mind. "Prayer is a ladder," says the Maggid, "rooted in the earth and reaching toward heaven."[125] The "ladder of ascent" (*sulam ha-'aliyah*) is a well-known kabbalistic image for the mystic quest, an image plucked from the Hebrew Bible (Gen. 28:10–19) and shared by many Jewish philosophers as well as religious thinkers from other traditions.[126] For the Maggid, this scriptural ladder becomes a symbol for the power of language to hold together the two sides of the paradox, bridging the gap between the ineffable and the realm of finite words. This same ability to translate God's infinity is embodied in the charismatic figure of the *tsaddik*, who "has the capacity to draw down the life-force (*shefa*) and bestow it on others. And so, too, can such an individual raise up his generation."[127] Far from retreating into contemplative silence, the mystic's sacred speech transforms the people around him and allows the world to shine with renewed divine vitality.

Language, as philosophers, poets, and mystics know full well, is graced with the power to reveal and conceal at the very same moment.[128] Words attenuate God's infinite vitality, but it is through piercing the illusion of their individuation that the attentive worshipper arrives at the infinite unity within. "The inspired person (*ish ha-nilbav*)," claims the Maggid, "makes no distinctions . . . for Speech itself is utter oneness. Through this, he unites the world above with the world below, rising up from level to level to the very source of them all. There everything is utter unity."[129] The inspired worshipper is undeterred by initial perceptions of multiplicity in language. Quite the opposite is true. Such a person understands that all multiplicity, whether in the particulars of language or the cosmos itself, reveals the infinite and ever-flowing well of divine vitality.

The worshipper journeys into this realm of creativity and inspiration that lies beyond words, tracing spoken words back to their roots in the mind, and then beyond. Yet this realm is restricted by its ineffable silence; flashes of insight have no expression until they are brought into language. Indeed, says the Maggid, the processes of cognition and intellection that lead to speech must also take place within the boundaries of words, since language governs the structures of the mind as well. A similar transformation characterizes all acts of divine revelation, including creation, which originated in a preverbal inner divine realm and was then accomplished through the pathways of language. It is to this theme that our exploration now turns.

PART II

The Divine Word

Chapter 4

Letters, Creation, and the Divine Mind

The sayings and sermons of the Maggid of Mezritch are the
outstanding example of an almost complete transformation of
all the spheres comprising the world of Judaism into spheres of
the soul, of a revalution of each and every one of its conceptions in terms of the personal life of the individual.

—Gershom Scholem

Everything, being and becoming, nature and history, is
essentially a divine pronouncement (*Aussprache*), an infinite
context of signs meant to be perceived and understood by
perceiving and understanding creatures.

—Martin Buber

Imbricated Mythologies

God's formation of the world through speech, and, more specifically, through
the twenty-two letters of the Hebrew alphabet, is central to the Maggid's
linguistic theology. His interpretation of the Genesis narrative offers a mystical exploration of the origins of human language through the coming into
being of God's sacred word. Dov Ber's homilies emphasize that God—and
God's language—comes into being anew, not as a one-time historical event,
but as creation is constantly revived. The process begins with the emanation
of the *sefirah keter*, representing the preintellect of the divine mind, which is so
far beyond description that it can be alluded to only by the tip of the smallest
letter (*yod*). This initial moment of divine self-disclosure was followed by

the emergence of *hokhmah*. This godly wisdom was sublime and ethereal, and is referenced by the *yod*, the first pointlike letter of God's most sacred and ineffable name. The divine language flowing into the cosmos originates in this *hokhmah*, which includes the potential for all letters and words. This original burst of divine energy takes on a more specific form in the realm of divine thought, or *binah*, and is continuously translated through the *sefirot* until it reached *malkhut*. This final stage of creation is the ten (or nine) divine utterances, which represent the emergence of spoken language from the pool of divine potential.[1]

The same twenty-two Hebrew letters through which God formed the world are the kernel of all human language as well. Perhaps the Maggid conceives of these letters as a universal set of phonemes, but he may instead consider Hebrew the metaphysical root of all other languages. The stages of human cognition and articulation mirror the emergence of the *sefirot* and the divine name in creation. Ideas originate in the ineffable and incomprehensible realms of *keter* and then *hokhmah*, either of which might be identifiable with the Maggid's term *kadmut ha-sekhel*. As one continues to contemplate and focus his mind on a single creative inspiration, he brings the idea into *binah* and surrounds it in a linguistic garment composed of the letters of thought. Only after becoming invested in these letters can he articulate his thought via the medium of spoken words.

Letters and words, like the physical world, focus and reduce infinite potential so that it may be expressed through limited structures. The Maggid generally refers to creation as an expression of God's kindness, describing the initial act of divine self-contraction as an act undertaken out of love. The unrestrained illumination of *Ein Sof* would have hopelessly overwhelmed any created beings, so it was necessary for God to diminish that expanse of divine light. However, the attenuation of God's light is neither permanent nor entirely insurmountable. A worshipper may attune his contemplative sense and thereby learn to see the divine word that sustains all elements of the physical world and gives them life. The same is true in the realm of interpersonal communication: a thoughtful and attuned listener may recover the deepest, even infinite significance of an idea that has been constricted into words.

The Maggid's teachings reveal that he holds together two very different myths regarding the place of language in the cosmos. The first of these, adapted from Lurianic Kabbalah, is that of the withdrawal of God's infinite light (called *tsimtsum*)[2] and the intradivine fracture that results from the "breaking of the vessels" (*shevirat ha-kelim*), the moment in which God's light poured into the sacred array of the *sefirot* with too much intensity. The vessels shattered, casting forth the light in the form of divine sparks. Key to the Maggid's theology of language is the fact that these kernels—or shards—of illumination are also described as letters, tiny seeds of divine vitality awaiting the worshipper's cultivation. The letters of idle chatter or mundane, dross-ridden conversations contribute further to this linguistic entropy. The efforts of the worshipper thus seek to heal or repair the cosmic cataclysm, restoring balance to the *sefirot* and channeling blessing and divine life-force into the world.

Yet many of the Maggid's homilies explore the lingering presence of God's sublime language in mythic terms without mentioning this ancient disaster described in Lurianic teachings. Drawing on a rabbinic tradition, Dov Ber refers to the cosmos as animated by the divine word because God created the world through the Torah itself. Reverberations of Scripture, manifest as sacred letters, thus continue to inhere in the physical realm and animate the cosmos. Through contemplating the works of creation, the worshipper is tasked with connecting these divine letters with their divine source. Dov Ber reinterprets the central Lurianic creation myth in a characteristically Hasidic key, arguing that God's contraction of the primordial divine light—a willing act of self-limitation into the letters of creation—was an expression of love akin to a parent speaking to a child.

Stories of Creation

The narrative of Genesis 1, in which God speaks the cosmos into existence through a series of utterances, implies a mythic account of creation through language.[3] This notion is echoed by later books of Scripture, including the psalmist's words "By the word of the Y-H-V-H the heavens were made, by the breath (*ruah*) of His mouth, all their host" (Ps. 33:6) and "Forever, O Y-H-V-H, Your word stands firm in heaven" (Ps. 119:89). Indeed, the idea that the Divine created the world through words is a common theme in the literature of the ancient Near East and in Jewish writings from late antiquity in particular.[4] The Bible does not refer to the role of specific letters or divine names in creation, nor does it make a claim about the Hebrew language in particular, but passages such as these are the scriptural foundations for many later mystical reinterpretations of Genesis.

Rabbinic literature includes a small but significant number of passages about God forming the world through various forms of language.[5] An early tradition claims that the world was created through ten divine utterances,[6] and rabbinic works occasionally refer to God as "the One who spoke and the world came into being."[7] A later tradition preserved in the name of Rav explains that Bezalel fashioned the Tabernacle by means of the twenty-two Hebrew letters through which the world was created.[8] This passage is particularly significant because it focuses on the linguistic character of the divine utterance rather than on God issuing an order. Creation is a common subject of inquiry in rabbinic literature, as the sages grappled with the absence of a systematic narrative in Scripture. But the role of divine speech or the Hebrew letters in God's formation of the world was not the subject of any sustained interpretation in Talmudic or early midrashic literature

Several traditions in rabbinic literature suggest that God formed the world through a sacred divine name, such as *yod* and *heh* (the first two letters of Y-H-V-H).[9] There are mentions of a secret forty-two-letter name of God, as well as names of twelve and seventy-two letters,[10] which became central to many later kabbalistic interpretations of creation. However, these mysterious divine names are not explicitly recorded, nor does the rabbinic material ascribe them a role in God's formation of the world.[11] But rabbinic texts also refer to the creative power of language with no explicit connection to God forming the universe through words.[12] The Talmud refers to Rabbah as fashioning a humanoid, and two other sages creating a young calf, after studying a work called *Sefer Yetsirah*. This particular book is not necessarily identical to the classical text of early Jewish mysticism bearing the same name,[13] but traditions such as these suggest that later Jewish works were building on preexisting attitudes about the creative power of language and letters.[14]

Rabbinic traditions portray God creating the world through Torah itself.[15] The classical midrash *Bereshit Rabbah* opens with a tradition in which God formed the world by gazing into Scripture, a creation myth that is obviously rooted in the language of Torah but different than both speaking the world into being and formulating the world by manipulation of letters.[16] The Mishnah preserves the following teaching in the name of Rabbi 'Akiva: "Beloved is Israel, for they have been given a precious tool; a deeper love is revealed to them in that they were given the precious tool of the world's creation."[17] Such traditions build on Proverbs 8:22–30 by identifying Torah as Proverbs' wisdom (*hokhmah*), though they are not necessarily connected to the Torah's linguistic makeup. But these teachings and their later interpretation represent a strand of thinking in which the Torah, and perhaps the language of Scripture more broadly, holds great creative power.

The opening section of *Sefer Yetsirah* describes the universe being formed by means of the "thirty-two pathways of wisdom," or the ten *sefirot* and the twenty-two consonant letters of the Hebrew alphabet. God created the world by combining these letters with one another, suggesting that the Hebrew letters are the fundaments of the world as well as the basic elements of language.[18] *Sefer Yetsirah* devotes very little explicit attention to personal mystical experience, though some recensions depict the biblical figure of Abraham attaining the divine wisdom necessary to create by means of the Hebrew letters. This reason, among others, has led scholars to identify the notion that human beings can also awaken the creative capacities of language as one of the central tenets of this work.[19]

Some texts of the *heikhalot* literature of late antiquity refer to God forming the world by means of divine names, and some mention letter permutation as a technique for inspiring mystical ascents. But neither of these themes may rightly be described as a central concern of *heikhalot* literature.[20] The writings of the early Provençal and Spanish Kabbalists, however, devoted much attention to the linguistic aspects of creation. They produced a huge number of commentaries on the first chapters of Genesis, many of which interpret the biblical narratives as a description of the emanation of the *sefirot*.[21] The names of God are associated with different *sefirot* and are also ascribed a particularly important place in this mystical remapping of creation.[22]

Commentaries on *Sefer Yetsirah* had emerged as an independent genre in the twelfth and thirteenth centuries, signaling the incorporation of this enigmatic work and its understanding of language into the mystical canon.[23] *Sefer Yetsirah* gives specific divine names a less prominent role in the creation story than the Hebrew letters more broadly. But the commentaries on *Sefer Yetsirah* authored by Kabbalists like Isaac the Blind weave together letter mysticism with focused speculation on the various divine names. The notion that God created the world through the Hebrew alphabet, and through the letters of Scripture in particular, became a cornerstone of the works of Avraham Abulafia and Yosef Gikatilla.[24]

The *Bahir* and the writings from the circle of Isaac the Blind were the first to describe divine "thought" (*mahashavah*) as a crucial phase of emanation.[25] Some early kabbalistic works refer to *mahashavah* as the first true *sefirah*, while others consider it the second emanated power.[26] Many of these texts describe human and divine thought as being intimately linked, and this *sefirah* came to serve as the focal point of meditation. These early Kabbalists argued that the realm of *keter*, which lies beyond *mahashavah*, cannot truly be described or understood, and, for this reason, thought must be the locus of mystical contemplation.[27]

Eitan Fishbane has recently highlighted an important theological shift in the writings of many of these early Kabbalists. He argues that their works do not describe God's words as hypostatic entities separate from the Divine, a position found in many prekabbalistic texts. Rather, Fishbane suggests that "the auto-emanation of the divine Being is . . . the vocalization of a silent cosmic reality. God does not just speak the word of creation. God *is* the word of creation."[28] That is, the early Kabbalists describe the emanation by means of the letters and words of divine speech as a manifestation of the Godhead within a delimited structure. God is embodied within the speech through which the world was created, much as the Divine is expressed through the framework of the *sefirot*.

The story of creation, the emergence of the *sefirot*, and the names of God are central concerns of the Zohar and later *Tikkunei Zohar*.[29] Several passages refer to the rabbinic legend of God forming the cosmos through Torah, reinterpreting this ancient myth through the symbolic associations of the *sefirot*.[30] Descriptions of the creation through the Hebrew letters more broadly also abound in Zoharic literature.[31] According to one account, the world was "engraved and established" (*itgelif ve-itqayyam*) by means of the letters of a forty-two-letter divine name.[32] This same passage refers to *shekhinah* as having been formed by a stream of letters issuing forth from the *sefirot* of *keter*, *hokhmah*, *binah*, and *hesed*.

One of the more elaborate stories in the Zoharic literature about the formation of the world through letters appears in what is now printed as the work's introduction.[33] Drawing on earlier midrashic traditions, this passage claims that the Hebrew letters preexisted creation by two thousand years.[34] God contemplated them and delighted in them long before using them to form the world, but eventually the letters came before Him in reverse order, and each pleaded to be used in the work of creation. Only the *aleph*, the quietest of all the letters, is too timid to enter before the Divine. God selected the *bet*, the first letter of *bereshit* (in the beginning), as the instrument through which to form the cosmos, but awarded the silent *aleph* with the gift of being the "head of all the letters" (*reish le-khol atvan*).

The teachings of both Moshe Cordovero and Yitshak Luria refer to the emergence of the Hebrew letters as a specific stage in the process of emanation.[35] The importance of the letters is underscored in particular in the traditions recorded in the works of Yisra'el Sarug and Naftali Bachrach.[36] However, the writings of the Safed mystics rarely invoke the myth of God creating the cosmos through gazing into the Torah. Cordovero and Luria devote far more attention to the specific role of the divine names of seventy-two, sixty-three, fifty-two, and forty-five letters in the various stages of emanation. They note how each of these divine names interfaces with the others, forming with them the intricate and complex theosophical matrix that undergirds the devotional practice of *kavvanot* and *yihudim*. The notion of God's self-unfolding through the Torah seems to have been less pivotal in their interpretation of the specific Genesis narrative, but it was key to Hasidic teachings on creation.

The Letters and the Ten Utterances

The notion that God used the letters of Hebrew alphabet to form the world is a fundamental element of the Maggid's theology. He is also concerned, however, with a question left unanswered in some earlier traditions: Were the letters—and thus language—coeternal with the Divine, or were they created at some stage as well?[37] The Maggid suggests that the Hebrew alphabet was indeed formed by God, and the letters originated in the very earliest moments of emanation. The letters emerged within the realm of divine thought, appearing long before God's first speech acts:

> [The Sages taught:] "In the beginning" (Gen. 1:1) was also an utterance.[38] But this explanation is difficult, since Scripture should then have written, "and He said." I heard an explanation for this:[39] It is known from the kabbalistic books that the letters were emanated in the very beginning, after which the Holy One used them to create all of the worlds. This is the mystery of, "In the beginning God created '*et*' [the heavens and the earth]," referring to all the letters from *aleph* to *tav*. Thus the letters were the first act of creation, emanated in thought alone and without any articulation.

> Speech (*amirah*) is composed of the letters [as they are articulated] through the five openings of the mouth. But the letters had not yet been emanated, for they emerged in thought alone and without any speech. Thus it was impossible to write, "and He said," since this [first act of creation] was accomplished without words. For this reason, the Aramaic translation[40] renders the verse as "with *hokhmah* [God created the heavens and the earth]."[41]

The initial word of the Torah indeed refers to a type of divine utterance, but one that is significantly different than the following nine creative speech acts. It happened entirely within the realm of God's thought (*mahashavah*), the region of the Godhead in which the Hebrew alphabet was first emanated. Only after they emerged in divine thought could God use these letters to form each element of the cosmos.

The Maggid is describing creation as a two-stage process defined by different forms of language. The first phase is that of the more abstract letters of thought, which the Maggid generally associates with the *sefirah binah*. This symbolic identification is less certain in our case, however, and he seems to refer to the emergence of the letters in *hokhmah*.[42] This would establish the roots of language in the very first stage of creation after the emergence of the unknowable *keter*. In either case, the letters of God's thought serve as the basis for articulated divine words, a second and more concrete category of language. In this later phase, God combined the letters with one another and thereby formed the series of divine utterances through which the cosmos was created.

Other sermons locate the origins of language at an even earlier stage in the process of creation. These homilies focus on the importance of the "primeval will" (*ratson ha-kadmon* or *ratson ha-kadum*). The Maggid explains that Scripture cannot describe this phase of creation as speech because it was too sublime, at once full of infinite potential and totally inexpressible. Only a lesser manifestation of the divine wisdom could be revealed through words:

> The Sages taught: "The world was created by ten divine speech acts; 'In the beginning' is also a divine utterance." In the creation story, Scripture says: "'*et*' the heavens and '*et*' the earth"—the particle '*et*' includes the rest of their kind (*toldoteihem*) [i.e., that which heaven and earth brought forth].[43] The Sages taught that

all of the acts of creation are alluded to in the first speech act, and afterward each one was spelled out in all of its particulars.[44]

The matter is thus: It is known that before the worlds were brought into being, it first arose in God's mind to create them. This cannot even be called a speech act, since it took place within the [divine] mind.[45] All of the worlds were included in it—that is, in the primeval Will—in abstract form, as were all the different levels [of existence]. Afterward, they were drawn forth into specification.

"In the beginning" (*bereshit*) is also related to the word for speech, as in the verse "[You have not denied . . .] the request of his lips (*areshet sefatav*)" (Ps. 21:3). However, this is a translation (*targum*). It refers to the primeval Will from which everything was drawn, and therefore it is in translation. This type of exalted level cannot be revealed except through a translation, which is the "back side" (*ahorayyim*) or *malkhut* of the world that is above it. This is the same of all levels. This is why the Aramaic translation [renders "In the beginning"] as "with Wisdom" (*be-hokhmata*).[46]

The initial emanation of the divine will included the potential for all of the later utterances. Each of the works of creation, formed through divine speech, emerged from the reservoir of this first emanation. But does this initial stage, the root of all subsequent language, represent *keter* or *hokhmah*? The answer is not entirely clear. It might be correlated to the idea that the cosmic divine *aleph* as *keter*, *ratson* (or "will") is almost always associated with *keter* in early Kabbalah,[47] but the conclusion of this passage suggests that the Maggid associates it with *hokhmah*. The ambiguity is striking and worth noting, for he often moves between terms such as *ratson* or *mahashavah* in a rather fluid manner. The instability of his symbolic language is one attribute of the Maggid's sermons that makes his teachings particularly difficult to interpret.

An additional element of the Maggid's homily remains somewhat puzzling. The word *areshet* seems to be pure biblical Hebrew, although it is a hapax legomenon, so presumably Dov Ber does not mean that it is a literal translation of *dibbur*.[48] The Maggid may be using the term *targum* to describe the physical world as a translation of the spiritual world,[49] but this is only part of Dov Ber's broader exegetical point. He is also claiming that *areshet*, and the related word *bereshit*, allude to the capability of language to bring wordless potential into concrete and specific articulation. Such translation refers to a process through which higher stages of emanation are adapted and communicated to lower levels.[50] In this case, it is the necessary linguistic medium through which the infinite potential included in the first "speech act" of creation could become fully manifest.[51]

Our interpretation of this sermon is complemented—and complicated— by a loose parallel found in another collection of the Maggid's homilies. The teaching begins with the construction of the Tabernacle, described as "life of all the worlds," through Bezalel recombining the letters of creation.[52] It then turns to the formation of the cosmos itself:

> We are taught: "the world was created by ten divine speech acts." The Talmud notes, however, that "God said" appears only nine times in the opening chapter of Genesis. It replies that "In the beginning" is also a divine utterance. But why doesn't the Torah use "God said" in this first case? Because this act of divine speech is beyond our grasp; only its lower manifestations can be known. This represents [an aspect of] translation, for the translation of "speech" (*dibbur*) is *areshet*. This primal utterance is the raw material (*hyle*) out of which all further speech was to emerge. [I.e., all divine speech acts are a "translation" of God's original unformed utterance.]
>
> The same must be true with regard to the Tabernacle. [Parallel to the primal utterance] is the menorah, which even Moses had difficulty in grasping. It could not be shaped by any human, but formed itself. The menorah bore witness to the fact that God's presence now dwelt in Israel's midst. This is the "oil"; the illumination dwells upon it [i.e., Israel] like the fire upon the [surface of the] oil. The rest of the utterances are the "olive," with the oil contained within them.
>
> That is why this chapter [of Scripture] does not open with "God spoke to Moses" or even "God said." This "olive oil" is beyond our grasp. Even "saying," which would imply thought, is not appropriate here.[53]

The description of the Tabernacle as a microcosm of the physical universe is common in Jewish literature.[54] The Talmudic sages drew a specific connection between the creation through language and the construction of the Tabernacle,[55] and later Kabbalists associated the different elements in the structure of the Tabernacle with various *sefirot*.[56] The Maggid's contribution, however, is found in the way he employs these symbols to describe the emergence of language from the infinite expanse of divine silence.

The menorah corresponds to *keter* or *hokhmah*, either of which may be identified as the first of the ten utterances of creation. This structure is a stage of emanation that remains so far beyond language that it cannot be understood by the human mind. It is a veritable pool of dynamic potential simply awaiting revelation, but without specific and finite vessels the illumination of God's first utterance would overwhelm everything before it. The first moment of *keter* or *hokhmah* is thus imperceptible because of its brilliance. This is true of the shimmering potential of God's initial speech act, too expansive and intense to be grasped by the human mind. Therefore, it must be contracted through the medium of language. All subsequent divine words emerged from the first creative utterance, just as light pours forth from the menorah when the oil's hidden potential is set ablaze. God's language, associated with the *sefirot*, is a tiered framework that mitigates the intensity of the divine light. This reduction, however, is precisely what allows for the revelation of the light.[57]

The initial divine utterance and the primal *sefirot* require a limited medium through which they can be expressed. These finite vessels, claims the Maggid, come in many forms: the Tabernacle, the physical world, the *sefirot*, and, most fundamentally, language itself. Each of these represents a manner in which infinite divine potential is embodied in something more concrete. In this context, the Maggid is highlighting the importance of "translation" as a way of mediating between the infinite, prelinguistic realms and the concrete realms of the physical world and of language.[58]

These sermons explore the order of creation, but they also explain the origins of language itself. Nine of the ten utterances in the opening chapter of Genesis represent divine speech, but they flow forth from a preliminary act in which God created the potential for all the letters. This first emanation is the foundation of all language, both human and divine. The letters emerged first within the deepest realms of God's mind, and only then could they be used to translate thought into the creative spoken word. This same dynamic, says the Maggid, holds true for human cognition. Ideas begin in *hokhmah*, the prelinguistic realm of the mind, but they receive structure and definition in *binah*, where they are embodied in the "letters of thought." Only then may an idea be contracted into words and articulated aloud.[59]

Let us move from the image of the Tabernacle to a different creation metaphor invoked by the Maggid. Forming the world demanded that God contract the ever-expansive flow of *hokhmah*, investing and expressing it through the lower *sefirot*. In order to accomplish this, however, it was necessary to diminish *hokhmah* to such a degree that the cosmos could withstand its brilliance. To illustrate this process, the Maggid offers the following parable about a father instructing his child:

> The child receives [ideas] from the father's wisdom. His understanding comes from his parent's words, since [otherwise] the father's wisdom is too great and hidden. The child can grasp something because his father has contracted his wisdom, lessening it and embodying it in words according to the child's
> · [level of] understanding. When the child truly devotes his mind to [contemplating] the words, he receives [the wisdom within them], since there everything is utter oneness. This is the meaning of, "The opening of Your words gives light" (Ps. 119:130),[60]—*hokhmah* shines forth from within the word, and through this it can illuminate another person and a student can understand it. This brings great pleasure to the father.[61]

The analogy of the father's wisdom to the *sefirah hokhmah* is crucial to understanding the point of this teaching: God contracted the divine wisdom into the ten (or in another sense, nine) utterances of creation so that the cosmos might endure, just as a parent must focus and restrict an idea into words so that it may be grasped by a child. In both cases this transformation is accomplished through embodying *hokhmah* in language.[62] The Maggid returns to this same parable of a parent and a child in order to describe revelation and the nature of Torah as well, for Scripture too represents an embodiment of the divine presence through language.

A second, more devotional nuance of the Maggid's parable should not escape our attention. The child may grasp his father's infinite wisdom by contemplating his words and focusing on their true inner content. Although the parent's language diminishes the original idea, such restriction into words does not erect an insurmountable hurdle. Far from preventing the child from attaining his father's thought, language actually grants him a way of understanding his parent's idea. Thus the image of the father and the child suggests that the Maggid is calling on his students to access this divine wisdom through contemplating the earthly realm. Finite vessels, whether a teacher's words or physical reality itself, provide a medium through which one may access the expansive and ineffable.

Divine immanence is central to early Hasidic theology, and these thinkers often describe God's presence in the physical realm by invoking the notion that the world was created through language. Clearly inspired by the theology of the BeSHT, many of the Maggid's sermons emphasize that God's creative speech acts did not simply disappear from the world once it was formed.[63] These initial divine utterances have remained in the earthly realm as the eternal sacred energy that animates and nourishes it:

> "Praise Y-H-V-H from the heavens" (Ps. 148:1). [We should
> interpret this] in light of, "Forever, O Y-H-V-H, Your Word stands
> in the firmament" (Ps. 119:89), and "by the word of Y-H-V-H the
> heavens were made" (Ps. 33:6). God created the worlds with speech,
> and the power of the Maker is in the made.[64] The power of
> [divine] speech is in the heavens, and through the power of this
> speech they endure and are sustained. This is the meaning of,
> "Your Word stands in the firmament"—[God's] speech stands in
> heaven. "Praise 'et' Y-H-V-H" refers to all the letters from *aleph* to
> *tav*. The letters [are articulated] through the five positions of the
> mouth, which is the *heh* of "the heavens" (*ha-shamayyim*).[65]
> You too should "praise" [God] with speech acts made up of
> the twenty-two letters and five positions [of the mouth]. The
> principle is that this [human] speech sustains the world, like the
> power [of God's word] in the heavens. "Y-H-V-H" [refers to] the
> Holy One's speech. "From the heavens" means with the power [of]
> the heavens, through which the world is sustained. The enlight-
> ened one will understand.[66]

The divine utterances of creation endure, giving vitality to the corporeal world. God's formative word is the divine "power" or lifeblood that courses through all created beings. But the Maggid's sermon links this notion of divine immanence to the nature of all language, arguing that human words are formed as the very same twenty-two Hebrew letters are projected through the five positions of the mouth. The essential affinity between human and divine language allows mankind to draw forth God's linguistic power from the physical realm. Proper worship must engage the sacred element of language that dwells infused within the earthly realm.

The Maggid occasionally draws an explicit connection between the di-vine word of creation, human language, and the importance of Israel's speech.

Dov Ber emphasizes that the original formative utterances continue to illuminate and sustain the earthly realm.[67] Israel, however, plays a crucial role
in renewing the cosmos through their sacred language. The words of their
supplications, described as a kind of prayerful song, infuse the divine utterances with new energy and thus revitalize the entirety of creation.

The notion that God's word remains in the corporeal realm becomes
the basis of a contemplative exercise. We read the following as part of a much
longer homily on the mystical dimensions of prayer:

> One's sole intent in speaking words of prayer and study should
> be to raise them up to their [divine] source. The creation of the
> world began with the twenty-two letters of the alphabet, and
> the Zohar describes God's creation through Torah, meaning the
> twenty-two letters of Scripture. Similarly, life-sustaining effluence
> (*shefa'*) flows from on high into all creatures by means of those
> [letters].
>
> One's task [in prayer] is to raise the words, causing them to
> flow upward into their source.
>
> This is the process: he must link word to [God's] Word, voice
> to Voice, breath to Breath, thought to Thought. These are the
> four letters Y-H-V-H. If one does this, all his words fly upward to
> their Source. This causes his words to come before the One,
> causing Him to look at them.[68]

One who worships or studies has the opportunity, and indeed the obligation, to attach the words to the sacred utterances of creation. The present
description of how to do so seems to be rather different than the unifications we noted in the previous chapter, where the quest to connect *kol* with
dibbur (*tif'eret* and *malkhut*) demands that one unify two of the most basic
physical sensations of speech, and that connecting *'olam ha-dibbur* with *'olam
ha-mahashavah* (*malkhut* and *binah*) requires one to align his spoken words
with innermost sacred thoughts.

In this text one must bind the words of prayer to the divine utterances
through which the cosmos was formed. This is true of each stage of linguistic unfolding, including the sound of voice (*kol*), breath (*hevel*), and
thought. All rungs must be connected to their divine counterpart, thereby
unifying the four letters of the name Y-H-V-H and ensuring the unobstructed
flow of divine vitality into the cosmos. Words spoken in this manner "enter

the presence of God," which the Maggid interprets as a metaphor for opening the inner channels of blessing.

This description suggests that accessing the divine quality of language requires more than awareness that speech is a gift from God. The worshipper must actively connect each linguistic faculty to its divine counterpart, starting with articulated words and progressing to the inner realms of thought and spiritual intellection. These four stages also correspond to the letters of the divine name Y-H-V-H, revealing also the fluidity of the Maggid's rich symbolic associations and further interweaving the tones of human and divine language.[69]

Israel Arose in Thought

Kabbalistic theology has long been dominated by a kind of ethnocentrism in which "Israel" and "humanity" are constantly conflated in this literature.[70] This is heightened in Hasidism, including the teachings of the Maggid, who often connects the role of language in creation to his interpretation of the rabbinic teaching that "Israel arose in thought." This phrase appears in the midrash and may suggest that God created the world for the sake of the Jewish people, but it is reinterpreted in classical Kabbalah in light of the *sefirot*. The divine mind or thought (*hokhmah* or *binah*) and the Jewish people (*kenesset yisra'el* or *malkhut*) each share a relatively stable web of symbolic associations.[71]

The Maggid interprets "Israel arose in thought" as a statement of cosmology, a description of the order of creation, and an illustration of the special love between God and the Jewish people.[72] His sermons often refer to the pleasure worshippers bring to God as arising in the divine mind long before these individuals were actually created.[73] Indeed, the initial divine thought that gave rise to the moment of *tsimtsum*, or the withdrawal and diminution of God's light so that creation might endure, was an expression of divine love for Israel.[74]

"Israel arose in thought" is often linked by the Maggid to the concept of God's primeval thought (*mahashavah*), the initial phase of creation from which all subsequent emanations proceeded. Although the Jewish people appear much later on the stage of history, the Maggid reiterates that something may be "last in deed, yet first in thought" (*sof ma'aseh be-mahashavah tehilah*).[75] God's first *mahashavah* held the potential for the entire project of creation, just as an artisan's preliminary plan includes all parts of his work long before it comes to fruition.[76] The Maggid explains this dynamic with a metaphor directly relevant to our subject: just as spoken words are the culmination of an extended process of intellection, Israel manifests an aspect of God's thought that emerged in the very first moments of creation:

> Israel arose in thought to be created first. Even though man appeared last in the works of creation, he was first in thought, as it says, "You have formed me before and after" (Ps. 139:5). It is known that all twenty-two letters and the five positions of the mouth exist in thought, which is the root of all the letters. One cannot speak something out loud without thinking of it first. If he does bring forth a word without thought, [his speech] will be incomprehensible, lacking wisdom and intelligence. So too is [God's] Thought the root of all the worlds, which were revealed through speech.
>
> For example, take someone who is writing letters. Before he outlines the shape of the letter [itself], he begins with a *yod*, the tiny point and smallest of all the letters. And even before writing the letter, he scores its shape. This engraving is called thought, like a thought that comes before a letter or word is spoken. As the thought is combined with the letter and the word, the letter and word become recognizable.[77]

Israel arose in God's mind before the world was formed, just as an idea first appears in the intellect before it is translated into written or spoken words. They were present in the earliest stages of divine cognition, which later became expressed in the sacred speech of creation. Indeed, the cosmos is a concrete, linguistic manifestation of the primal divine thought. It is no surprise that this excerpt comes from a sermon addressing the ways in which Israel's special capacity for language empowers them to arouse the worlds above and below. Their prayers awaken and illuminate the divine utterances in the earthly realm, but the Maggid is also describing Israel as the thought at the heart of the language of creation.

This particular interpretation of "last in deed, yet first in thought" sheds some light on a theme noted above. Israel appeared in the first divine thought, the initial phase of emanation that included the potential for the elements of language that would later emerge in the process of creation. Like Israel, the letters used by God to form the world "arose" in the first stage of emanation.[78] They emerged first as part of God's will, an abstract thought that was then expressed through the stages of emanation and the physical world. The Maggid takes the verse "I am the first and I am the last; there is none but me" (Isa. 44:6) to mean that the divine will is equally present in all aspects and phases of creation, giving it form as the once-inchoate letters of thought come together into the enduring structures of the cosmos.

The Maggid takes "Israel arose in thought" to refer to the meditative faculty possessed by the Jewish people.[79] Israel has an innate connection to *hokhmah*, through which the world was created. This natural bond grants them the ability to ascend on high through contemplative thought. Such is clear in the Maggid's reinterpretation of God's reply to Moses in the famous Talmudic legend about the martyrdom of Rabbi 'Akiva.[80] God commands, "Silence, for so it has arisen in my mind (*shtok, kakh 'alah be-mahashavah*)!" but the Maggid reads the perfect *'alah* as the imperative *'aleh*. God thus responds: "Be quiet—raise everything up with the mind."[81]

Complementing this meditation on the mind with an emphasis on speech, Dov Ber also describes creation and the emergence of letters as fully coterminous:

> Israel are truly one with the blessed God. It is taught that before creation, He and His name were united in *keter* . . . and Israel was not yet a part of the world. Afterward, after it arose in His good Will [to create the world], this Will moved from level to level, until the letters came into speech.
>
> Through this [process] Israel was created, just as they are today. There is no separation between them and their Maker. Even their corporeal [aspects] were brought into being and fashioned from the letters. Before the world was created, these letters existed with His name in *keter*.[82]

Israel was created directly by divine speech. Their physical form is composed of God's letters, and they possess a unique capacity for sacred language.[83] This notion, claims the Maggid, also explains Israel's enduring connection to God. Nothing can sever the bond because their very being embodies the sacred word. This homily even refers to the potential letters as included in *keter*—not *hokhmah*—suggesting that language is rooted in what is often described as a totally prelinguistic stage of emanation.

The Maggid interprets the idea that "Israel arose in thought" in reference to an image of the Jewish people permanently engraved in God's mind.[84] This likeness hewn into God's thought signals more than an eternal bond between God and Israel. The image itself transforms over time—it shifts as Israel changes and matures—just like the picture a child preserved in the mind of a parent. The image responds and evolves in keeping with their actions. And the Maggid extends this notion in the opposite direction: the image of Israel affects the ways in which they imagine God. The homily began with the rabbinic teaching of God appearing to the Israelites as a young man at the Sea of Reeds, and as a wizened sage at Sinai. The Maggid explains this seeming change in the divine form by attributing the shift to Israel: in a kind of intellective double-projection, the Jewish people see the face of God as a projection of their own image as it is enshrined in the halls of divine thought.

The intimate connection between the workings of God's mind and human cognition is underscored in the first sermon of *Maggid Devarav le-Ya'akov*. It begins with a familiar interpretation of "Israel arose in thought," namely, that God created the world in search of the future pleasure sparked by deeds. The Maggid then offers a very different reading of this phrase:

> The Sages taught that Israel arose in thought. The earliest desire (*kedimat ha-ratson*) was that Israel be righteous in each and every generation. . . . The Holy One delights in the deeds of the righteous, and [therefore] contracted Himself [and allowed for creation]. This withdrawal [or focusing] is called *hokhmah*, for *hokhmah* emerges from Nothing (*ayin*), as it is written, "*hokhmah* comes forth from *ayin*" (Job 28:12). This contraction was for [the sake of] Israel, performed out of [God's] love. . . .
>
> One must make all of his thoughts and intention into a throne for the Holy One. When one thinks of His love, this causes God to dwell in the world of love. The same is true when one thinks of awe—it causes Him to dwell in the world of awe. One must never cease thinking about God for even a single moment. . . .
>
> This is the meaning of, "The eyes of Y-H-V-H are upon the righteous" (Ps. 34:16). When a child does some childish act, he

draws his father's attention to those [seemingly trivial] deeds. *Tsaddikim* can do the same thing, as it were, by causing God's Mind to dwell wherever they are thinking. When they contemplate love, they bring the blessed Holy One into the world of love. This is the meaning of the Zohar's comment on [the verse] "the King bound up in tresses" (Song 7:6)—the tresses of the mind.[85]

This is the explanation of, "God concentrated (*tsimtsem*) His *shekhinah* to rest between the two staves of the ark."[86] They are the two lungs, or *shekhinah*.[87] God dwells wherever [the righteous one] is thinking. "Eyes" refers to the mind; the Mind [of God] is in the hands of the righteous. But how do they attain this rung? Only by considering themselves as mere dust, thinking that they can do nothing without the power of God. Anything they do is really being performed by God.[88]

This homily ascribes a remarkable degree of power to the contemplative abilities of the *tsaddikim*. Here the Maggid makes a claim beyond Israel's vision of God being a reflection of their own likeness within the divine mind. The thrust of this sermon is prescriptive: when a *tsaddik* contemplates a certain *sefirah*, God's presence is drawn into that realm. This *tsimtsum*, an act of simultaneous diminution and focus, expresses God's love for Israel.

The Maggid is arguing that *tsimtsum*, the process through which the infinite *Ein Sof* is contracted into limited vessels, is more than a historical stage in creation. *Tsimtsum*, the translation of the Divine, constantly transpires in the human mind.[89] Cognition draws God's presence into the finite structure of the *sefirot*, a map that exists in parallel within the human mind and the Godhead. Rather than supplanting the idea of *tsimtsum* as a stage of creation, this psychological interpretation grounds the cosmic narrative in the religious life of the individual.

It also returns us to a fundamental question that is intimately related to our analysis of the Maggid's understanding of language: Do processes of human and divine self-disclosure simply mirror one another, with each embodying a kind of revelation through language? Or might human intellection and speech actually represent a manifestation of this process as it is simultaneously taking place within the Divine? This homily lends itself to the latter interpretation. Cosmic *tsimtsum*, the constriction and revelation of God, happens through the ongoing contemplation of human worshippers.

Creation Through *Yod*

The letter *yod*, first letter of the sacred name Y-H-V-H, has long been an important kabbalistic symbol in the context of creation and language. The early Kabbalists often associate it with the *sefirah hokhmah*, a very early stage of emanation described as a single "point" of divine wisdom holding the potential for all aspects of creation before they unfold.[90] Many of these classical mystical sources refer to the uppermost tip (*kots*) of the *yod* as alluding to the *sefirah keter*, an even more abstract phase of creation that is classically understood as lying beyond linguistic reference.[91]

The Maggid's sermons frequently invoke these ancient associations, but often do so with subtle shifts in meaning. He explains that *yod* is the smallest of letters because it alludes to divine wisdom, signifying a realm that can neither be understood nor expressed in words.[92] It represents the infinite potential that appeared in the very first moments of creation, as well as the divine *hokhmah* that continuously flows through the earthly realm, the human mind, and all language. Thus the *yod* also refers to the abstract stages of cognition, human as well as divine, and it is the ultimate source of all language. The *yod* is the most basic shape from which all other letters are drawn, and *hokhmah* is the prearticulate realm out of which all speech emerges.

Yet the Maggid notes that the kabbalistic description of creation through the *yod* conflicts with a famous rabbinic midrash. A tradition in the Talmud claims that God formed the present world with the letter *heh*, and the World to Come (*'olam ha-ba*) with the letter *yod*.[93] The Maggid explains this contradiction as follows:

> It is written, "You made them all with wisdom (*hokhmah*)" (Ps. 104:24). The Zohar teaches that everything was created through Thought, which is the letter *yod*, called *hokhmah* and *mahashavah*. Thus this world must have been created with the letter *yod* as well! . . .
>
> Everything was created with *yod*, which represents the ten utterances,[94] but the *yod*, which is *mahashavah*, is described as

contemplative [or conceptual] (*'iyyunit*). This is like an artisan
who makes some sort of vessel. He puts all of his thought and
contemplative energy into the form and shape of that vessel. Now
the power of the maker is in the made, and therefore the power of
his contemplative mind is present within the form and the shape
of the vessel. Before the vessel was made, the thought [of it] was
sealed and hidden . . . but after he makes the vessel, [the artisan's]
thought is revealed and the power of thought is contained within
[the object]. Thus the vessel initially existed within thought, but
afterward the thought is contained in the vessel. . . .

The *yod* is divided and becomes two *heh*s [of the name
Y-H-V-H], an upper *heh* and a lower *heh*. But the letter *yod* is not
totally uprooted [when it is split], since everything was created by
the ten utterances. This world, which was created with a *heh*, was
first concealed within [God's] Thought. It was like the vessel that
was initially hidden within the mind of the artisan. So too the
heh, which is speech (*dibbur*) and the five positions of the mouth,
was hidden within the *yod*. Then the vessel, meaning this world,
"was created with the *heh*" (*be-heh baram*, Gen. 2:4) . . . and the
lower *heh* was revealed. This is speech, as is known. Yet the power
of the *yod* remains within it.[95]

The Maggid confirms that God formed the earthly realm with the letter *yod*,
which alludes to the ten creative utterances as well as *hokhmah* and *mahashavah*.
However, the initial burst of divine thought was intense and unformed. Like
an artist's concept that must someday be embodied in a physical work, God's
mahashavah required a more concrete medium in order to achieve definition
and expression. Therefore, the *yod* was translated into two of the letter *heh*.
The first of these represents *binah*, the realm of structured cognition, and the
second corresponds to *malkhut*, the region of articulated language.

The process through which God's initial thought is expressed through
the unfolding stream of the cosmos has several linguistic dimensions. Indeed, creation represents a multistage transition from infinite—but
silent—potential into well-defined speech. The energy of *hokhmah* first tran-
sitions into *binah*, where it is expressed through the letters of thought (*otiyyot ha-mahashavah*). But the divine wisdom must be further translated before
it can become manifest as the physical world, and therefore it is projected
into concrete speech (*dibbur* or *malkhut*).

The Maggid is careful to underscore the enduring connection between the original divine thought and its vessels of expression. By analogy, the potential wisdom of an artist's initial design is revealed through the physical object he creates; his wisdom continues to animate the creation even after it was formed. This principle holds true in the creation of the cosmos as well. The power of the initial divine *mahashavah* never recedes from the earthly realm, and the limited physical world diminishes the intensity of *hokhmah* while also allowing it to become expressed.

Several of the Maggid's sermons trace the relationship between creation, the names of God, and the stages of human cognition and language. A selection from one of his longest teachings on the subject illustrates this aspect of his theology:

> The letter *yod* is called the "point in the palace" from which the world was created,[96] for "You made everything with wisdom" (Ps. 104:24). All existence came into being from *yod*. . . . All of the worlds came into existence by means of the four letters of Y-H-V-H; there is nothing in the world that did not come into being (*nithaveh*) by it. His name [Y-H-V-H] refers to this.
>
> The twenty-two letters and all words were brought into being by it as well, as the verse says, "with the fullness of Your name, You have empowered Your word" (Ps. 138:2).[97] That is, the name Y-H-V-H must be embodied within each word and utterance, for this [sacred name] brought it into being. The Holy One had to focus the light of Y-H-V-H into every word and utterance. This makes it seem as if the utterance is greater, and thus "with the fullness of Your name, You have empowered Your word."

The Zohar interprets the diacritic within the *bet* of the word *bereshit* ("in the beginning") as a *yod*, the initial "point" of creative *hokhmah* that is surrounded by *binah*. The other letters of the divine name Y-H-V-H proceed from the first *yod*, as do each of the four worlds. Indeed, all twenty-two letters of the Hebrew alphabet were drawn forth from the primordial *yod*. Thus the formation of the worlds and the emergence of language out of the sacred name Y-H-V-H were parallel, and perhaps even simultaneous, processes. The creative energy of the first divine thought, symbolized by the original letter *yod*, dwells within the physical world as well as inside each word and utterance.

It was necessary for God to reduce the divine *hokhmah* before language and the worlds could be brought into being, but this seeming diminution actually magnifies the divine presence by granting it expression through the physical realm. The Maggid's sermon then illustrates another aspect of this transformation in greater detail:

> Let us explain, making this accessible to the mind, how the name Y-H-V-H must be within every word. The letter *yod* is *hokhmah*, and it is [God's] Thought (*mahashavah*). But Thought must be empowered by a still higher intellect (*sekhel 'elyon yoter*), as we have mentioned in previous teachings.
>
> In order to make this comprehensible, let us say that it is known that thought is contemplative (*'iyyunit*) [and fluid] by nature. A person thinks constantly, and his thoughts roam over different places; one thinks about whatever he sees. . . . One is never devoid of thoughts, for his mind constantly skips and darts from thought to thought. This is the mind's nature. If a person wants to think about one single thing, he must focus (*le-tsamtsem*) his mind in an act of great concentration, not thinking about anything else.

The realm of cognition is associated with *binah* in many of the Maggid's sermons, but the correspondence between *mahashavah* and *hokhmah* is quite clear in this homily. *Mahashavah* is defined by its irrepressible dynamism and constant motion, for the Maggid claims that one's mind never truly falls silent. Contemplation of a single object or idea therefore requires that a person rein in his naturally effervescent intellect, restraining it and focusing it into more defined structures. But *keter*, an unstructured region of the mind that is beyond deliberate cognition, represents a higher realm of intellection that sustains even *hokhmah*.

This identification of the first stages of creation with *keter* and *hokhmah* is confirmed later in the homily:

> The supernal Emanator (*ha-ma'atsil ha-'elyon*) ordered the emanation as follows. First the highest Intellect (*ha-sekhel ha-'elyon*), which focuses the thought, was emanated. This refers to the tip of the *yod*. From there it came into the general *mahashavah* . . . which is the *yod* itself. This is the cognitive vitality (*mohin*), as is

known, which is a thought as it occurs to someone in its general form.

Nevertheless, after he considers the idea for a while and focuses his thought, he can consider it in terms of specific letters. But this [type of cognition] is called specific only in relation to the Thought and the Intellect. In regard to the specific forms of the letters (*tsiyyurei ha-otiyyot*) it is still pure potential, without any real manifestation. The forms [of the letters] are completed in the first *heh*, which is *binah*. . . .

The beginning of the revelation of the letters, which are the five (*heh*) positions of the mouth, [already] happens in Thought. This is the meaning of "as they were created" (*be-heh baram*, Gen. 2:4) [reading it as "they were created with *heh*" (*be-heh bera'am*)][98]—some [aspect] of the *heh* was revealed even at the very beginning of creation, which is *hokhmah* and *yod*. But the shapes of the letters were only revealed in the first *heh* itself. . . . Then the voice, which is the *vav*, emerges from the first *heh* and expands through the windpipe and its six rings. It then enters the lungs, which contain the five lobes that are adjacent to the heart . . . [99]

The heart understands and combines the letters, as it says, "the word of Y-H-V-H is refined (*tserufah*)" (Ps. 18:31). This refers to a combination (*tseruf*) of the letters that results from the five positions of the mouth. This is the meaning of *tserufah—tseruf heh*. [The letters] arrive at the mouth, where the four letters [or stages] of Y-H-V-H are finished and revealed. The word is completed; His first thought may be seen through the word. Thus the word is called *malkhut*.[100]

This homily offers one of the Maggid's fullest descriptions of the three inter-twined processes we have been tracking throughout this chapter: the creation of the world, the unfolding of language from the name of Y-H-V-H, and the stages of human cognition and verbal articulation. All of these begin with the emergence of the *sefirah keter*, the primal emanation that can only be alluded to with the tip of the *yod*. *Keter* is elusive, imponderable, and inef-fable; nothing that transpires therein can be understood or expressed.

This phase is followed by *hokhmah*, associated with the letter *yod* itself. The energy of *keter* flows into *hokhmah*, where intellection begins to take place in a recognizable form. However, in this realm cognition is still indistinct and rather fluid, because it lacks the specific features of the particular letters. These emerge only in the next stage, *binah*, represented by the first *heh* of Y-H-V-H. *Binah* is a region of contemplation and intellection of a very different order; in it ideas are first embodied and shaped by means of the letters of thought. In *binah* the forms of specific letters, indeed the roots of all later language, are revealed in full for the first time.

Ideas are drawn out of *binah* through *kol*, which corresponds to the *vav* of Y-H-V-H and the *sefirah tif'eret*.[101] This stage marks the beginning of an idea being revealed in relatively concrete terms. In the human analogy, *kol* is a voiced sound without any articulated words, a necessary physical element of language production. The thought finally moves on to the five positions of the mouth, thus attaining full expression through verbal articulation (*dibbur*). This is the final stage of emanation, the moment in which the *sefirot* have finally emerged and the cosmos is created through the divine word.

The Maggid's description of the various stages of emanation and cognition in the previous sermon seems well ordered and stable, although there is some inconsistency in his use of the term *mahashavah*. But some of the Maggid's other sermons invoke the *yod* not in reference to conscious thought, but as an allusion to the deeper realm known as *kadmut ha-sekhel*, or the pre-cognizant mind (see above). The Maggid suggests that this region is the purest form of *hokhmah*, an endless font of creative potential from which the physical world and language emerge:

> We must understand why the Torah mentions gold before silver [in Ex. 25:3].[102] Doesn't water come before fire?[103] We can say that this refers to a general [type of] gold that includes seven different types.[104] The letters of "gold" (*zahav*) represent seven (*zayyin*) days that emerged from the five (*heh*) positions of the mouth; this means that they came from speech.[105] [The letter] *bet* includes all the words of Torah, since Scripture begins with a *bet*. All subsequent letters of Torah must have been included in the first *bet*.
>
> The first letter is the general principle (*kelal*) of what one wishes to say later on. The details are all rooted in this idea as well, but they are in the pre-cognizant mind (*kadmut ha-sekhel*), the hylic *yod*.[106] We ourselves see this happen when something suddenly occurs to a person. He thinks about it afterward in his mind, [considering] a number of things that were hidden from

him. This idea that occurred to him was drawn from the pre-
cognizant mind.

Thus it is with the *bet* of *bereshit* ("in the beginning"). It
includes the potential for all the words that follow. Therefore, the
bet has a diacritic, referred to by the Zohar as the "point within
the palace."[107] The *bet* is called a "palace" because it includes
all the letters, but they exist there as *hyle*. The point within
it alludes to the hylic *yod*, the unformed Wisdom (*golem
hokhmah*). This unformed potential (*golem*) corresponds to the
large *mem*,[108] a sealed *mem* of [the verse] "for the abundance of
the kingdom" (Isa. 9:6).[109] This is the gold that includes seven
types, and is therefore mentioned before silver.[110]

This sermon illustrates the parallels between the creation through the divine word, the emergence of Torah, and the pathways of human cognition
that lead to speech. Each of these processes of revelation follows a similar
pattern in which potential energy, or inspiration, is drawn forth from a realm
that is beyond conscious thought or language. Pure *hokhmah* lacks any distinct shape. It is formed through *binah*, the structure through which it begins to achieve articulation. Then *holkhmah* is drawn through the seven *sefirot*
of *hesed* to *malkhut*, the final stage of expression.

The Maggid has described creation as the incremental translation of divine wisdom through the structures of language. In the next chapter, we
will see that his portrayal of revelation is quite similar, for the events of Mt.
Sinai represent a moment in which God's *hokhmah* entered words and was
embodied as Scripture. The Maggid illustrates this point by explaining that
human cognition happens in the same way: the first flash of inspiration is
the potential for an idea, but the initial insight cannot be understood or
articulated. A person can only grasp this thought after considering and
contemplating it, slowly bringing it into the framework of language in his
mind. Then the insight may be described in words and eventually communicated verbally.

But the careful reader will have noticed that the symbolic associations
in this homily conflict with those generally found in the Maggid's teachings. Here the seven lower *sefirot*, called the "seven days," are said to come
from *dibbur* and the five positions of the mouth. Yet the latter two elements
are associated with *shekhinah* and *malkhut*, the very last of the *sefirot*, which
cannot rightly be described as the origin of the seven *sefirot*. The Maggid

often refers to *binah* as home to the letters of thought and the origin of concrete language, but, in this case, he seems to associate *dibbur* with *binah* and thus the first *heh* of Y-H-V-H. Some kabbalistic traditions correlate *binah* with *dibbur*, but this association is relatively rare.[111] This inconsistency, similar to the ambiguity in the Maggid's use of *mahashavah*, is important and worth noting.

Creation by Means of Torah

The Maggid frequently refers to the midrashic tradition of God creating the world through the Torah.[112] In several homilies he explains the importance of this myth for understanding revelation and the origins of Scripture, themes that will occupy us in the upcoming chapter. But the Maggid often explores the impact of this notion on his interpretation of the creation narrative itself. In some cases, he simply cites God gazing into the Torah as proof that the world was indeed formed through the letters of the Hebrew alphabet.[113] And the idea that God created the world through the Torah is one of the conceptual foundations for his understanding of how God may be served through physical deeds. He claims that the letters of Scripture animate the corporeal world, for "the Maker and the made are totally one, and are not separate at all. Were it not for this power of the Maker that is in the made, there would be nothing at all."[114] Of course, studying Torah brings new energy to the letters of Scripture found in the works of creation, but engaging with the physical world also uplifts these letters and returns them to their divine source.[115]

Many of Dov Ber's homilies offer a sophisticated, detailed explanation of how the world was formed by means of Scripture:

> God created the world through the Torah. Before the worlds were formed, there was nothing other than the infinite light of *Ein Sof*. The worlds could not [yet] come into existence, since they would have been unable to bear the light of *Ein Sof*. Those [who would] receive [the divine light] needed it to be diminished. But the lower worlds were unable to receive [the light] even after the initial reduction, since its illumination was still too great. There needed to be a total of four reductions (*tsimtsumim*) [of the divine light]. These are the four worlds of which we know: Emanation

(*atsilut*), creation (*beriyyah*), Formation (*yetsirah*) and Action ('*asiyyah*), until this world came to be. All of this was accomplished by means of Torah, with which the world was created.

There were four [stages] of diminishment (*tsimtsumim*) before [the Torah] came into speech,[116] since the illumination and wisdom (*sekhel*) were still too great after the first act of contraction. Speech could not withstand it, and therefore all of them were necessary.[117]

In a development and restatement of earlier kabbalistic ideas, Dov Ber argues that the Torah that preexisted creation was too expansive and brilliant for it to be embodied in language. Therefore, this Scripture was beyond the grasp of all finite beings. In fact, this primordial Torah was so great that a single act of withdrawal, a contraction of the light of God's wisdom, could not sufficiently reduce it into a form that could be understood by those who were to receive it. This could only be accomplished through a series of *tsimtsumim*, each of which reduced the light of the primordial Torah and paved the way for it to enter a linguistic configuration.

But the Maggid is making a broader point as well. He identifies the *tsimtsum* of the preexistent Torah's illumination with the reduction of the divine light of *Ein Sof* that happened during creation. That is, the diminishment of the primordial Torah represents the simultaneous translation of God's infinite wisdom into the letters, words, and stories of Scripture, just as the emanation of the *sefirot* and the physical world required a series of reductions in divine light. These two momentous events, the creation of the world and the revelation of Torah, allow limited beings to engage with an embodiment of infinite divine Wisdom.

This sermon, however, leaves an important ambiguity unresolved. Was creation a divine act parallel to the contraction of Torah into language, or was the physical realm actually created *by means* of a preexistent Scripture? The Maggid's sermon implies the first, but the rabbinic tradition he is interpreting clearly suggests the latter. Perhaps there is a third way of understanding his comparison of these two sacred processes: the formation of the world and the emergence of Torah may reflect the same divine act as viewed from two different perspectives. From one angle, the embodiment of *hokhmah* into finite vessels is manifest as the physical world. From a different perspective, however, the same divine translation resulted in Scripture being drawn forth from the infinite expanse of divine wisdom and infused into a garment of letters and words. If this reading is correct, which I suspect that it is, then for the Maggid the terms "Torah," "language," and "word" have become almost interchangeable. This is possible, however, because Dov Ber's teachings on creation through Scripture are—at heart—deeper reflections on the genesis of language through the unfolding of the Divine.

The Torah is an embodiment of divine wisdom that God has focused into the defined structures and limitations of language. This sacred book, the textual expression of endless *hokhmah*, was the only fitting tool through which God could accomplish creation. One of the Maggid's teachings refers to the Divine gazing into Scripture literally, likening God to a person who peers into an actual text: "[The realm of] thought (*mahashavah*) is like a book. [Just as] one says what he has seen in a book, so too does he say what he sees[118] in his thought. It seems to me that I heard[119] this explanation of [the sages' teaching,] 'God looked into the Torah and created the world.' The Torah emerged from *hokhmah*, meaning that whatever He saw in His thought, as it were, if He desired it, it was created."[120] In this short teaching the Maggid employs personal terminology, an analogy taken from human experience, to illustrate a theological point about the details of creation. A person must conceive of something in his mind before he can articulate it through language. In order to find the correct words for expressing his idea, he must gaze into the depths of his intellect. Speaking is thus likened to reading from a book; to articulate a thought out loud is to recite the words that are inscribed on one's mind.

This model, argues the Maggid, is a fitting description of the manner in which God created the cosmos. The physical works of creation were formed by means of the sacred word, and thus represent an articulation of the linguistic pattern engraved on the divine mind. God gazed on the "text" of His thought in order to speak creation into being. In this context the Maggid identifies the divine thought as the Torah. God looked into Scripture, which is a textual fabric held together by the structures of language. Of course, the linguistic form of Torah is not synonymous with the *hokhmah* from which it emerged. The Scripture composed of words, stories, and laws, presumably associated with the *sefirah binah*, is a crystallization of God's wisdom.

We should note that Israel's special capacity for sacred language, while imbued within them from the beginning of creation, should not be interpreted as a natural phenomenon. The Maggid emphasizes that their capacity for holy speech is a divine gift, a position that is in keeping with his positive embrace of language.[121] In this vein, he reinterprets a midrashic teaching about God placing an extra *heh* in Abram's name, transforming him into Abraham. This *heh*, argues the Maggid, represents the five positions of the mouth and thus a new capacity for language:

> [Abraham] was given the five positions of the mouth. This is the essence of what sustains the world (*'ikar kiyyum ha-'olam*), and the most important element of divine service: raising up the words and the letters to [their source in the] holy realm.
>
> This the meaning of what is written, "He imparted the power of His deeds to His people" (Ps. 111:6). "The power of His deeds" refers to [divine] speech, through which the world was created, as it is written, "with the word of Y-H-V-H the heavens were made" (Ps. 33:6). The Holy One created the world with the twenty-two letters of the Torah. He conveyed (*higid*) this same power to His people, meaning that He drew it down for them.[122] This refers to the letter *heh* [given to Abraham], which represents the five positions of the mouth, so that they too would have the power to uplift the words.[123]

Abraham was infused with a special linguistic capacity when God changed his name. The additional letter *heh* granted him, and all of his descendants, an immutable ability to return the divine word of the physical world to its holy source. Indeed, this act of uplifting the letters of creation is the very essence of religious service. This homily thus reinforces the connection between the cosmological or theological elements of the Maggid's thought and his devotional goals. The speech of Israel sustains the cosmos, and this intrinsic facility for returning sacred language to its holy origin is the ultimate goal of the project of creation.

Chapter 5

The Nature of Torah and Revelation

Some people may wonder: why was the light of God given in the form of language? How is it conceivable that the divine should be contained in such brittle vessels as consonants and vowels? . . . And yet, it is as if God took these Hebrew words and breathed into them His power, and the words became a live wire charged with His spirit. To this very day they are hyphens between heaven and earth.

—Abraham Joshua Heschel

The Maggid's theology of language shapes, and is shaped by, his understanding of Torah as an expression of the sublime depths of God's silent mind. Scripture, he suggests in a clever reinterpretation of rabbinic traditions, predated creation as an endless expanse of divine wisdom. Perhaps the primordial Torah was even beyond language, a surging font of sacred illumination undefined by words. The Maggid concludes that this limitless Torah could not be apprehended by the human being. God therefore constricted—or focused—this primordial Scripture into letters and words, an intricate latticework of narratives and laws.

The Torah thus becomes God's infinite wisdom expressed through the structures and limitations of language. Dov Ber also invokes the Zoharic maxim that Torah and God are one, taking it to mean that Scripture is a finite, textual embodiment of the divine presence itself. The Torah, though seemingly fragmented into pericopes and laws, remains united by the divine wisdom that was safeguarded in every letter. This dynamic mirrors the manner in which the divine *hokhmah* undergirds all aspects of the physical cosmos. This parallel is no coincidence, for it is the result of God's creating the world through Torah. Each word of Scripture represents a gateway, a textual portal through which the discerning student of Torah may penetrate its linguistic facade and approach the infinite divine essence that continues to course through it. In this way the garbing of Torah in language, suggests the Maggid, reveals as well as conceals. Like spoken words that diminish an expansive thought while allowing for communicative expression, Scripture translates the ineffable expanse of God's mind into language for Israel.[1]

This conception of Torah is bound up with the Maggid's descriptions of revelation as the emergence of Torah from divine silence into words and letters. Torah embodies God's infinite wisdom and is to some extent even coterminous with the Divine. Then by what means—and at what point— was Torah first brought into the structures of language? Dov Ber also grapples with the role of language in the experience of revelation. Was the encounter between man and God at Sinai defined by the medium of language, or did some element of the sacred communion of revelation transcend words entirely? The Maggid's answers to these questions pivot on his understanding of the relationship between God's word, human language, and the boundaries of intellection.

The Roots of Revelation

The centrality of Torah, and the craft of scriptural exegesis in particular, in classical rabbinic works cannot be overstated. Passages throughout rabbinic literature suggest that the Bible is replete with nearly infinite shades of meaning, both theological as well as legal. Such reflections on the nature of Torah are closely linked to emergent notions of a canonized Scripture.[2] This likely builds on ancient associations of Scripture with the sophia of Proverbs and Job in the literature of late antiquity, and the Torah itself is sometimes personified in rabbinic literature.[3] But classical rabbinic literature has also preserved a small—but significant—number of traditions that describe the Torah as more than a divinely revealed text of laws and narratives, referring to Scripture as predating the world and as the instrument through which God created the cosmos.[4] Such traditions become the centerpieces of later kabbalistic descriptions of the Scripture.

Explorations of the essence of Torah have long been part of Jewish mystical literature.[5] This is because biblical verses and their exegesis are a central part of the symbolic vocabulary of the Kabbalah. But it goes deeper, for the medieval Kabbalists portray Scripture as a linguistic embodiment of the invisible and ineffable Divine.[6] Such an understanding represents a fundamental theological shift. The earlier *heikhalot* and *merkavah* literature includes both experiential and exegetical elements, since many of these works are themselves a mystical expansion of key passages of the Hebrew Bible.[7] Rather than the visionary encounter with God found in some earlier texts, medieval Jewish mystics, from the twelfth- and thirteenth-century Rhineland Pietists to the sixteenth-century masters of the Safed renaissance, depict the text of the Torah as the central medium through which the chasm between the human and divine realms may be bridged. The early medieval German Pietists conceived of Scripture as a manifestation of the names of God and an embodiment of the divine glory (*kavod*).[8] And the *Bahir*, the earliest font of Kabbalistic symbolism, describes Torah as an incarnation of divine wisdom and perhaps even a hypostatic power.[9]

Nahmanides' commentary on the Torah was an important stage in the development of mystical conceptions of Scripture.[10] His work includes a significant number of explicit kabbalistic references, and although his allusions are generally fragmentary and cryptic, Nahmanides brought these mystical traditions into the spotlight for the first time by citing them in his commentary. Furthermore, in his introduction Nahmanides refers to the rabbinic teachings about the preexistence of Scripture, but he also reveals that he possessed a tradition (*kabbalah shel emet*) that the Torah is entirely composed of the names of God. These are formed by breaking down the divisions between the words of Scripture and recombining them in new ways.[11] For this reason, says Nahmanides, a Torah scroll with misspelled words, or even one that lacks a single necessary letter, is rendered unfit for ritual use. It is interesting to note, however, that Nahmanides' own commentary does not engage in that sort of exegesis.[12]

Like the Jewish philosophers before them, medieval Kabbalists viewed Sinai as a revelation of God's own self (for them, as represented by the *sefirot*), not just the commanding divine will. In the case of Sinai, this is depicted as the emergence of the divine word out of the recesses of mysterious inner silence.[13] The thirteenth-century Zohar, undoubtedly the most influential work of medieval Jewish mysticism, describes Scripture as a verdant textual garden overflowing with secrets. Each letter of the Torah blossoms into an untold number of new interpretations, and the exegesis of its sacred words is reckoned a mystical experience second to none.[14] "Letters without vowels," writes the thirteenth-century Bahye ben Asher, "bear many different interpretations which fracture into many different sparks. For this reason, we are commanded not to add vowels to the Torah Scroll. . . . Without them, a person may understand many wondrous and exalted things. Understand this."[15]

The Zohar's authors refer to the Torah as a sacred text that is composed of divine appellatives and whose every word is, in some sense, a name of God.[16] The work even describes the relationship between the Scripture and its divine Revealer in more intimate terms, declaring that the Torah and the blessed Holy One are identical.[17] The Zohar also connects the different elements of Torah to the symbolic matrix of the *sefirot*: the written Torah is associated with *tif'eret*, the oral Torah with *malkhut*, and the preexistent Torah with *hokhmah*.[18] These conceptions are reflected in the Zohar's well-developed conception of Scripture's inner and outer layers of meaning.[19] An oft-cited passage in the Zohar depicts the Torah as having taken on a narrative "garb" when it came into the world, suggesting that the language of Scripture both reveals and conceals the divine essence expressed through—and hidden within—its words.[20] This meant that, for the medieval Kabbalists, the Torah is the central nexus through which the chasm between the human and divine realms may be bridged.[21] The theophany of Sinai and disclosure of God's essence is, in some respect, recreated through the act of sacred study. And the flowing translation of divine wisdom into language, a dynamic that characterizes the Sinai revelation, is a continuous process rather than a single historical event.[22]

Similar notions of the Torah as a woven gossamer composed of infinite layers of meaning continue in the works of the Safed renaissance. These thinkers offered many esoteric interpretations of scriptural verses, although the mythological elements of the Hebrew Bible were particularly important for Yitshak Luria.[23] Their writings reveal an awareness that the present form of Scripture (called *Torah de-Beriah*, or the "Torah of Creation") is not identical to the Torah that existed before the creation of the world. They reflected on the possibility of reconstructing this primordial source of inspiration, which they referred to as the *Torah de-Atsilut* (the "Torah of Emanation").[24] This notion was further developed in the literature of the Sabbatean movement, whose thinkers sought to grasp the nature of the Torah as it would be revealed in the age of redemption.[25]

But many other seventeenth- and eighteenth-century Kabbalists continued to grapple with the relationship between the luminous preexistent

Torah and the current mundane form of Scripture.[26] In a rare moment of autobiographical reflection, the seventeenth-century Kabbalist Naftali Bachrach recounts his astonishment at the seeming banality of many of Scripture's narratives. Receiving no satisfying explanation from the sages of his day, the young Bachrach was comforted only after reading the works of Lurianic Kabbalah. These mystical texts opened Bachrach's eyes to the mysteries of Torah, pushing him to study the Zohar and eventually to attain a new way of seeking spiritual and religious meaning in the timeworn texts of tradition. The vast and dramatic scriptural narratives, claims Bachrach, are simply a garment for the meatier elements of *halakhah*. But the legal dimensions of Torah are simply yet another cloak for the true soul of Torah—the spiritual riches of Kabbalah, which infuse Scripture's every word with spiritual mysteries and devotional meaning.[27]

The Torah of Creation, the Name of God, and the Divine Text

These kabbalistic teachings on Torah's emergence at Sinai nourished Dov Ber's conception of the primordial Torah. The idea of an ethereal Scripture that predated the world and was used by God in the formation of the cosmos is a cornerstone of his language. This preexistent Torah is described by Dov Ber as timeless, enduring—like the Divine—beyond the temporal matrix.[28] We might have assumed such an eternal Scripture to be entirely beyond language, but the Maggid's teachings are more complicated on this point:

> It is taught that the Holy One created the world through the Torah. Not only this world, but all the worlds were created through the letters of Torah. We cannot say that each part of the world was formed from a particular part of the Torah. The Torah is preexistent (*kedumah*). It is above time and totally unified (*ahdut pashut*) [i.e., a simple, non-composite unity]. It has no parts. According to this, it necessarily follows that each section of the Torah includes the entire Torah; all the worlds contain its entirety as well. . . .
>
> This is [the explanation of], "the Holy One created the world with the Torah"—with the Torah, just as we have it, but it has become embodied in all the worlds according to [that particular world]. [Scripture] itself does not change.[29]

The preexistent Torah was essentially undifferentiated and unlimited, dwelling within the divine mind and perhaps unrestricted by the structures of words and language. Yet the Maggid refers to God forming the world with the letters of Torah as His instruments, which suggests that the primordial Scripture included some sort of an inchoate linguistic structure, a potential reservoir of vital and dynamic energy drawn on in the formation of the cosmos. These are perhaps analogous to the "letters of thought" that govern cognition both human and divine, but it seems more likely that we are meant to associate the letters of the primordial Torah with *hokhmah* (rather than *binah*), the infinite reservoir of potential from which God's language emerged.

In trying to determine the relationship between the primordial Torah and the "garments" of language that eventually surround it, the symbolic associations invoked by Dov Ber are suggestively ambiguous. Some of his homilies associate the primeval Scripture with *hokhmah*, whereas in others the Torah is described as having emerged from *hokhmah*.[30] Ze'ev Wolf of Zhitomir, one of his key disciples, recalls the following: "I heard from the Maggid that during the Torah's descent from its source, it became garbed in this world, for in truth the Torah came forth from *hokhmah* or *binah*."[31] This point of tension endures throughout the Maggid's corpus and is never clearly resolved.

The Maggid draws a striking analogy between the inner unity of Torah and the divine energy that joins all aspects of the created world. The physical realm and its multiplicity of organisms and phenomena are immediately visible to the worshipper, but the cosmos is home to an infinite number of nested worlds. Just as the primal energy of *hokhmah* is garbed in all the trappings of creation as the world emerges from the sacred word, so is the primordial Torah garbed in the mantle of words and letters—the narratives and commandments of Scripture. The commandments may appear to be specific actions with very clear limitations and boundaries, but because they contain the full infinity of the Divine within them, each *mitsvah* can lead the worshipper to *devekut* with God. A similar sweep of divine unity lingers in each element of Scripture even after the Torah was invested in the form of language. Scripture's translation into specific laws and stories occludes this fact for the casual reader, but the careful student will be able to pierce through the text by means of his contemplative study, thus arriving at the limitless expanse of sacred vitality expressed within its words.

Dov Ber notes that the primordial Torah assumed an appropriate form as it entered the physical world. He does not, however, specify that God's wisdom was so transposed during creation and revelation alone. This act of cosmic self-translation is taking place continuously, manifest as the ever-unfolding of God's sacred being. This framing is suggestive of the way in which the Maggid's teachings often posit explicit connections between creation and revelation, describing both as parallel processes by which divine thought is translated into language and thus brought within the threshold of human understanding. Several homilies link the two processes even more fundamentally, correlating the ten creative utterances of Genesis and the Ten Commandments issued at Sinai as two stages in a continuous unfolding of the divine word: "Creation lacked strength and endurance until the Torah was given. This is because the world was created by ten utterances (*ma'amarot*),[32] as it is written, 'and He said' (*va-yomer*, Gen. 1:3 et al.). [Such] speech (*amirah*) takes place within the heart,[33] in the deeper realm of Thought (*sod ha-mahashavah*). But after the Torah was given, [the world] was brought into the mystery of speech (*sod ha-dibbur*), as it is written, 'And God spoke (*va-yedabber*) all of these words . . .' (Ex. 20:1)."[34] God's initial formation of the worlds through divine speech was itself a type of revelation. This original genesis of the cosmos proved too sublime to endure in perpetuity, however. Much like the fleeting dynamic activity of the human mind, in which ideas are reborn and continuously transformed, the created world was somehow unstable until the theophany at Sinai transformed these original divine utterances into a concrete form of language. The divine word inborn in the cosmos through creation was thus only partially fulfilled until revelation, for it was only at Sinai that the divine thought was drawn into language and communicated to the world through God's speech.[35]

But why did God contract the preexistent Scripture by compressing it into language? The answer, argues the Maggid, is that such a Torah cannot be comprehended by the finite mind. The Lurianic creation mythos maintained that God needed to withdraw the infinite expanse of divine light in order to generate an empty space for creation. So too, says that Maggid, the Divine tempered the pure illumination of the primordial Scripture: "The Torah is called a 'folded scroll' (*megillah 'afa*, Zech. 5:1–2),[36] greater than all of the worlds. God needed to contract the Torah so that its light could shine in the worlds."[37] The primeval Torah was too expansive and luminous; its brilliance would have been overwhelming, so God diminished its light by contracting it into specific words.

Revelation and creation, recast as two stages in a single process of the cosmic unfolding of God's essence, are thus critically intertwined in

the Maggid's theology of language. Other homilies draw a more explicit
conceptual parallel between the two events, both of which required that God
temper the infinite divine light:

> It is known that the ultimate reason (*takhlit*) for the creation of
> the worlds is that there can be no king without a people.[38] This
> [divine] Thought caused the *tsimtsum*.
>
> "And Y-H-V-H came down upon Mt. Sinai" (Ex. 19:20).
> What need was there for any descent? Isn't "the world filled with
> His glory" (Isa. 6:3)? A parable: a father who wishes to delight in
> his child must talk to him. Now the intellect (*sekhel*) of the father
> remains just as great as it was before he spoke to his child. It does
> not change, and the father does not descend from his expansive
> mind. But this mind is hidden and unseen when he is speaking
> with his child; the words he exchanges with the small child
> [express] a smallness of mind (*katnut ha-sekhel*). This is referred to
> as contraction (*tsimtsum*) and descent (*horadah*) for the father—[if
> not for the child], he would have no reason to contract his
> intellect and to draw it into these sorts of diminished words.
>
> Therefore, when the Holy One wanted to speak to Israel, it is
> called a descent for Him, as it were. The same is true when it
> arose in the primeval thought (*mahashavah kedumah*) that there
> can be no king without a people.[39]

Elsewhere the Maggid refers to the giving of the Torah on Sinai as an act of
divine love. God allowed His ever-expansive mind to become restrained
within the structures of language out of his great love for the Jewish people.[40]
Though this type of translation does not change the divine essence, which
remains perpetually infinite, it does represent a moment in which God's
unbounded potential becomes concretized in finite vessels. However, the
Divine's willing self-limitation—both in creation and in revelation—fulfills
a divine need as well. Without revealing the Torah or forming the worlds, some
prospective element of God's identity, here described as kingship, would have
remained forever unexpressed.

The power of the Torah to convey the ineffable through the boundaries
of language is about more than God's thought or wisdom. The Maggid frequently refers to the Torah as an expression of sacred divine names. Yet for
Dov Ber, unlike his medieval kabbalistic forebearers, this understanding of

Scripture does not mean that the Bible constitutes a single, extended name of God, nor does it imply that the Torah is a textual composite that fuses together different divine appellatives. Instead, the Maggid offers a proposition grounded in the divine nature of *all* language: the Torah in its current form is expressed in words, and the name Y-H-V-H is present in all language, and therefore the sacred divine name must be included throughout the Torah:

> "The Tree of Life in the midst of the garden" (Gen. 2:9). The Tree of Life is the holy name Y-H-V-H, as is known.[41] "The midst of the garden" means that this name is embodied within the fifty-three[42] portions of the Torah. Earlier we have taught that this name is clothed within all of speech.[43] It has endless masks and degrees of hiding. It is expressed first within the five points of articulation, then successively within letters, combinations of letters, words, and narrations. The Zohar says that one who has eyes [referring to the mind's eye] looks at the inner nature of things; one who lacks such eyes sees only the royal garments.[44] This is especially true of seemingly profane narratives.[45]

The sacred name Y-H-V-H, the root of all language, is concealed within all words or speech acts as a sublime life-giving force. Here the Maggid applies this notion to the text of Scripture as well, showing that the same creative power that animates all human words is present in the Torah. Y-H-V-H is embodied within each word of the Torah, imbuing it with the infinite quality of divine vitality, and therefore none of Scripture's stories can be essentially mundane. The properly attuned student is mindful of the inner nature of Scripture that is manifest through its words and letters. Just as the name Y-H-V-H animates all language, and the sacred creative word remains within the physical world, divine wisdom continuously fills the Torah. This sustaining vitality inheres as "the power of the Maker within the made,"[46] and awareness of the fact that Y-H-V-H reverberates within Scripture should spark a feeling of revelatory wonder in the student.[47]

The Maggid also notes that the stories of the Torah express divine names as well. They need not be reduced to alluding to specific *sefirot*. Instead of reducing the Torah into letters or tiny symbolic units in an attempt to unearth esoteric names, the Maggid interprets the Torah's narratives as an articulation of God's different qualities.[48] The Maggid underscores that the literal meanings of the stories hold inspirational lessons for the spiritual life. "The entire Torah," claims the Maggid, "speaks the names of God. For example, one section speaks about the attribute of love—how to love the blessed Creator, recounting how the patriarchs loved Him and walked with Him always, suffering injustices for this love."[49] This conception of the entire Torah as composed of the names of God, like all elements of the Maggid's theology, has critical repercussions for devotional practice. Each scriptural narrative thus brings a divine name to life by revealing how it may be embodied in the course of human devotion.

Dov Ber also describes reading the sacred text as a dialogue between man and God, a conversation in which one calls to the Divine by name:

> When a child calls his father by his name, or even when a villager calls him by the description of "king," as is fitting for him, it arouses his compassion. So too, as it were, the blessed Holy One focused (*tsimtsem*) Himself into the Torah. Along with the constant compassion that He bestowed on Israel because of His pain at their great suffering, they arouse extra compassion when they read Torah. [This is true] even of a "villager," meaning someone who reads Torah with great awe and love [but] without understanding its inner dimensions (*penimiyyut*).
>
> The Holy One and Torah are one. The entire Torah is names of God. One called by name will set aside all affairs and turn to the person who called to him, answering his question because he is bound by his name. So too, as it were, did God focus Himself into the Torah. We draw Him down when we read the Torah, arousing compassion and loving-kindness. He and His name are united and one.[50]

This teaching makes a devotional, even theurgic, element of Torah study highly accessible. Even someone with no knowledge of kabbalistic wisdom receives an additional measure of divine mercy when he reads Scripture with enthusiasm and passion. The Maggid is not suggesting that God's mercy is aroused by intoning magical formulae or secret divine names that have been mined from the biblical text. Divine compassion is inspired through reading, or perhaps better, *reciting* the words of Torah with great fervor.

This teaching comes rather close to transforming study into an act of prayer. The intellectual content of the biblical text and the plain-sense meaning of the Torah's words, in contrast to what we saw above, are much less important than the simple act of reading Scripture. We might have expected the Maggid to be consistent in emphasizing that a student must have proper inner intention. But in this homily he attributes power to reciting the words and letters of Torah even without full understanding.

The Maggid's descriptions of the divine heart of Scripture venture beyond the notion that the Torah is composed of God's names. Drawing on the Zoharic teaching that identifies the Torah with the blessed Holy One, Dov Ber explores the essential link between them:

> It is taught that the Torah and the blessed Holy One are one.[51]
> This means that the essence of His divinity can be withstood only
> by means of the Torah. God created the world through Torah,
> meaning the letters, saying, "Let there be light,' and there was
> light" (Gen. 1:3). This was an act of contraction (*tsimtsum*) for
> God, who focused (*tsimtsem*) Himself into the letters and created
> the world.
>
>   Now, a person is not entirely separate from the letters that he
> speaks; his physical body is distinct, but not his life-force. So it is
> with the blessed One, Who is not separate from the letters [of
> Torah]. Nobody can withstand His Divinity except through them.
> This is the meaning of "He and His causes [i.e., a linguistic
> medium that attenuates God's intensity] are one."[52]

The notion that God focused the infinite divine light into the letters of Torah appears frequently in the Maggid's teachings.[53] Here he provides a clear reason for this contraction: the divine essence can be accessed only through Scripture, because without the vessel of the letters the light would be far too intense. The linguistic structures of Torah are a filter necessary to prevent the world from being overwhelmed by the overabundance of God's light. The words of the Bible are thus like a partial veil, which conceals the enormity of the divine essence while at the same time allowing for human beings to perceive—and engage with—that sacred cosmic light through the intermediary framework of language.[54]

The identification of God with the Torah returns us to a striking theological problem: How can an infinite God be embodied in a limited number of words? The Maggid answers that although its text does not express the true fullness of the Divine, the words of Torah are filled with the divine energy and thus provide a link to the infinite expanse beyond. Just as a worshipper's thoughts continue to enliven his spoken language long after the idea has taken shape in words, so does God's vitality, "the power of the Maker in the made," constantly breathe new life into the cosmos.[55]

The Maggid argues that the preexistent Torah, like *hokhmah*, refers to the infinite well of divine energy that animates the physical realm. The words of Scripture, despite their capacity to mediate between the Divine and the temporal world, still compose a limited text. God is immanently manifest within the language of Scripture because these words provide concrete vessels for the vast and unformed potential of divine energy, but the Bible itself does not restrict the infinite number of potential ways that the divine essence could be expressed. In recasting this Zoharic tradition, Dov Ber has added a new dimension to the kabbalistic identification of the Torah with the Divine: the text of Scripture and its language.[56]

This understanding of the Torah as the linguistic expression of the divine presence is critical to the Maggid's conception of the commandments as deeds through which the worshipper enters the infinite expanse of the divine presence. The various elements of Scripture and its many precepts may appear to be entirely distinct and disparate from one another, a jumble of unrelated narratives and injunctions. But the Maggid emphasizes that the words of Torah are united by the same *hokhmah* that undergirds all creation. This sacred vitality is, according to the Maggid, rendered accessible to the worshipper through sacred deeds: "When one performs a commandment with fiery passion and desire, and his will is to do the blessed Holy One's Will, they [i.e., his thought and his deeds] rise up to the primeval Will. There all of the six hundred and thirteen commandments and all of the letters of the Torah are totally united, for the holy books teach that what lies beyond *hokhmah* cannot be depicted, even with the 'tip' of [the letter] *yod*."[57] Fulfilling the commandments with enthusiasm, devotion, and contemplative focus allows the worshipper to move beyond the perceived multiplicity of the physical world by ascending to the divine Will. This realm, a reference to the *sefirah keter*, is one in which the worshipper's recognition of division melts away entirely. It is therefore a region of experience that can be alluded to only by the most sublime of all symbols: the tip of the letter *yod*. This semantic gesture is the final footstep on the peninsula of language, gesturing toward the infinite beyond.

But sacred deeds connect the worshipper to the limitless pool of the divine will precisely because the Torah is, in essence, the divine presence manifest in language. Scripture and God are united in what the Maggid describes as a "single holiness and spiritual vitality" (*kedushah ahat ve-ruhaniyyut ehad*). It is through engagement with language, through the performance of the precepts, that the access point to infinity opens up before him. As a part of the Torah, the commandments are rooted in the infinite realm. God contracted the infinite, preexistent Torah into the finite structures of language so that it might be grasped by the limited human mind. So too must the worshipper concentrate his energy (both physical and contemplative) through focus on a single devotional act of sacred reading.[58]

The Formation of Torah and the
Commandments Before Sinai

The Maggid describes the Torah as a linguistic expression of the boundless Divine. It holds untold secrets and endless layers of meaning, and Scripture's words, claims Dov Ber, are the garment through which the sacred name Y-H-V-H is revealed. Given this lofty origin, the Maggid frequently questions why the Torah is host to so many apparently banal—and occasionally profane—narratives. Such tales seem to have little to do with grand moments of theology, philosophical reflection, or specific commandments.[59] In some instances, the Maggid's homilies point out the concealed spiritual significance of these stories, thus attempting to demonstrate that the Torah's narratives are conduits for divine wisdom despite their apparently prosaic surface.[60] Elsewhere the Maggid suggests that the entire Torah is timeless because its stories constantly take place within each human being, understood to be a microcosm of the divine superstructure of the *sefirot*.[61] Scripture is thus eternal not only because of the constant relevance of its words and injunctions, but because the narratives of Torah are constantly unfolding in the ongoing experiences of human devotion.[62]

The Maggid claims that certain narratives were included in Scripture as a part of the ultimate quest to redeem human language by raising it up to God.[63] But several traditions from the Maggid suggest that human beings have an active role in shaping the linguistic fabric into which the infinite divine wisdom is contracted.[64] This is among the more striking and original elements of Dov Ber's teachings on the nature of the Torah, one that reveals the worshipper's power to effect God in ways that we have not yet touched on:

"A new teaching (*Torah*) will go forth from Me."[65] It is known that the blessed Holy One created the world with Scripture . . . [but] the Torah itself (*Torah 'atsmah*) has not yet been revealed.

The entire Torah is collected from [the actions of] righteous persons, like Adam, Noah, the patriarchs and Moses, upon whose deeds the *shekhinah* rested. This is the full Torah (*Torah shelemah*). But the light of its essence will not be revealed until the arrival of our righteous redeemer (may it be quickly, in our days!); then we will understand the illumination. This is [the meaning of] "a new Torah . . . from Me"—from its [i.e., Torah's] essence.

The secret is why the Torah's essence cannot be truly attained in the present. Why is this so? At present, the Torah is only that which is taken from people, some of the Torah was taken from Laban, meaning the stories about him, and some was taken from Balaam, and some from the stories of the other people that are written in the Torah. But in the future the blessed Holy One will be connected to Torah, and then we will understand its essence. This is the meaning of "[Torah] will go forth from Me," and not as it is now, when the Torah is just stories.[66]

The Torah is composed of many textual layers, and its essence will be revealed only in the future. The Maggid does not seem to be arguing that an entirely new Scripture will emerge in the messianic age. Dov Ber is suggesting that a new level of understanding will be yielded as readers of Scripture penetrate through the obscuring "shells" of the biblical text, attaining the sacred vitality within.[67]

This homily also implies a radical detail, one that is not often adduced in the Maggid's teachings: at the present time God and Torah are, to some degree, disconnected from one another. We have seen that the Maggid generally identifies a close and largely positive affinity between Torah and God. Scripture shapes the course of cosmic vitality as it flows into letters of the Torah, providing a linguistic medium through which the divine presence is manifest in the earthly realm, but the words of Torah do not themselves effect the infinite divine essence that lies beyond. And yet, in this teaching the Maggid insinuates that the connection between God and the Torah has been sundered.[68] Only in the future will the bond be restored, as the faithful once more turn to the letters of Scripture and realize that they are an endless font of sacred life-force.

This teaching also argues that the true depths of Torah cannot currently be grasped because its narrative garb was shaped through acts of people. The Maggid notes that every part of Scripture, including the narrative sections describing the actions of biblical characters, are pathways through which the blessed Holy One is revealed.[69] But Dov Ber clearly suggests that these garments are shaped, at least in part, through the deeds of man. This discussion of the narratives of Torah as formed from human action is generated by a riddle: How can Scripture be described as preexistent if the specific narratives in the Torah, whether banal or sacred, took place long after creation? The text of Scripture is not identical to that of the primordial Torah, which was linguistic only in the most rudimentary sense.

The Maggid, for example, imagines Laban pursuing Jacob (Gen. 31:23) because "some letters [of the Torah] remained with him. These letters thus added a section (parashah) to the Torah."[70] Laban runs after his nephew because there remained a few sparks of holiness, sacred wisps of the divine word, that needed to be uplifted. These lonely fragments of sacred language were to be redeemed, and the story of the interaction of Laban and Jacob—and their linguistic conversation—thus expanded the countenance of the scriptural text. Indeed, says Dov Ber, the seemingly mundane deeds of the biblical ancestors were included in the Torah because these individuals performed them with extraordinary devekut. This left an impression on the text of the Torah, and on the generations of worshippers that followed: "Even the intercourse of the patriarchs is [part of the] complete Torah (Torah shelemah).[71] Indeed, it is written in the Torah! The Torah scroll is invalid if 'and he [Jacob] came unto Rachel as well . . .' (Gen 29:30) or 'and Jacob loved Rachel' (Gen. 29:18) is missing. [The patriarchs] did everything with great attachment to the blessed One, Who delighted in them, and from this Torah was created. The Torah and the blessed Holy One are one."[72] Attaining devekut is one of the foremost goals of the Maggid's spiritual path, and here we see that Scripture was formed from the patriarchs' deeds because they performed all of their actions with such great attachment to the Divine. This passage is excerpted from one of the Maggid's most important sermons, in which he describes God and mankind as two "half-forms" that complete one another.[73] Dov Ber means that God delights in human actions, but also that such deeds complete the divine structure. The patriarchs' ordinary actions—performed with contemplative focus and devotion—were translated into the linguistic garment of Scripture. Human deeds, even if physical and coarse, may thus become part of the Torah.

This presentation is quite striking, and is indicative of Dov Ber's understanding of human deeds and their great power.

The Talmudic sages taught that the patriarchs observed the precepts of the Torah and studied its words with great reverence.[74] But this tradition seems incomprehensible when placed alongside the notion that the Torah predated revelation and even existed long before creation, found in many of our teachings thus far. How could the biblical characters fulfill the demands of a text before it was formed? Many early Hasidic masters took up this theme, and the question of spiritual devotion before Torah—and the possibility of spiritual uplift outside of the normative framework of *halakhah*—seems to have been an issue that much preoccupied them.[75]

Hasidic responses to this quandary emerge in three general categories, all of which are represented in the Maggid's teachings. First, the patriarchs followed the precepts of Torah through the power of their contemplative minds even before it was revealed. Second, other sources suggest that the patriarchs performed all of their deeds, even those that are seemingly mundane or profane, with such great mystical attachment that they were able to connect themselves to the essence of Torah through those actions. Finally, some Hasidic masters describe the patriarchs as fulfilling the entirety of Torah through a single commandment that had already been prescribed to them by God.[76]

The Maggid suggests that since the world was created through Scripture, the patriarchs were able to grasp Torah—identified with God's essence—before Sinai:

> It is known that Abram the patriarch fulfilled the Torah before it was given. The explanation is such: the blessed Holy One created the world through Torah. . . . There were four [stages] of contraction (*tsimtsumim*) before [the Torah] came into speech, for the illumination and wisdom (*sekhel*) were still too great after the first act of contraction.[77] Speech could not withstand it, so all of them were necessary.
>
> It is known that [the sages interpreted] "when they were created" (*be-hibaram*, Gen. 2:4) as "for Abraham" (*be-avraham*),[78] meaning that all of this was done out of love. This caused the stages of diminishment (*tsimtsumim*), for "love pushes aside all flesh."[79]
>
> Abraham is called "Abraham, My lover" (Isa. 41:8); by virtue of his love, he was found worthy of an immense [act of] *tsimtsum*

(for "as face answers to face [in water, so does one man's heart to another]," Prov. 27:19).[80] He grasped the essence of divinity (*etsem elohut*) that had been forgotten in the generations before him. The Torah and the Holy One are one, and he apprehended the Torah before it was given—before it entered into language.

But for us, who live in a world that was created through [these stages of] diminution, the Torah was given to us in contracted form as well. Even though "the Torah of Y-H-V-H" (Ps. 19:8) is complete, including all the hidden lights, it is concealed in it, contracted and hidden. Understand this very well.[81]

Scripture was given in language for the first time at Sinai. But Abraham accessed the primordial Torah even before it was articulated in words. His achievement is not linked to fulfilling a particular commandment, however, or even to performing ordinary deeds with attachment. Precisely how he grasped the ancient Scripture is not entirely clear, but in this teaching, unlike many others, the Maggid makes no effort to demonstrate that Abraham performed the commandments in any physical way. The focus is rather on Abraham's contemplation—of the world around him, and of his own inner self—and his love for God. These qualities enable him to grasp the undiminished essence of Scripture before it came to inhabit language. Perhaps Abraham then fulfilled the precepts of Scripture, but this sermon highlights the patriarch's apprehension of the preexistent, and prelinguistic, Torah.

The Maggid's homily draws an important distinction between the questing Abraham and those who live in the post-Sinai era. After the giving of the Torah and the theophany at Sinai, the text of Scripture has now become the sole access point for attaining knowledge of the divine essence. Revelation was an act of divine limitation, a moment in which the ever-expansive primordial Torah was garbed in words and stories for those who lived after Abraham and could not attain his unique rung of spiritual excellence.

The notion that the patriarchs fulfilled the entire Torah, as it were, through performing a single commandment in the most perfect form is also well represented in the Maggid's sermons. Exploring this notion sheds light on Dov Ber's understanding of the nature of religious praxis and the relationship of human deeds to the infinite Torah. In this case, Abraham was given the commandment of circumcision (Gen. 17). This single devotional act serves as an access point for a deeper mode of worship:

Abraham fulfilled the entire Torah. We must understand how this
is possible. We may explain it as follows: it is a great principle that
all six hundred and thirteen commandments are branches of the
Torah. Each part of the Torah is a commandment. Now before
the Torah was given, he had only the commandment of circumcision. This commandment included the divine vitality of all Torah;
all of Scripture was concentrated within it (*derekh tsimtsum*). After
the giving of the Torah it spread out through the various
branches. Before this, the vitality and all the parts of Torah were
contracted within it. Therefore, when he understood circumcision, he understood all the branches connected to Torah and
intended [to fulfill][82] all of them.[83]

This notion that a single commandment includes the entire Torah, indeed
all of existence, is fundamental to understanding this passage. Maimonides
suggests that it is possible for one to achieve a place in the world to come
by performing a single *mitsvah* "as it ought to be done," likely referring to
inner intent and a lack of consideration of temporal reward.[84] Medieval
Kabbalah ascribes great significance to the act of circumcision in particular, which is interpreted as a physical deed that mirrors—and inspires—
divine revelation.[85]

However, the Hasidic version of this idea subtly shifts the focus toward
its own notion of *devekut*, emphasizing that one may indeed arrive at a state
of perfect communion with God through performing a single *mitsvah* with
focus, fiery enthusiasm, and contemplative presence. Each precept is a microcosm of the whole Torah, which is itself a linguistic expression of God's
very essence, and therefore a single commandment can lead the mystic to
achieve unspeakable intimacy with the infinite Divine. Circumcision fulfilled
this role for Abraham, but after Scripture was delivered on Sinai all of the
other commandments serve as "branches" that lead one to perceive the deeper
nature of Torah.

If the Torah—and the commandments—was fully accessible to the patriarchs, why was it necessary to be revealed at Sinai? In a sermon preserved
by one of his disciples, the Maggid suggests that although Torah was part
of the world from the moment of creation, the villainous generations of
Enosh, the flood, and the tower of Babel sundered the connection between
Torah and the world.[86] Generations passed, and people came to view Scripture and the physical world as separate from their divine origins. The people

of Israel were compelled to descend into Egypt in order to redeem the fallen elements of Torah that had become trapped there, a metaphor for attuning oneself to the Scripture found in all aspects of the physical realm. This teaching thus offers a mystical explanation of the exile and subsequent redemption of the Jewish people from Egypt. However, when read carefully it also implies that the Scripture had to be given on Mt. Sinai because mankind gradually lost the ability to see Torah in the world around them. Israel had forgotten that Scripture and the cosmos are interwoven, and that both are indelibly connected to God.

The Maggid does not erase the distinction between the devotional modes of pre- and post-Sinai. But some of his teachings suggest that one may access the Torah in its pristine form even after revelation:

> The following is the meaning of "your commandment is broad beyond measure" (Ps. 119:96), and, "Open my eyes, that I may perceive the wonders of Your Torah" (Ps. 119:18), referring to those wondrous worlds hidden within Your Torah. This is [the explanation of,] "the blessed Holy One created the world with the Torah"— with the Torah, just as we have it, but it has been garbed in all the worlds according to what it is. [The Torah] itself does not change.
>
> This is how the patriarchs studied Torah, and how Noah studied Torah. They attained the Torah just as it is, even though at that time it had not been clothed in a garment as we have it. This is like a sheath for the Torah itself.
>
> This is "in the future the blessed Holy One will remove the sun from its sheath."[87] It will be grasped as it is, without any garment, since right now its illumination cannot be withstood on its own, and not every mind can bear it.[88] But the tsaddikim, who have removed themselves from physicality, can grasp it, each one according to the degree he is divested from the corporeal.[89]

The patriarchs studied Scripture in its most essential form, before Torah was recast in the later linguistic mantle of narrative and laws. This garb acts as a shield that preserves one from the unbearable illumination of the Torah, since most people cannot withstand this light. And yet, the Maggid has reiterated that the Torah of creation is—in some essential sense—synonymous with the post-Sinai Scripture. The garment has been changed, but the nature of Torah remains exactly the same.

The throbbing heart of Torah may still be accessed by certain righteous individuals that have successfully divested themselves from the physical world. In the future, Torah's inner nature will be revealed to all, but even now it is accessible to those who seek it. Some of the Maggid's teachings allow for the possibility that certain people of later generations will emulate the patriarchs' type of contemplative service.[90] Through their deeds and their thoughts they unite the *sefirot*, bringing together the World of Thought and the cosmos, and can even transform the physical world around them. Rather than an alternative to the normative structures or an antinomian thrust in the style of the later Sabbateans, these traditions suggests that the Hasidic masters—the Maggid among them—were exploring the manner in which the passionate eros of devotion is expressed through the ritual practices of rabbinic Judaism.[91]

The Role of Moses

The Maggid's sermons link the possibility of human actions shaping the garments of Torah to his description of Moses' role at Sinai, the moment in which God translated the primordial Torah into language. The Maggid builds on the ancient image of Moses as a unique prophet and lawgiver, one rooted in Hebrew Bible and developed significantly in later rabbinic sources and Jewish mystical texts.[92] Kabbalistic sources generally associate Moses with the *sefirot* of *tif'eret* and, less frequently, *da'at*; he is often described as the "husband of *shekhinah*" or the "bridegroom of *malkhut*."[93] The Maggid's teachings variously associate Moses with the higher *sefirot*.[94] He claims that Moses' divestment from the corporal, including refraining from sexual relations with his wife, allowed him to train his mind on God at all times and thus access the divine *hokhmah* that animates the cosmos.[95]

For the Maggid, the uniqueness of Moses and his prophetic capacity is most visible in the fact that he was the one who delivered the primordial Torah into language.[96] Moses' understanding of the Divine exceeded that of all other prophets. Scripture could have been given only by someone who grasped the most intimate and powerful divine name, the one that animates all others and signifies the aspect of God that sustains all existence:

Our teacher Moses grasped the essence of divinity, which is the vitality of all the names [of God], where there are no distinctions

and all is utter oneness. Therefore, the Torah in all its breadth
(*bi-kelalutah*) was given through him. This was not the case with
the other prophets, who grasped the essence of divinity only [as it
was projected through] the divine attributes and names (*middot
ve-kinnu'im*). . . .

Moses grasped [divinity] through the name Y-H-V-H, the
all-encompassing vitality, such that the entire Torah, in general
and particular, including all that a faithful student would inno-
vate,[97] was given through him.[98]

Moses possessed an understanding and an apprehension of God the likes of
which was achieved by no other prophets. He had access to the divine name
Y-H-V-H, the liminal point that is a bridge between the linguistic structures of Torah and the prelinguistic fountain of divine energy, and for this
reason it was he who could bring the Torah into speech. Moses was connected to Y-H-V-H—the source of all language—rather than to any other
subsidiary divine names, thus mediating between the infinite preexistent Torah
and the Scripture he delivered at Sinai.

The key to Moses' singular vision of God was his humility.[99] The prophet's modesty was a kind of *imitatio dei*, enabling his limited self to become
filled with the infinite expanse of the true Self.[100] The attenuation of the
Torah at Sinai was a demonstration of God's modesty. Moses' lack of ego
and pride enabled him to apprehend the self-humbling God and thus serve
as the conduit through which Scripture was given. For the Maggid, such
humility has mystical and ethical components: only through becoming as
nothing, may one come to enter the Naught. Moses is one of the few who
enters into the *ayin* because in his reverent humility before the divine
majesty he saw himself as nothing (*ke-ayin*). At Sinai, Moses was granted
an immediate vision of the infinite sweep of *hokhmah*, ascending beyond
even his ordinary contemplative sight, momentarily glimpsing God and the
Torah beyond the various stages of contraction.[101]

The primordial Torah was invested in language at Sinai, lacking words
until Moses gave them to it. A teaching from the Maggid preserved in *Me'or
'Einayim*, the work of one of Dov Ber's foremost disciples, offers some insightful reflections on this process:

I heard my teacher [the Maggid] interpret the verse, "She made
him a basket (*teivat*) of reeds [and she covered it with pitch],

placing it in the grass (*suf*) at the banks of the river" (Ex. 2:3) in this way. The Torah was originally in the World of Thought. When the world's patriarchs studied it, they grasped it as it was in the World of Thought, as we have said elsewhere. It was through Moses, who represents awareness (*da'at*), that Torah was drawn into speech, the final [stage] of the seven "days of building."[102] Thus the Torah frequently says: "God spoke to Moses" or "God spoke all these words" (Ex. 20:1). This means that he [Moses] drew the primordial Torah into speech and it became dressed in material garb.

This is, "She made him a *teivah* [meaning both 'basket' and 'word']." The words of Torah became that "basket" of speech. *Gomeh* or "reeds" can be derived from *gemi'ah*, which means "drawing forth," drawing forth the pleasure within Torah, which comes from *hesed*, by means of speech, as in "The teaching (*torah*) of compassion (*hesed*) is upon her tongue" (Prov. 21:36). "She covered it with pitch" (*hemar*) means that she dressed it in corporeal (*homer*) garb. "Placing it in the grass" (*suf*) means that she drew it into the end (*suf/sof*), the final one of the cosmic rungs, that of speech. "At the banks" (*sefat*) refers to the lips, also the place of speech. "River" refers to that ancient cosmic flow, originating in thought, but being drawn into speech at the hour when the Torah was given.

Therefore, everyone should become accustomed to contemplating the Root of our thought and to raising it up to its Source. Even if one is not a *tsaddik*—meaning that he cannot recall the blessed Creator as thoughts come to him, since he does not have that worthy habit of mind—still, he should study God's Torah at such times [of lower spiritual attainment]. Then he will begin to cleave to goodness with whatever quality had been aroused [by that thought]. In this way, he will repair it [i.e., that attribute]. Understand this.[103]

The pre-Sinai Torah was abstract and unknowable. God created the world through this infinite Scripture, composed of divine names and indeed identified with God. At Sinai, Moses drew this primordial Torah into its current linguistic form and brought God's wisdom into words. We should remember the idea of primordial Scripture does not necessarily mean that it was totally prelinguistic; the "letters of thought" are of course an essential part of cognition. Dov Ber's depiction of creation stresses the role of language in establishing the order of the cosmos, and revelation might then be described as a development within the linguistic realm, moving from the unarticulated to the articulated realm.

Certain homilies imply that Torah emerged from divine silence into human language even before Moses. Revelation, thus construed, starts as the cosmos first arose in God's mind, unfolding through the words and letters of the creative speech acts. This transposition, the unfettering of the divine source, began with the first act of divine self-limitation into *hokhmah*, alluded to by the letter *yod* of Y-H-V-H.[104] In this stage God's essence was still unformed and prelinguistic, only taking on the shape of the letters as it entered the realm of *binah*, associated with the first *heh* of God's name. According to the Maggid, this stage represents the formation of the world through the ten divine speech acts. It was through these utterances that God created the world, but the revelation of His essence was still unstable and incomplete, like a thought before it has been expressed in verbal language. Moses, associated with *tif'eret* and the *vav* of Y-H-V-H, finally drew God's essence into language and brought it into speech. This final stage, represented by the final *heh* of God's name, was accomplished through the giving of the Ten Commandments at Sinai. These correspond to the ten utterances through which the world was created, thus completing a cosmic process of revelation that spells out the sacred divine name. On one hand, Moses simply continued the process, but he is the one who draws it from potential into speech, giving it words.

Moses' unique mastery of language and contemplative attachment to God enabled him to bring forth the Torah from the realm of divine thought into speech. This notion raises the following questions: To what degree did Moses actually shape the textual fabric of Scripture? Was it he who chose the words of the Torah's linguistic garb, were they directly revealed to him by God, or did he simply intuit the correct words through his communion with divine thought? The Maggid never directly addresses this issue, though as we have seen, he suggests that some of the narrative garment of Torah came from the deeds of the patriarchs. Some scholars have detected a fascinating conception of revelation in later Hasidic texts, which describe the theophany at Sinai as prelinguistic and without specific content.[105] If we interpret the Maggid's teachings as suggesting that Moses was the origin of the specific words of Torah, then his description of revelation seems to anticipate this radical idea found in the later Hasidic works.

Building on ancient traditions, the Maggid describes the written Torah and oral Torah—that is, the body of rabbinic teachings—as having been conterminously revealed. In doing so he makes a very interesting point: the primordial written Torah existed in the realm of pure divine thought, only entering into words as the oral Torah was given at Sinai.[106] This suggests that the Torah revealed to Israel at Sinai was, in fact, the oral Torah, considered thus at least vis-à-vis the written Torah, the sacred primordial Torah beyond language. Indeed, the Torah articulated aloud at Sinai was the oral Torah, for the purely abstract written Torah is forever concealed and unspeakable.[107] This nonliteral interpretation of the term written Torah is rather striking. Indeed, according to the Maggid it represents Torah as it exists in the mind of God. While we may rightly speak of its letters, for thoughts are also constructed from *otiyyot ha-mahashavah*, the written Torah cannot ever be revealed. This reservoir of divine wisdom is accessible only to the discerning contemplative who can journey into the World of Thought.

Moses' importance as a master of sacred speech began long before the Israelites arrived at Sinai. Indeed, the Maggid interprets the entire story of the exodus as the redemption of language in which God charged Moses with the dangerous task of freeing the fallen, or "exiled," capacity for "holy speech" (*ha-dibbur ha-kadosh*) that was trapped in Egypt.[108] This courageous act of restoring the exiled speech enabled the Jewish people to receive the Torah on Sinai. But some of the Maggid's sermons describe even speech as being difficult for Moses, since he was intimately connected to the contemplative realms higher than speech.[109] Dov Ber thus interprets Moses' proclamation "I am of uncircumcised lips" (Ex. 6:12) as an admission that his spiritual attunement belies any compromise by expressing it through language.[110] Indeed, suggests the Maggid, Moses' constant state of attachment to God through contemplation almost prevented him from taking part in the redemption of Israel from Egypt.[111] But God "commanded" (*va-yetsavem*) Moses and Aaron to forge a "bond" (*tsavta*) with Israel in order to lead them out of Egypt.

Moses' singular connection to the prelinguistic realms of the Divine also means that he was less connected to the physical world. For this reason, Moses left the performance of deeds and wonders to the other leaders of his day:

The Zohar teaches that "had Moses spoken to the rock, there would have been no forgetting [i.e., Torah would never be forgotten]."[112] The reason is that all the miracles Moses performed were accomplished by speech alone rather than by action. He was told, "lift up your staff" (Ex. 14:16), but the Sea was subdued by the word alone. This was not the case with Joshua. Moses represents "awareness" (*da'at*), drawn into speech.

His generation was also called "the generation of awareness" (*dor de'ah*). For this reason they are referred to as *dor ha-midbar* ("generation of the wilderness"), which can mean "the generation of speech" (*medabber*).[113] Speech is drawn forth from the mind, and thus they received the Torah in speech. . . .

But when the first generation of the wilderness, the "generation of awareness," had died out and a new generation had come, Moses saw that they were people of deeds. They would come to inherit the land, as is known, and therefore he struck the rock. But the blessed Holy One told Moses that the opposite was true! He should have established and raised up this second generation as a generation of speech, following the inheritance of their forefathers. With speech alone water would have come forth from the rock, and they too would have been a generation of awareness. This [mistake] led to forgetting, or a descent from speech into deeds. The sages of the Zohar spoke well, teaching that there would be no forgetfulness if he had not hit the rock.[114]

Moses and his generation possessed a special combination of awareness and speech (called *da'at* and *dibbur*). The Torah was therefore revealed to them in its linguistic garment for the first time. The next generation, however, was attracted to deeds, and Moses erred in hitting the rock in order to sate their desire for action. This well-intentioned mistake caused them to lose their sacred awareness of God.

This particular text is of historical importance as well as theological interest. Arthur Green has convincingly argued that this text should be read in the context of a historical "debate" among the Maggid's circle regarding how—if at all—their spiritual path might be broadened from a small group of scholars into a mass movement.[115] The sermon also recalls the Maggid's response to the accusations of the *mithnaggedim* as recorded in a letter by Shneur Zalman: "Our great master chose to take no action against them, since the power of Israel lies entirely in their words, to cry out to God to disrupt their wicked thoughts and prevent their hands from doing anything. And just as he interpreted it for us, so it was."[116]

The Kiss of Sinai

The Maggid's homilies represent Sinai as an intimate encounter between God and Israel. The Decalogue was of course central to that experience, but Dov Ber also describes revelation as an overwhelming and radical theophany that fundamentally transformed the Jewish people and their relationship to the word. Drawing on the Zohar's notion that speech (*dibbur*) had been cast into exile in Egypt,[117] the Maggid refers to Sinai as a critical step in restoring Israel's capacity for sacred language:

> The Israelites were like a newborn baby when they left Egypt. When they arrived at the sea, they were like a freshly weaned child.[118] They had only a small capacity for speech, and were not yet fully mature. This is the deeper meaning of why they could not recite the song on their own; Moses had to sing first and they sang after him.[119] This is the explanation of why Moses said, "and you should be silent" (Ex. 14:14)—they could not yet speak maturely, but rather as a young child. . . .
>
> When they came to Mt. Sinai they had understood how to learn, saying, "we will do and we will understand" (Ex. 24:7). They themselves achieved the supernal wisdom.[120]

The encounter between Israel and God at Sinai was far more sophisticated than the theophany because when the Jews left Egypt, they were immature and could not yet speak. As the people matured throughout their journey in the wilderness, their capacity for sacred speech as well as their conception of God transformed and evolved. In crossing the Sea of Reeds they could only mimic the song of Moses, distinguished by his command of language and his singular apprehension of God. However, Israel had matured by the time they reached Sinai. They redeemed their ability to speak as well as to listen, thus preparing themselves to receive the Torah:[121] "When one achieves [true] awe, coming to know the revelation of divinity, he sees God's sovereignty in all places and there is no place devoid [of him], as our sages said: 'The words "I am Y-H-V-H your God" were heard in all places, in each and every place. Even the stone in the wall cried out and the rafter in the woodwork answered: "I am Y-H-V-H your God."[122] They grasped His divinity in every place, crying out 'I am' and 'there is none other.' Consider this and ponder it well."[123] At Sinai all living beings, and indeed even inanimate creations, were stirred to awareness of God's presence in the physical world. This attunement, however, was not simply a onetime awakening: it is accessible to any spiritual adept or worshipper who gazes on the world—and the threads of language—with the awareness that everything reveals the Divine.

One remarkable Hasidic teaching from one of the Maggid's students frames the encounter between Israel and God at Sinai as an erotic moment of communion that took place through the medium of language. This homily was delivered by Levi Yitshak of Barditchev in 1773, just a few short months after the Maggid's death, and is filled with terms and images plucked from Dov Ber's theological vocabulary. We read:

> "You have been shown to know [that Y-H-V-H is God, and there
> is nothing else]" (Deut. 4:35). . . . The matter [may be understood]
> by first [interpreting] this teaching from the sages about the
> giving of the Torah: as each utterance left the mouth of the
> blessed Holy One, he made it kiss the mouth of each and every
> person.[124] But we must make this understandable to the human
> mind, how can speech be a kiss? . . .
>
> It is known that there is an aspect of voice (kol) and an aspect
> of speech (dibbur). Speech is the external part of voice, which is
> more internal. When someone speaks to another person, it is
> possible for his lips to deceive and his mouth to lie to him; his
> heart may be inconstant.[125]
>
> But if he speaks from the depths of his heart, he will arouse
> all of his powers into this speech, for the heart is the root of his
> strength. The dwelling place (mishkan) of the aspect of voice is in
> the heart, as is known, and therefore this sort of speech arouses a
> great response all on its own even without his intention.[126]
>
> This is the meaning of "words that emerge from the heart,
> enter into the heart."[127] Since he speaks from his heart, the voice
> emerges and is garbed in the speech, and he differentiates the
> letters by means of the organs of articulation. This arouses the
> love in his fellow's heart. It means that he wishes to give his love

to his friend, and thereby the corresponding love in his friend's heart will be aroused, greeting him with a smiling countenance.

This is the meaning of kisses—when they kiss one another, they reveal the love in their hearts. Their kisses bring their loves close to one another, and they become one. This is the idea of the "soul to soul" connection (*hitdavkut ruha be-ruha*) mentioned in the Zohar.[128] . . .

But when He came to give [the Torah] to us, for whom His love was hewn into [the divine] Heart from the earliest days of the earth and the [emergence] primordial thought . . . He spoke to us out of great and eternal love (*ahavah rabbah ve-ahavat 'olam*). The voice that leaves the heart was aroused with great love, and each [divine] utterance was of the type of voice that dwells within the heart. He revealed the secret hidden in His heart to us, which is the fullness of Torah (*shelemut ha-Torah*) and its pleasantness. Our souls departed as He spoke (cf. Song 5:6),[129] since the love in the hearts of the Jewish people was aroused to greet the love of the blessed One. "He went and met him at the mountain of God, and he kissed him" (Ex. 4:27)—the two loves cleaved to each other, becoming one.[130]

Revelation at Sinai was an intimate, loving encounter between God and Israel. The author of this source describes the experience in erotic, evocative terms drawn from the rich language of the Song of Songs.[131] These images are used in earlier rabbinic kabbalistic literature to refer to the intense relationship between master and disciple, the members of a spiritual fellowship, and, of course, between God and the Jewish people.[132] In this teaching, at Sinai Israel is so overwhelmed and aroused by this love that their souls break free and reach out for the Divine.

Language is the point of connection that allows for this loving bond between God and Israel. The words of the Ten Commandments, filled with love, emerge from the heart of the Divine and inspire a mutual embrace. This sermon makes no explicit reference to any of the *sefirot*, and the focal point is the unification of *kol* and *dibbur*. Both of these terms are associated with *sefirot*, though they have been simplified in Dov Ber's teaching. *Dibbur* (or *malkhut*) represents verbalized, audible speech, and *kol* (*tif'eret*) refers to the passionate love with which it has been imbued. Such homilies suggest that the semantic content of revelation was of secondary importance to its emotive core. The divine voice was aroused and ignited love within the hearts of Israel. The words themselves were only a garment for God's love, serving as a vessel through which an otherwise unspoken feeling could be expressed.

The theophany at Sinai left an impression within the minds of the Jewish people, becoming imbued in their collective memory as a reserve of spiritual vitality awakened in worship.[133] The biblical commandments thus become gateways of arousing the memory of the encounter with God. Each *mitsvah*, says Levi Yitshak, must unite "deed, thought, and speech."[134] The triad is familiar from earlier Jewish literature,[135] but here it is interpreted to mean that the worshipper must bring together the Torah (God's thought born into speech) with human action (deed). God's mind entered language at Sinai, but the third and final stage—performing the commandments— was left to Israel. The *mitsvot* effect a union of the human and divine realms that began at Sinai, a merging of sacred deeds and sacred language into an eternal moment of spiritual uplift.

In bringing our discussion of the Maggid's theology of revelation to a close, we should reflect on *why* the subject of Sinai was so important to this eighteenth-century Hasidic figure. Elsewhere I have argued that for Dov Ber and his students this issue is directly linked to the legitimacy of the project of Hasidism, emerging in these very years, as an innovative social movement as well as an exegetical approach that calls for—and is grounded in—new interpretations of canonical texts.[136] The Maggid's sermons define the momentous significance of Sinai as the emergence of divine wisdom from the concealed and ineffable realms into the garment of letters and words. He was deeply interested in plumbing the nature of sacred study, and, for this reason, his homilies frequently highlight the echoes of Sinai in contemporary devotional practices.

The figure of Moses, here afforded such an important role in the formulation of revelation, is surely a stand-in for all future interpreters. This includes the Hasidic *tsaddik*, whose sermons were moments of theophany akin to the unveiling of God's self at Sinai. But the Moses of these homilies may also be the Maggid himself, an inwardly driven mystical thinker whose rich spiritual life leads him to meet the Divine in the murmuring depths of the mind. He is called on, however, to reach into this sacred ineffable and shepherd forth the insights and cloak them in language for his students.[137]

PART III

The Devotional Life

Chapter 6

Study and the Sacred Text

Without reviving spiritual exegesis, it is not possible to rediscover *scientia sacra* in the bosom of a tradition dominated by the presence of sacred scripture. Scripture possess an inner dimension which is attainable only through intellection operating within a traditional framework and which alone is able to solve certain apparent contradictions and riddles in sacred texts.

—Seyyed Hossein Nasr

Our inquiry into the Maggid's teachings on creation, revelation, and the nature of Scripture has paved the way for exploring one of the fundaments of his devotional path: Dov Ber's approach to sacred study. We cannot hope to encompass all of the Maggid's teachings on this subject, for Torah and study are central themes in nearly all of his sermons. The following discussion will instead highlight those of his homilies on the power of religious scholarship that forward our exploration of his teachings on language itself. The Maggid's conception of devotional study is rooted, as may be expected, in his understanding of Torah as the linguistic expression of the divine presence.

God's wisdom, though it remains hauntingly beyond words, has been translated into language and recast as Scripture. The scholar must always strive for the *penimiyyut*, the inner dimension of *hokhmah* expressed through its words. *Devekut* through study thus depends on the scholar's approach rather than the specific identity of the religious text at hand. The passionate, enthusiastic study of any religious work, "Torah" in its most broadly construed form, reenacts the intimate encounter between God and Israel at

Sinai. In this moment of sacred communion, the scholar is linked to the prelinguistic realm of divine thought. A flood of inspiration or creative illumination flows through him, giving rise to new interpretations of sacred texts.

Religious Study and *Torah Lishmah*

The study of Torah lies at the very heart of the rabbinic project, and the importance of learning in rabbinic culture cannot be overestimated.[1] Such learning was not simply a matter of accruing knowledge for the sages of the Mishnah and Talmud, who were keenly aware of the sapiential and ethical dimensions of devotional study.[2] Numerous traditions in rabbinic literature reveal erotic elements to this study, with some texts suggesting a commitment to learning that borders on a mode of asceticism in which devotion to sacred study supersedes the scholar's intimate physical relationship with his wife.[3]

Scholars debate the extent to which there were mystical elements of rabbinic Torah study, in terms of both subject matter and the experience of learning.[4] Opaque references to "works of the chariot" (*maʿaseh merkavah*) and "works of creation" (*maʿaseh bereshit*) may indeed refer to the study of esoteric subjects.[5] Yet some rabbinic texts describe the act of Torah study itself as an illuminated moment of rapture, a phenomenon that scholar Nehemia Polen has termed "performative exegesis,"[6] suggesting that the interpretation of Scripture was understood as an act of communion with the Holy Spirit.

Many rabbinic traditions underscore that the motivation and intention of the student are of utmost importance. Some of these refer to the highest, or perhaps purest, mode of learning as *Torah lishmah*, or study "for its own sake."[7] But the precise definition of this phrase remains unspoken, and the parameters of *Torah lishmah* continued to be the subject of debate in later Jewish mystical and philosophical thought.[8] Most medieval authors agree that it refers to a type of study that is undertaken neither for the sake of reward, either in this world or the next, nor to exhibit and demonstrate the powers of one's intellect.[9] For some, *Torah lishmah* was an attempt to grasp, in practical terms, how to perform the commandments with the greatest precision and utmost fidelity. For others, it referred to a purely intellectual quest of understanding and knowledge of God through the sources of

Torah. For still others, *Torah lishmah* represented a "devotional" path or spiritual praxis by means of which the scholar becomes connected to the Divine.[10]

The debate regarding the contours of *Torah lishmah* may be linked to the question of which sacred texts should form the core of Jewish curriculum. Medieval Jews argued whether traditional subjects like the Bible, Talmud, or *halakhah* should be the sole focus of one's studies, or if other bodies of knowledge like Kabbalah or philosophy should be admitted—or even demanded.[11] Some medieval mystics went so far as to claim that only the study of kabbalistic works could be deemed truly *lishmah*; only through these works, they said, can one truly come to know God. Indeed, there are voices in *Tikkunei Zohar* and the later strata of the Zohar itself that call for the study of Kabbalah over and above all other religious texts.[12] For the authors of the Zoharic corpus, biblical interpretation and creative exegesis remained a key locus of mystical experience, as well as a theurgic practice.[13]

The later works of Safed Kabbalah continue many of these threads, describing study, and *Torah lishmah* in particular, as a praxis intended to mend the cosmic fracture through healing the rift of the *sefirot* and uniting the divine name Y-H-V-H.[14] It was to be performed for the sake of *shekhinah*, associated with the final *heh* of Y-H-V-H and the same letter in the word *lishmah*.[15] Many of these texts describe studying the casuistic patterns of Jewish law as breaking through the "husks" (*kelippot*) that obscure and surround the holy sparks, or divine wisdom, hidden deep within the Scripture. Although many Lurianic sources evince preference for the study of Kabbalah, called the "inner dimension" (*penimiyyut*) of Torah, works such as Isaiah Horowitz's *Shenei Luhot ha-Berit* in the sixteenth century blend together exoteric (legal) and esoteric (kabbalistic as well as midrashic) elements of Jewish thought into a single corpus of devotional literature replete with spiritual meaning.[16]

Hasidism absorbed many elements of the kabbalistic approach to engagement with Torah, though in doing so Hasidic thinkers subtly shifted the orientation away from mystical metaphysics or theosophy and toward the devotional elements of sacred study. Teachings from the BeSHT on the nature of study often underscore the experiential dimension of religious scholarship, including quasi-magical and theurgic elements.[17] Such a paradigm clearly undergirds the tale of the Maggid's first meeting with the BeSHT, which we took up in Chapter 1. The reader should recall that although the Maggid offered a series of technical explanations of a mystical source, the BeSHT accused his words of being "without any soul." This is mirrored in one of the Maggid's own sermons on the experiential dimensions of study, a homily that describes scholars wrapped in a sacred fire surrounded by words that are filled with divine vitality and rejoicing just as when "given at Sinai."[18] Rather than isolating the study of a particular corpus, even that of Kabbalah, the early Hasidic masters argued that the devotional *how* of sacred study should outweigh the scholastic question of *what*.

The polemics of the *mithnaggedim* include biting criticisms of Hasidic disdain for scholars and, in more extreme cases, of neglecting and even deriding study as a hindrance to the true goals of the spiritual life.[19] This backlash from the *mithnaggedim* may have inspired the Hasidim to reinforce their study of *halakhah* and tighten up on certain matters of ritual practice, while still levying a powerful critique against prideful and narcissistic scholars.[20] But the emphasis on *devekut* as the pinnacle of religious service and a particularly strong approach to prayer were key to the emerging religious ethos of Hasidism. This shift in values away from the primacy of study, among others, sparked the ire of Talmudic scholars and the Lithuanian rabbinate.[21]

The Maggid's teachings offer a rich account of study as a spiritual praxis.[22] His sermons often cite the neglect of Torah as a particularly grave transgression.[23] Several homilies suggest that study is a unique opportunity for attaining *devekut*; the true intensity of God's majesty, says the Maggid, can only be withstood when it is filtered through the lens of Torah.[24] Drawing on the sacrificial imagery of the Temple, the Maggid suggests that the fire of the onetime altar has been transformed into the scholar's flames of devotion. The sacrificial gift is, of course, none other than the passionately recited words of study: "We are urged to study Torah, that which rises higher than any burnt offering. What sort of Torah study is this talking about? 'The offering upon its stake,' (Lev. 6:2), meaning teachings offered in ecstasy and close attachment to our blessed Creator, not things that flow only outward from the lips. 'Any word that does not come forth in awe and love does not fly upward,'[25] and is not called an ascending offering."[26] The Maggid has thus internalized workings of the Temple as a symbolic vocabulary for loving acts of personal, inward devotion.[27] These letters are likened to the "ascending offering" (*'olah*) because they rise up through the spiritual attention of the scholar. The words of study are consumed by the fires of passion, returning to their sacred origin in the Divine. This process is derailed and the letters fail to ascend, however, if the language offering is no more than the lip service of overly cerebral intellection or vapid recitation.

The small but significant number of homilies in the Maggid's corpus evincing some reticence toward study bespeak a concern that certain foci, like exclusive concentration on abstruse Talmudic dialectics, will mire the student in an endless swamp of textual sophistry.[28] One particular tradition suggests that the scholar must take periodic breaks from study in order "to sequester himself in his mind" (le-hitboded be-mahshavto) and thus attain devekut.[29] Introspection and moral development were an important part of the Maggid's spiritual path, and some traditions suggest that such inner work cannot take place when one is focused on textual study.[30] Scholarship, suggests the Maggid, may hinder one's connection with God to the extent that it is tinged with intellectual conceit rather than the quest to know the Divine.[31]

The intertwined questions of what was to be studied and how it was to be approached return us to an issue raised in Chapter 1: What was Torah study for the Maggid's circle of early Hasidic thinkers? Was it focused Talmudic scholarship, despite a lack of evidence for many—thought not all—of the figures in this group? Was it mostly Hebrew Bible and rabbinic legends, the focal point of nearly all of the sermons that have been preserved? We might argue that Talmudic giants like Shmelke of Nikolsburg (and his brother Pinhas), Levi Yitshak of Barditshev, and Shneur Zalman of Liady would never have respected the Maggid unless he was learned in traditional rabbinic discourse. This line of thinking would also account for the attempts to attribute such knowledge to the Maggid in even the very earliest hagiographical stories in Keter Shem Tov and Shivhei ha-BeSHT. And yet, Yaʿakov Yosef of Polnoye—a prodigious scholar—was deeply shaped by the spiritual teachings and religious personality of his master the BeSHT despite the fact that the latter's teachings reveal rather little intensive Talmudic knowledge. This critical question will accompany us throughout the current chapter.

Study as Devotion

The Maggid's depictions of sacred study as a religious discipline frequently refer to the encounter with the text as an immediate and personal experience. "Each day they [i.e., the words of Torah] must be as new as if they were given on that very day.[32] Just as [the experience of] Sinai was 'face to face,' so too must it be each day as you are studying."[33] Spiritual study entails a direct and intimate meeting with the infinite divine wisdom that reverberates in the words of Scripture. The Maggid's formulation of this encounter as "face to face" echoes an account of Sinai in the Hebrew Bible (see Deut. 5:4), thus drawing a direct link between the act of study and revelation, but the Maggid has also invoked the erotic Lurianic terminology for the proper coupling of the *sefirot*.[34] This communion—of the student with the Torah, and the *hieros gamos* of the Godhead—takes place as the scholar devotes himself to scriptural study and interpretation with a sense of perpetual newness.

A sermon preserved in the writings of Meshullam Feibush Heller, a disciple of Dov Ber as well as of Yehiel Mikhel of Zlotshev, offers the fullest account of mystical study and *Torah lishmah* attributed to the Maggid:

> I heard from the mouth of that holy man Dov Ber, on the
> Sabbath I spent there during his lifetime, his reply to a question
> someone asked about a passage in the Midrash. That text com-
> pared a student of Torah to a pearl-encrusted clapper inside a
> golden bell.[35] He said that this refers to those who study Torah
> truly for its own sake (*lishmah*), in order to be attached to God.
> Their thoughts are only of God. When Scripture says "May this
> book of teaching never depart from your mouth; contemplate it
> (*bo*) day and night" (Josh. 1:8), the text really meant to "contem-
> plate *Him* day and night;" your thoughts should be of God.[36]

Interpreting the ambiguous *bo* (it) of Joshua 1:8 as a reference to the Divine, rather than the Torah scroll, the Maggid stresses that all religious scholarship must be reimagined as a deeply personal quest to achieve intimacy with God. Such study goes far beyond absorbing knowledge or ideas, says the Maggid, because in such efforts one comes to meet God amid the letters of Torah. For a devoted student, indeed, such a divine revelation transpires in the language brought forth in study:

> God is concentrated right there in the spirit-breath of Torah
> (*ruhaniyyut hevel ha-Torah*) as it comes forth from a person's pure
> mouth. If one can purify both his mouth and heart, he may
> become a chariot for God. So attachment to God is the innermost
> part [of this act of study]; the teachings one learns are the
> external form in which this devotion is garbed. That is a proper
> understanding.

This is not true if your desire and love are for anything other
than God—if you are still attached to temporal matters or seek
even some bit of self-glorification. Then your innermost thought
is of that glory, and your learning surrounds that thought. Woe to
the disgracing of Torah, making her into a garment for your own
foolish thoughts that she has to cover up![37]

Intention and mindful contemplation transform the very letters and words
intoned in the act of Torah study into a garment for the Divine. The elements of speech, from the unformed breath that animates language to the
letters and words themselves, become vessels of an immediate manifestation
of the divine presence. Yet Torah study may itself become idolatrous if allowed to stoke the fires of pride rather than fostering humility in the quest
for the Divine. One cannot achieve communion with the Divine if any shred
of pride or self-aggrandizement remains; only through expunging the ego
and engaging in pure *Torah lishmah* does *shekhinah* emerge and become invested in the letters of his contemplative study:

That is why the midrash compared the student of Torah to a
golden bell. The bell is the external section, while the clapper is
within it and makes the sound. "Woven gold is her garment," but
"the full glory of the king's daughter lies within" (Ps. 45:14). That
glory consists of awe before God and the indwelling presence of
shekhinah, within the heart of every Jew. The "woven gold" is the
letters of Torah, in which she is dressed. But the pearl-studded
clapper (*'inbal*) is our attachment to God, which is possible only
where there is true humility (*'anavah*).[38]

Dov Ber's metaphor, plucked from the pages of the midrash, operates on several levels. Like the clapper that brings forth sound by striking against the
external structure of the bell, the letters serve as a linguistic frame through
which the resonant inner spirit—of the text and the student—comes to be
revealed. The Maggid uses the same image to describe the inner world of
devotion and *devekut* within the disciple. Like the interior of the bell, this
spiritual vitality is clothed within the specific teaching being studied at that
moment. The particular subject, however, is of secondary importance to the
devotional yearnings of the student, which become garbed in the words of
Torah and thus come to manifest the divine presence.

We shall see that interpretive creativity is a fundamental part of the Maggid's approach to sacred study, but he is also deeply wary of the pride and hubris that can accompany scholarly accomplishments. Nullifying the ego and unshackling oneself from all personal desires are cornerstones of Dov Ber's mystical theology and moral teaching, extending to the study of Torah as well.[39] The teacher, says the Maggid, must always remember that new exegesis is a gift: "Even though this is a bit of Torah that no ear has ever heard, it comes not from you, but from God."[40] New interpretations of Scripture flow into one's consciousness from the hidden depths of God's mind. These ideas are a bestowal of divine inspiration, and the scholar must not forget that their ultimate source lies beyond the self.

Torah lishmah, for the Maggid, is described as study for the sake of redeeming *shekhinah* from the cosmic exile.[41] As noted, *shekhinah* (or *malkhut*) is linked to divine indwelling as human capacity for sacred speech (*dibbur*), suggesting that the goal of all study is to redeem the word from its fallen and debased state.[42] The Maggid frequently suggests that impassioned and inspired engagement with Torah has cosmic implications. He argues that God receives pleasure from study rooted in passion and enthusiasm rather than simple intellectual curiosity.[43]

The world was created through the words and letters of Scripture, and therefore, says the Maggid, reading the words of Torah with love and awe draws new vitality into the physical realm.[44] Study unites the *sefirot*, for the scholar's contemplative inquiry draws the words of the text into his mind and infuses them with new meaning and vitality. This type of study links the realm of external words with the deepest source of language within the self. It unites the World of Speech (*malkhut*) with the World of Thought (*binah*), generating a new torrent of cosmic divine vitality that courses into the words of the text and the mind of the scholar.

The Maggid's descriptions of the theurgic power of study occasionally point toward the magical properties of language. Yet healing and other miracles, according to the Maggid, are accomplished not through incantations or magical formulae, but through enthused prayer, supererogatory acts of piety, and passionate and fiery Torah study.[45] In this context the Maggid offers an interesting explanation of the famous Talmudic phrase "Israel has no constellation" (*ein mazal le-Yisra'el*).[46] Rereading *ein* as *ayin* (the words are indistinguishable when written without vowels), he explains that Israel transcends the astrological forces by penetrating the inner divinity of Scripture.[47] Cleaving to this godly wisdom, the infinite Naught that is the fundament of all linguistic being and the source of the letters of Torah allows them to transform the physical world.

Many traditions describe the BeSHT as having attained clairvoyance by gazing into the letters of Torah.[48] References to similar powers appear in the Maggid's teachings and in the legends of his life, though they crop up far less frequently. "Torah and the Holy One are one. Therefore, one who is connected to the letters of Torah will automatically know what happens within time, since he himself is beyond time. . . . He wants to see nothing but Y-H-V-H alone, which he glimpses by means of Torah's letters."[49] The scholar does not begin his studies with the intent of acquiring any type of magical sight. He longs only to attain a vision of the divine presence within the depths of the Torah, but the connection he forges with God also grants him knowledge of the full expanse of the temporal world.

Delving into Torah allows one to gaze on the world from the divine perspective in which everything is known, and clairvoyance is simply a by-product of this mystical study.[50] We should thus note the difference between passages such as this, in which clairvoyance is a result of cleaving to the divinity of language but not the primary goal, and the ascents of the soul or the magical powers typical of *ba'alei shem* or popular Kabbalists. The Maggid is not entirely disinterested in clairvoyance, of course, but such teachings have him apologizing for the ability as nothing more than a by-product of *devekut*. Like miracles, visions beyond the cosmos—and beyond time— emerge from such impassioned piety but should never be misconstrued as the true aim of devotion.

Among the ultimate goals of sacred study, says the Maggid, is the cultivation of attunement to God's presence in all aspects of the cosmos. Dov Ber suggests that a scholar who has truly ascended to the heights of sacred study, becoming clothed in the holy words, comes to see that everything is God—in ordinary language as well as mundane activities. "This," claims the Maggid, "is the meaning of 'the word of Y-H-V-H is pure'[51] . . . [everything comes] from the supernal Word. 'Pure' (*tserufah*) refers to the person who knows to connect (*le-tsaref*)[52] all words and deeds to the Holy One."[53] Purity is thus measured not by scholastic aptitude or even ascetic commitment, but in the scholar's ability to perceive the world as an ever-reverberating manifestation of God's sacred language. In this same teaching, the Maggid presents a very different interpretation of the kabbalistic tradition that the Torah is the names of God: through studying Torah and tracing language back to its divine source, the scholar understands that the cosmos—formed by God through Scripture—is saturated with divine vitality.[54]

The Maggid was well aware of earlier kabbalistic and rabbinic traditions that emphasize the need to withdraw from the world in order to cultivate a pious, ascetic approach to study. In one sermon, he quotes a meditative technique, found in the work *Reshit Hokhmah*, in which the scholar is to imagine himself standing in the Garden of Eden, stepping away from other people—and the physical world at large—and retreating in contemplative solitude.[55] The Maggid then remarks:

> But we must understand, how can he think this? One must surely know that he is in the world, amid people that he recognizes!
>
> The matter is thus: When one studies or worships with fear and love, connecting and binding his mind to the Creator, he contemplates that He fills all of the worlds and there is no place devoid of His glory, and all is filled with the life-force of the blessed Creator. Therefore, in everything that he sees he will see only the divine life-force that is drawn into it.[56]

Though he quotes the source with reverence and struggles to make sense of it, the Maggid is subtly challenging the original meditative technique. Dov Ber shifts the emphasis rather dramatically by calling on the scholar to visualize God's life-force as manifest through the physical world and the people around him as suffused with sacred vitality. Elsewhere he notes that one who "withdraws (*parush*) from the world and studies Torah always, but does so without attachment to the blessed Creator, [intending] only to grow haughty and be called 'rabbi,'—this is utter foolishness."[57]

Rather than seeking to escape from the chains of world, the Maggid puts forward an embracing vision of the world as saturated with God's word. In doing so Dov Ber suggests a metaphysical basis for serving God through corporeal deeds, which, as we have noted, occupy a place of tension in his theology. The cosmos reverberates with the divine word and is filled with the radiant letters of God's formative utterances—as well as the thundering command of Sinai—but engagement with these aspects of the Divine requires prudent circumspection. This, he suggests, is what it means to inhabit the Garden of Eden: an experience cultivated through devotional investment in the ever-present sacral quality of language.

The words of Torah may themselves be holy, says the Maggid, but accessing or activating the divinity within them does not happen automatically. The letters of Scripture are drained of their power when recited by rote. One who reads them without the correct contemplative attention is misusing a divine gift: "One must not say, 'I am immersed in God's Torah and commandments, which are complete holiness; even without [my] intention they are holy.' Do not say this! On the contrary, in particular with holy things your intention must be fitting; your thoughts must be pure and your word complete, for 'they are life to those who speak them' (Prov. 4:22).[58] It [one's intention] should be clear in each and every word that leaves your mouth, in each and every letter, vowel and sound."[59] The Maggid seems to understand that a theology that bespeaks the divinity of language easily allows the claim that inner intention during studying, while perhaps laudable, is relegated to second place. If the very letters of Scripture themselves hold God's presence within them, then is it not sufficient to speak them aloud? The Maggid's answer is resoundingly in the negative. Though he does not demand that one soar to brilliant heights of scholastic achievement, the Maggid clearly argues that the potential divinity of each and every speech act can be unlocked only through intense focus and intention.

One cannot always be immersed in sacred texts, of course, but the Maggid notes that the avenues of language provide an unrestricted mode of *devekut*: "It is possible to think constantly of the letters of Torah, and Torah is God's garment. Even when in conversation with people, you should contemplate only the letters that comprise those words being spoken. They too are derived from the twenty-two letters of Torah."[60] Since Scripture is a linguistic expression of the divine presence, contemplating its letters allows the scholar to commune with God even if he is not formally studying. But the Maggid moves one step beyond, noting that the letters of all speech are those of Torah. One who meditates on human words will soon discover the Torah within them as well.

The Maggid thus understood that the spiritual life includes natural vacillation between the states of *katnut* and *gadlut*, or "constricted" and "expansive" consciousness.[61] Moments of heightened awareness cannot be sustained indefinitely, and other modes of serving God remain accessible in these times of lesser illumination. This holds true for study as well, for it is impossible to attain spiritual or intellectual uplift each time one begins to read a religious text. In one teaching, he notes that even "one who studies Torah

without any understanding" accrues merit and accomplishes something of
lesser—but not inconsequential—religious significance.[62]

The Maggid explores this dynamic in a sermon exploring the different
intensities of Torah study as a journey through a multi-tiered garden. The
image of Torah as a verdant expanse awaiting textual exegesis is an ancient
one, appearing in many medieval kabbalistic works, including the Zohar.[63]
Dov Ber invokes the notion of two Gardens of Eden, one higher and one
lower, as a metaphor for different modalities of engaging Torah. An ever-
flowing river of inspiration (see Gen. 2:10), associated with the *sefirah binah*,
flows forth from the realm of *hokhmah* and irrigates the letters of Torah with
God's vitality. This slakes the thirst of the one studying the words of Scripture, but such study still represents a lower level, for the scholar is but a passive recipient of the inspiration. One who journeys back into the headwaters
of *hokhmah*, however, will attain a higher rung of spiritual awakening: "The
'upper Garden of Eden' refers to one who studies and arrives at great depths.
The idea (*sevara*) is so sublime that he knows that he cannot understand.
It is the most sublime—in his mind, it 'runs and retreats' (Ezek. 2:14) [i.e., it
cannot ever be grasped in full]. Yet he delights (*mit'aden*) in the depth of the
idea, though it is too subtle to be expressed in letters. It is a voice (*kol*)[64]
that cannot be conveyed with any letter (*ot*)." Through cultivating an attitude of awe before the sublime mystery, the scholar reaches into divine wisdom itself and attains a moment of total rapture in encountering the sweep
of *hokhmah* beyond the limits of language or active cognition. In peering into
this abyss, the scholar delights in his own unknowing even as he is overwhelmed by majesty. This stage of transcending the intellect and stretching
beyond words is only temporary, however, for the contemplative attains a still
greater level of knowledge as he translates the insights of his ineffable encounter into the structures of language.

We should remember that the Hebrew word for "letter" (*ot*) may also
refer to a "sign," a semantic gesture that alludes to the worlds beyond language. Scripture, says the Maggid, is infinite just as the infinite Divine;
therefore, the journey to understand and interpret Torah is a quest without
end.[65] When approached correctly, the practice of *Torah lishmah* will open
the mind of the scholar and transform his intellect into a channel through
which divine *hokhmah* gushes forth: "The Torah is endless (*ein sof*), for the
Torah and Holy One are one. So too will [the properly attuned scholar] earn
'many words' (*devarim harbeh*)[66]—the depths of the Torah—flowing forth like
a river constantly and without interruption."[67]

The notion that *Torah lishmah* is rewarded with rushing streams of inspiration is found in the rabbinic sources quoted by the Maggid. His innovation, however, lies in the explanation for why this is so: such a scholar links his mind to the infinite source of language in the Divine, thus channeling a torrent of new interpretations of Torah that veritably flood the mind. These ideas spill forth from *kadmut ha-sekhel*, the precognizant region of God's mind and the human intellect, as well as from the divine wisdom concealed within every word of the Torah itself. This deeper, preconscious level of mind meets the same level—called *sod* or *penimiyyut*—within Torah, since both the human mind and the Torah text are manifestations of the multi-tiered *sefirotic* universe within God. Both soul and Torah are cast in the divine image, as it were. As like finds like and the words of the text echo within the heart and mind of the worshipper, together they journey back to the source.

Creativity, the Origin of Ideas, and Religious Law

The priority assigned to *hiddushim*, or novel interpretations of Torah, is a critical element of the Maggid's approach to devotional study. The deepest power of sacred learning is found not in the memorization or recitation of canonical texts, says the Maggid, but in the generation of new ideas. The quest to summon up *hiddushim* may entail reading the same sacred texts with a fresh sense of vitality and inspiration, thus imbuing threadbare texts with additional life-force while drawing forth new meaning from the well of potential.[68] In some instances, he describes *hiddushim* as a divine gift, coming upon the scholar like an unexpected spark of intuition. In other teachings, Dov Ber refers to a creative interpretation as the hard-won result that emerges after a prolonged period of diligent and devoted study. The sublime flashes of illumination that are the core of creativity, whether spontaneous or deliberate, are then formulated into language by the cognitive mind and the "letters of thought." Only after this can they be spoken aloud and conveyed to another. The Maggid often compares such generative creativity through the unfolding of language to God's formation of the world, but, as with all elements of study, it also reenacts the sacred process through which God's ineffable wisdom was translated into language at Sinai.[69]

This link between the emergence of the Torah and the processes of human creativity is crucial. Indeed, as noted, Dov Ber refers to sacred study as recreating the Sinai theophany, further suggesting that one who approaches

Torah with a contemplative mind will continue to hear the voice of God in the present. The echo chamber for this reverberation, suggests the Maggid, is the voice of the scholar as he intones the sacred words:

> I heard the following from my teacher [the Maggid]: ". . . if you listen, [hearkening to My voice]" (Ex. 19:5). As you listen, meaning that you understand and pay attention to the words, even to *your* words—when you pray or study with great attachment and additional discernment (*binah yeterah*), then "you shall hear My voice"—it will be as if I am speaking to you.[70]
>
> From amidst your words you will understand great and awesome secrets of Torah in each letter and vowel. [This will happen] very quickly, [so fast] that it is impossible for the simple mortal mind to understand it. This is the meaning of "and now"—by means of your attachment, "if you listen, you will hear My voice."[71]

The scholar must focus on the words of study or worship, intending to hear the divinity garbed in human language. The inspiration and "great and awesome secrets" attained through such efforts, which fill even the semantic fundaments of the scriptural text, are divine recompense for the student's attention. So powerful and vital that they transcend the cognitive boundaries of the human mind, the *hiddushim* rush forth from *kadmut ha-sekhel* so rapidly that they cannot be fully understood in the moment. Attunement to the inner divinity of such language thus generates an outpouring of creative vitality, suggesting that, in some sense, revelation stretches beyond the one-time event of Sinai and into the present.[72]

The Maggid's teachings identify the origins of *hiddushim* in the realm of *kadmut ha-sekhel*. In an extended homily exploring the translation of thought into spoken language, Dov Ber notes:

> The first *bet* [i.e., the initial letter] of the Torah includes all of the following letters, for the first letter is the general [principle] of that which one then wishes to speak about. All of the particulars are rooted in this initial general rule, but they exist only in the pre-cognizant mind (*kadmut ha-sekhel*), the *hyle* or *yod*.
>
> We ourselves see this in a person who suddenly attains some idea or knowledge. He thinks about it afterward in his mind,

[considering] many things that were hidden from him. This idea that occurred to him was drawn forth from the pre-cognizant mind.[73]

New interpretations of Torah, like all creativity, emerge from the very deepest recesses of the human mind. *Hiddushim* may be consciously drawn from this reservoir, but *kadmut ha-sekhel* is the fountain of creativity without the structures or linguistic frameworks necessary for purposeful intellection. Like the first letter of the Torah, associated in earlier Kabbalah with the *sefirot* of *hokhmah* and *binah*, an idea is unformed and incomprehensible in and of itself, though it is the seed that contains all the future unfolding. The flash of inspiration or awareness must be turned over and considered at length before it can be communicated.

The Maggid's teachings reveal an ongoing tension regarding whether *hiddushim* are the result of spontaneous inspiration, or of sustained and purposeful study. Dov Ber's homilies outline two different modes of intellection. According to the first, the scholar begins by taking up a specific text and achieves a measure of inspired creativity only after engaging with its words and bringing them into his mind. But the Maggid also notes that a sudden flash of inspiration may occur to a scholar before opening the book or beginning to recite the text: "If an idea (*sekhel*) suddenly occurs to someone,[74] and he does not know what to do with it, he should begin to clarify it. He contradicts it, and then stands it up once more, breaking down [the idea] and then building it up. [This is] the secret of 'touching and not touching,'[75] [which continues] until he fashions a garment and a contracted vessel for the idea."[76] Religious inspiration, argues the Maggid, does not always begin with a text. An idea may be the result of spontaneous generation, a divine gift bestowed on the student or scholar in a moment of loving grace. God thus delivers *hiddushim* into the mind of the devoted worshipper as a token of divine affection. In at least one teaching the Maggid suggests that one who is firmly bound up with God has no need to struggle painfully for new interpretations of Torah; such a person simply repeats what the Divine has whispered in the hushed murmurs of his contemplative mind.[77]

By contrast, many of the Dov Ber's other homilies describe creativity as a moment of inspired liberation at the culmination of an extended and challenging process. One begins to study by engaging the passions in loving reverence before the Divine, opening up a sacred book and looking to find the Creator expressed through the words spelled out across the page.[78] The initial moments may be smooth, but soon enough such a person will be confronted by the difficulties of the text. "What should one do?" queries the Maggid. "One must fall silent in his study and begin to contemplate within the mind (be-mahashavah) . . . bringing [inward] the words that he could have spoken [aloud]."[79] Instead of releasing one's words in vocalized study, the Maggid recommends that one raise language to its root in the mind through a moment of temporary contemplative silence.[80] The Maggid continues: "This matter is wondrous and clear. If one cannot understand something, he begins to think about it and through this a thought suddenly occurs to him; the idea strikes him like a lightning bolt of sudden illumination.[81] This idea comes from the pre-cognizant mind (kadmut ha-sekhel)."[82] This spark of illumination, here associated with hokhmah, enlightens the scholar's mind and clears away the seemingly insurmountable difficulties in the text. But, adds the Maggid, the idea remains a "simple" or "unformed" idea (sekhel pashut), an inchoate flare of understanding, until the scholar finds the words with which to describe and expand it. This contemplative process sparks a momentary flash of inspiration, verily described by the Maggid as a bolt of lightning. One searching for an answer is thus enjoined to clear a passage of communication by turning his faculty for language into a bridge spanning the depths of his preconscious mind and the regions of active cognition. Then, after the initial glow of the idea has been broadcast through the linguistic structures of the mind, the scholar returns to speech through vocalized study and even communicating the hiddush to others. The creative process, thus construed, takes place in the return to the origins of speech and beyond. But the formerly perplexed scholar, now confident with the idea that has emerged from this extended creative process, must reveal it through spoken words and release the internalized energy.

The Maggid frequently notes that hiddushim are not the work of a moment. The human mind, he says, naturally flows freely from one thought to another; it drifts hither and thither without alighting upon a single subject, question, or issue.[83] Focusing on a particular idea for an extended period of time requires much concentration, which the Maggid describes as a type of tsimtsum in both senses of the word. Contemplative study requires that the scholar withdraw from all distractions, be they earthly or conceptual, and simultaneously focus the totality of his mind on a single difficulty or problem arising from the text. Only such attention may elicit a burst of inspiration, powerful though vague and undeveloped until it begins to be filtered through the medium of language. Yet this lengthy process, which translates the primary fodder of the preintellect into the cognitive mind (*hokhmah* into *binah*, or *mahashavah*, in the Maggid's *sefirotic* terminology), represents only a partial revelation of the scholar's creativity; both stages take place within the mind of a single individual. Only as the idea moves into the realm of voiced sound and articulated speech (*kol* and *dibbur*) do *hiddushim* reach their fullest expression.

This understanding roots creativity in the deepest recesses of the mind, a realm where, as we have seen, the boundaries between human and Divine are quite thin. The delicacy—and permeability—of this separation is critically important in those homilies that describe *hiddushim* as a divine gift. In one such sermon, the Maggid claims that the Divine, like a loving teacher or parent, cannot bear to stand idly by and watch someone struggle forevermore with a textual quandary:

> A parable about a son beloved by his father. Once a guest came to test him, but the son could not understand the *halakhah* [of the test] at all because of its great depth and sharpness. But on account of his great love for the child, the father could not bear his beloved son's pain from encountering such great difficulty.
>
>   What did the father do? He gave him a hint[84] about the *halakhah*, showing him the path upon which to walk and demonstrating how to discursively "give and take"; he very nearly told him all the contents of the *halakhah*.[85]

The child, continues the Maggid, astounds the guest with his knowledge of the subject, "correctly answering and dismantling (*mefarek*) [the questions] with his clarified and illuminated intellect." Such skilled demonstrations fill the father with delight, although he recognizes that he is the ultimate origin of the child's ability. The guest redoubles his efforts in an attempt to stump the child, but the child, "trusting his father, became independently inspired (*hit'orer me-'atsmo*) and, growing wise, explained all the questions."

Hiddushim, thus construed, are a divine gift bestowed on an embattled or immature scholar whose devotional yearnings have outpaced his ability to unpack the meaning of a source. That God is the source of the scholar's initial inspiration does not diminish the divine joy in seeing such an individual succeed in his studies. But the thrust of the Maggid's parable shifts significantly toward the end. The child remains secure in believing that the parent can help, but he no longer needs to receive explicit instructions. As the child has grown wiser and more self-reliant, his scholastic abilities have now matured. He can now generate his own solutions to the textual or conceptual difficulties that emerge from his studies. Building on the classic Zoharic concept of it'aruta de-le-tata or the "arousal from below" in which God delights, the Maggid notes that this final independent and creative mode of study brings the Divine infinitely more joy than the mere parroting with which the parable began.

This fascinating ambiguity regarding the origin of ideas brings us to a related point: several of the Maggid's sermons describe hiddushim as concepts or ideas concealed within the Torah, or even within the divine mind itself:

> As soon as the notion of Israel arose in the divine mind, God was already deriving joy and pleasure from the deeds of each tsaddik. . . . The sages said, "Everything a faithful student is ever to say was already given in the law of Moses at Sinai." God said to Moses: "Thus will scholar so-and-so innovate in that generation."[86]
>
> The teachings and deeds of each tsaddik give pleasure and delight to our blessed God. This is the sort of love and joy brought about in the parent by the child's power. This is what the Zohar means when it says that "Israel sustain their Father in heaven."[87] This is like the parent being given joy by that beloved child. In the fullness of pleasure the parent may cry out: "I am made strong and healthy by this pleasure!" So it is with the blessed Holy One: the pleasure is so great, it is as though they were sustaining Him!
>
> This is also the meaning of "I was (va-ehyeh) His nursling, His pleasure day by day" (Prov. 8:30). RaSHI explains that the Torah [or "wisdom," the subject of this verse] grew up in God's bosom for two thousand years before creation. But the simple meaning of this verse claims that wisdom was God's nursemaid or teacher. It is difficult even to say this. Isn't God the First of all firsts?
>
> But we can understand it in our way. Torah prides herself on being God's teacher, as it were. This refers to the great pleasure God derives from Torah, from the teachings of each and every tsaddik and the good things each one does. These are the commandments that make up the Torah; this becomes a nursing and sustenance for God.[88]

The *hiddushim* of later sages were included in the original Sinai revelation. Moreover, like the Torah itself, these creative interpretations existed as hidden potential concealed within the divine wisdom undergirding the primordial Scripture of creation. Study and worship bring God pleasure even before they transpire in the physical world, for linear time and temporality itself are utterly inapplicable to the Divine.[89] This suggests that all *hiddushim* existed within the heart of Torah long before they were "revealed" by later sages, whose role is one of cosmic disclosure rather than fundamental creativity.

Hiddushim bring delight to God, and this pleasure, says the Maggid, is mutual.[90] There is a theurgic element in the Maggid's conception of Torah study, for *hiddushim* unify the *sefirot* of *hokhmah* and *binah*, creating a generative flow of blessing into the mind of the scholar.[91] The Maggid often underscores that *hiddushim*, like *Torah lishmah*, transform the worshipper. Employing an image drawn from the conceptual world of Safed Kabbalah, one of the Maggid's teachings claims that every new interpretation of Torah becomes a *makif,* an encompassing light that surrounds the person in whom it originated.[92] This radiant aura may even be communicated to others, sparking a chain reaction of joy that begins within the individual human heart and extends forth to other people as it is communicated in language. Elsewhere the Maggid extends this notion to language more broadly, saying that one becomes enveloped in the cloud of illumination formed by each word spoken with devotional longing and truth.[93]

The Maggid describes the act of Torah study as a way of entering into a realm of conceptual freedom that renews the scholar. The primordial Torah is rooted in the highest *sefirot*, beyond the realm of *shevirah* or "cosmic brokenness." Its words, therefore, grant one access to the spiritual plane beyond sickness, death, and exile, allowing the scholar to enter regions of the Godhead in which divine unity of the *sefirot* was never fractured: "One who enters Torah, where there is no brokenness, becomes totally free."[94] Entering this realm of spiritual renaissance, found in the innermost reaches of the text and the self, requires the correct contemplative attunement. In doing so the scholar may reach through the limited linguistic garb that Scripture currently occupies and go to the deepest place of Torah in *hokhmah* and *binah* and, like Moses, shepherd forth a new host of meanings and inspiration.

These sermons, and many others like them, demonstrate that the Maggid attributes tremendous power to human creativity and exegetical agency.

He often underscores that the *tsaddikim* actually shape God's thoughts, determining—and even overturning—the divine will.[95] Dov Ber's more radical formulations describe righteous individuals as "teaching" God what to do.[96] Rather than angering God, however, this demonstration of independence brings Him great pleasure:

> The sages taught: "the righteous perform (*'osim*) the will of God."[97] They did not say, "perform His word or utterance." Now, of course the blessed One's Will cannot be grasped.
>
> A parable: a father articulates some point of *halakhah* or new interpretation of Torah to his son. The son can contradict his father's words, because of his sharpness and erudition. The child opposes his father by arguing against him, but the father is delighted and filled with great joy, as in [the verse], "become wise, my son, and gladden my heart" (Prov. 27:11).[98] The parent desires this much more than if [the child] remained in silent agreement with his words.
>
> So too, the *tsaddikim* rule [through] fear of God, as it were.[99] This is: "they make the will of God"[100] rather than "perform His word or utterance."[101]

Reinterpreting the word "perform" as "make" (both *'osim*), the Maggid argues that *tsaddikim* form God's will through textual reasoning and logic. Their interpretations may oppose God's initial desire, but such exhibitions of exegetical independence that invert the divine will actually bring Him great joy. God, it seems, delights in the interpretive liberty rendered—or relinquished—to human beings.[102]

The Maggid's parable about the child whose exegesis contradicts that of his parent thus delivers us to the boundary of hermeneutical freedom. *Hiddushim* emerge from the sages' gift of reinterpreting the divine writ anew in each generation. Although some of Dov Ber's homilies describe them as coming from God, many of the Maggid's sermons emphasize that *hiddushim* in fact create the divine will because righteous individuals use the letters of Torah, the fundamental building blocks of all language both human and divine, exactly as they wish.[103]

We should ask, however, if the Maggid also extends this interpretive freedom to the realm of Jewish law. Sources extolling theological freedom and exegetical creativity that do not change the practices of *halakhah* are relatively common in rabbinic scholarship as well as Jewish mystical litera-ture.[104] The words of Torah, says the Maggid, are an inexhaustible wellspring of new ideas waiting to be revealed by human scholarship. But does he be-lieve in a single ideal *halakhah* to which all worshippers are beholden, or might there be an infinite number of possible and equally valid legal interpreta-tions as well? Do the *tsaddikim* have the power to refashion Jewish law, cre-ating an alternative *halakhah* in line with the goals of spiritual life? These questions are critical both in light of the nearly limitless creativity the Maggid allows (and even demands) in interpreting Scripture, and the au-thority he accords the *tsaddikim* who evidently determine God's will.

I have elsewhere argued that the Maggid and his students did indeed extend the license of human creativity into the realm of *halakhah* in addi-tion to homiletics—at least theoretically.[105] Social and intellectual commit-ments prevented wholesale change, of course, but we should underscore that the complex relationship between Hasidism and Jewish law does not rise or fall on the question of legal change. Hasidism looked to reinfuse the struc-tures and rituals of rabbinic Judaism with devotional meaning. This meant using the classical *mitsvot*—with some variations—in order to cultivate and further the inner spiritual quest of the individual.

These sermons on the nature and function of Jewish law suggest that scholars must fundamentally rethink the relationship between Hasidism and *halakhah*. Spirituality and law are often juxtaposed as opposing forces in the religious life of devotion: the spirit inspires the mystic to new levels of inti-macy with God, while the nomos restrains and binds him to the norms of a particular community. This binary framing, while perhaps reflective of some religious thinkers, is unsatisfactory for explaining the place of law in Ha-sidic piety. Many members of the Maggid's circle were deeply immersed in the world of *halakhah*, and they offered a vision in which nomos, eros, and mystical piety often merged in distinctive ways, and that these are visible in novel forms of Jewish legal method and discourse.

A few salient illustrations of Dov Ber's thinking on this subject will suf-fice for the present discussion, which focuses on the Maggid's theory of language rather than his relationship to *halakhah*. In one homily, the Mag-gid interprets the Talmudic dictum "These and those are the words of the living God"[106] as instructing that any ruling on a specific point of law may be changed by returning it to its source in the supernal realm—the highest seat of concrete human knowledge—and drawing forth another conclusion.[107] Another tradition has the Maggid suggesting that the legal creativity of the

Talmudic sage Rabbi Meir stemmed from his access to *kadmut ha-sekhel*, "the world that flows into *hokhmah*."[108]

Despite this dazzling brilliance, however, the *halakhah* is not generally formulated in accord with his opinion. This is noted in the rabbinic sources, which explain that his colleagues could not fully grasp his decisions,[109] but the Maggid offers a more kabbalistic explanation regarding why the *halakhah* is not decided in accord with Rabbi Meir. Dov Ber argues that his soul was rooted in a realm beyond the origins of *halakhah*, which deals with specifics and particularities. Therefore, Rabbi Meir's brilliant dialectics are a lens through which he projects wisdom that flows from a creative font beyond the discursive logic that defines Jewish law and its formulation.

The Maggid's extended teachings on creativity and *halakhah* have much to do with our discussion of language. In one sermon, he notes that the primordial Torah exists—continuously—in abstract unity within the divine mind. Scripture takes on a recognizable linguistic and legal form only as it is translated through the lower *sefirot* and enters our world. The plurality of different opinions regarding any point of *halakhah* represents this emergence from ineffable abstraction into the structures of language. The oral Torah, says the Maggid, is an approach to legal dialectics that by its very nature encourages multiplicity rather than conformity or harmony, seeking to identify multiple viewpoints and preserve their integrity whenever possible. He notes that God delights in this quest for new ideas, yet the Maggid seems bothered by the possibility that human interpretation may lead sages to decide the *halakhah* contrary to what exists in the pure or ideal Torah on high:

> How can the *tsaddikim* use their reasoning to come up with something that is against the Torah above?
>
> It is as we have elsewhere explained. "The *tsaddik* rules by the fear of God" (2 Sam. 23:3)[110]—because of the greatness of his connection to God, the *tsaddik*'s will is the Will of the blessed One. Just as we have seen the supernatural miracles performed by *tsaddikim*, who decree and the blessed Holy One fulfills, the same is true here. Because they were so deeply attached to the blessed One, Joshua said that we pay no mind to a heavenly voice.[111] The Torah has already been given to Israel, meaning that it is from our perspective. It says, "to incline after the majority" (Ex. 23:2). If so, we must follow these positions, since certainly the Torah [as we

see it] from our perspective includes dialectics. We are the
majority, and we have the power to transform the combination [of
the letters] above so that the *halakhah* follows us.

This is [the meaning of]: do not read "ways" (*halikhot*) but
"laws" (*halakhot*).[112] Those below have the power to change the
"cosmic ways" above, so that they are like the laws that we have
decided. This is [the meaning] of the statement, "My children
have defeated me," by changing the combination [of the letters of
the heavenly judgment] to agree with them. "He smiled," since
God receives great pleasure and delight from this, as it were.[113]

Earlier in this same teaching Dov Ber implies that there are ideal—or perhaps even correct—interpretations of Scripture to which all other *hiddushim*
are compared: "One who learns with fiery passion, great joy and attachment
to the blessed One, will certainly align his words to their truest sense."[114]
Yet in this suggestion he argues that there can be no intractable gap between the supernal Torah and its manifestations in the world of language
because the heavenly Scripture changes in accord with the ruling of the
earthly sages. This suggests that there cannot be a single, ideal manifestation of *halakhah*—be it that of the natural world or the divine Will—to which
all legal decisions must conform, for the preexistent Torah shifts, as it were,
in response to the rulings of the *tsaddikim*.[115] Thus the primordial Torah,
which remains abstract, fluid, and bursting with an infinite number of possibilities, is not entirely prelinguistic or devoid of specific content. The wisdom held within God's mind is indeed home to some combinations of letters,
which mirror those established by human scholars.

The Maggid did not serve as an official judicator of *halakhah*, either in a
court or in written decisions. But a significant number of his students were
scholars steeped in traditional works of Jewish law, writing important texts
on law and deciding cases of *halakhah* in the decades after the Maggid's
death. The presence of traditions about the nature and function of Jewish
law in the Maggid's teachings suggests that the question of practice and the
boundaries of human creativity was of critical importance to the Maggid
and his circle. These texts, which offer an interesting way of conceptualiz-
ing Jewish law, are part of a theological worldview in which the changes in
halakhah are part of a much broader project of renewal and creative reinterpretation of canonical texts. These sermons suggest that the Maggid offered
his students new ways of thinking about the system of *halakhah* and how its

laws had been determined thus far, though they do not necessarily represent an engine for change in making future legal decisions.

Dov Ber's emphasis on exegetical creativity is, no doubt, part of his inheritance from the legacy of rabbinic scholarship and kabbalistic exegesis, but it also reflects the quest for personal renewal that dwells at the heart of Hasidic spirituality.[116] As a pietistic and mystical revival movement, Hasidism sought to infuse timeworn practices, religious texts, and concepts with devotional significance that is at once old and new. The ideal Hasid strives to perform all deeds with total devotion, yearning to fulfill the divine command with focus and intensity rather than out of rote obligation. The Baal Shem Tov is remembered as interpreting the psalmist's words, "Do not cast us into old age" (Ps. 71:9) as a soulful petition: may our service never become stale, and may our sacred actions and words never fade into old shells empty of meaning.[117] This tireless quest for perpetual newness, held as an aspiration for communities as well as private individuals, is as old as Hasidism itself.

Speaking Torah and the Boundaries of Language

Thus far we have explored the Maggid's presentation of Torah study as a mystical practice. At this point we may pivot, approaching the issue from a different perspective and examining his descriptions of how spiritual ideas may be transmitted from a teacher to the student. Language represents a unique nexus between God and man in the Maggid's theology; words and letters are a concrete medium in which the infinite divine wisdom may become expressed. Extending this principle into the human realm, the Maggid also refers to language as a channel necessary for the exchange of ideas between two people. Dov Ber is keenly alert to the fact that one's thoughts can never be fully expressed in words. Wisdom, whether human or divine, is attenuated, diminished, and transformed as it becomes articulated in language.

Key to this is Dov Ber's description of the teacher's relationship to his student as parallel to that of God and the *tsaddik*. The divine mind contracted into language and poured itself through the "funnel" of words and letters so that they may inhabit the thoughts of the worshipper. We should remember that the Jewish God is often described as a teacher, an image captured succinctly in the rabbinic blessing recited before study: "Blessed are

You . . . Who teaches Torah to His people Israel."[118] In the Talmudic imag-ination, God's teachings are, of course, Scripture and the ever-expanding discourse stemming from it. The Kabbalists describe the Teacher as both embodied in the sacred text but also hovering just beyond the endpoints of the letters. God's Wisdom has been—and is continuously—contracted into these words, a revelatory act of self-limitation that allows the listeners and readers of the divine writ to pierce through the language and reclaim the sacred vitality within its boundaries.

Much recent scholarship has focused on the Hasidic sermon as an event and an exegetical experience.[119] Hasidic sources often compare the emergence of these teachings, often in a deeply spiritual atmosphere during the third Sabbath meal, to the giving of the Torah at Sinai. And in Hasidic texts *tsad-dikim* are not described simply as delivering a homily, but as quite literally "speaking Torah"—the words of the master thus represent a new stage in divine revelation and the constant unfolding of the divine word.[120] One par-ticularly well-known and oft-quoted tradition preserved by a disciple of the Maggid offers some personal reflections on how one may prepare himself for this moment:

> Once I heard the Maggid say to us explicitly, "I will teach you the best way to speak Torah. You must not sense yourself as anything at all. Be a listening ear attuned to the way the World of Speech is speaking in you, for you yourself are not speaking. As soon as you hear your own words, stop."
>
> We saw this many times. When he [the Maggid] opened his mouth to speak, it was as if he was not of this world at all. *Shekhi-nah* was speaking from within his throat.[121] Sometimes he would stop and wait for a while, even in the middle of an idea or a word.[122]

In order to correctly "speak Torah," claims the Maggid, the preacher must transcend the confines of the self. Any residual self-awareness interferes with the flow of divine wisdom through his mind, and, more specifically, prevents *shekhinah* from being able to speak from within him. Once more we find the Maggid invoking the familiar symbol of the World of Speech, the divine in-dwelling within the human in the form of language; only through arousing this sacred capacity for language can the human preacher truly begin to "speak Torah." Evidently Ze'ev Wolf of Zhitomir, the student in whose work this tradition is preserved, witnessed Dov Ber do this on many occasions.

The Maggid's teachings reveal him to be a contemplative and introspective mystic. They consistently outline a spiritual journey in which the worshipper begins with letters and words, moving through the physical sounds of speech to the innermost reaches of the conscious mind and heart and eventually arriving at a sublime realm beyond words. It thus comes as no surprise that we find teachings that underscore the difficulty of speaking in public. An interesting tradition from Yisra'el of Kozhenits, to which we briefly referred earlier, reads as follows: "We received [the following teaching] from our teacher and master [the Maggid]: At times the *tsaddik* is connected to the upper worlds in his mind. He cannot open his mouth to share a teaching (*halakhah*) with them [i.e., his students], descending from his level to theirs. Therefore, they must prepare the way and open the channel with their questions or other such things."[123] A teacher, notes the Maggid, may become so enraptured by his own contemplative meditation that the ability to converse with others melts away. When all of the master's energy is focused inward, he is left with no points of connection to his community of students. His disciples can inspire their master to begin speaking, but this type of communication is described as a sort of spiritual "descent" for the teacher who must cut short his meditative journey in order to share his wisdom with others.

Other homilies of the Maggid claim that one who is engaged in speaking cannot listen to voices either human or divine; therefore, such a person cannot understand or receive any new interpretations of Torah from the heavenly streams of inspiration.[124] Teaching disciples, thus depicted, comes at the expense of the master's own intellectual and spiritual creativity. More fundamentally, the Maggid argues that anyone who truly understands the breadth and subtlety of an idea must also realize that it cannot really be spoken aloud or communicated to another in all of its brilliance or glory.[125] Thoughts originate in the dynamic realm of *hokhmah*—the unformed and prelinguistic potential of ideas—and only once they have come into *binah*—the region of conscious intellection—can they be translated into words and then conveyed to others. A flash of creativity retains its luster only within the mind in which it was originally conceived. Inspiration, by its very nature, cannot ever be fully communicated.[126]

And yet, as we have noted throughout this book, the Maggid repeatedly returns to the conclusion that worshippers and teachers alike must embrace language. It is not enough for such individuals to remain in silent contemplation in the deepest recesses of their mind. One sermon compares teaching to giving birth, whereas silence and solitary contemplation are likened to tragic infertility.[127] In some instances, this use of language seems primarily utilitarian: a master must speak to his students in order to instruct them, offering constructive rebuke and shepherding their religious growth.[128] But the Maggid avers that all acts of revelation, both human and divine, take place in language; spiritual instruction can be accomplished only through words. Dov Ber describes speaking and teaching as far more than purely selfless acts in which the master sacrifices his own intellectual growth in order to help his students. The *tsaddik*, claims the Maggid, receives from this communication as well; new elements of divine wisdom and secrets of Torah flow through his mind when he connects to the people around him.[129]

The mandate for a teacher to share his wisdom through language does not change the fact that spoken words cannot convey the fullness of his thoughts. But this limitation is also what allows for communication to take place. A master's knowledge can be so great that it would totally overwhelm the student, were he to reveal it all at once; therefore, he must contract his wisdom by focusing it into words.[130] In one sermon, we read:

> "A teacher should always teach his student succinctly" (*derekh
> ketserah*).[131] If a master wants his disciple to understand his
> expansive wisdom, but the student cannot receive it [in its current
> form], the teacher must focus his mind (*metsamtsem sikhlo*) into
> words and letters. For example, when one wants to pour some-
> thing from one vessel into another and is afraid lest it spill, he
> uses another vessel called a funnel (*mashpekh*). The liquid is
> contracted into it, and therefore the [second] vessel can receive
> without any of it spilling outside.
>
> The matter is just the same with a teacher whose intellect is
> contracted into words and letters. He speaks them to the student,
> and through them the student can receive the master's expansive
> mind.[132]

A teacher must constrict his wisdom into words if he is to transmit something of it to his students. This is the Maggid's interpretation of instructing one's disciples "succinctly," cleverly reading the Talmudic phrase *derekh ketsarah* as "by way of contraction." Like creation and the emergence of Torah from divine silence at Sinai, the teacher's embrace of language is an act of *tsimtsum* undertaken because of love for others. The teacher must bring forth ideas from his mind and garb them in spoken language so that they may be absorbed by his students. In order to explain this dynamic, the Maggid offers the image of pouring water through a funnel; the vessel constricts the stream of the liquid, but enables its seamless transfer into a second receptacle. Thus, the teacher's letters and words form a linguistic channel through which his wisdom may flow into the mind of the student.

The brief passage above is taken from a longer sermon on creation and the ways in which divine wisdom is embodied in physical reality, a major concern in the Maggid's theology. Dov Ber offers the story of the teacher and his student, and then the image of the funnel, as parables for illuminating these cosmic processes. Indeed, throughout his teachings the Maggid frequently emphasizes the central importance of the parable (*mashal*, pl. *meshalim*) as one of the teacher's most important tools for overcoming the inherent limits of language.[133] Of course, the *mashal* has an important pedagogical and rhetorical role in rabbinic literature,[134] the works of medieval philosophy,[135] and especially classical kabbalistic texts.[136] Parables are a central feature of many early Hasidic homilies.[137] But, as scholar Aryeh Wineman has demonstrated, they are particularly critical in the Maggid's sermons, almost all of which employ *meshalim* in some form.[138] Of these, the image of a father and a child or a student and his master are by far the most common. If all words are a type of vessel for ideas and meaning, the parable is the linguistic vessel par excellence, and for this reason parables are one of a preacher's greatest assets. A few brief examples will allow us to illustrate the Maggid's understanding of the nature of *meshalim* and their significance in the process of teaching through language.

In the midst of a homily about the manner in which the *sefirot hokhmah* and *binah* unfold out of the expanse of *keter*, the Maggid returns to the question of how human knowledge (also *hokhmah*) may be transmitted from one person to another. He explains:

> By means of a parable: a father wishes to help his child under-
> stand some matter of wisdom, but the child cannot understand
> this wisdom as it is, in all of its profound depth. The father must
> instruct him by means of a parable, and through this he [the
> child] can reach the wisdom itself. Looking at this carefully, we
> can see that the father himself is wise and understanding. The
> letters and the idea of the parable are extraneous, since he knows
> the wisdom without the parable.

But the child forces the father [to use] the letters and the idea of the parable. For the child's sake, the father grafts the element of supernal wisdom onto the letters and new idea of the *mashal*. The wisdom is hidden within the parable. The child imbibes (*yonek*) from the letters and the idea of the parable until he understands the *mashal* quite well. Then, if the child is wise, by means of the parable he can grasp the wisdom. The letters of the *mashal* are conduits through which the waters of supernal wisdom flow.[139]

The father's wisdom is too expansive for his child to grasp without an intermediary. He must therefore imbue his ideas into a vessel—in this case, a parable—so that they may be understood. But this limitation is not permanent. By plumbing the depths of his father's words and looking beyond the simple meaning of the parable, the son can actually recover the wisdom that lies concealed deeply within. Elsewhere the Maggid notes that teachers or homilists must clothe their ideas in simple explanations and stories. These straightforward words engage the listener and allow him to receive the master's teachings, struggling with them and eventually coming to attain the wisdom just as it once existed in their teacher's mind.[140]

In another sermon, a homily describing the Lurianic notion that the lowest level of a higher world becomes revealed as the uppermost element of the world below it,[141] the Maggid offers the following remarks:

To make this more understandable, let us give the parable of a master instructing his student. The teacher's wisdom is unfathomably great, and moreover, it is sealed away and hidden within his mind. Surely the disciple cannot comprehend it. A student can only grasp the words that he hears from the master's mouth. And even so, if he does not train his mind upon the teacher's words, he cannot receive [even those] words. Therefore, the words spoken by the teacher, which are the lowest level [i.e., the lowest expression of his wisdom], enter into the mind of the student, meaning his cognitive vitality (*mohin*).

At the beginning of his studies, the disciple absorbs the words just as they are. But as he grows wiser, the teacher can explain the matter with greater complexity—its continuation and meaning. Yet the inner essence, the hidden wisdom, can neither be grasped by the student nor communicated by the teacher. But

the teacher's act leaves an impression of this sealed wisdom
[within his student]. Since the power of the maker is in the made,
this impression grows and develops, and little by little it expands
in his mind.[142]

A student cannot apprehend the teacher's knowledge in all of its fullness and
intricacy, for as such it remains locked away in the master's mind. Therefore, the teacher must convey his wisdom by contracting it into words, even
though in doing so he diminishes it by withdrawing and focusing the expanse of knowledge into discrete language. These words are within the disciple's threshold of apprehension, but, in Dov Ber's parable, they serve as far
more than a medium or conduit through which the teacher's ineffable wisdom becomes revealed.

The master's language enters into the mind of the disciple and infuses
him with a burst of cognitive inspiration. The master's ideas remain restricted
by the words, but the Maggid's use of the kabbalistic phrase "the power of
the Maker is in the made" reminds us that the teacher's original wisdom
continuously inheres in letters of his speech. The very act of teaching through
language impacts the disciple, revealing at the same moment that it conceals and steadily filling the student's mind with a flare of illumination. The
disciple then continues to mull over the words of his teacher, and his master's ineffable "hidden wisdom" that has been impressed in his mind begins
to awaken and mature.

One of the Maggid's sermons offers a more precise description as to how
an attentive student may set about plumbing the depth of his master's instruction. We read:

> At first [the student] does not consider these words deeply,
> grasping them only according to their simple meaning because of
> his small degree of understanding. However, then he begins to
> take up the content of the matter and turns his mind away from
> everything else. With the fullness of his intellect and his power of
> contemplation he delves into the matter, [immersed in his study]
> to such a degree that he would not answer even if someone calls
> to him. It is almost as if he cannot see something that lies before
> his eyes, for he has diverted his attention so much into the heart
> of the matter. Then he comes to the ultimate understanding and
> truth of the matter.

> This type of removing his mind [from all other things] is
> almost like a type of death or slumber, which is one sixtieth of
> death.[143] All of his vitality ascends above, and through this he
> receives new cognitive vitality (*mohin*), as in "they are renewed
> [i.e., he receives new understanding], each morning [after medita-
> tive 'slumber']" (Lam. 3:23).[144]

The student must divert his attention from all distractions and withdraw
from all physical stimuli if he is to grasp the true profundity of his teachings' words. Only this type of intense concentration allows the contemplative focus necessary for him to understand the meaning of his master's
teaching. We should note, however, that in this passage the Maggid does
not describe the disciple's quest for understanding as receiving or revealing
a hidden element of wisdom that has been embodied within his master's
words. This homily portrays the flood of comprehension as happening within
the student. After he has turned inward and "risen above" language, to employ the vertical metaphor of the homily, the student achieves a new level of
understanding.

The Maggid's understanding of parables informs his own interpretation
of earlier texts. He says quite explicitly that the anthropomorphic language
of Lurianic Kabbalah is a *mashal*, a vocabulary of physical terms used to refer to a divine reality that is spiritual.[145] Furthermore, the Maggid claims
that the entire Torah, even the nonnarrative sections, is composed of parables that communicate divine wisdom.[146] However, he draws a key difference
between the *meshalim* of Scripture and all other parables. In most *meshalim*
the letters and words are only a vessel for the idea within them; they become superfluous once the student has penetrated to their wisdom. The letters of the Torah, however, are intrinsically holy, for they too are saturated
with the divine presence.

These brief examples are indicative of the Maggid's overall approach to
parables, which operate on several simultaneous levels. First, Dov Ber's *meshalim* function on their own as short narratives embedded within his homilies. They are entertaining and illuminating asides that add texture to the
homily as a whole. Second, the Maggid employs parables to illustrate and
embody the message of the homily. In the teachings above, cosmological processes are described through an analogy to the realm of human cognition.
In many cases his parables appear to have a reflexive and self-referential
element. The Maggid often employs a parable in order to demonstrate the

necessity of such pedagogical tools. Third, parables about the art of teaching appear with striking frequency in the Maggid's homilies. These seem to refer to what the Maggid himself is doing. Surely it is no coincidence that the Maggid often employs *meshalim* of master and disciple, or parents educating their children, in explaining the flow of divine energy or spiritual wisdom from one realm to another. This was, after all, the very same task that lay before him, and one perhaps best explained to his listeners through parabolic example.

But might the Maggid's *meshalim* have an additional rhetorical function as well? Parables are often more than a pragmatic technique employed by homilists to entertain their listeners. The pedagogic importance of the closely related phenomenon of metaphors in determining the way we think and experience the world has been analyzed by scholars of philosophy, religion, and linguistics.[147] George Lakoff and Mark Johnson have argued for a particularly close-knit imbrication of metaphorical language and the processes of the mind:

> Since communication is based on the same conceptual system that we use in thinking and acting, language is an important source of evidence for what that system is like. . . .
> The human conceptual system is metaphorically structured and defined. Metaphors as linguistic expressions are possible precisely because they are metaphors in a person's conceptual system.[148]

In most cases, the textual witnesses of the Maggid's teachings are unstable enough that close-knit philological work rests on shaky ground.[149] But skepticism seems less apt when it comes to the many hundreds of parables across Dov Ber's corpus of homilies. These *meshalim* are largely stable, presenting a coherent picture of a spiritual educator committed to the power of language to convey theological truths and religious experience. According to Lakoff and Johnson, the evocative language and metaphorical formulations invoked by such an educator should not be misconstrued as poetic flourishes or reduced as incidental to meaning. Parables and metaphors reflect and construct the processes of human thought, revealing the mind's murmurs in spoken language because the two realms are so intimately intertwined.

The discussion of parables and metaphors returns us once again to the works of Johann Georg Hamann, the Maggid's eighteenth-century contemporary. In considering the stratified development of human art and language, Hamann comments: "Poetry is the mother-tongue of the human race, as the garden is older than the ploughed field; painting, than writing; song, than declamation; parables, than logical declamation. . . . A deeper sleep was the repose of our most distant ancestors. . . . Seven days they would sit in the silence of thought or wonder;—and would open their mouths—to winged sentences."[150] The roots of language are, in some sense, found in the vital parables that predate philosophical investigation. Like poetry and painting, the expressive power of such rhetoric is raised up by the romantic Hamann. And, in Dov Ber's formulation: "Link word to [God's] Word, voice to Voice, breath to Breath, thought to Thought. These are the four letters Y-H-V-H. If one does this, all his words fly upward to their Source. This causes his words to come before the One."[151] Focused contemplation and awareness of the echoes of God's language in all language allow the words of study, prayer, and spiritual education to take wing in their flight home to the Divine.

William Kirkwood has offered some insightful remarks about the parable that will help us understand the Maggid's teachings. He writes that parables "challenge listeners' established beliefs and attitudes, but also evoke in them certain feelings and states of awareness significant in their own right as the ends, not mere means, of religious discipline. The operation of these motives is one of the particularly interesting features of parables as rhetorical devices."[152] Parables are, by most definitions, brief vignettes primarily found in oral teachings, and they function as engines of spiritual self-confrontation. Storytellers, preachers, and religious masters all employ parables to overturn their listener's assumptions and inspire growth, and in some cases, even provoke an experience. In the Hasidic case, there may also be instances where the parabolic form allows the preacher to go farther than he would dare without it, somehow shielding theological radicalism with an approachable form and well-known rhetorical strategy.

The Maggid's teachings called his students to a different type of spiritual consciousness: all being is rooted in the infinite *ayin*, but the silent divine Naught is continuously expressed through the ever-flowing expanse of cosmic language rooted in creation, revelation, and the fundamental process of human intellectual and speech. We might thus add a fourth dimension to the Maggid's usage of parables: they effect change in the student through awakening him to a new awareness of the Divine as manifest in human words. Of course, this does not happen immediately. Like the practice of the Zen koan, the student must work hard in order to contemplate and consider the teaching received from his master.[153] Only then does the ineffable wisdom embedded in the parable blossom and stimulate a fundamental transformation of consciousness in which the student comes to see all language—and all being—as bespeaking the Divine.

"Each According to His Level"

The Maggid understood that a teacher whose disciples have a range of intellectual interests and capabilities must speak to them differently.[154] He notes that God, too, encountered this difficulty, thus giving Israel a multivalent text that is accessible to different readers and seekers. Presumably Dov Ber's own sermons or homilies shifted to meet the needs of his varying audiences; the homilies offered to an intimate group of his disciples would not have been identical to those given in more open public settings. In one sermon, Dov Ber alludes to this issue directly, saying that while a master can reveal more of his expansive wisdom to his advanced students, he must adapt and even diminish his teachings in order to match the abilities of his less accomplished disciples.[155]

However, the Maggid argues that some gifted teachers are able to go beyond the ability to tailor their sermons for different kinds of audiences. The most talented spiritual educators, says the Maggid, can engage every one of their listeners at the very same time by delivering sermons that are sublimely—and intentionally—multivalent.[156] This notion is echoed in Solomon Maimon's experience of the sermon he heard from the Maggid during his brief stay in Mezritsh: "Each of us felt the part of the sermon dealing with his verse contained something referring directly to his own pressing personal concerns. Naturally, we were amazed."[157] Each individual at the Maggid's table came away from the homily with the feeling that he had been personally addressed, even though the sermon itself was the same for all listeners. The task before the homilist, it seems, is to engage with the unique circumstances of different individuals simultaneously. I suspect this phenomenon is grounded in the Maggid's understanding of the nature of language and the process through which teachers convey their ideas. A master focuses his knowledge into words and letters, and this wisdom remains unbounded until it is expressed in specific language. It must then be unpacked by his various students, and the results of these efforts differ from disciple to disciple.

Two important traditions from the Maggid cited by his student Ze'ev Wolf of Zhitomir will shed further light on the means by which a teacher can deliver a single instruction that is appropriate for many students. We read:

> The Maggid offered a parable about someone who travels to a faraway land with his merchandise, etc. There he sees wondrous and elevated things. At the time of the holidays, he returns home and tells his loved ones and relations what his eyes have beheld. Even while on the road, he speaks quite a bit to the people and the community, [telling them] about the wondrous things he has seen, as is the way of the world.
>
> Of course, there are significant differences between the opinions of those who have been listening to his words. Each one [hears them] according to his understanding and the level of his contemplative connection to God. According to this, he inclines his ear to listen and bring forth for himself some hint of wisdom, for "there are no words without the voice being heard, which calls out, 'Turn to the path of Y-H-V-H!'"[158]

This parable seems to represent a thinly veiled autobiographical account of the Maggid's own spiritual journeys.[159] His inward contemplative quest led him into the depths of consciousness and religious inspiration, and, as he returns, the traveler cannot but communicate to others the amazing sights he has witnessed. Rather than becoming stunned into inscrutable silence by his experience, the journeyer into the "faraway land" of the innermost spirit is practically overfilled with words in his joyous desire to share this vision with others. His various listeners, however, each grasp the storyteller's account differently. His students interpret his words through their own epistemological framework, and each of his students extracts a different kernel of wisdom from the same account of the master's journey. This unique message is the "voice," a bit of divine inspiration hovering just within the specific words.

This passage is complemented by another tradition from Ze'ev Wolf, one that is explicitly biographical in its description of the Maggid. He writes:

> Once we were sitting in the Maggid's house, where all sorts of people, young and old, had assembled. He opened his mouth to

speak works of Torah, [saying]: a parable referred to in [the sages'] teaching: a person who has two wives, one young and the other old. The old one plucks his black hairs, the young plucks his white ones, and between the two of them he becomes bald.[160]

So it is with words of Torah. The sages were aroused to say that the Torah was given as black fire on white fire.[161] "Black fire" refers to words of awe, such as ethical instruction (*divrei mussarim*), which applies to the youth who have not yet grasped the secret of Y-H-V-H. They must be frightened by matters of awe and a terrifying whip.[162] "White fire" refers to matters of love, allusions and secrets of Torah that apply to those enlightened people, teaching them the sublime taste of intellectual apprehension of God.

Many people come before the master to ask things of him. Some pull him [in one direction] by asking about awe, a name for black fire. Others inquire after matters of love. Between them all, he becomes "bald"—he cannot speak about anything.

However, if he is an all-encompassing sage (*hakham ha-kolel*),[163] with a broad soul and expansive consciousness, he can bring forth words that are equal before all, [understood by] each according to his rung and understanding. [Each disciple] can find rest for his soul, searching the intention of the master for [the lesson that] applies to his particular divine service.[164]

Many teachers are rendered speechless by an audience of students requiring different—and contradictory—spiritual instruction. A more wide-ranging and expansive master, however, will find the words necessary to inspire each of his disciples in the appropriate way. Rather than being forced to retreat into silence, such a teacher imbues his words with a shimmering spark of radiant wisdom. Building on the plain-sense meaning of the Talmudic story cited by the Maggid, we thus find Dov Ber adding an extra layer of mystical interpretation. The teacher is bringing his ineffable wisdom into language, using the power of words to deliver a single sermon that is fitting for all of his students.

We might wonder, however, if in this case Ze'ev Wof of Zhitomir may have interpreted the Maggid's parable with a rather heavy hand.[165] The Maggid may well have been suggesting to his various students that their many and disparate needs were pulling him in every direction, leaving him exhausted and bare. Such an interpretation fits quite well with the stories depicting Dov Ber as a reluctant teacher and a rather shy, recalcitrant leader scornful of honor and concerned with the spiritual costs of such public ministry. Similar worries surface in some of the Maggid's sermons about the *tsaddik*, which were offered in the third person but likely reflect his own experience. Ze'ev Wolf, confronted with this complicated incident and complex legacy, subtly changes the thrust of the master's words by offering a reading of the parable that both valorizes diversity and emphasizes that great spiritual educators may indeed transcend such dichotomies.

Solomon Maimon and Ze'ev Wolf were not the only ones to remember the Maggid's ability to speak on multiple levels and to diverse audiences at once. A tradition appearing in a work attributed to his great-grandson, Yisra'el of Ruzhin, offers a reflection on this element of Dov Ber's legacy from a slightly later point in the history of Hasidism. We read:

> When the Maggid spoke Torah at the table, his disciples would go over the teaching (*Torah*) as they returned home. This one would say, "I heard the teaching in such a way." Another would say, "I heard it in a different way." Each of them heard it differently.
>
> But I say that is no great surprise, for the Torah has seventy faces. Each student heard the teaching from the Maggid according to his particular face of the Torah.[166]

The Maggid's various students, says Yisra'el, heard the same sermon in different ways. This tradition does not attribute the diverging interpretations of the Maggid's disciples to their individual spiritual attainments. Yisra'el of Ruzhin claims that each student was essentially linked to a particular "face," a distinct way of approaching Torah, and that this connection shaped the manner in which they absorbed the Maggid's teachings.

Words and letters are necessary vessels through which a teacher may communicate his ideas to a student. Dov Ber draws a connection between the revelation of the Torah on Sinai, the moment in which the infinite divine wisdom took on a linguistic garb, and the manner in which the master's *hokhmah* is focused in language so that it might be understood by his disciples. The Maggid acknowledges that a teacher may be so caught up in his own contemplative efforts that it is difficult for him to begin to speak, but he underscores that it is vital for him to do so. A master's words give wisdom to his students, but he too is graced with new insight and inspiration as he begins to teach.

The parable is perhaps the most important medium through which a teacher may focus his wisdom and convey his thoughts to his students. Like all words, these short anecdotes are a necessary linguistic intermediary between the minds of the master and his disciple. Parables articulate ideas in a manner that allows the diligent student to contemplate and interpret them and eventually recover the ineffable wisdom imbued within them. Yet because all communication of ideas requires the master to contract his wisdom into words, his teachings may be interpreted in many different ways. Furthermore, great preachers have the capacity to offer sermons and instructions that are compelling and appropriate for many different students at once. As is revealed in the testimony of the Maggid's disciples, his audiences were at times quite varied. Instead of allowing himself to be shocked into silence, says the Maggid, in cases like this the teacher must garb his wisdom within words in such a way that it may be correctly understood by each and every one of the assembled students.

These traditions offer an image of the Maggid as a leader who addressed a range of different people, not simply a small group of elite disciples.[167] This notion is supported by the variety of teachings attributed to him, which range from short, incisive snippets of spiritual advice to long, complicated, and rather abstract sermons. Furthermore, textual evidence suggests that in some cases several of his disciples wrote down the same teaching. Each of these students did so in his own particular way, capturing different aspects of that sermon.[168] This image of the Maggid as a preacher whose words reach multiple audiences simultaneously may also be reflected in the fact that he attracted nonintellectual figures as well as scholars.[169] A wide variety of people, from talented scholars to spiritual charismatics, were drawn to explore the new vision of the spiritual life flowing forth in Mezritsh. In Dov Ber's teachings each one of them found "something referring directly to his own pressing personal concerns," said Solomon Maimon. "Naturally, we were amazed."

Chapter 7

The Languages of Prayer

At no point in the life of a sacred book is it likely to elicit more
varied responses than when it is being chanted, sung, or recited
in some meaningful context such as that of worship or
meditation.

—William Graham

If thou could'st empty all thyself of self,
Like to a shell dishabited,
Then might He find thee on the ocean shelf,
And say, "This is not dead,"
And fill thee with Himself instead.

—T. E. Browne

The Maggid's understanding of prayer is the heart of his religious vision.[1]
Daily worship is a journey, the path along which one uplifts language to its
root in the mind of God. We have seen his glowing references to sacred
study as an act of spiritual illumination. Dov Ber finds that same light in
prayer, the other verbal art cultivated within classical Judaism. Prayer, however, presents its own challenges. He notes that one may be drawn to Torah
study by the thrill of chasing new ideas. The liturgy, however, is repetitive,
causing some to lose their desire to pray. Dov Ber presents prayer as a singular opportunity for contemplative awakening, self-transcendence, and
spiritual uplift.[2] In worship, says the Maggid, one must strive to "bind and
connect the mind to the blessed Creator," a moment of contemplative unity
with the Divine.[3]

Devekut, cleaving to God in prayer, is attained as the worshipper articulates the words of prayer and concentration. This, taught the Maggid, awakens the divine vitality within the letters of the liturgy. In such moments of illuminated worship, the divine word (*shekhinah* or *'olam ha-dibbur*) speaks through the worshipper, revealing once more that human language embodies the divine quality of sacred speech. Awareness of this power, linguistic as well as contemplative, brings the worshipper to a state of humility and self-transcendence, allowing one to pray for the needs of *shekhinah* instead of his own personal desires.

In his teachings on prayer, the orality of the Maggid's theology of language is once again raised to the fore. Spoken words have the power to draw forth this sacred vitality within the letters, and therefore prayer must be articulated aloud. In rarified moments of contemplative prayer, the mystic may venture beyond words. But this elation is followed closely by the worshipper's return to the structures of language. Only through the medium of words may one's illuminated experience be concretized, expressed, and shared with others. Tracing the language of worship to its roots is an internal, contemplative journey back to its original Source. In doing so the worshipper forges a bridge between the *sefirot*, uniting the Worlds of Speech and Thought in the cosmic structure as embodied in the speaker.[4] Accessing the sacral quality of language in prayer, however, requires the worshipper to strip away all attachments to the physical world and enter into the state of *ayin*. This means a posture of total humility and lack of ego, and in many of the Maggid's sermons entering the *ayin* also entails an experience of the divine presence. This encounter results in an overflow of blessing and divine vitality that leads the worshipper back to the spoken word.

Prayer in Jewish Mysticism

Prayer in the Hebrew Bible generally appears as a spontaneous offering given by an individual in response to a particular triumph or tragedy. There seems to have been no clear obligation to pray regularly in the biblical period, nor is there evidence of a standard or fixed liturgy.[5] Only in the rabbinic period did the structure, specific formal requirements, and most importantly for our purposes, the text of Jewish prayer crystallize.[6] Rabbinic sources demand attention and concentration in worship. The Talmudic rabbis were well aware that obligatory prayer and fixed liturgies can easily lead to rote worship, and an obligation to employ a set text may interfere with, or even preclude, spontaneous prayer.[7] We should note that for the rabbis of the Talmud, as in the Bible, worship was not purely a cerebral or philosophical exercise. Prayer was to be recited aloud, and many parts of the liturgy were accompanied by physical movements.[8] Several rabbinic descriptions of prayer even include descriptions of ecstatic or visionary experiences as well, presaging developments in later Jewish mysticism.[9] Rabbinic literature also evinces tension on the religious significance of prayer when compared to study of Torah, a subject that remained a point of debate into the modern period.[10]

Prayer was a foundational element of kabbalistic religious practice from its earliest stages, and had long been a focal point of Jewish mystical speculation, even before the early medieval Kabbalists.[11] The ascents of the *hekhalot* literature were often accompanied by hymns, and in some cases the mystic joins along with the angelic choir in reciting the heavenly liturgy before God.[12] The later Rhineland Pietists of the twelfth and thirteenth centuries emphasized the importance of prayer, with the liturgy and act of worship replacing the ascent to the Throne of Glory as the locus of mystical experience.[13] The Pietists offered no systematic doctrine comparable to that of the highly specific *kavvanot* or *yihudim* ("intentions" and "unifications") found in later Kabbalah, but their teachings attributed special significance to one's inner state during prayer.

Perhaps reflecting a broader European cultural change toward texts and away from orality, the Rhineland Pietists also emphasized that great secrets were to be found in the words of the liturgy itself.[14] These were to be unlocked through tallying the numerical values of letters and words, or counting the total number of words in a particular unit. This approach to prayer often removed the words of the liturgy from their literal context, since their symbolic association and numerical values were more important than their plain-sense meaning, and at the same time it transformed the prayers into a canonical text to an unprecedented degree.[15]

The thirteenth-century Provençal Kabbalists developed new types of mystical prayer, emphasizing the need for *kavvanah*, defined as intense meditative concentration during prayer, as well as contemplation of the associations between the words of the liturgy and the *sefirot*.[16] According to these thinkers, the central work of prayer takes place within the mind, described as the realm of *mahashavah*.[17] The highest form of prayer entails leaving the physical realm behind, tracing one's own thoughts back through the divine *sefirot* until achieving communion (*devekut*) with the Naught (*ayin*).[18] This doctrine of prayer included theurgic elements together with these experiential aspects, for the mystic's prayers affect the flow of divine vitality through the *sefirot* and the cosmos more broadly.[19]

The Zohar expanded the associations of the *sefirot* and divine names with different parts of the liturgy. Its authors developed new customs (or resuscitated older ones), and introduced small changes in the liturgy; many of these innovations were incorporated into the prayer books of Europe, North Africa, and the Middle East.[20] The Zohar is a work of devotion in addition to theosophy, and its various strata offer a range of stirring visions of prayer as moments of intense intimacy and contemplative communion with the Divine.[21] This heightened state of consciousness must be embraced, but only temporarily, for the siren- song of such illumination can overwhelm the worshipper and draw him, like a moth to the flame, toward a rapture that exacts the ultimate cost.[22] For our purposes, we should also note that the Zohar emphasizes the orality of prayer, perhaps in a polemic against the spiritualizing rationalists who advocated a more silent form of contemplative prayer.[23]

The Kabbalists of Safed introduced several significant liturgical rituals and compositions, many of which became quite widespread in the following centuries.[24] Such liturgical creativity was accompanied by a new interpretation of the existing prayers and indeed of the very act of worship. Building on the Zohar, the Safed sources describe prayer as undertaken for the sake of *shekhinah*, in order to lift up the divine presence from its present exile and thus heal the cosmic fracture.[25] The many writings of Moshe Cordovero, for example, evince both the theurgic and the meditative, contemplative elements of worship.[26] Prayer with the proper intention, claims Cordovero, unites the cosmos with the spiritual expanse of the Divine through aligning and illuminating the *sefirot*.

The Lurianic legacy of mystical prayer also includes relatively accessible ritual practices (*hanhagot*), but Luria's chief contribution was an elaborate system of specific *kavvanot* or "intentions."[27] The goal of these formulae accompanying the liturgy, contemplated or envisioned by the worshipper, include uniting *sefirot* (and the corresponding divine names), and shattering the husks in order to redeem the fallen sparks.[28] These *kavvanot* circulated in various recensions and were eventually printed, serving as the basis for significant commentary and expansion across the next two centuries in the works of Kabbalists like the influential Shalom Shar'abi of Yemen and Jerusalem.[29] This array of ritual practices spread throughout Europe, together with the theosophical writings of Safed Kabbalah, shaping the emergence and development of Hasidism in the eighteenth century.[30] Despite the relatively swift diffusion of many kabbalistic customs of prayer and liturgy, for many religious intellectuals the *kavvanot* themselves had begun to stagger under the weight of their own ever-increasing complexity.

Hasidism upheld the traditional attitude toward study and worship as devotional pillars of the religious life, but its teachings further elevated the significance of prayer to a place of unrivaled centrality.[31] This stemmed from a belief in attaining *devekut* as the highest religious ideal. Whether striving for overwhelming and impassioned communion should be reserved for the elite—that is, for the *tsaddikim*—or upheld as a goal for all worshippers was a matter debate among different Hasidic thinkers, but their united emphasis on prayer indicates a broader turn toward a more accessible modality of religious devotion.

Popular Hasidic teachings about prayer and stories of the illuminated and effective prayers of the *tsaddikim* played a very important role in the spread of the Hasidic movement.[32] They were also a flashpoint of controversy with the *mithnaggedim*, who denounced the eclipse of the distinction between prayer and study and condemned offenses such boisterous shouting and bodily gesticulations during worship. They decried these as wild antics together with the Hasidic rejection of Ashkenazi liturgy for the Sephardic prayer rite (*nusah*), and the formation of separate prayer quorums (*minyanim*) was singled out in the earliest anti-Hasidic bans.[33]

This renewal of worship, shared by all Hasidic communities into the present day, is rooted in the spiritual ethos of the BeSHT. Many tales recount his ecstatic service and the effectiveness of his prayer, but these hagiographical stories are complemented by his innumerable teachings about the art of worship.[34] Following the earlier Kabbalists and in keeping with his approach to the spiritual life, the BeSHT emphasized that prayer should be offered for the sake of *shekhinah* alone.[35] But he also underscored that prayer, though it must be taken seriously, need not be accompanied by sadness. Joy rather than morose contrition holds the keys for opening the heart and mind to the spirit of God.[36]

The BeSHT's notion of cleaving to the letters of prayer as a spiritual technique is of particular relevance to Dov Ber's take on language.[37] The BeSHT is said to have described the words of prayer, and especially those spoken aloud, as vessels filled with divine vitality. The worshipper penetrates through the shell, becoming attached to the spiritual kernel within the letters through intensive *kavvanah*. In prayer one thus blends pious enthusiasm, fresh passion, and contemplative focus with the vocal recitation of the liturgy.[38] Some teachings attributed to the BeSHT even suggest that letters recited without such *kavvanah* are suffused with divinity, just as the physical cosmos is saturated with the ever-sustaining divine word.[39] Such an approach thus opens the doors to mystical prayer to a wide variety of people beyond the elites.

Worship as *Devekut* and the Prayer of *Shekhinah*

The Maggid's teachings, in keeping with those of the BeSHT, extoll *devekut* as the core of his spiritual vision. This type of sacred communion is by no means restricted to worship, but his sermons often describe prayer as a singular opportunity for connecting oneself to the Divine.[40] "*Devekut* is speaking a word," claims the Maggid, "extending it for a very long time; one yearns not to part from the word because of this *devekut*."[41] Each word of the liturgy is to be cherished as a "complete structure" (*komah shelemah*) that simultaneously conceals and discloses the Divine, and the Maggid calls each worshipper to enter into the spoken letters of prayer with every fiber of his being.[42] Meditating on the fact that the language of the liturgy draws on the same cosmic pool of energy used in God "speaking" the world into existence inspires a posture of awe and reminds the worshipper that words have remarkable creative power.[43] This effort requires such great concentration that the Maggid is moved to declare it a wondrous miracle that the human being does not totally expire after such an experience. Continued existence after the breathtaking rapture of impassioned prayer is an act of divine grace.

The Maggid's understanding of devotional prayer requires the worshipper to undergo a process of *hitpashtut ha-gashmiyyut*, withdrawing from external stimuli and any attachment to the physical world.[44] Focusing on the words of speech represents a technique for achieving this release from corporeal desires, shuttling the worshipper toward the state of *ayin*.[45] The experience of Naught is often described as the abandonment of the ego and consciousness of the self.[46] But in many homilies he points toward a moral radical understanding of reaching *ayin* as an overwhelming awareness of God's infinite expanse, an encounter with the Divine that stretches beyond even the most basic semantic gestures or images:

As a *tsaddik* stands up to pray before the blessed Creator, surely he connects (*medabbek*) and binds (*mekasher*) his mind and vitality to *Ein Sof*—utter unity (*ahdut pashut*) that cannot be depicted.

When he begins to speak, he draws forth the vitality of the blessed Creator into the words that emerge from his mouth. He is truly attached to his vitality and breath that have been focused through articulation into the letters he is speaking. It seems as if his breath and vitality, which are connected to *Ein Sof*, are articulated and focused through the articulation of those letters.[47]

The words of the worshipper manifest his own inner vitality and thoughts, focusing the rush of the mind into specific letters and speech. But by turning inward and thus becoming firmly and inscrutably connected to the infinite Divine, these same words also become vessels that hold God's spirit. The moment of unspeakable rapture is thus recast in language through the return to liturgy as a focal point for spiritual meditation. God comes to dwell within the letters, and these words of prayer are a gift for channeling new divine vitality into the worshipper and the cosmos.

The Maggid's homilies often depict illuminated prayer as a moment in which *shekhinah* speaks from within the worshipper.[48] When one worships God with great passion and enthusiasm, he claims, "the words leave his mouth of their own accord (*me-'atsmam*)."[49] This flow of language, a rushing river returning to its source in God's mind, originates in the Divine as well: "As soon as one says, 'My Lord, open up my lips' (Ps. 51:17) [at the beginning of the *'amidah*], *shekhinah* becomes garbed in him and speaks the words. When one holds faith that the *shekhinah* recites these very words, he will be overtaken by awe and the blessed Holy One focuses himself (*metsamtsem et 'atsmo*) and dwells with him."[50] *Shekhinah*, or the World of Speech in the Maggid's vocabulary, becomes invested in the worshipper through contemplative prayer and thus is the source of all words. Human speech has essential power precisely because it is an expression—or better, an embodiment—of divine language. That this is true even of prayer means that worship is in some sense an act of intradivine worship, accomplished as God's word and human speech become intertwined (see above).

This vision of prayer in which *shekhinah* speaks through the worshipper is closely connected to the Maggid's interpretation of petitionary prayer, a key component of the rabbinic liturgy.[51] The notion that the worshipper must come before God in order to plead for his material success seems to stand in conflict with the goals of *devekut* and self-transcendence.[52] Many of Dov Ber's sermons underscore that petitionary prayers should instead reflect concern for the fractured existence of *shekhinah*. This indwelling aspect of the God-head, he teaches, is redeemed from exile as the World of Speech is embodied in the worshipper:

> When one arises to pray before the blessed One, this is how he should act: the sole intention of his prayer should be to bring blessing to God's *shekhinah*.
>
> This is the meaning of the Sages' statement: "pray only with a serious demeanor (*koved rosh*)[53]—be mindful of the Beginning of all beginnings (*resha de-kol reishin*)."[54] Even though he asks for something he needs, the intention should be that whatever it is not be lacking above. His soul is a part of God, and it is one of the limbs of the *shekhinah*. The goal of your prayer is that the lack be fulfilled on high.[55]

Shekhinah is revealed—and redeemed—through the act of worship, and therefore one must not be so crass as to use the sacred connection forged by the language of prayer for personal desires. The Maggid quotes the *Tikkunei Zohar*'s derisive portrayals of supplicants who "act only for themselves and bark out, 'give, give.'"[56] Even amid the liturgical petitions, the worshipper should plead for nothing other than blessing and healing for the wounded *shekhinah*.

Prayer for the sake of redeeming *shekhinah* is, in the Maggid's view, another way of describing the ultimate goal of all religious life: restoring language to its sacred root. In devoting his words to God, the worshipper returns a fallen or lost element of the Divine. "One must pray only in order to bring language to Him," says the Maggid. "If one does so, all the guards will let him through. There is a parable about a peasant bearing the signet ring of the king. Although he is unworthy of coming before the king, the guards let him through because the king longs for the signet. They rush him to the king so that the king can enjoy his pleasure more quickly. In this way the blessed Holy One longs for the Word."[57] *Shekhinah*, the divine word, languishes in exile, and can only be restored to the palace of the Divine through human prayer. The worshipper bearing the godly gift of language, like the villager with the signet ring, is granted access to the deepest realms of God's mind.

Forgetting the self and praying for the sake of *shekhinah* allows the worshipper to transcend the limits of his particular needs. One bounded by individual identity cannot become a dwelling place for the infinite God, but, says the Maggid, when one moves beyond the self and prays for *shekhinah* one becomes connected to the infinite expanse of the Divine: "Thus one may ascend higher than time, to the World of Thought, where everything is equal."[58] Prayer is thus a moment in which the divine breath and sacred language course through the worshipper, whom the Maggid likens to a shofar: "The sound he gives forth comes from that which is blown into him. If the person blowing stops, the voice will stop as well. Without God, it is impossible to speak or think."[59] Just as breath passes through the ram's horn and is transformed into sound, so does *shekhinah* appear in the words of the worshipper's supplication.

Such a theory of prayer accords well with the Maggid's depiction of the worshipper becoming increasingly still as he moves deeper and deeper into the mind, an instruction that stands in contrast to the frenetic movements that characterized the style of prayer of the BeSHT and some of the Maggid's students.[60] But does this cluster of ideas regarding the language of *shekhinah* and self-abandonment necessarily lead to a kind of passive resignation, as Weiss and Schatz-Uffenheimer have contended?[61] We shall see that things are not so simple.

While deeply introspective, the Maggid conceives of prayer as a dynamic journey in which the worshipper's thoughts and words speak the Divine into being.[62] The ultimate goal of prayer, says the Maggid, is to draw God's presence into the human body as an investment of the divine word, thus linking the physical and the spiritual realms together through the medium of illuminated language.[63] This process, though trained inward, requires contemplative activism combined with physical—if nearly automatic—intonation of the liturgy as well as temporary renunciation of the ego.

This returns us to the question of whether the Maggid's homilies evince an approach to divine service that prides contemplative silence as the highest form of worship.[64] Such an interpretation cannot be sustained, though a few of the Maggid's teachings lend themselves to this reading. "'Silence is a fence for wisdom'[65]—when one is silent," argues Dov Ber, "he can become attached to the World of Thought, which is *hokhmah*."[66] A similar point emerges in his reading of Hannah's supplication in 1 Samuel, the story invoked in the Talmud as the source for quiet prayer.[67] The biblical heroine, he says, prayed with the full power of her contemplative mind by moving beyond the letters in order to overturn the laws of nature. Yet even in this case the Maggid notes that potential transformations effected in the World of Thought *must* be subsequently drawn into the medium of speech. Some ambiguity remains as to whether this verbalization is a later stage of prayer or if it takes place simultaneously with contemplation, but the Maggid never retreats from his emphasis on the crucial connection between the contemplative mind and the spoken words of prayer into which the illuminated inspiration flows.

One tradition has Dov Ber suggesting that only beginners need to pray amid the written letters of the prayer book, for more experienced contemplatives should close their eyes and focus their sight inward.[68] He also notes that prayer should be recited in a low voice, without any ecstatic shouts or movements: "One may perform the service of prayer to God without it being visible to others at all. He makes no motions with his limbs, but the innermost parts of his soul burn within his heart. He cries out quietly (*be-lahash*). This type of inner service is much greater than that which can be seen in the limbs."[69] This teaching is, first and foremost, a guarded admonition against the dangers of pride and self-aggrandizement that might accompany visibly ecstatic prayer. Such is the context of the counsel to pray *be-lahash*. Although this term may be translated either as "quietly" or as "silently," as Schatz-Uffenheimer would have it, the second is the weaker reading on both conceptual and philological grounds. Rabbinic and medieval Jewish sources frequently invoke *lahash* in reference to whispered supplication or instruction rather than soundless contemplation; a similar use is preserved in another of the Maggid's sermons.[70] The volume of one's supplication may diminish in times of heightened spiritual uprush, and perhaps language may even become extinguished for a brief moment. "Inner service" and soulful passion, however, find their fullest expression through illuminated speech.

The Maggid's sermons often refer to the unity of God and man achieved in the language of prayer. Special note, however, must be made of the following teaching. The homily that follows is often pointed to as a microcosm of Dov Ber's theology, and, most relevant for our purposes, it offers one of the fullest descriptions of the intertwining of divine and human self through the power of words:

> "Make for yourself two trumpets (*shtei hatsotserot*) of silver" (Num.
> 10:2)—this means "two half forms" (*hatsi tsurot*), and may be read
> as linked with, "On the image of the throne was an image with
> the appearance of a man, from above" (Ezek. 1:26).

A person is really only *dalet* and *mem*, [two letters] which stand for *dibbur* and *malkhut* [both names of *shekhinah*].[71] But when one attaches himself to the Holy One, who is the cosmic *aleph*, he becomes *adam* [i.e., a complete "person"].

The Holy One entered into multiple contractions, coming through various worlds, in order to become one with humans (*ahdut im ha-adam*), who could not have withstood God's original brightness. Now the person has to leave behind all corporeality, also traveling across many worlds, in order to become One with God. Then his own existence is itself negated. Such a person is truly called a "person" (*adam*), the one on the image of the throne (*kisse*), for God Himself is hidden (*mekhuseh*) there.

Shekhinah, the indwelling presence of the Divine and the tenth *sefirah mal-khut*, comes to rest as an element of God imbued within the human form and gives mankind its capacity for sacred language. All human speech is— or at least, may become—an expression of God's ever-repercussive word. One isolates and degrades this faculty for language by speaking thoughtlessly or without intention, disconnecting *shekhinah* from the other *sefirot* hidden within the Godhead as well as within the deepest realms of the worshipper's own mind. Doing so thrusts the divine presence further into exile and renders the human form tragically incomplete, undoing the ultimate goal of creation and concealing the potential divinity within the individual being:

This follows the prophet's description of "cloud and crackling fire." At first the person is in a "cloudy" state, filled with darkness, unable to pray with enthusiasm. But then along comes the "crackling fire," when he attains such passion. This is the "image of the throne," where the blessed God is hidden. He discovers it in a *mar'eh* ("appearance" or "mirror"). Whatever is awakened in him is awakened within God as well. If love is aroused in the *tsaddikim*, so too is it aroused above. The same is true of any quality. This is true of those who are very pure, rising across all those worlds to become one with God (*ahdut 'imo*). . . . All of the upper worlds and all the divine attributes are in his hands, and he is like the king amongst his legion. . . . Just as the *tsaddik* wishes, so does God desire. . . .

These are the "two trumpets (*hatsotserot*) of silver (*kessef*)." A person is only a *hatsi tsurah* ("half of the whole form"), or *dam*.

But the *aleph* by itself, as it were, is also an incomplete form. Only when attached to one another are they made whole. *Kessef* can mean "longing." One must always long for the blessed Holy One, and God will love him as well.[72]

As the worshipper raises up his or her quality of speech, understanding on the deepest level that human language is a divine gift, the elements of the Godhead are brought into alignment. This attunement on behalf of the one praying is more than theurgic cosmology, however, since through this process Dov Ber clearly suggests that the contemplative becomes one with God.

Scholars disagree starkly regarding the thrust of this teaching. Scholem suggested that it valorizes the "transfiguration of man" through *devekut*, such that the climax of the contemplative journey is in the worshipper's abandonment of the self "within the divine mind."[73] Yet others, including Moshe Idel and Ron Margolin, have noted that the Maggid's emphasis lies in the call of such a person to return to the physical world after his transformative, ecstatic communion with the Divine.[74] The moment of unification with the Divine as described by Dov Ber does not seem to permanently eclipse the worshipper's personal identity. The meditative ascent—or inward journey—and the bonds of love between God and the human being allow the *tsaddik* to reign over the world; the divine will reflects his deeds and wishes like the image in a mirror. Nor does unity with God suggest that the *tsaddik* abandons his connection to the physical world or seeks to transcend language itself. The playful interpretation of *adam* (man) as a combination of the Divine (the cosmic *aleph*) and *dam* (*dibbur/malkhut* and "blood") demonstrates that the proper alignment between God and man comes about precisely through unifying the physical and the spiritual through the nexus of language.

This text, as elsewhere, has the Maggid describing the *tsaddik* as united with God and as the veritable fulcrum of the universe; such individuals are linked to the very life-force that unites the *sefirot*. The *tsaddik* sustains the cosmos through drawing forth divine vitality in worship, and the prayers of such individuals are uncannily effective.[75] The *tsaddik* unites heaven and earth through harnessing the power of language and thought, seeing these faculties as embodiments of elements of the Divine and then devoting them solely to God. "All of his deeds, words, and thoughts," says the Maggid of the *tsaddik*, "are perpetually united with and connected to the blessed One; he does not separate from God for even a moment."[76]

Dov Ber describes the *tsaddik*'s power as grounded in humility rather than a magical command of language or divine names, for pride or self-aggrandizement derails the *tsaddik*'s spiritual attunement and severs his connection with the infinite Naught.[77] The *tsaddik*'s prayer may not always yield a visible result, and the Maggid refers to the power of worship to unite the *sefirot* as a matter of faith even for such elect devotees:

> Complete *tsaddikim* (*tsaddikim gemurim*) are those whose words of holiness—of prayer and Torah—are all in order to unite Speech with the World of Thought. In each prayer and every word of Torah, one must believe that he certainly unites the World of Speech with the World of Thought, if he does so with intention (*be-kavvanah*). Even though he prays and his request is not granted, by means of the arousal below he unites the World of Speech with the World of Thought, causing the same thing to happen above. These people, whose sole intention is to unite the World of Speech and the World of Thought, are true *tsaddikim*.[78]

Tsaddikim, claims the Maggid, align the Worlds of Speech and Thought in their prayers, which are offered for no reason other than bringing unity to the Divine. Such words restore harmony to the Godhead and redeem *shekhinah* from the cosmic exile, healing and drawing divine energy into the world, but may not necessarily result in the *tsaddik*'s own wish being fulfilled.

A few of the Maggid's teachings justify the *tsaddik*'s ability to overturn God's will through his prayer by comparing the enraptured worshipper to a prophet. Invoking the biblical model of the prophet as an intermediary standing between God and Israel, this recasting of the *tsaddik* depicts his role as combining that of worshipper and exegete.[79] The *tsaddik* chooses the melody according to which liturgy is recited, a decision that impacts— and may even totally transform—the semantic meaning of the words; in some instances he is given permission to rearrange the letters that emerge from the divine mind and thus determine how God's message is to be manifest.[80]

The Maggid's particular take on the theology of language is critical for explaining how *tsaddikim* may challenge and change the will of God. Through their words such individuals become connected to the infinite Naught, and thus peer into the primal reservoir of creative vitality and divine language:

It seems astonishing that we find the prayer of a *tsaddik* compared to a pitchfork that can overturn even the thought of God,[81]
as in [the Talmudic adage], "Who rules over Me? *Tsaddik!*"[82] How
can the speech of the *tsaddik* ascend so high that it becomes
something different!? . . .

    This is the meaning of, "And he took from the stones [of the
place]" (Gen. 28:11). It is known that the letters are called
"stones."[83] When a *tsaddik* prays with the letters, he connects
himself to the higher wisdom. This means that he has entered the
gateway to the Naught, considering that were it not for the power
of the blessed One, he would be nothing at all. All is thus the
power of God. Speech is the blessed One's World of Speech,
through which the world was created. The World of Speech is
drawn forth from *hokhmah*, referring to the pleasure and delight
that God receives from the worlds. Even now he speaks only for
the delight of the blessed One, returning the letters to their
Source in *hokhmah* whence they were drawn. . . . Through this the
tsaddik connects to the higher [rung of] Wisdom, which becomes
garbed in his words. With this intention and his desires, he draws
forth divine energy and the supernal will into *hokhmah*, and from
there to the very lowest of the levels.[84]

The *tsaddik* picks up the letters of prayer, as it were, and returns them to
their origin in God's mind. The worshipper then journeys onward even
unto the realm of *ayin*, setting sail upon the infinite sea of God's wisdom but
returning in order to draw forth new possibilities from this expanse of sacred vitality and shape the contours of their earthly manifestation.[85] There is
activism in this account, to be sure, for the *tsaddik* praying with contemplative devotion and fervor unites with God. This effort shapes and defines the
divine will, which would otherwise remain formless and inert.[86] But some
of the Maggid's teachings qualify this power, noting that the *tsaddik*'s desire
to overturn the heavenly decree—and indeed, his ability to do so through
prayer—comes from the Divine.[87] This approach fits well with the Maggid's
definition of the *tsaddik* as one who attains the state of *ayin*, shedding personal motivations and thereby becoming a vessel through which the divine
word speaks.[88]

    But if the illuminated prayer of a *tsaddik* does not necessarily achieve
its goal, is there perhaps another rubric by which to measure the success of

worship? Indeed, says the Maggid, a prayer that has been "answered" is manifest through the worshipper's experience of passion:

> Just as the world's creation began with the twenty-two letters of
> the alphabet, as the Zohar speaks of God's creation through
> Torah, so does life-sustaining energy flow down into all creatures
> by means of those letters. One must raise up these words from
> below to their root on high, causing words and letters to flow back
> upward into their Source. This is the process: he must link word
> to word, voice to voice, breath to breath, thought to thought.
> These represent the four letters Y-H-V-H. If he does this, all his
> words fly upward to their Source. He brings his words into God's
> presence, causing God to look at them.
>
> This is what it means that prayer is "answered." This looking
> is itself a sort of flow downward, reaffirming the existence of all
> the worlds. There is no passage of time above.
>
> The divine wellspring gushes forth in each instant. The flow
> is constant, and its nature is to do good and give blessing to God's
> creatures. But if one prays or studies in this way, he may become a
> channel for that spring, bringing its blessing and goodness to the
> entire world.[89]

This homily extends a marvelously rich description of prayer as a contemplative exercise in which the worshipper connects the words, sounds, and thoughts of his supplication to the corresponding *sefirot*. This is possible, of course, because divine language saturates creation from the moments of its formation. A prayer that has been "answered" is one that opens up the channels of energy between God and the cosmos, causing divine vitality to cascade into the world. In an earlier chapter, we noted that a person's contemplative gaze (*histaklut*) may inspire a renewed flow of sacred energy, but in this sermon, it is God's glance that is trained on the worshipper's words and showers him with a stream of blessing. This coursing life-force may take the specific form of fulfilling a particular petition, but the primary goal of worship, says the Maggid, is to restore language to the Divine and thus inspire a stream of vitality.

The Maggid also looks beyond the boundaries of articulated language to a different kind of embodied sound: the wordless call of the shofar.[90] The BeSHT is remembered as having used the moments before the shofar blowing on Rosh Hashanah to give a now-famous parable of a king who set up a series of walls, and, depositing treasure before each gate, commanded his subjects to come and witness his majesty.[91] Only the king's child, the true spiritual seeker, stays the course and realizes that the barriers were only an illusion. The Maggid's teachings on the call of the shofar, also offered as accessible parables before the blasts were sounded, take a very different tack.[92] Rather than focusing on God's immanence in the cosmos, his parables underscore the sound of the shofar as bridging the ineffable realm beyond the conscious mind and the unique qualities of spoken sounds.[93] Levi Yitshak of Barditshev, for example, presents the following:

> A fine parable partly by my holy teacher Berish [i.e., Dov Ber]:
> There was a king who sent his only son away to a distant land, for
> some reason known only to him.[94] As time passed, the son
> became accustomed to the ways of the villagers among whom he
> lived. He became a wayward fellow, forgetting the niceties of life
> with the king. Even his mind and his most intimate nature grew
> coarse. In his mind, he came to think ill of the kingdom.
>   One day the son heard that the king was going to visit the
> province where he lived. When the king arrived, the son entered
> the palace where he was staying and began to shout out in a strange
> voice. His shout was in wordless sound, since he had forgotten the
> king's language. When the king heard his son's voice and realized
> that he had even forgotten how to speak, his heart was filled with
> compassion. This is the meaning of sounding the shofar.[95]

This parable may be interpreted as referring to either the national exile of the Jewish people, or the individual soul as it is uncoupled from its origin in the Divine and cast into the physical world. In this strange new environment, the prince loses his ability to communicate with the king, perhaps even forgetting the royal language itself. The two are reunited only after the king leaves his palace and ventures forth into the forsaken land, where he is greeted by his son's wordless but stirring cry.[96]

The message for the Maggid's eighteenth-century listeners seems to be as follows: even though God's compassion cannot be aroused through well-articulated supplications, for Israel has forgotten how to pray effectively with words, divine kindness may be inspired by the primal, wordless cry of the shofar. It shatters all complacency and opens the heart of the Divine together

with the mind of the worshipper, thus accomplishing a spiritual renewal beyond the capacity of articulated language.

Ze'ev Wolf of Zhitomir offers a similar parable in his teacher's name,
though his account has a number of significant differences.[97] In his presentation of the parable, the king's children are "exiled from their father's table"
rather than dispatched to a faraway land on a holy mission, and this version
notes that children dearly long to return to the palace.[98] And, unlike the prince
whose voice is muted as he becomes entrenched in physicality, these children
attempt to appease their father by sending him articulate messages filled with
love: "They kept calling out and begging for his mercy, but they were met with
silence." The children therefore assume that their knowledge of the royal language has been obscured by the tongue of the coarsened peasantry around
them, and they opt for a different technique: "They decided to stop calling out
in words or language. They would just let out a simple cry to arouse his mercy,
since a cry without words can be understood by anyone."[99] Here the thrust of
the parable suggests that the princes' supplication fails even though they never
forgot the royal language itself. A worshipper can recite the liturgy with technical correctness, suggests the Maggid, but such prayer is ineffectual if the
inner intent has become coarsened through distraction or inattention. The
wordless call, of course, returns them to their father's benevolent glance.

These stirring parables about the king and his children offer a vision of
the shofar blowing as a relatively accessible devotional practice. This graceful simplicity is further accented when compared to the intricate *kavvanot*
associated with the shofar in Lurianic sources. As noted in the previous chapter, parables accomplish more than communicating religious information or
values through narrative; they provoke and arouse students to new levels of
spiritual awareness. In his metaphor of the palace and the king, the BeSHT
sought to awaken his listeners to God's immanence in the cosmos. The Maggid's parables, however, evoke the sound of the shofar as a repercussive
wordless cry, an avenue for returning to God even when words have failed.
The shofar's voice, which includes the sacred potential energy of all language,
opens the heart and mind to a vision of God's resplendent majesty.

Kavvanah of the Heart and the Lurianic Kavvanot

The teachings of Hasidism draw inspiration from the terminology and conceptual structures of Lurianic Kabbalah, but these thinkers generally recast

the earlier mystical traditions in simplified and devotionally oriented form. The Hasidic conception of *kavvanah*, perhaps best translated as "focused intention" or "contemplative attunement," during prayer shares many elements in common with the kabbalistic *kavvanot*. These include the goal of uniting the *sefirot* and the letters of God's name, drawing spiritual vitality into the letters, and raising up the fallen sparks. But most early Hasidic thinkers underscored the importance of heartfelt worship and service amid *devekut* rather than the elaborate and staggeringly complex system of Lurianic *kavvanot*. Even those Hasidic leaders that continued to use the *kavvanot* argued, either explicitly or implicitly, that their use be reserved for certain elect individuals.[100]

This issue of Lurianic *kavvanot*, and the related shift to a new kabbalistically inflected liturgy, are therefore important ones for understanding the thrust of Hasidic spirituality. Small circles of Pietists in Europe had long been praying according to a version of the Sephardic liturgy influenced by the Lurianic *kavvanot*, but the *mithnaggedim* grew irate as more people began to forsake the traditional Ashkenazi liturgy and adopt this version of the Sephardic rite.[101] The Lithuanian scholars were surely offended by the pretentiousness of large numbers of people praying in the manner once reserved for the elite. But accepting a new liturgy further escalated tensions because it meant that the Hasidim disrupted the traditional communal structure by forming new prayer quorums.[102]

The early Hasidic change to the Sephardic rite favored by the Safed Kabbalists likely reflected their desire to mirror the smaller circles of earlier Pietists. Adopting a different liturgy also served to establish a distinct identity for the nascent Hasidic movement, distinguishing their prayer quorums from the communal synagogue, and, because they adopted the liturgy *en masse,* from the prayer circles of the Pietists as well. But the shift to the Sephardic rite also demonstrates the importance of the world of Lurianic Kabbalah to the early Hasidic masters. Their interpretations of Lurianic systems were simplified, emphasizing spiritual uplift, devotion, and inner psychology rather than metaphysics or cosmology, but their conceptual framework is drawn directly from terminology and structures of Safed Kabbalah. The venerated figure of the holy Kabbalist Luria was quite important to the Maggid and his students, as was imitating some of the customs associated with him. But many complicated practices such as the *kavvanot* were consciously left behind for most people even if they were reserved for certain elites.

Dov Ber's sermons emphasize the importance of maintaining *kavvanah* in all speech, an awareness of the divinity of language and its capacity to unite God and man. Cultivating this vision of language is particularly important in worship, for words spoken without *kavvanah* fail to rise up and be connected to the Divine.[103] But his sermons have largely dislodged the term *kavvanah* from the complicated Lurianic formulae (see above). His interpretations of specific sections of the liturgy or verses included in the statutory prayers, though often including kabbalistic terms, are relatively accessible.[104] They require intense contemplative, intellective, and emotional focus, but they are a far cry from the complexity of the *kavvanot* assigned to the liturgy by earlier Kabbalists. We read, for example, as follows: "When a person prays according to the simple meaning [of the liturgy], the words are not alive. Only the name [of God] gives vitality to the words. For example, when one says, 'Blessed are You,' there is no vitality in 'Blessed are You' until he mentions the name [Y-H-V-H]. But when one prays according to Kabbalah, 'Blessed' is a name, 'are You' is a name, and so it is with all the words of prayer, since this is the World of Speech."[105] The words of the prayer are at first animated only by the appearance of God's name in the liturgy. Without these explicit mentions of the Divine, the text of the liturgy would be otherwise lifeless; the worshipper accomplishes something only because God's name appears in the liturgy and thus grants meaning and impact to the words around it. A worshipper who prays with a deeper level of understanding and vision, however, realizes that each word of the liturgy radiates with meaning and spiritual vitality. This indwelling is perhaps intensified in the names of God, but not restricted to it.

A cursory reading of this sermon might imply that the Maggid endorsed the Lurianic *kavvanot*, which connect all words of the liturgy to various permutations of the different divine names as well as the *sefirot*. But we should not assume that "according to Kabbalah" would be restricted to Lurianic *kavvanot*, as it could refer to other types of mystical teaching like the more ecstatic approach of other medieval Kabbalists. Furthermore, the conclusion of the teaching suggests otherwise. The Maggid argues that holiness is to be found in all language of worship. "Prayer according to Kabbalah" thus means something deeper. It reflects a deeply mystical understanding of the nature of language, but it does not necessarily mean that each word of prayer must be accompanied by a specific cluster of *kavvanot* in order to awaken this power.

All language, avers the Maggid, embodies and expresses the name Y-H-V-H. Knowledge of this enables the worshipper to approach each word of the liturgy, whether or not it is formally a divine name, as magnifying and bringing to life God's ineffable and sacred name. While this type of contemplation does not necessarily supplant the traditional Lurianic *kavvanot*, it is a devotional vision of the liturgy that is vastly more accessible. Our interpretation is confirmed by another important and well-known teaching: "One who prays with all the *kavvanot* familiar to him, can only do so with those that he knows. But if one speaks a word with great connectivity (*hitkashrut gadol*), all the *kavvanot* are automatically included in that word.[106] As he speaks the word with this great attachment, those worlds above are certainly aroused, and it accomplishes great feats. Therefore, one should be careful to pray with attachment and fiery passion. Surely he will accomplish great things in the world above, since each and every letter arouses [the realm] on high."[107] Traditions such as this source suggest that the Lurianic *kavvanot* actually limit or inhibit prayer, without ever undercutting their authority. The *kavvanot* are inaccessible to individuals who have not committed years to advanced study of Safed Kabbalah. But their highly developed complexity is also their undoing, for the *kavvanot* limit the otherwise infinite devotional capacity of language.[108] One of the Maggid's students quotes him as teaching that one who does not know the *kavvanot* should be mindful of the fact that the language of the prayer-book is composed of letters, cantillation marks, crowns, and vowels, which correspond to the four worlds. Attention to the multivocal reservoir of the language of prayer thus allows for spiritual uplift even for those without knowledge of the *kavvanot*.[109]

The Maggid's longest and best-known teaching on the interface of liturgy, language, and *kavvanot* is a curious text structured more like a written responsum (a rabbinic response to a legal question) than an oral homily.[110] He explains that there were thirteen gates leading into the Jerusalem Temple, one for each of the twelve tribes and an additional entrance for individuals unsure as to their tribal identity. Prayer, says the Maggid, brings the worshipper into God's presence just as the onetime sacrifices in the Jerusalem Temple did. The many and various liturgical traditions function like these portals to this sacred structure, but only the Lurianic rite, says the Maggid, is universally relevant. The conceptual underlay of the kabbalistic liturgy may be incredibly recondite, but at the same time it is accessible because it pertains to the soul-root of the entire Jewish people rather than of a particular tribe.

God's ineffability should render prayer impossible, but, says the Maggid in a different homily, liturgical worship focuses the Divine into the spirit-breath of prayer. This causes God to inhere within human language and draws divine vitality to the world.[111] Dov Ber refers to a Lurianic tradition, claiming that only the rabbinic prayers and a few liturgical poems by the early Eliezer ha-Kallir were composed with prophetic inspiration. Only such liturgical structures have the power to summon forth God's life-force and express it through the language of prayer. In making this point, however, the Maggid suggests a deeper point about the importance of fixed prayers: the liturgy delivers the worshipper from a feeble and ultimately unsuccessful search for words after such a radical experience of the Divine.

Even such teachings that laud the specific liturgy of the Kabbalists make no mention of the intricate name-permutations or other *kavvanot*. The Maggid endorses the kabbalistic version of the Sephardic rite, but describes it as a wide-open "gate" through which all may reach toward the Divine. The mystics of previous generations, says the Maggid in a famous parable, knew the correct keys for opening all the divine channels. Contemporary worshippers have lost this knowledge, but they need only break open the lock of heaven's door through passionate devotion and heartfelt worship.[112]

Uplifting the Fallen Letters

The notion that "strange" or "alien thoughts" (*mahshavot zarot*) must be raised up to their source in God was an important—and controversial—component of early Hasidic thought.[113] In this realm the Maggid was deeply influenced by the holistic approach of the BeSHT. Instead of combating bizarre, distracting thoughts during prayer with ascetic practices or by repressing the thoughts outright, the Maggid, like his teacher, requires that they be uplifted and sanctified.[114] All human thoughts and emotions derive from one of the seven lower *sefirot*, and may therefore be raised to their origins in the divine mind and expressed in a new way.[115] For example, love—or even lust—for physical pleasures can be restored to its truest form, which is the love of God. Similarly, thoughts of pride and self-aggrandizement may be cultivated as the awareness of God's glory as well as human dignity.[116] Because of his emphasis on inward contemplation and nullifying the ego, the Maggid notes that prayer is the ideal time for effecting this transformation.

The Maggid often explains that the divine quality inherent in language makes the process of uplifting *mahshavot zarot* possible. All thoughts and emotions are composed of letters, including even strange or wayward thoughts, and sacred contemplation and alien thoughts are separated only by their permutation.[117] The letters of distracting thoughts have fallen into cosmic "brokenness," the realm of the "husks," an exile that is prolonged if one speaks words of prayer without the correct attunement.[118] These letters trapped in the distracting thought remain sacred, and the worshipper must thus return them to the divine mind (the *sefirah binah*), whence they may be recombined by the worshipper into something positive.[119]

When traced back to its divine origin, physical lust for some physical object may be transformed as love for God; the unchaste thought is thus reformulated into a spiritual desire. Lifting up these fallen letters accomplishes something far more important than simply banishing a distraction, for strange thoughts accost one in prayer in order to be uplifted, and God delights in this process.[120] Rather than an encumbrance to be avoided at all costs, they offer the worshipper a unique possibility with a unique opportunity for healing and return to God.[121] One who lifts up the wayward thought will achieve an even higher level of religious service, and the joyful energy received from the transformation of these thoughts stokes the fires of his impassioned prayer.[122]

The Maggid frequently likens the act of prayer to a journey through a series of palaces. Drawing on the teachings of the BeSHT and the Zohar, Dov Ber describes prayer in much the same terms as ancient *heikhalot* texts, which chronicle the mystic's ascent through the heavenly palaces in order to glimpse the Throne of Glory.[123] The Maggid's homilies internalize this journey, focusing on the words themselves as palaces or rungs of ascent. The worshipper is examined at each station, says the Maggid, to see whether or not he is worthy of continuing:

> "I have seen servants riding on horses" (Eccl. 10:7). The letters of prayer are called "horses." When a strange thought rides upon them, one is astonished to see a servant riding on the king's horse. But when one attunes himself to the fact that these are holy letters, for only their [specific] combination is negative, one can return the letters to [their origin in] Thought (*mahashavah*)—to the world of "transformation" (*'olam ha-temurah*).[124] New combinations are then made from them—words of Torah instead of silly words. . . . [125]

The BeSHT said the following about the Zohar's teaching that a person is judged in each and every palace, and he is cast out

of the palace [if found unworthy].[126] He explained that the words
are called "palaces," since the intellect (*sekhel*) dwells within them.
One who prays moves from letter to letter, and word to word. If
he is not worthy, they cast him out. This means that they send
him a strange thought, automatically placing him "outside"[127] [the
journey of contemplative worship].[128]

The worshipper moves from stage to stage in an ever-deepening journey
toward the Divine. Although the search for God's presence takes him
into the recesses of the contemplative mind, these interior palaces are more
than imagined meditative stations.[129] The Maggid identifies them as the letters
and words of prayer—the written liturgy as it is breathed to life in spoken
prayer—and, with every utterance, the worshipper is judged to see if he is
worthy of continuing. If he is truly distracted by a strange thought, he is
cast out, and the inward quest terminates; the letters of prayer can no longer be raised up.[130] Understanding the precarious nature of the contemplative journey, says the Maggid, allows the worshipper to overcome the strange
thought. It results in constant vigilance, granting one the audacious confidence
needed to strip the distracting thought down to its fundamental letters and
raise them up.

This contemplative approach to wayward thoughts is linked to the Maggid's treatment of repentance and rituals of confession in particular.[131] Sacred letters are born in the performance of commandments, suggests the
Maggid, but the same is true of transgressions. Only verbal expiation has
the power to lift up these fallen letters cast into the "husks" through sin.[132]
A teaching preserved in a disciple's work offers the following reflections on
the transformative power of spoken confession:

> I heard from my teacher [the Maggid]: Why is it that in the
> confession we have to mention each sin? Is it not enough to leave
> the sin behind and to heartfully regret having done it? Is that not
> the essence of repentance? After all, everything we have done is
> revealed to God.
>
> He said that when we transgress we do so using our strength
> and vitality. We actually draw the energy of the letters of that act
> we commit into the deed itself: "Theft," "cheating," "harlotry,"
> and the like. Therefore, when we repent, we have to speak them
> out with those same letters, reciting them with a broken heart

and in tears. We have to follow them down to the low place called "sadness" and "weeping," raising those letters up by reciting them in both fear and love, with great devotion, before the world's Creator. This allows them to fly upward, as the Zohar teaches.[133]

Afterwards I heard from the late sage Shlomo of Karlin that he also heard our teacher explain the word *viddui* ("confession") in this way. *Viddui* has the spelled-out letter *yod* within it. You are raising all those letters back up to their root in *yod*, the root of all the letters.[134]

Prayers must be spoken aloud, claims the Maggid, even though God understands the petitions of the heart and the murmuring depths of the mind. The liturgy must be vocalized and spoken aloud in order for its words to draw vitality into the worshipper and the cosmos. Furthermore, one must gather together the letters of a transgression and return them to their original source in order to heal the fracture caused by sin. The Maggid is interpreting the word *viddui* (confession) as "re-making into a *yod*"—returning the letters to *hokhmah*, which is the reservoir of potential from which all language, and indeed all creation, unfold.

Contemplative attachment to God within the mind should, ideally, be a permanent state.[135] Prayer is thus a time of personal and spiritual danger. The quest to redeem the broken shards of the self and the world through uplifting the roots of language is Maggid's understanding of verbal confession. It is related also to the doctrine of uplifting fallen thoughts, and to Dov Ber's mystical interpretation of the ritual of *nefilat apayyim* or *tahanun* (prostration) recited after the *'amidah*.[136] There is great hazard in going down to the lowest realms, since one's internal connection to God may be shattered in the process. Such a descent is necessary, however, in order to redeem the exiled letters. The worshipper must gather together these holy words and sacred fragments of the Divine, drawing them into the self and then raising them up to the ultimate source in the mind of God.

Prayerful Echoes

The central importance of worship and its vital power, suggested the Maggid, does not end with the conclusion of the formal prayer service. Such scripted devotion sets the tone for one's words throughout the day, reminding the worshipper that *all* language may be an expression of the Divine and must therefore be sanctified:

> One must guard his mouth and tongue from any speech, even that which is permitted, before worship. Even greeting another person before prayer creates a blemish.[137]
>
> The world was created through thought, speech, and deed. First came thought, speech is a branch of thought, and deed is a branch of speech. So too, when one becomes a new creation when he arises from his sleep. . . .
>
> One must therefore be careful to sanctify and purify his first word, and clarify his first thought so that it will be connected to holiness, so that this will be true for all the subsequent words drawn from it. Afterward, when he stands up to pray amidst the joy that comes from performing a commandment, he will certainly be answered because he has sanctified his initial words and thoughts.[138]

One's initial words each day are likened to the formative utterances with which God created the world. Those original traces of divine speech contained within them the roots of all language; and so too, the first words of a particular day include subsequent unfolding of speech. If these letters are uttered in a mind-set of the profane, or even the mundane, that quality will be imprinted in all later words emerging from those initial sacred moments. But if a person sanctifies his capacity for language immediately upon arising, devoting his words and his thoughts to God by means of prayer, this spirit of holiness is drawn forth into his words throughout the course of the day.

Prayer transforms the individual worshipper and his relationship to language, but the gift of inspiration extends beyond his private interior world. Impassioned prayer is a moment of cosmic importance:

> When an Israelite stands up to pray with love and awe, the various angels in all the worlds break out in song. All of them are included in him [i.e., in the worshipper]. . . . All the worlds are drawn together, giving themselves over and cleaving together into a single unity. Then surely all are united in single unification and included in one, as in a tiny point. . . . After prayer, during which

they all ascend as one and cleave to the blessed Creator, effluence
and vitality are drawn down to all the worlds.

It is known that all the worlds were brought into being
through permutations of the letters, as it is written, "by the word
of Y-H-V-H the heavens were made" (Ps. 33:6). These utterances
have remained in the worlds from the time they were created,
illuminating them and imbuing them with life-force, in keeping
with the deeper meaning of "as long as there is heaven over earth"
(Deut. 11:21).[139] This is the meaning of "Forever, O Y-H-V-H, Your
word stands in heaven" (Ps. 119:89).

The prayers of Israel draw new energy and vitality into the
[divine] letters, permutations and utterances within the worlds.
They are forever renewing these utterances with new life-force
and illumination. This is the meaning of [Israel's] song, and
perhaps this was the reason for establishing the daily custom of
reciting *Perek Shirah* after each prayer service.[140] The enlightened
will understand.[141]

The prayers of Israel, spoken with contemplative focus, unite the heavens
in a moment of sacred exaltation. The Maggid suggests that this is the reason
behind reciting *Perek Shirah*, an ancient text describing the song of creation
both animate and inanimate, at the conclusion of the prayers. Worship infuses new life into the physical world, drawing together the human, divine,
and cosmic songs into the breath of prayer.

We might therefore expect the Maggid's teachings to include many reflections on the power of song in worship. Music had a very important place
in Hasidic life and theology from the very beginning, and Solomon Maimon
reports that the sermon he witnessed in Mezritsh was begun by a stirring
wordless melody started by none other than Dov Ber himself.[142] Music is
rarely mentioned in the Maggid's homilies, and his sermons rarely give theoretical descriptions about the power of songs in religious life.[143] This lack
of mention is quite interesting, and may reveal something about the restrained
tenor of the Maggid's religious personality.

One remarkable exception, however, is found in a gloss appended to a
teaching in *Maggid Devarav le-Ya'akov*, the first printed compendium of the
Maggid's homilies. In this marginal note, Dov Ber's son—Avraham "the
Angel"—quotes his father as explaining that song, like the trop of the Torah, has the power to lift the worshipper above the letters into the divine

mind where all the letters originate, beyond time and beyond language. The worshipper then returns to the letters bearing a new charge of sacred illumination.

Prayer was, it seems for the Maggid, a rather lonely affair. Dov Ber's teachings emphasizing the place of solitude in the spiritual journey dovetail with the very small number of references to communal prayer in his homilies. This does not mean he devalued communal worship, of course, but it is suggestive of Dov Ber's retreating personality and the radically inward glance that characterizes his teachings. One of the sermons on communal prayer compares the individuals of a prayer quorum to words, describing the prayer-leader (*sheliah tsibbur* or *hazan*) as the mindful vision (*hazon*) that unites them all.[144] The contemplative property of the leader uplifts those around him.

This depiction of the community as an embodiment of sacred language is reflected in a tradition cited by one of his students. Shlomo of Lutsk wonders how an illuminated spiritual individual can pray with ordinary people with different degrees of spiritual attainment. It is all the more difficult, he says, for an advanced worshipper to serve God in a state of *devekut* while functioning as the prayer-leader for such a variegated community, which includes people focused on the vanities of this-worldly pleasure. But Shlomo notes: "I heard in the name of my teacher and master a bit of faithful advice: one should not connect to their life-force [i.e., the coarse vitality of the broader community]. He should, rather, ascend in his mind (*ya'aleh be-mahshavto*) to push aside the dross and slag in them, connecting himself to the pure and refined sacred quality within them, which is the name Y-H-V-H [that inheres within each person]."[145]

The community, like all language, is united as an expression of God's most sacred name. Each member of the quorum, even coarse individuals connected more to the corporeal than to flights of the spirit, is an element of this expression of the Divine. It is the job of the leader to lift up these sacred sparks, the inherence of divine language within each individual, and bring it to the surface. Expanding his teacher's advice, Shlomo notes that the prayer-leader's spiritual enthusiasm spills out, illuminating and inspiring even the distracted members of the community:

> We see this in our very own experience (*ba-hush*). They [i.e., the quorum] are aroused to chant the words of prayer loudly and with abundant yearning, even though they themselves know nothing.

The prayer-leader, who raises up the holiness within them, brings
this about. . . .

This is the meaning of the verse: "when you raise up (be-
ha'alotkha) the lamps, [the seven lights shall be facing the Meno-
rah]" (Num. 8:2). When you lead the prayers, worshipping
together with the children of Israel, who are called "lamps," see to
it that you raise up this sacred quality within them.

They, too, shall receive inspiration.

Their words will become illuminated as well.[146]

Thus the words of prayer-leader, the throbbing heart of the liturgical community, surge forth and bring light and inspiration to the worshippers. In
detailing this dynamic, Shlomo of Lutsk informs his readers that he is drawing upon his own lived experience. Perhaps, then, we might stretch his description and apply it to Shlomo's own teacher—the Maggid—and the
Mezritsh circle. Hasidism was carried aloft by the religious personalities and
charismatic presence of these figures, some of whom remained in close-knit
devotional fellowships while others emerged at the helm of large and variegated communities. All of them, however, understood Dov Ber's legacy as
demanding that a leader's world of inner piety must spill into the community through his words.

The Maggid remained a private and introspective mystic, but at times
he was surrounded by a circle—or circles—of disciples and travelers who
journeyed to hear his words and simply to witness his conduct. Dov Ber's
sustained attention to the sacred quality of human language was key to this
allure. Like the High Priest charged with "raising up" the lamps of the Menorah, the Maggid's spiritual educator has been tasked with translating inner devotion into communal inspiration. Just as the prayer-leader must set
the hearts of his flock aflame through chanting and worship, the teacher or
religious leader must illuminate his speech and polish his words until they
reflect the sacred vitality in all human language. These words, claims Dov
Ber, expand the fiery yearning and passion of one's spiritual life even unto
those who would otherwise stand beyond its warmth.

Epilogue

Moving Mountains

After the death of the holy Maggid, the disciples began to speak among themselves and contemplate his deeds and service. The Rabbi from Liady asked, "Does anyone here know what our master used to do each day when he went walking by the river bank and wandered among the croaking frogs in the lakes and pools?" Nobody knew the Maggid's intention. The Rabbi from Liady answered, "I will tell you. He went there to learn the song that the frogs sing to the blessed One, as described in *Perek Shirah*. He wanted to hear how they praised and exalted the One."

—*Kerem Yisrael*

We have seen that the Maggid's theology is much concerned with creation and revelation, the sacred processes through which God enters language. The divine word became expressed through the cosmos by means of the utterances of creation, and this vital life-force inheres in the physical and animates it. The infinite pool of divine wisdom entered into language on Sinai in the moment of revelation, becoming expressed through the sacred text. Both creation and revelation are seen as ongoing process through which the Divine breaks the bonds of endless silence and enters the mantle of language in order to be known by humanity.

The Maggid's sermons have also shown us that the bestowal of the divine Self is by no means a one-way street. Words and letters are to be restored to their source through study and worship. "God created the world as 'being' (*yesh*) from the Naught (*me-ayin*)," claimed the Maggid, "and it is the role of the *tsaddikim* to summon forth the Naught from that being."[1] This renewal of God's word through human language, the unpacking of the infinite from finite words and letters, represents the Maggid's fullest vision of redemption.[2]

As is the case with early Hasidic thinkers, the Maggid's sermons emphasize the quest for immediate personal awakening rather than the kabbalistic goal of cosmic *tikkun*, which is laden with messianic implications.[3] Inner spiritual arousal may well be described as a sort of "private" or "personal redemption," though the notion as such does not appear in his sermons.[4] But the Maggid's homilies are indeed concerned with the reawakening of sacred speech as a historical process in which humanity's relationship to language is radically transformed. This redemptive elevation of human speech and thought operates on personal, communal, and cosmic planes. In the Maggid's longest teaching on the subject, we read:

> "A song of ascents. As Y-H-V-H restores the fortunes of Zion, we see it as in a dream. [Our mouths will be filled with laughter, our tongues, with songs of joy"] (Ps. 126:1–2). We can explain this according to what is written in the Zohar [about the verse]: "Who scorns a day of small beginnings? [Even they will see with joy the plummet in the hand of Zerubbavel]; even these seven, which are the eyes of Y-H-V-H, ranging over the whole earth" (Zech. 4:10).[5]
>
> This is the general principle: the letters that fell into the realm of brokenness (*shevirah*) during the seven days of creation come to a person in prayer as thoughts of love, awe, splendor, glory and beauty.[6]
>
> These [letters] are the lower waters that cry out, "We too wish to stand before the King."[7] For this reason they come [to him], each according to his level. But they arrive when he is totally unaware, as he is reciting [well-known] words, such as from Psalms. The thoughts come to him [at this time] because he must be in a state of [spiritual] smallness (*katnut*) in order to repair them; therefore this must happen without any prior intention (*da'at*).
>
> This is the meaning of, "Who scorns a day of small beginnings? . . . even these seven, which are the eyes of Y-H-V-H, ranging over the whole earth." We must raise up [these letters] until the arrival of our blessed redeemer, may he come speedily in our days. The word is in exile. In the future, however, all speech

will be for God alone, and all of the elements of brokenness will be uplifted. Understand this.

Strange thoughts accost the worshipper during prayer in order to be repaired and uplifted in their source of God. They are composed of fallen divine letters, cast into the "husks" after the sacred vessels shattered and scattered sparks of holiness throughout the cosmos. Raising these broken fragments is the ultimate goal of all prayer.

To do so the worshipper must descend into a temporary state of *katnut*, a moment of limited or constricted consciousness allowing him to reach into the realm of brokenness and draw up the divine vitality. One is not permitted to enter this dangerous place intentionally, so God sends these wayward thoughts when the worshipper is occupied with reciting the words of prayer. When one's concentration is focused elsewhere, suggests the Maggid, the broken letters take him by surprise and may thus be transformed. The Maggid continues:

> Do not object [by saying], "And what will come of those words [of prayer] that were recited without awareness (*da'at*)?" The matter is thus: One [should] consider that he is not speaking at all, but rather that *shekhinah*—called the World of Speech—is speaking from his throat. His memory (*zikaron*), for he has memorized the words [of the liturgy] to which he has become accustomed, will raise them up. *Shekhinah* is truly in exile, which means that the Word is in exile. Understand this very well.

Given the Maggid's insistence on *kavvanah* in contemplative prayer and intensive mystical study, we might think it strange that this sermon recommends that the worshipper recite the words and allow them to flow forth without additional focus. The key to this practice lies in cultivating an awareness of *shekhinah*, the indwelling divine spark, speaking though the worshipper.

The worshipper does not redeem the holy letters simply through intellection or contemplation, but through the organic fusion of mind and heart with the spoken word as the focal point of his attention. Rather than calling for close deliberation of the liturgy's ideational content or the far-reaching symbolic associations of the *kavvanot*, the worshipper is to allow the exiled fragments of sacred language to arrive as he recites the care-worn words of the prayer book long since committed to memory:

Here is a parable about a king that commanded his servants to
raise up a mighty mountain, one that is too large to lift. The
servants came up with the idea of boring into the mountain and
breaking it down, separating it into smaller pieces. Each person
lifted a little bit, according to his strength. Through this they
performed the king's command.

So too, the [supreme] King of kings commanded us to uplift
the sparks of holiness, for this is the ultimate goal of all service. It
brings great pleasure to the Divine for the lower levels to be
uplifted, as we have explained elsewhere. This is the reason for
the breaking [of the vessels], so that each person would be able to
raise up an [element of divine vitality] according to his level.
Understand this parable very well. . . .

Know that holiness dwells within the letters of Torah.
Holiness and spiritual energy rest upon it, for the Torah and God
are one. Therefore, Scripture says, "A song of ascents. As Y-H-
V-H restores the fortunes of Zion, we see it as in a dream. Our
mouths will be filled with laughter (*sehok*)," which is related to
"worn-out clothes" (*begadim shehukim*)[8]—the language that had
been in exile until now, is in "our mouths." "Our tongues, with
songs of joy"—[redeeming the letters will] bring great pleasure
[to God].

"Then shall they say among the nations, Y-H-V-H has done
these great things for them" (Ps. 126:2)—those who were [in
exile] among the nations, will do great things for Y-H-V-H.[9]

The divine word languishes in exile. What is called for here is a fundamental reorientation in humanity's relationship with language. In the future,
as the Maggid imagines it, all speech shall be linked to the Divine, uttered
for the sake of God alone. This overarching transformation cannot happen
all at once, nor will it be the result of the efforts of a few select *tsaddikim*.
Each person is commanded with the task of uplifting his own words, but
all of these infinitesimal changes link together into the monumental transformation.

The Maggid's parable of the king and the clever plan to accomplish the
impossible also demonstrates that the shattering of the cosmic vessels, the
moment that resulted in the divine word being sent into exile, was not purely
a tragedy. Dov Ber describes the descent of these holy letters as an essential,

necessary stage in the unfolding of God through the cosmos, one that paved the way for the ultimate redemption of both humanity and the Divine. In his interpretation of Psalm 126, the Maggid has overturned the plain sense of the verse, which originally refers to the great power and beneficence of God's deeds in redeeming Israel.

Dov Ber reads the verse from Psalm 126 in just the opposite way: Israel will deliver the divine word from the "husks" and thus perform a task both wondrous and great, uniting human words and letters with the origin of all language and being. In fact, the shattering of the vessels and the dispersal of the sacred letters allow everyone to take part in a great project, from the elite *tsaddikim* to the ordinary worshippers. The king's servants can successfully lift an impossibly large mountain only as they work together, for each individual has a crucial role in the redemption of language.

This parable about the devotional life of a sacred community could, without stretching the fabric beyond recognition, easily be extended to the emergence of Hasidism from among the Maggid's many disciples. The BeSHT may have come to be the imagined paterfamilias of this movement of renewal, but in many respects Hasidism as we know it was born in the teachings of the Maggid and his many disciples. Each of these students carried Dov Ber's teachings in new directions, theological as well as geographic, despite the lack of any "marching orders" from Mezritsh and probably without any united decision to translate the ethos of Hasidism from the teachings of a small, elite circle into the theology of a relatively widespread mass movement.

The argument that there was indeed a loose-knit fellowship that may be described as the "school of the Maggid," correctly advanced by Rivka Schatz-Uffenheimer, has been strengthened by Arthur Green.[10] He suggests that the homilies of the different figures in the Maggid's school may be read together as an internal conversation, or debate, regarding the major issues of theology and practice.[11] While the Maggid's students cohere on many points, they disagree sharply in their understanding of key theological ideas as well as specific devotional practices like prayer and study. These ideational dissimilarities, claims Green, emerged most acutely as Hasidism was transforming from a circle of elite devotees into a mass movement.

The differences between the Maggid's disciples surely reflect the changing social reality of Hasidism, but they may also have contributed to and driven forward its transformation into a full-blown movement in the years after Dov Ber's death. Without assuming that the homilies printed in early

Hasidic books are transcriptions of actual discussions that took place in the Maggid's *beit midrash*, we may thus read their teachings as the medium through which the Maggid's disciples explored and articulated their conceptions of what Hasidism would become. The various students of the Maggid each developed their own theological vision, influenced by their master's teachings and perhaps by those of their colleagues as well.[12]

The significant emphasis on personal creativity in the Maggid's circle gave rise to a blossoming of different theological positions and spiritual paths, but it also led to fierce disagreements. Conflicts inevitably arose among the Maggid's many and varied students, sometimes erupting between disciples who had formerly been quite close. These disputes also contain elements of economic and territorial rivalry, but the intellectual or spiritual elements at the heart of these conflicts should not be discounted.[13] The Maggid seems to have understood that his disciples would not—and should not—see eye to eye on every religious issue, but several of his homilies underscore the need for mutual respect and tolerance in the wake of such disagreement. In a sermon explaining a curious Talmudic teaching that Israel attained divine inspiration because of their modesty, the Maggid notes: "This is relevant to a group of scholars who sit around one table. They all offer teachings about a particular verse or rabbinic statement, one explains the verse one way and another explains it differently. If, Heaven forbid, they are in competition with each other, each claiming: "my explanation is better than the others"—woe to them, it is better they had never been born. But if their sole intention is to develop and enhance Torah, they are very fortunate."[14] It is hardly surprising that the push for scholarly and spiritual creativity in such a close-knit environment led to competition.[15] In many cases this emerged as debates over the authentic legacy of the Maggid's teachings and his mode of spiritual leadership. Teachings such as this homily may be read as the Maggid's attempt to foster a group of disciples who valued creativity and developed their individual religious visions without seeking to compete with or undercut one another.

The study of Hasidism has only recently begun to track the theological and ideological gulfs that distinguished the Maggid's students from one another. Future research is needed to demonstrate that the ways in which Dov Ber and his students daringly reconceived of the religious life should be seen as differing perspectives within what was emerging as a shared theological project. But there is something that they shared: the image of the Maggid and his contemplative vision of sacred words, now deeply rooted in the fertile soils of early Hasidic thought. The story of Dov Ber and his theory of language has unfolded across history. His teachings on sacred speech echo in the works of his many disciples and descendants from the eighteenth century into the present day. But theirs is a different story, and it will be told at a different time.

Appendix

The Sources: A Bibliographic Excursus

> Some of the works ascribed to the Gaon [of Vilna] were really composed by his disciples, who put into writing the lectures and remarks of the master, and are therefore to be used with great care. No teacher would like to be held responsible for the lecture notes of his students—even the cleverest of them.
> —Louis Ginzberg

Printed Compendia, *Regimen Vitae*, and Manuscripts

Speaking Infinities constructs an argument about the Maggid's theory of language as it emerges from the teachings preserved in his name in early Hasidic literature. These include teachings found in a variety of printed books, unpublished manuscripts, and the works of his immediate students. I have not attempted to reconstruct Dov Ber's *ipsissima verba*, which, in all likelihood never existed in written form. I remain wary of any attempt to synthesize the entire body of teachings attributed to the Maggid, and, in the present book, I have taken care to acknowledge the diversity, tension, and discontinuity among these sources along with highlighting their consistency. The following remarks are far short of an exhaustive study. They are intended to help the reader navigate the works listed in the notes and, more broadly, to shed some light on the complexity of early Hasidic sources and the deeper issues at play in writing the intellectual history of the movement's formative period.[1]

The problems of transcription, transmission, and translation that plague the teachings attributed to the Maggid are by no means unique to him. With very few notable exceptions, early Hasidic leaders did not choose to put their own teachings into writing. Throughout the late eighteenth and early nineteenth centuries it was far more common for a *tsaddik*'s homilies to be transcribed, edited, and printed by his disciples.[2] In general, we know rather little about the specifics behind the production and publication of these texts.[3] The homilies may have been written down shortly after being delivered, or pieced together from memory long afterward. These textual artifacts may represent the work of a single disciple, but some may be composites that were stitched together from multiple witnesses.[4]

Motivations likely varied among the disciples as well. The focused activity of transcribing can improve one's recall of an oral event, and students may well have taken notes on Hasidic homilies intended solely for personal use.[5] Other disciples may have committed a master's teachings to writing in order to share them with others, whether giving them to students who could not attend the sermon or perhaps even to curious outsiders.[6] The different intended audiences of the final text must have had a measured impact on its formation.[7] In sum, the Hasidic teachings were transformed—variously edited, shortened, expanded, and perhaps even censored—as they were committed to writing and later assembled into printed compendia. In most cases, we simply cannot retrace these developments in full.[8]

These textual issues are further compounded by the fact that, with few exceptions, written accounts of Hasidic homilies were published in Hebrew. This means that the textual sources represent a translation from the original Yiddish, the vernacular in which the teachings would have been delivered. This rift between the language of the sermons' delivery and that in which they were recorded makes the study of Hasidic texts even more difficult. The contemporary scholar, relying only on the written texts, has no way to access the original oral homily on which Hasidic books are based.[9] A few sermons—such as those of Ya'akov Yosef of Polnoye—were probably written and intended for readers, but the vast majority of early Hasidic homilies represent textual artifacts produced in response to an oral event.

The Hasidic preference for spoken language in devotional and educational contexts is indeed noteworthy, but we must remember that exclusive depictions of orality often reflect their own romanticized mythos.[10] Early Hasidism was driven by a hybridized culture, one in which spoken words and written language interface in complex and often surprising ways.[11] Scholars across various disciplines have given considerable thought to the complicated relationship between spoken and written language. Such research has noted the significant differences between these two modes of communication and their cultural significance.[12] Oral speech is often distinguished from its written counterpart by its rhetorical style, linguistic register, and semantic structure. But oral speech, from public sermons and political orations to hushed whispers, includes another dimension: the *experience* of hearing—or uttering—the words. Hasidic sources understand this element as part and parcel of a homily's spiritual significance and the meaning of the sermon as a religious event, often describing the words of a *tsaddik* as a theophany akin to the revelation at Sinai.[13] Reading a text, whether penned by a disciple or even by a *rebbe*, is portrayed as a very different sort of religious experience than hearing the sermon delivered by the master himself or receiving a living oral tradition from a fellow Hasid.[14]

Written sermons, both printed and unpublished, are intensely problematic and yet unavoidable for the modern scholar of Hasidism. But these homilies were by no means the only medium through which Hasidic ideas and practices were spread. Valuable Hasidic sources also include letters, hagiography, theoretical treatises (extremely rare in the movement's early years), and early *hanhagot* ("conduct" or "*regimen vitae*") literature. The power of the *hanhagot*, argues Zeev Gries, lay in their translation of pietistic spiritual customs of elite fellowships into a readily accessible literary format.[15] Unlike the predominantly oral genre of sermons, these short works often include exhortations that people read them regularly; this literary element became part of their sacred or ritual status.

The *hanhagot* were a very important element of Hasidic self-definition, offering a literary forum in which the ethos articulated in the sermons could, and *should*, be embodied through the practices and ritual performance of the individual members of the spiritual community. Rivka Schatz-Uffenheimer argued that the full radicalism of early Hasidism—that is, what she perceived as antinomian piety—is found in these *hanhagot*, whereas Gries has suggested that, on the whole, these sources represent a relatively conservative element of the Hasidic movement.[16] The radicalism of the *hanhagot* is found in providing a mode of ritual practice and piety that depends primarily on the individual rather than communal legal norms, thus incurring the fury of the *mithnaggedim*.[17] Together with the homilies both printed and oral, these sources represent a crucial channel through which the theology of Hasidism moved beyond the small circles in which it began.

The Teachings of the Maggid

The only sources that seem to have been written by Dov Ber include a handful of brief letters and a short approbation (a brief written gesture of rabbinic approval) for a work on the laws of ritual slaughter.[18] These epistles and encomia offer important historical information about the Maggid's reputation for piety and the regional authority it conferred. They give some inkling of Dov Ber's relationship with his students, and with other scholarly figures of his day, but they provide little in terms of his thought or theology. The contemporary scholar interested in the intellectual world of early Hasidism, therefore, must turn to the wealth of homilies and *hanhagot* attributed to Dov Ber.

The first and most important collection of Dov Ber's sermons is *Maggid Devarav le-Ya'akov—Likkutei Amarim* (Korets, 1781).[19] This anthology, the third Hasidic book to be published, includes long, intricate sermons, as well as short, incisive teachings on the devotional life or instructions for proper conduct. The sermons in *Maggid Devarav le-Ya'akov* are not arranged according to an easily discernible order, and the division between one homily and the next is often unclear.[20] The compendium was edited from an assortment of manuscripts by Shlomo of Lutsk, a close disciple and relative of the Maggid. Shlomo of Lutsk acknowledged that the teachings were marred by issues of transmission and lamented the impossibility of rewriting them, but his editorial hand must have shaped the final form of this book in significant and largely invisible ways.

Shlomo of Lutsk also wrote two interesting and important introductions to *Maggid Devarav le-Ya'akov*.[21] The first offers a brief history of Kabbalah from the dawn of Jewish mysticism through the Safed renaissance, leading up to the BeSHT and culminating with the Maggid. This attempt to trace the sacred lineage of Hasidism puts Dov Ber at the head of the list of important—and authoritative—mystical figures. Shlomo of Lutsk's second introduction offers a remarkable summary of the core issues of the Maggid's thought, including a few notes on Dov Ber's theory of language.[22]

Maggid Devarav le-Ya'akov circulated widely and was reprinted no fewer than eight times before the editor's death in 1813. The fact that this book was republished significantly more often than the writings of Rabbi Ya'akov Yosef of Polnoye, volumes that include so many traditions from the BeSHT, reveals the centrality of the Maggid in early Hasidic culture. *Maggid Devarav le-Ya'akov* was consistently reprinted throughout the nineteenth and early twentieth centuries. Rivka Schatz-Uffenheimer's 1976 edition, based on early printings and a variety of different manuscripts, was an important milestone in the study of Hasidic texts.[23] Though it has been critiqued by scholars such as Zeev Gries, Schatz-Uffenheimer's edition remains a standard for scholarly work on early Hasidism.[24]

Avraham Yitshak Kahn, a modern Hasidic leader, published a new edition of the work in 1971. His version attempted to correct the text based on manuscripts, in addition to providing helpful indices and listing parallels in the works of the Maggid's students.[25] Kahn's republication of the Maggid's works reveals an interesting historical note about the modern Hasidic world. Sensing the decline in Hasidic spirituality and the caliber of its leadership, Kahn hoped that the study of this book would spark a renewed sense of mystical devotion in contemporary Hasidic society. The teachings of the Maggid are particularly suited for this task, argues Kahn, because they serve as an "introduction to many great and precious matters."

The other major collection of Dov Ber's homilies is *Or Torah* (Korets, 1804). This work presents the Maggid's sermons in the order of the weekly Torah reading, followed by homilies on parts of Scripture and portions of the Talmud.[26] Many of the homilies in this work also appear in other earlier compendia with small differences, but this collection includes a number of original homilies to which there are no other textual witnesses in the Maggid's corpus and was likely published from an independent manuscript. Although Schatz-Uffenheimer ungenerously suggests that this division of homilies began the "atomized understanding of the Maggid's teachings"— that is, broken down into fragments and thus misunderstood—the editorial decision reflects the fact that many, if not all, of the Maggid's sermons were homilies grounded in the weekly Torah portions.[27] *Maggid Devarav le-Ya'akov* was itself stitched together from a variety of sources, a point made by Shlomo of Lutsk and confirmed by examining the extant manuscripts. We should not assume that the structure, divisions, and textual content of *Maggid Devarav le-Ya'akov* are any more authentic than other volumes or manuscript stemmata.

In some cases, the Maggid's teachings were bundled together and printed alongside traditions from other Hasidic masters. The highly influential

Likkutim Yekarim (Lemberg, 1792), for example, includes teachings from several different early Hasidic figures in addition to those of the Maggid. This presents significant issues in determining attribution, though in this case it seems that the anonymous material stems from the Maggid.[28] Many of the teachings in this book, edited by Meshullam Feibush Heller of Zbarazh,[29] had already appeared in *Maggid Devarav le-Ya'akov*. The importance of this collection lies more in its overall accessibility than its originality; *Likkutim Yekarim* includes both *hanhagot* and sermons and offers many short, pithy statements clearly intended to inspire and awaken the reader.[30] The book was frequently reprinted over the next two centuries, and in 1973 Abraham Isaac Kahn published an excellent new edition. Kahn's version is corrected against manuscripts and includes indices and lists of parallels with the other printed collections of the Maggid's teachings.

Many *hanhagot* attributed to the Maggid were integrated into these sermonic collections, appearing alongside lengthy homilies and intricate theological teachings. Similar *regimen vitae* appeared in other books, including those of Dov Ber's disciples, and a few, such as *Darkhei Tsedek* (Lemberg, 1796), appeared as independent works.[31] Foremost among the *hanhagot* treatises was *Tsava'at ha-RiVaSH* (Zolkiev, 1793), a short and frequently reprinted compendium. The title suggests that the work represents the ethical "will" (*tsava'ah*) of the BeSHT, but scholarship has demonstrated that *Tsava'at ha-RiVaSH* preserves teachings and ritual practices from the Maggid's school along with those of the BeSHT.[32] Some of this work's more radical elements, such as the exhortation to pray loudly, to uplift "strange thoughts," and to elevate devotional worship over and above the traditional value of study, sparked the ire of the *mithnaggedim*; *Tsava'at ha-RiVaSH* seems to have been among the early Hasidic writings to be burned by the opponents of Hasidism.[33] The compendium was drawn from a much larger pool of late eighteenth-century *hanhagot*, and its various printed editions were heavily edited and perhaps even censored by the Hasidim in light of the controversy with their opponents.[34]

The early anthology *Keter Shem Tov* (Zolkiev, 1794) is also presented as a compendium of the BeSHT's teachings, though closer inspection reveals that it includes a significant body of material from the Maggid. The work's editor, Aharon ha-Kohen of Apt, culled these teachings from previously printed works as well as unpublished traditions (whether oral or in manuscript).[35] The misattribution of many of these teachings, seemingly deliberate, may represent an effort to recast the BeSHT as the ultimate source of the

Maggid's theological creativity, though Aharon ha-Kohen was surely not unaware of the prestige and commercial value commanded by a sizable—and
accessible—collection of teachings from the revered BeSHT.

Printed Hasidic literature began to circulate in the 1780s, but for years
handwritten manuscripts had played a crucial role in the dissemination of
Hasidic ideas—including those of the Maggid.[36] Disciples continued to
use these manuscripts even after Dov Ber's homilies were published as
printed compendia. Such works were rather expensive, and some early
Hasidic communities even preserved a sacrosanct place for handwritten texts
after they had been printed.[37] And, of equal importance, transcriptions of
Dov Ber's teachings clearly circulated within the Maggid's lifetime,[38] and
were quoted by his disciples as "copies" (he'etakot)[39] or "manuscripts" (kitvei
yad).[40] Many of his prominent disciples possessed such copies of his sermons, including Levi Yitshak of Barditshev, Shmu'el Shmelke of Nikolsburg, and Menahem Mendel of Vitebsk, as well as Shlomo of Lutsk and
Yisra'el of Kozhenits.[41]

Fundamental questions regarding the authorship, provenance, and
textual interdependency of these manuscripts remain unanswered.[42] These
manuscripts bear witness to the fact that the printed collections, though
extensive, are only a small sampling of the Maggid's legacy—even that which
was committed to writing. Several of Dov Ber's important disciples, most
notably Levi Yitshak and Shlomo of Lutsk, evidently had a hand in transcribing the Maggid's homilies. It is curious, however, that Levi Yitshak's
approbation of the Barditshev 1808 edition of *Maggid Devarav le-Ya'akov*
makes no mention of his efforts to write down his master's teachings.[43]
Stranger yet is the fact that these students make no explicit mention of one
another's efforts to capture their master's words in writings.[44] They may
have been involved in transcribing the Maggid's teachings at different
times. Shlomo of Lutsk, however, makes veiled reference to individuals
who abbreviate and misunderstand Dov Ber's teachings in their attempt to
put them into writing. The near silence may well indicate some rivalry between them, suggesting that the struggle for the Maggid's legacy began as
the very first written texts were produced.

The wealth of manuscripts led to the publication of new compendia of
the Maggid's teachings throughout the nineteenth and twentieth centuries.
Kitvei Kodesh (Lemberg, 1862), *Or ha-Emet* (Husyatin, 1899), *Sefer Likkutei Amarim* (Lemberg, 1911), and *Shemu'ah Tovah* (Warsaw, 1938), all printed
from privately held manuscripts, present otherwise unknown material from

the Maggid together with teachings from other Hasidic thinkers.[45] These works should be distinguished from posthumous "works" of early figures that are nothing more than late composites of oral (or literary) traditions printed in response to the increasingly central place of books in Hasidic culture.[46] But many of the extant manuscripts with sermons and *hanhagot* attributed to the Maggid remain unpublished, in part or in full, as do traditions embedded in handwritten compendia or texts by later Hasidic masters.[47] Only a careful comparative study of these manuscripts will demonstrate the overlap or degrees of variance between them, and reveal which sections have not yet been published.[48]

The recently published volume *Dibberot ha-Maggid* (Jerusalem: Mechon Genuzim, 2018) is an excellent example of this phenomenon. The editors of the printed book explain that this new collection is based on an early manuscript, which, they claim, served as the source of many of the early books of teachings printed in the Maggid's name. The manuscript runs some two hundred folios, including several hundreds of sermons of varying lengths and complexity. The pagination, the locutions, and the names of the other figures mentioned (including Levi Yitshak of Zelekhev/Barditshev) demonstrate that *Dibberot ha-Maggid* is based on the same manuscript (Scholem MS RS 28) employed by Rivka Schatz-Uffenheimer in her critical edition of *Maggid Devarav le-Ya'akov*, although they decidedly neglect to mention Schatz-Uffenheimer's work. *Dibberot ha-Maggid* includes some otherwise unattested sermons and some interesting dated material, adding complexity to the role of Levi Yitshak in the transcription and editing of Dov Ber's homilies. However, the producers of the new volume reordered the homilies to reflect the order of the Torah readings and holidays. This anthological choice undermines the value of the work for scholars of early Hasidism, revealing the vast extent to which editors reshape and transform Hasidic teachings when moving the homilies from manuscript to print.

One further compendium of the Maggid's teachings deserves note, although it includes relatively little new material. Yisra'el Klapholtz's late anthology *Torat ha-Maggid* (Tel Aviv, 1969) draws together the full range of sermons and *hanhagot* from printed books as well as a few unpublished manuscripts. Klapholtz's goal was to unite the variety of traditions attributed to the Maggid for the first time, without identifying *which* book is the most authentic representation of the Dov Ber's teachings or attempting to decide which of the various versions of the teachings is the most correct.[49] *Torat ha-Maggid* thus serves as an interesting example of how multiple traditions from the Maggid may be juxtaposed in order to illuminate their consistency and contradictions.[50]

Klapholtz's work is also important because it drew on a significant and often underappreciated corpus of teachings: the works of the Maggid's disciples. Traditions preserved in works of Dov Ber's students must be used with caution, of course, because the words of a teacher undergo a process of interpretation whenever they are shaped by a student's memory or writing.[51] The manner in which the Maggid's disciples cite their teacher's words speaks to the various complexities of such oral transmission, from errata and misunderstandings to the simple fact of imperfect human memory.

In some instances, Dov Ber's students reproduce teachings from the Maggid and then puzzle over their meaning. Others disciples lament having forgotten key parts of the homily or being unable to fully recast the sermon in written form.[52] In a few cases, a student offers a summary or paraphrase of his master's words, acknowledging that this secondhand account is laconic and imprecise.[53] Students evidently relied on each other for explanations of the Maggid's cryptic oeuvre, for at least one disciple refers to struggling with a homily until finding an explanation in the work of another student.[54] Such dynamics left their imprint on the contours of the Maggid's thought as presented in the works of his disciples.

For the purposes of the present book, I have defined a disciple of the Maggid's as an individual who met him on at least one occasion and was therefore in a position to cite his teachings firsthand. Although homilies, stories, and traditions quoted by nineteenth- or early twentieth-century Hasidim may very well represent an oral legacy not yet committed to writing, such transmission is difficult to chart. This does not mean, however, that all of Dov Ber's immediate disciples absorbed the master's ideas directly. Some surely did, either as a public sermon or in personal instruction. But other students heard traditions as quoted and transmitted orally by another of the Maggid's disciples.[55] In a small but significant number of cases, even students who knew the Maggid reveal that they absorbed a teaching from a handwritten manuscript or even from a printed collection. All of these avenues are represented in the works of his students, though the first two are by far the most common, suggesting that the oral pathways of communication were more important—and perhaps more accessible—than those of written language.[56]

Given the issues presented by citations of the Maggid in his disciples' work, what argument could be adduced for welcoming such teachings into our study of his thought? At times, we can explore a certain teaching presented by a disciple by comparing it to the various other witnesses of the same homily. This is particularly useful if the tradition can be juxtaposed with a sermon printed in one of the published collections of Dov Ber's teachings. Even without seeking a single *Urtext* for each of his homilies, this comparison might allow us to verify which ideas originated with the Maggid himself. But this tack demands that we exclude valuable teachings that appear in the works of a disciple—or two—but lack a parallel in the printed sermons attributed to Dov Ber. Accepting only those teachings that appear in many works assumes that all of the Maggid's teachings were delivered publicly to a large group of his disciples, a fact that is not borne out in the sources. And, perhaps most problematic of all, weighing the students' homilies against the sermons printed in Dov Ber's name falsely attributes a "gold standard" to the published compendia. These books are equally fraught with textual problems and uncertainty.

Moshe Rosman's helpful distinction between scholarly "usability" and historical "reliability" in regard to the teachings of the BeSHT will be of significant assistance in grappling with these questions. Though they would be deemed unreliable if our task were to reconstruct the original sermons as delivered by Dov Ber, these important traditions reveal much about how the Maggid's theology was remembered—and recast—in the decades immediately after his death.[57] We must also remember that a significant degree of mediation is present in *all* extant written records of the Maggid's homilies; the teachings quoted in his students' works are not necessarily more heavily interpreted than the written sermons printed in his name. Furthermore, in a small but significant number of instances, students cite traditions from the Maggid but then immediately offer a different interpretation of the biblical verse or rabbinic teaching that opposes the exegesis and message of their teacher.[58] Teachings that are presented against the grain, as it were, may in fact be some of the very best textual witnesses.

On the Shores of Language

These problems are by no means unique to the study of Hasidism or even to Judaism.[59] Similar issues of transmission, textual diffusion, conceptual fluidity, and a near-total lack of stable *Urtexts* confront scholars of most religious traditions.[60] In Buddhism, the teachings of Gautama were surely transformed by his disciples, as these students put them into writing or circulated them orally, often transposing them from language to language—and from culture to culture. These processes sculpted the structure and form of the Buddha's words and shaped the ideational content of his teachings. The past decades have seen the rise of a vast subfield examining the prehistory—and underpinnings—of Christian scripture, showing that key parts of the New Testament emerged from a "synoptic orality" rather than a single, stable pre-Gospel textual source.[61] Scholars continue to debate to what extent—if any—we may use the teachings attributed to Muhammad and the *hadith* traditions to reconstruct the formative period of Islam.[62]

Religious literatures the world over have thus emerged from an intricate gossamer of sources, both oral and written, rather than the strict *ipsissima verba* of their central leaders, teachers, and in some cases, their founders.[63] Scholars must be mindful of the limits of such sources, exploring the usability of various texts in constructing different narratives rather than attempting to pinpoint or suss out their strict historical accuracy or authentic kernel.

The complex hybridity of Hasidic attitudes toward the written and spoken word is another shared feature linking this investigation to broader issues of historical significance. William Graham, a noted scholar of the Qur'an, has unveiled the largely unappreciated oral dimensions of Scripture in religious cultures across the globe. His argument, though elegant and erudite, is essentially quite simple: scholars all too often misconceive of sacred sources purely as "texts"—as self-sufficient written artifacts—either because of categorical assumptions about the nature of reading or study in a devotional community, or simply because it is easier to study written words than to inquire into their place at the hub of a cultural universe of signs, sounds, and performative gestures. "A sacred text," writes Graham, "can be read laboriously in silent study, chanted or sung in unthinking repetition, copied or illuminated in loving devotion, imaginatively depicted in art or drama, solemnly processed in ritual pageantry, or devoutly touched in hope of luck and blessing."[64]

This is surely true of Jewish relationships to the classics of the canon—the Hebrew Bible and the Talmud—but many of these performative features apply equally to the sacred books of Hasidism. For the faithful reader, devoted study of these works includes "affective" and sensory—or "sensual"—elements of religious experience.[65] Hasidic inspiration is generated by face-to-face encounters with living teachers, but such uplift is also born in the pious encounter with the text. This relationship to the sacred book expressed through embodied practices, from illuminated prayer tied to its words to the simple act of kissing the book when replacing it on a shelf or slipping it under a pillow to alleviate the dangers of childbirth. The words of a Hasidic book are not just silently perused: for the Hasid, the words are imbibed into the innermost reaches of the soul, and, moreover, they are recited aloud.

Moderns often forget that vocal reading was the standard for much of our history, and that it remains such in many cultures across the globe (including Hasidic society). Changes in reading practices were one of the many shock waves that ripped through traditional communities with the advent of print culture. Published books fundamentally transformed the relationship to oral speech and written words: the increased accessibility of written materials and the relative independence of the reader shifted the way that people cultivated, processed, and dispersed knowledge.[66] Moses Mendelssohn, whose classic philosophical treatise *Jerusalem* (1783) appeared just a few decades after the death of the Maggid, was aghast at the overreliance on printed words in his day. Though acknowledging the benefits of the outpouring of knowledge heralded by such a cultural shift, Mendelssohn laments that the pivot toward written words was far-reaching and by no means entirely positive: "We teach and instruct one another only through writings; we learn to know nature and man only from writings. We work and relax, edify and amuse ourselves through overmuch writing. The preacher does not converse with his congregation; he reads or declaims to it a written treatise. The professor reads his written lectures from the chair. Everything is the dead letter; the spirit of living conversation has vanished. . . . Hence, it has come to pass that man has almost lost his value for his fellow man."[67] Mendelssohn decried the loss of a sense of vital engagement with other human beings that resulted from the turn toward printed books as the arbiters of knowledge and culture. He describes the focal point of Berlin intellectual society as trained to the written word, rather than to communion between two living souls. Painting this transition in such dire terms served Mendelssohn's own philosophical goal of defending the validity of the oral Law, but his mournful complaint reveals an important aspect of the cultural reformations in early modern western Europe.

The words of Kalonymous Kalman Epstein (d. 1823), a Hasidic leader who flourished in Krakow some decades after Mendelssohn, offer a very different picture of the relationship between books and education. In accounting for why so few of the great Hasidic masters of the late eighteenth century committed their teachings to writing, Kalonymous explains:

> They did not produce books inscribed in writing. But they accomplished something even greater: they instructed their disciples and raised up many students. . . .
>
> Each of these disciples is an illuminated work (*sefer*), as it were, like the word "luminous" (*sapirut*) and "clear" (*bahir*)—their hearts clearly shine with the service of the Divine. . . . This is [the meaning of the verse] "there is no end of making many books" (Eccl. 12:12)—each of a *tsaddik*'s students, and the disciples of those students, are individual books whose hearts radiate divine service.[68]

Hasidic leaders and thinkers continued to assign pride of place to oral spiritual instruction rather than the written word well into the twentieth century, long after the emergence of printed Hasidic literature. The evocative power of the Hasidic sermon is found precisely in its oral quality and in the enduring charismatic presence of the leader. The delivery of these homilies, likened to the theophany at Sinai, was a momentous occasion of religious significance.

And yet, though preference is given to the oral sermon, the Hasidic book has also become a locus of spiritual experience conjured up through the act of reading. For much of literary history, reading was essentially an oral activity in which texts were read *aloud* rather than being silently—and privately—perused.[69] Hasidic attitudes toward the written word suggest that performative, vocal forms of reading have not entirely disappeared from the modern landscape. Josef Balogh argued for the prominence of voiced reading well into the nineteenth century, and, in Hasidism, it exists still.[70] These sources note that the originally oral revelatory moment may be recreated, if with somewhat diminished intensity, through the embodied act of carefully attuned study.

This devotional approach to reading recalls the point made with such felicity by Michael Polanyi, who notes that our claim to "read or listen to a text, and . . . not merely see it or hear it, is precisely to imply that we are attending focally to what is indicated by the words seen or heard and not to these words themselves."[71] The task of the reader, thus conceived, is not simply to fixate on the written words but to look beyond—or within—the text and into a reservoir of meaning accessed through personal experience. Similar descriptions of sacred study abound in Hasidic works from the eighteenth century into the present day, as Hasidic thinkers reflected on the importance of reading religious texts through opening the mind—and heart—to the spiritual grasp of the written word.

The Hasidic sermon is, with few exceptions, a literature beset with issues of translation. The homilies were delivered in Yiddish but generally preserved only in Hebrew, which has long functioned as the primary language of Jewish scholarship across the generations. But the Yiddish lurking behind these texts has not been entirely effaced. A layer of Yiddish dwells deep within Hasidic homily even after these oral discourses were translated into Hebrew and committed to writing. Yiddish inheres in the structures, diction, and syntax of the Hebrew, and, as Arthur Green has noted, the "accent" of the original continues to loom in the translated source.[72] Returning to Zeev Gries's claim that the written Hebrew source is but a "weak echo of a living experience,"[73] we might say that a trace of the Yiddish continues to resonate in the Hebrew homily. Yiddish remains veiled within the shroud of Hebrew words, a linguistic simultaneity that complements the Hasidic commitment to both oral language and written words.

This issue of language choice brings us to a larger question about the role of translations within a single polyglossic culture vis-à-vis transpositions that "move" a text or sermon from one language community to another. In her pathbreaking work on Jewish theories of translation, Naomi Seidman has explored the cultural religious performativity of language through showing that many modern—that is, Western—notions of translations are essentially grounded in an assumption of linguistic equivalence. She argues that Jewish translation projects, like all such efforts, cannot be separated from politics and historical cultural surroundings, noting that "Jewish translation . . . takes its shape within particular cultural settings, in conversation with others—indeed, it is an exemplary expression as well as the privileged conduit of these conversations."[74] Rather than an abstract literary, philosophical, or theological problem, translation is a process that is indelibly linked to the boundaries of human communities. And, for that reason, Seidman argues: "Translation more particularly appears as a negotiation of an unavoidably asymmetrical *double*-situatedness. As such, it both complicates and is informed by issues of identity. Because translation is necessarily also a political negotiation, it appears not strictly as a linguistic exercise but also in a variety of relational modes: translation as colonialist, imperialist, or missionary appropriation but also translation as risk, as assimilation, as treason, as dislocation, as survival."[75] This certainly holds true of translations in which there is an attempt to permeate the boundary of one culture through rendering a text or speech act comprehensible—and accessible—to another community. But the notion of "*double*-situatedness" is expressed differently when the translation effort navigates between two languages, each with their own cultural place and resonances, within a single diglossic or multilingual group. Seidman astutely notes that Jewish ambivalence—and, more than occasionally, outright antipathy—toward the project of intercultural translation manifests differently in regard to intracultural translation.[76] Translations intended to serve individuals outside of the safe borders of Jewish linguistic culture, such as the Septuagint, have suspicion levied against them that is shot through with political concerns.

Intracommunal translations occupy a different cultural role, though such projects may also raise questions of power and authority. The near-universal Hasidic choice to translate its teachings into Hebrew and preserve them thusly in writing seems to have been undertaken in order to increase respectability (internally as well as in the face of its detractors), but the preference for Hebrew may also represent an attempt to establish a Hasidic literature that is linked to ancient Jewish exegetical and literary traditions. A choice to preserve the sermons in Yiddish, by contrast, might have been driven by considerations of audience and accessibility, as well as an attempt to guard the teachings in as pristine and unchanged a form as possible.

Recent scholarship has emphasized that the classical trope of "Hebrew for sacred subjects, Yiddish for the mundane" is insufficient for explaining the place of Yiddish in Hasidic society. Chava Turniansky has shown that intended audience, rather than content, often drove an author's choice of languages in eastern Europe. The Yiddish sermon, in both oral *and* written forms, mediated between the scholarly intellectual culture and that of the broader community.[77] This is all the more complicated in Hasidism because the religious significance of each of these languages, which share a common alphabet, is firmly implanted in the Hasidic imagination.

Hasidic homilies were first put into writing in handwritten manuscripts, and it was from these sources that the printed books of the Hasidic library were generated. Many of these textual witnesses—with few exceptions, only in Hebrew—have endured, and comparison to the printed books demonstrates that in the transition from manuscript to book the teachings were often significantly transformed. In many cases this process continued across different printings and editions of books: new material was added, other

elements were taken out, and seemingly minor changes like print format-
ting, divisions between sermons, and apparatuses of notes or commentary
were introduced. Each of these shifts impacts the way these theological
teachings are interpreted by the reader.

The printed book, for all of its smooth coherence, is a deceptively marbled object. Historians of material culture have long argued that even the
most finely produced printed book conceals untold stories, visible to the per-
ceptive reader whose eyes are trained beyond the meaning of the words. As
Adrian Johns has highlighted in his study of printing in early modern
England, "The appearance and even the content of printed pages could be
closely affected by the skills and conceptions of the printers producing them.
In the final appearance of the page were implicated the compositor's knowledge, dexterity, interpretation of authorial meaning, and anticipation of
readers' competences."[78] The breadcrumbs of typography and style reveal much
grander movements of print culture. But they are equally true of words committed to writing that endure in unpublished manuscripts. Daniel Abrams
has argued quite adamantly that just as books must be seen as multilayered
cultural and religious constructs with a delicate history and prehistory, such
is also the case with manuscripts, which are never picture-perfect represen-
tations of an idealized *Urtext*: "As literary artifacts of material culture, manuscripts should not be viewed as the raw data that scholars process in order
to produced critical editions. . . . Manuscripts *are* processed data, signposts
of the particular stages of composition, editing and textual reactions accomplished by readers, copyists and assorted other commentators who did not
share the modern sensibility of 'what is an author' and the literary integrity
of a work."[79] The page of a book or the face of a manuscript is an aggre-
gate of influences, expectations, and commitments, which are manifest
in the physical form of the book and the choices that lead to the way it
looks. The text is far more than a book: in addition to the semantic meaning of its words, it gestures toward an entire world of other matters that
must be taken into account when interpreting the ideational content of the
teachings it holds.

Parting Words

The Maggid may not have committed his own teachings to the written word,
raising them up "upon the altar of print" in the rabbinic idiom, but sources

attest that Dov Ber was well aware that his sermons were circulating in written form.[80] In fact, Shlomo of Lutsk claims that he began to transcribe the Maggid's teachings at the behest of the master himself:

> The Lord knows that the truth is with me, witnessing that I write these words in this holy compendium. I have written all this so that God's people will understand that even in this bitter exile, in this impure land, our God has not forsaken us. We have been sent sainted individuals (*tsadikkim gedolim*), interrogators of hearts, to revive us as on this very day. . . .
>
> I thought to put neither hand nor foot toward publishing this holy work—even to write down words such as these seemed utterly distant in my eyes, for they are wisdom [as fine] as coral,[81] such that they cannot even be spoken. . . . [82]
>
> But once my master and teacher asked me why I was not writing down what I heard. I responded to him as above. I also said that I have noticed that those who do transcribe [the sermons] abbreviate [i.e., and misconstrue] the master's intention. They often lack comprehension, writing according to their own understanding. He told me, "Nevertheless, however they will be written down, it will be for the good, so that it may be a reminder for the service of the blessed Creator" (*mazkeret le-'avodat ha-bore barukh hu*).[83]
>
> I asked him, "Why does our master and teacher want such a thing?" He said, "Is what King David asked for such a small matter, saying 'May I dwell in your house forever' (*'olamim*, Ps. 61:5)—in this world and in the next."[84]
>
> But I [i.e., Shlomo of Lutsk] still did not want to write them down, and certainly not publish them, because of the abovementioned reasons [of fear of misinterpretation and oversimplification].[85]

Shlomo of Lutsk balks at the idea of writing down the Maggid's teachings, lamenting that others have tried and that their work is riddled with misunderstanding and hopelessly bland when compared to the original living word. Perhaps, as Gries has argued, Shlomo was afraid to publicize the Maggid's teachings because of the many references to Lurianic Kabbalah. But this reading seems a stretch, given that the issue at hand is simply the act of *transcribing* the Maggid's sermons, not necessarily publishing or distributing them to a wider audience.[86]

Unlike Shneur Zalman of Liady, who tightly controlled the written versions of his teachings,[87] we find no trace of the Maggid editing or standardizing the texts written by his students. The Maggid seems to have had no interest in establishing a single authoritative or authentic written form of his teachings, and certainly not a printed book. The vicissitudes of transcription, translation, abbreviation, and even misunderstanding seem not to have concerned him as they did his disciple. This introduction suggests a different explanation for Shlomo's silent quill: the impossibility of capturing the depth of the Maggid's sermons and the rapturous experience of hearing them directly from the illuminated master in written language.

Even with the shortcomings inherent in transcribing his teachings, Dov Ber suggests that these records will be "a reminder for the service of the blessed Creator" (*mazkeret le-'avodat ha-bore barukh hu*).[88] This elliptical formulation bears many possible interpretations. The Maggid's request may reflect his understanding that ideas must be preserved in written form in order for them to endure beyond the span of his life. Such texts would enable disciples to review his teachings after his death, and new students might become exposed to his sermons through the transcriptions. However, I suspect that the Maggid may have sensed the impending transition from oral pathways of communication and foresaw the role books would play as the Hasidic movement began to take shape. In this context I would like to offer the following understanding of the phrase *mazkeret le-'avodat ha-bore barukh hu*: these oral sermons-cum-textual artifacts, although written in abbreviated and altered form, are an access point for continued religious inspiration for once and future students.

The Maggid's trust in the written word as a finite vessel that can nonetheless hold an infinite reservoir of meaning appears in the many homilies in which he explores the correct "intention" (*kavvanah*) one must have in studying a written text. Dov Ber suggests that a scholar must imagine that the sage to whom a particular teaching is attributed is standing before him and reciting it anew. Through contemplating these words and speaking them aloud as well, the scholar begins to unearth an even deeper source of inspiration—the original sage's wisdom, which remained dormant within the words of the text until being reawakened by the scholar. Quoting a Talmudic maxim, Dov Ber claims that this process causes the sage's lips to murmur in their grave.[89] The meeting of the wisdom that has been derived from the written text with the vitality imbued in it by the contemporary scholar simultaneously extends the life of the teacher and brings the reader to a new state of enlightened redemption.[90]

Such homilies suggest that a student can attain the wisdom of his master through contemplating his written words even long after his death. We might distinguish between reading a canonical text such as the Talmud, whose words are taken to be authoritative and authentic, and reading the teachings of a Hasidic master as they were copied down by one of his students. We have seen, however, that the Maggid describes all acts of communication between a master and a disciple in a similar manner. The teacher focuses his ineffable wisdom into language, but through contemplating his master's words the student can reach beyond the letters and recover the original idea.

The Maggid makes no ultimate distinction between written and oral language. Delving into a transcription of a teacher's ideas does not hinder the process of recovering the wisdom, for the written words come to life once more as they are spoken aloud. The text and its study re-evoke the *tsaddik* as a person and an illuminated human being. This realization returns us to Scholem's comment that Hasidism essentially produced remarkable original religious personalities more than it did new ideas, which has been challenged and largely overturned in recent decades.[91] Texts, and the ideas with which they are imbued, return their readers to the charisma of the living person.

The Maggid does not explicitly extend this model to his own readers, but such may be the intention behind his application of the term "reminder" (*mazkeret*) to the copies of his homilies. Written texts gesture toward the riches of oral speech, and a master's words change radically as they are filtered through the disciple's mind and are entered upon the page. Such transformations, however, are not grounds for dismissal. The psalmist's yearning to dwell in God's house, says the Maggid in light of the Talmudic interpretation, is nothing less than a teacher's impassioned call to be remembered after the length of his days. To dwell in language, to enter the written words together with illuminated sacred speech, is also to stand in the presence of the living master who first spoke them. Embracing the gift of words is to attain eternity by slaking one's thirst from the flow of sacred vitality, dipping into the rushing river of language that is at once human and divine.

Notes

Works frequently cited have been identified by the following abbreviations:

ABBREVIATIONS OF COLLECTIONS OF THE MAGGID'S TEACHINGS

MDL	Maggid Devarav le-Ya'akov
LY	Likkutim Yekarim
TSVHR	Tsava'at ha-RiBaSH
KST	Keter Shem Tov
OT	Or Torah
KTVK	Kitvei Kodesh
OHE	Or ha-Emet
ST	Shemu'ah Tovah
SLA	Sefer Likkutei Amarim
THM	Torat ha-Maggid
DHM	Dibberot ha-Maggid

OTHER COMMON ABBREVIATIONS

m.	Mishnah
t.	Tosefta
y.	Jerusalem Talmud
b.	Babylonian Talmud

Note to epigraph: Zelda Schneurson Mishkovsky, "Heavy Silence," in *The Spectacular Difference: Selected Poems*, trans. Marcia Falk (Cincinnati: Hebrew Union College Press, 2004), 221.

PREFACE

1. Abraham Joshua Heschel, *Moral Grandeur and Spiritual Audacity: Essays*, ed. Susannah Heschel (New York: Farrar, Straus and Giroux, 1996), 275.

2. Charles Taylor, *The Language Animal: The Full Shape of the Human Linguistic Capacity* (Cambridge: The Belknap Press of Harvard University Press, 2016), 4.

INTRODUCTION

1. The only complete account of the movement's history is the recently published Biale et al., *Hasidism*.

2. See Idel, *Hasidism*, 57–58, 83–84, 92–93, 160–170; idem, "Modes of Cleaving," 299–317; Elior, *Mystical Origins*, 41–45.

3. See Pedaya, "Baal Shem Tov," 58–59, 66–69; idem, "Two Types," 86–87.

4. Durkheim, *Elementary Forms*, 36–40, 227; and Eliade, *Sacred and the Profane*.

5. See Goody, "Religion and Ritual," 142–164, esp. 151; Jay, "Gender and Dichotomy," 38–56.

6. Seligman et al., 180.

7. Ibid., 7.

8. See Berger, *Sacred Canopy*, esp. 26–27.

9. See also Mayse, "Expanding the Boundaries."

10. See Magid, *Hasidism Incarnate*, 1–14 and 31–50; and Wolfson, *Language, Eros, Being*, 190–260.

11. See Garb, *Manifestations of Power*, esp. 142–173; and Lachter, *Kabbalistic Revolution*, esp. 15–44, 100–158.

12. This Hasidic embrace of the vernacular, explored in greater detail below, echoes seventeenth-century Sabbatianism. On Shabbatai Tsevi singing melodies (including Christian songs) in the *lingua franca*, claiming they contained mystical secrets, see Scholem, *Sabbatai Sevi*, 397 and 313. See also Papo, "From Messianic Apologetics"; Sisman, *Burden of Silence*, 154–156; and Mayse "Expanding the Boundaries." This potential connection between Sabbatianism and Hasidism, a broader issue that remains the subject of scholarly dispute, requires further inquiry.

13. On paradox, see Elior, *Paradoxical Ascent*; and Liebes, "Zohar and Eros," 67–119.

14. See Matt, "*Ayin*," 67–108; Elior, "Paradigms of *Yesh* and *Ayin*," 168–179.

15. See Lorberbaum, "Attain the Attribute," 169–235. Cf. OT, *pesukim*, no. 348, p. 385; and MDL, no. 199, p. 324.

16. This paradox was identified and explored, in brief, by Weiss, "Mystical Hasidism," 278–282.

17. See Sells, *Mystical Languages*; Franke, *On What Cannot Be Said*; and Putnam, "On Negative Theology," 407–422.

18. McGinn, *Essential Writings*, 146–147.

19. See also Turner, *Darkness of God*; and Proudfoot, *Religious Experience*, esp. 119–154.

20. Maimonides, *Guide of the Perplexed*, 1:59, interpreting Ps. 65:2; and the devastating critique in Crescas, "Light of the Lord," 104–105.

21. See also Marmur, "God of Language," 267–292; and Fishbane, "Mystical Contemplation," 1–27.

22. Sells, *Mystical Languages*, 3.

23. Ibid., 15; cf. 12.

24. Ibid., 10.

25. Perhaps Dov Ber sensed the dangers inherent in the BeSHT's notion of radical divine immanence. See Green, "Hasidism: Discovery and Retreat," 104–130.

26. See Sells, *Mystical Languages*, 11: "Part of the modern misunderstanding of classical apophasis is due to the projection back upon late antique and medieval writers of a monomic, generic God divorced from particular traditions and language."

27. See, for example, James, *Varieties of Religious Experience*, esp. 370–420; Underhill, *Mysticism*, esp. 83–113, 427–452; and Otto, *Idea of the Holy*, 5–51, 62–73.

28. Inge, *Christian Mysticism*, 4–5.

29. See Schmidt, "Making of Modern 'Mysticism,'" 273–302; de Certeau, *Mystic Fable*, 1–26; Dupré, "Spiritual Life," 21–31; and, more broadly, McGinn, "Theoretical Foundations," 265–343.

30. See Katz, "Language, Epistemology, and Mysticism," 22–74; idem, "'Conservative' Character," 3–60. See also Forman, *Problem of Pure Consciousness*, 3–49; Hollenback, *Mysticism*, 33–132.

31. On Buber's use of Hasidism, see Shonkoff, "Sacramental Existence."

32. Buber, *Ecstatic Confessions*, 5.

33. Buber, *I and Thou*, 89.

34. See Buber, "Word That Is Spoken," 353–360.

35. See Biale, *Gershom Scholem*, 112–146.

36. See also Idel, "Reification of Language," 42–79; Wolfson, *Language, Eros, Being*, esp. 1–45; and Idel, *Absorbing Perfections*.

37. See Biale, *Gershom Scholem*, 112–146.

38. See his reference to Buber in Scholem, *Major Trends*, 354 n. 13; and Biale, *Gershom Scholem*, 122–123.

39. Scholem, *Major Trends*, 354 n. 13.

40. See Scholem, "Meaning of the Torah," 32–86.

41. See Scholem, "Name of God," 59–80; idem, "Name of God (Part 2)," 164–194. See also Ben-Sasson, "'Name of God . . . Revisited," 1–28.

42. Dan, "Gershom Scholem," 13; cited in Wasserstrom, *Religion After Religion*, 23.

43. Scholem, "Name of God," 62–63.

44. Ibid., 61.

45. Benjamin, "On Language as Such," 74. A similar theory emerges from his much-read essay "The Task of the Translator," where Benjamin describes translation as returning to the primordial language beyond words; see Benjamin, "Task of the Translator," 258–259.

46. Benjamin, "On Language as Such," 69.

47. Ibid., 71.

48. Scholem, *Major Trends*, 338. Italics in the original.

49. See Scholem, *"Devekut,"* 214–222; Weiss, *"Via Passiva,"* 69–94; and idem, "Mystical Hasidism," 277–285.

50. For a recent reappraisal of Buber's impact on Scholem, see Meir, "Hasidism," 93–120.

51. See Schatz-Uffenheimer, *Ha-Hasidut ke-Mistikah*; translated as *Hasidism as Mysticism*. See also idem, "Contemplative Prayer," 209–226.

52. Schatz-Uffenheimer, *Hasidism as Mysticism*, 185.

53. Ibid., 61.

54. See also Schatz-Uffenheimer, *Hasidism as Mysticism*, esp. 65–69, 184–188, 111–143, 185–186, 190–192, 204–214.

55. See Idel, *Hasidism*, 1; Brody, "Open to Me," esp. 25; and Margolin, *Human Temple*, 6–51, 176–191, 202–215, 280–283.

56. See Piekarz, *Between Ideology and Reality*, esp. 154.

57. See Pedaya, "Baal Shem Tov," 58–59, 66–69; and idem, "Two Types," 86–87.

58. See Kauffman, *In All Your Ways*, esp. 426–466.

59. Ibid., 19–20.

60. On language as a sacred bestowal, see also Wolfson, *Giving Beyond the Gift*.

61. Benjamin, "Language as Such," 67, cites Hamann's programmatic declaration "language—the mother of reason and revelation," as does Scholem, "Name of God," 62. See, more broadly, Horwitz, "Hamman and Rosenzweig," v–xxviii.

62. See German, *Hamann on Language*.

63. See Sparling, *Johann Georg Hamann*, 139–156; and Levy, "Johann Georg Hamann's Concept of Judaism," 295–329; and Forster, "Herder's Philosophy of Language," esp. 325–328.

64. Hamann, "Aesthetica in Nuce," 66.

65. See also Terazakis, *The Immanent Word*.

66. Hamann, "Last Will and Testament," 99.

67. See Girón-Negrón, "Dionysian Thought," 693–706.

68. See, in particular, Key, *Language Between God and the Poets*; and Frank, "Hearing and Saying," 611–618.

69. See Germano, "Poetic Thought."

70. Smith, *Imagining Religion*, 21 (italics in the original). See also Patton, "Juggling Torches," 153–171.

71. Garb, *Yearnings of the Soul*, 15, comments: "When dealing with theories and images, as opposed to the more socially embedded world of practices and experiences, one can draw on the entire range of religious and mystical writing. . . . However, one must then make every effort to relate the resultant insights to specific social and cultural contexts."

72. As quoted in McGinn, *Essential Writings*, 414.

73. Wolfson, *Language, Eros, Being*, 371–372.

74. See Idel, "White Letters," 169–192; and Bloom, *Kabbalah and Criticism*.

75. Schleiermacher, *Hermeneutics*, 97.

76. See Bono, *Word of God*.

77. See de Grazia, "Secularization of Language," 319–329.

78. See Wodziński, *Haskalah and Hasidism*.

79. See Stern, *Genius*, 1–12, 63–82.

80. See Feiner, *Origins of Jewish Secularization*, esp. 20–21.

81. Maimon, *Autobiography*, 97.

82. On modern Kabbalah as one of multiple Jewish modernities, see Garb, *Yearnings of the Soul*, 16–18, building on the iconic work of Eisenstadt, *Comparative Civilizations*.

83. See Rosman, *Founder*, 42–94; Hundert, *Jews in Poland-Lithuania*, 32–56; Dynner, *Men of Silk*, 25–88; and idem, *Yankel's Tavern*.

84. See Petrovsky-Shtern, *Golden Age Shtetl*.

85. Together with the bibliographic excursus in the appendix of the present book, see Mayse and Reiser, "Territories and Textures," 127–160.

86. Scholem, "Thoughts About Our Language," 27–28.
87. Scholem, "Name of God (Part 2)," 194.

CHAPTER 1

Notes to epigraphs: Heilman, *Beit Rabbi*, 189–190, translated in Green et al., *Speaking Torah*, 1:vii; Twersky, *Introduction to the Code*, 76.

1. See Petrovsky-Shtern, "Master of an Evil Name," 217–248; idem, "You Will Find It in the Pharmacy," 13–54; and Rosman, *Founder*, 1–42, 173–186.
2. See Rosman, *Founder*; and Etkes, *Besht*.
3. On this shift, see Green, "Hasidic Tsaddik."
4. See Rapoport-Albert, "Hasidism After 1772," 76–140; and cf. Dubnow, "Maggid," 58–66.
5. For a helpful study of the ritual complexity life among courtiers, nobility, and monarchs, see Elias, *Court Society*.
6. See Ehrman, *Lost Christianities*; and Dunn, *Unity and Diversity in the New Testament*. See also Magid, *Hasidism Incarnate*, 131–170.
7. On *Shivhei ha-BeSHT*, the most important collection of Hasidic tales, see Rosman, *Founder*, 143–158; and Etkes, *Besht*, 203–248; and Fishbane, "Perceptions of Greatness," 195–221.
8. See *Bi-leshon Hasidim Tithadesh*.
9. See Bodek, *Seder ha-Dorot ha-Hadash*, 31–32; Berger, *'Eser Orot*, 12a–14a; Buber, *Tales*, 98–112. Heilman's *Beit Rabbi* offers an image of the Maggid from the perspective of the Habad Hasidic community; see Karlinsky, "Dawn," 20–46.
10. See Gries, *Book in Early Hasidism*, 35–40; Dan, "Bow," 175–193; Meir, *Literary Hasidism*.
11. On Hasidic tales and their use, see Buber, "Interpreting Hasidism," 218; and cf. Scholem, "Martin Buber's Interpretation," 228–250. See also Green, "Buber, Scholem"; Kauffman, "Hasidic Story," 101–126; Rapoport-Albert, "Hagiography with Footnotes," 119–159; Nigal, *Hasidic Tale*; and Dynner, "Hasidic Tale," 655–675.
12. Dynner, *Men of Silk*, 132–134, notes that lineage swiftly became determinative for Hasidic leadership in Poland. For attempts to construct an illustrious pedigree for the Maggid, see *Kerem Yisrael*, 7–8; *Ner Yisra'el*, 6:424–428; and *Ohalei Ya'akov*, 89.
13. Despite his distaste for all things Hasidic, Graetz, *History of the Jews*, 5:402, was moved to write: "He was well read in Talmudical and Kabbalistic writings, was a skillful preacher (Maggid) . . . [and] removed from the Chassidim the stigma of ignorance." The claim that the youthful Maggid studied with the renowned Talmudist Ya'akov Yehoshua Falk (1680–1756) lacks evidence. See Dynner, *Men of Silk*, 232. Cf. *Ner Yisra'el*, 6:413; and Lederberg, *Gateway*, 318.
14. See *Igra de-Pirka*, ch. 1; and *Ner Yisra'el*, 6:430.
15. See SLA, 35–36; and Pedaya, "Social-Religious-Economic Model of Hasidism," 343–344.
16. The account in *Kerem Yisrael*, 11a, has the Maggid living in Rovno before Mezritsh.
17. See Weiss, "Beginnings of Hasidism," 125–128; Piekarz, *Beginning of Hasidism*, esp. 42–44, 114–115, 142–146, 163–168; Saperstein, *Jewish Preaching*, 44–63; and Katz, *Tradition and Crisis*, 144–147, 186–187, 194, 208.

18. The Maggid's name does not appear among the scholars mentioned in the introduction to *Mahberet ha-Kodesh* (Korets, 1783), a kabbalistic work printed from a manuscript in the Mezritsh *beit midrash* by Shlomo of Lutsk. See Gries, "Hasidic Managing Editor," 150–151.

19. See Reiner, "Wealth, Social Position, and the Study of Torah," 287–328; Kahana, "Changing the World's Measures," 29–53.

20. See Scholem, "Tradition and New Creation," 118–157; Werblowsky, *Joseph Karo,* 38–83; Hallamish, *Kabbalah.*

21. On the state of Kabbalah in eastern Europe, see Idel, *Hasidism,* 33–44; idem, "One from a Town," 79–104; and Hundert, *Jews in Poland-Lithuania,* 119–185.

22. See Piekarz, *Beginning of Hasidism,* esp. 11–174, 269–302, 361–377.

23. See the letter in Rosman, *Founder,* 114–115.

24. See, for example, LY, no. 191, fol. 58a; and *Ner Yisra'el,* 6:432.

25. See *In Praise,* 81; and Lederberg, *Gateway,* 81 and 342 nn. 117–118. The impetus behind the Kherson Geniza forgeries, the purported correspondence between early Hasidic figures, demonstrates how little is known about their relationships; see Rapoport-Albert, "Hagiography with Footnotes," 131–137.

26. *Yihudim* or "unifications" refer to the kabbalistic practice of uniting divine names and the *sefirot;* see below.

27. MDL, 2.

28. See b. Sukkah 28a. See Zohar 3:228a, 1:11a; *Bereshit Rabbah* 79:6; Zohar 2:6b, 3:201a-b; *Shivhei ha-Ari,* ed. Hillel, p. 20. See also Rapoport-Albert, "Hagiography with Footnotes," 123; Fishbane, "Perceptions of Greatness," 205–206; and *In Praise,* 242–244.

29. On *Sefer Razi'el ha-Malakh,* see Idel, *Hasidism,* 381 n. 55.

30. See Verman, *Books of Contemplation,* 49; and Avivi, *Kabbala Luriana,* 1:204–208; 2:564–568. See also *Or Ne'erav,* 3:3, 24; and *'Emek ha-Melekh,* 24.

31. See Scholem, *Major Trends,* 348–350; Idel, *Hasidism,* 9–30, 65–81, 206–207. See Ruderman, *Kabbalah, Magic, and Science,* esp. 102–160.

32. MDL, 2–3.

33. See OT, *va-era,* no. 79, p. 111.

34. See also Cooper, "But I Will Tell of Their Deeds," 127–163.

35. See *In Praise,* no. 36, p. 51.

36. See Nigal, "Primary Source for Hasidic Tales," 349–364; Lederberg, *Gateway,* 81–113; and Amshalem, "Stories in My Praise," 27–64.

37. See Nigal, "Primary Source for Hasidic Tales," 349–364.

38. See Idel, "Besht Passed His Hand," 79–106; Garb, *Shamanic Trance,* 113–114, 144, 214 nn. 104–106.

39. Mention of this key work of Lurianic Kabbalah, first published in 1782, is a telltale anachronism.

40. KST, no. 424, 264. See Lederberg, *Gateway,* 86–89; Amshalem, "Stories in My Praise," 34.

41. See *In Praise,* no. 62, pp. 81–84.

42. See the note in *In Praise,* 81.

43. See Thomas, *Literacy and Orality.*

44. Graham, *Beyond the Written Word,* 6.

45. The usability of *Shivhei ha-BeSHT* is further complicated by the fact that it circulated almost simultaneously in Hebrew and Yiddish versions. See Mondshine, *Shivhei ha-Besht;* and Grözinger, "Source Value," 354–363.

46. *Ner Yisra'el*, 6:423. Cf. *Ohalei Ya'akov*, 87.

47. See *Sefer Likkutei Amarim*, fol. 9a; and Mondshine, *Migdal 'Oz*, 368.

48. See Dubnow, "Maggid of Miedzyrzecz," 58–66.

49. The 1765 will of a certain wealthy man connected to the BeSHT lists the Maggid of Mezritsh as the beneficiary of a small sum of money together with many others, including Pinhas of Korets and Yehiel Mikhel of Zlotshev. This text neither singles out the Maggid nor implies that he is the BeSHT's primary disciple, but it confirms that the Maggid's connection to his teacher was publicly known during Dov Ber's lifetime. See David ben Israel Halperin, *Darkhei Tsiyyon*, unpaginated; and Etkes, *Besht*, 200–201.

50. See *Seder ha-Dorot ha-Hadash*, 19b–23b; *Imrei Pinhas ha-Shalem*, 1:484; Heschel, *Circle of the Baal Shem Tov*, 19–29. See, for example, the story *Kahal Hasidim ha-Hadash*, fols. 11d–12b, in which Ya'akov Yosef admits the following after witnessing Dov Ber deliver a sermon: "Since the day our master the BeSHT died, *shekhinah* departed with her pack and established her place with the Maggid." See also *Ben Porat Yosef*, vol. 2, *derush le-shabbat ha-gadol*, 606; and *Imrei Pinhas ha-Shalem*, 1:391.

51. See MDL, no. 95, p. 164; and *Dibrat Shlomo, pekkudei*, 210; ibid., *shemini*, 262.

52. See Idel, "Your Word," 235–236 and n. 69; cf. idem, *Ben*, 536.

53. Here the brief contrast of a phenomenon from the Islamic world will be instructive. Since the eighth century Muslim scholars have sought to establish an authentic *isnad*, a chain of tradition, for each *hadith* that supports and verifies its authority. See Juynboll, *Studies on the Origins*, esp. 155–175, 343–383; and Robinson, "Study of Islamic Historiography," 201, 205–208, 211.

54. See Dinur, "Origins of Hasidism," 139–140; Chone Shmeruk, "Hasidic Movement, 182–192, esp. 187; Ettinger, "Hasidism and the *Kahal*," 66–67.

55. See *Kahal Hasidim*, fol. 41a. In his *Ve-Tsivah ha-Kohen*, 84, a certain Aharon ha-Kohen recalls visiting the Maggid in Torchin and Rovno, suggesting that Dov Ber was already a public leader before moving to Mezritsh.

56. See *Ve-Tsivah ha-Kohen*, 84, suggests that some disciples remained with the Maggid for weeks at a time. See also Wilensky, *Hasidim and Mitnaggedim*, 1:308; and cf. *Ner Yisra'el*, 6:413. For later attempts to list the Maggid's students, see Walden, *Shem ha-Gedolim*, 11a–b; *Seder ha-Dorot ha-Hadash*, 31–49; Alfasi, *he-Hasidut*, 1:139–192; Berger, *'Eser Orot*, 17b–18a.

57. See Maimon, *Autobiography*, 86–100; Weiss, "One of the Sayings," 107–109; Assaf, "Teachings of Dov Ber," 99–101.

58. Socher, *Radical Enlightenment*, 76–78, argues convincingly that, despite his many criticisms, Maimon respected the Maggid's teachings and the high level of self-perfection they demanded.

59. Maimon, *Autobiography*, 95.

60. The custom of a personal audience with the *tsaddik*, known as *yehidut*, became an important and widespread Hasidic practice in the generations after the Maggid's death; see Etkes, *Rabbi Shneur Zalman*, 31–47, 94–95; and Pedaya, "Social-Religious-Economic Model," 353.

61. Maimon, *Autobiography*, 96–97.

62. See Socher, *Radical Enlightenment*, 134–135.

63. See Maimon, *Autobiography*, 106–107 where he notes the importance of understanding the "language of animals" in mystery cults. See also Melamed, "Spinozism, Acosmism, and Hassidism," 75–85.

64. See Etkes, "Early Hasidic 'Court,'" 157–169.

65. See Weiss, "Beginnings of Hasidism," 129, and 179–181. See also Rosman, *Founder*, 117–119; Etkes, *Besht*, 218–223; and Wolfson, "Walking as a Sacred Duty," 180–207.

66. For a firsthand description of the Maggid's house as filled with people varying in age and scholarly ability, see *Or ha-Me'ir*, vol. 2, *devarim*, p. 160.

67. See Gellman, *Emergence of Hasidism*, 101–145.

68. See *Seder ha-Dorot ha-Hadash*, 35; cited by Scholem, *Major Trends*, 344.

69. See Heilman, *Beit Rabbi*, 8 n. 2; and Scholem, *Major Trends*, 338.

70. See *Kahal Hasidim ha-Hadash*, fol. 11a; Maimon, *Autobiography*, 96–97; *Kahal Hasidim*, fol. 45b; *Imrei Pinhas*, 1:267; *Divrei David*, fols. 4b–5a; and Amshalem, "Stories in My Praise," 42–49.

71. See Heilman, *Beit Rabbi*, 12.

72. See Stampfer, *Families, Rabbis, and Education*, 252–274.

73. See Reiner, "Wealth, Social Position, and the Study of Torah," 287–328. Gries, *Hebrew Book*, 68, argued that the sermons printed in MDL loosely follow the order of the Babylonian Talmud. This suggests that the scholars assembled in the Maggid's *beit midrash* were studying Talmud, and he addressed them regularly, grounding his homilies in the shared text. See *Kahal Hasidim ha-Hadash*, 18d–19a.

74. See LY, nos. 137–159, fols. 46a–53b.

75. Barnai, *Hasidic Letters*, no. 65, 244. It is worth recalling that this letter, like that of Shneur Zalman described below, was written amid the conflict between these two disciples of the Maggid.

76. See Etkes, "Zaddik," 159–167.

77. See Green, "Typologies of Leadership," 127–156; idem, "Zaddiq as Axis Mundi," 327–347.

78. See Green, "Zaddiq as Axis Mundi," 338–339. Cf. Weiss, *Studies in Braslav Hasidism*, 104–107; and Rapoport-Albert, "God and the Zaddik," 318–320.

79. See Pedaya, "Social-Religious-Economic," 351–352; and Piekarz, *Hasidic Leadership*, 92–94.

80. See Green, "Around the Maggid's Table," 85–86. This interpretation is epitomized by the well-known story in which the Maggid demands to know why God has punished him with fame; see *Kerem Yisrael*, 8a.

81. See Etkes, "Zaddik," 163.

82. *Yesod Yosef*, *hakdamah*, unpaginated, includes a letter from Zusya of Hanipoli that mentions a rabbinic figure in Rovno who adopted some Hasidic practices under the influence of the Maggid.

83. The conflict with the *mithnaggedim* may have started as early as the 1760s; see the sources cited in Wilensky, *Hasidim and Mitnaggedim*, 1:27 n. 1; and Dynner, *Men of Silk*, 284 n. 198.

84. See Wilensky, *Hasidim and Mitnaggedim*, 1:27.

85. See Wilensky, *Hasidim and Mitnaggedim*, 1:42–43, 66, 182, 252–267; ibid., 2:201. See also Dubnow, *Toledot ha-Hasidut*, 165; and Gries, *Book in Early Hasidism*, 19. See, however, Wilensky, *Hasidim and Mitnaggedim*, 1:150, for an anti-Hasidic ban from 1787 that explicitly mentions MDL (citing it as *Likkutei Amarim*).

86. See Wilensky, *Hasidim and Mitnaggedim*, 2:259–260.

87. Ibid.

88. See Gries, "Hassidic Conduct Literature," 198–236, 278–305.

89. See *Iggerot Kodesh—Admor ha-Zaken*, vol. 1, no. 51, 125–126; Barnai, *Hasidic Letters*, no. 68, 255–256; and Etkes, *Rabbi Shneur Zalman of Liady*, 240–241.

90. On the conflict, see Gries, "From Myth to Ethos," 117–146; and Etkes, *Rabbi Shneur Zalman*, 208–258.

91. *Iggerot Kodesh*, pt. 2, 19–20. This account is mirrored in a letter from Pinhas Horowitz in Hillman, *Iggerot Ba'al ha-Tanya*, 117–118. See also Mondshein, *Migdal 'Oz*, 246–248.

92. See below; and ST, 61.

93. See Wilensky, *Hasidim and Mitnaggedim*, 2:237, 247; and Heilman, *Beit Rabbi*, 19 n. 6.

94. See Wilensky, *Hasidim and Mitnaggedim*, 1:40 n. 24. See also *Ner Yisra'el*, 6:416–417.

95. Hasidic tradition records a special relationship between the two, so perhaps Zusya moved there to help his teacher in the final months. See *Kerem Yisrael*, 11a; and see *Kitvei Yoshiy Shub*, no. 16, pp. 92–93.

96. See *Yoshiya Shub*, no. 3, p. 89. See also *Kerem Yisrael*, 11a.

97. See Green, "Levi Yizhak of Berdichev," 254–268.

98. A fascinating—though admittedly late—tradition claims Dov Ber and his son were no longer on speaking terms because of Avraham's unwillingness to be intimate with his wife. This tradition appears in a note in box 294 of the Abraham Joshua Heschel Papers, David M. Rubenstein Rare Book & Manuscript Library of Duke University. See also *Seder ha-Dorot ha-Hadash*, 33–34.

99. See *In Praise*, no. 72, pp. 91–92.

100. See *In Praise*, no. 75, pp. 94–99. See Dynner, *Men of Silk*, 232–233.

101. *Sivhei ha-BeSHT* includes a lengthy story—one of the longest in the book—that was preserved and retold by Gittel. See Margolin, *Human Temple*, 206–210; and Kauffman, "Hasidic Women," 223–257.

102. The story of Gittel was the subject of a recent Israeli novel, appearing in English as Herzfeld, *Trail of Miracles*.

103. Snippets of his teachings appear in the works of Dov Ber's disciples, and a collection of Avraham's sermons was published as *Hesed le-Avraham* in 1851. See also the manuscripts in Mondshine, *Migdal 'Oz*, 389–398; and Gries, *Conduct Literature*, 132. For later Hasidic traditions claiming that Avraham was the study-partner (*havruta*) of Shneur Zalman of Liady, see *Beit Rabbi*, 9–10, 178–179.

104. See Kauffman, "Typology of the Tsaddik," 239–272; and Stillman, "Transcendent God, Immanent Kabbalah," 310–330.

105. See *Hesed le-Avraham*, *noah*, 26; *va-yetse*, 43–45; *va-yishlah*, 46; and *ha'azinu*, 87–88.

106. See *Hesed le-Avraham*, *toledot*, 42; and cf. ibid., *likkutim me-shir ha-shirim*, 89.

107. On the emergence of Hasidic dynasties, see Polen, "Rebbetzins," 53–84.

108. See *Hesed le-Avraham*, *hakdamah*, 21; ibid., *lekh lekha*, 30–32; *va-yishlah*, 45; *va-yeshev*, 47–48; and *ki tavo*, 86.

109. See *In Praise*, no. 72, pp. 91–92; and Assaf, *Regal Way*, 32, 47–56.

110. See Shor, *Ketavim*, 242–297.

111. Rapoport-Albert, "Hasidism After 1772," 76–140.

112. See Rapoport-Albert, "Hasidism After 1772," 98.

113. See Etkes, *Besht*, 113–202, 249–258; Rosman, *Founder*, 166–168.

114. See *Orah le-Hayyim*, vol. 2, *va-ethanan*, 293; *Kedushat Levi*, vol. 1, *likkutim*, 481.

115. For example, see the letters in Hillman, *Iggerot Ba'al ha-Tanya*.

116. It is curious that Shlomo of Lutsk, a relative of Dov Ber as well as an important editor and transcriber of the Maggid's teachings, is scarcely mentioned in any of the hagiographic traditions or theological works by the other disciples. For a rare story in which Shlomo is a minor player, see *Kahal Hasidim ha-Hadash*, fol. 11b.

117. See Wilensky, *Hasidim and Mitnaggedim*, 1:43, 28, 64–65; and idem, 2:101–102.

118. For example, the grandson of Levi Yitshak of Barditshev married the granddaughter of Shneur Zalman of Liady; see Shneur Zalman's letter of consolation to Levi Yitshak after the death of the latter's son, included in *Sefer ha-Tanya, iggeret ha-kodesh*, ch. 28, fols. 147b–148b.

119. Here I find myself agreeing with Schatz-Uffenheimer, *Hasidism and Mysticism*, 260: "There were many disciples in Mezhirech [*sic*], each one of whom clearly derived his own personal message from the teaching of the Maggid, but who nevertheless shared a common ground giving meaning to the concept, 'the school of the Maggid.'" See the epilogue in the present book.

120. See Mayse, "'Moving Mezritsh.'"

121. See Green, "Around the Maggid's Table," 73–106; and Stampfer, "How and Why Hasidism Spread," 201–219.

CHAPTER 2

Notes to epigraphs: Scholem, "Thoughts About Our Language," 28–29; MDL, 6.

1. See Savran, "Seeing Is Believing," 320–361.

2. See Boyarin, "Gospel of the *Memra*," 243–284; idem, *Border Lines*, esp. 86–226; and Wolfson, *Language, Eros, Being*, 190–261.

3. See Yadin, "Hammer on the Rock," 1–17; and Halbertal, *People of the Book*, 1–89.

4. For an overview, see Zwiep, *Mother of Reason and Revelation*.

5. See Scholem, "Name of God," 59–80; idem, "Name of God (Part 2)," 164–194; and Dan, "Name of God," 228–248.

6. See Wolfson, "Negative Theology," v–xxii; idem, "*Via Negativa*," 393–442; Fishbane, "Mystical Contemplation," 1–27.

7. See Fishbane, "Speech of Being," 485–521. This blossoming of theological explorations into the nature of language took place at the moment in which Kabbalah was shifting from oral traditions into a written literature. See Idel, *Kabbalah*, 250–256; idem, *Absorbing Perfections*, 390–409; and Wolfson, "Beyond the Spoken Word," 166–224.

8. See Idel, "Reification of Language in Jewish Mysticism," 42–79; and cf. Hallamish, "On Silence," 79–89.

9. See Sells, *Mystical Languages*, 1–13.

10. See Green, *Guide to the Zohar*, esp. 55–59.

11. See Pedaya, *Name and Sanctuary*, 69–76. On the interweaving of linguistic and visual mysticism in Kabbalah, see Pedaya, *Vision and Speech*. Cf. b. Shevu'ot 26b; m. Berakhot 2:3; b. Berakhot 24b; b. Shabbat 150a, 113a-b; and b. Bava Kamma 73a–73b.

12. On the notion of *yihudim*, see Fine, "Contemplative Practice of Yihudim," 64–98.

13. See Idel, *Hasidism*, 11–29, 41–65; Scholem, *Major Trends*, 320–325; idem, "*Devekut*," esp. 208–213; Sack, "Influence of *Reshit Hokhmah*," 251–257; Lorberbaum, "Attain the Attribute," esp. 87–195, 201–217; and Avivi, *Kabbala Luriana*, 2:557–566, 816–842, 861–865. See also Scholem, *Origins of the Kabbalah*, 460–474; Idel, "Multiple Forms of Redemption," 47–51; and, more broadly, Izmirlieva, *All the Names of the Lord*.

14. See Idel, "Martin Buber and Gershom Scholem," 395–396. More broadly, see Idel, *Language, Torah, and Hermeneutics*, esp. 1–28; and idem, *Mystical Experience*.

15. See, for example, *Pardes Rimmonim*, 27:2, 30:3. The word *heikhal* may also be trans-lated as "sanctuary," for the *heikhal* was a part of the Temple structure; see 1 Kings 6:3; Jer. 7:4. The term *kelim* is a very common one for the vessels used in the Tabernacle and the Temple, and the word *makhon* is also associated with the Temple, as in Ex. 15:17; and 1 Kings 8:13, 39, 43. Noting this, perhaps, Cordovero is drawing a subtle association between the presence of God in the Jerusalem Temple and the divine immanence manifest in language.

16. See *Pardes Rimmonim*, 27. Bracha Sack argues that he was influenced by, and se-lectively quotes from, *Sefer ha-Temunah*; see Sack, *Kabbalah of Rabbi Moshe Cordevero*, 279–290.

17. See *Limmudei Atsilut*, 32a, 1a–b; and Shatil, "Kabbalah of R. Israel Sarug," 158–187.

18. See *Ben Porat Yosef*, vol. 1, *bereshit*, 64. See Idel, "Your Word," 219–286; idem, *Hasi-dism*, 57–58, 83–84, 92–93, 160–170; idem, *Absorbing Perfections*, 155–163; idem, "Modes of Cleaving," 299–317; Etkes, *Besht*, 147–150; Elior, *Mystical Origins*, 41–58; Kauffman, *In All Your Ways*, 77–82; and Wacks, "Yihud in Speech," 143–163.

19. On the various recensions of this letter, see Rosman, *Founder*, 97–113; idem, "He-brew Sources," 155–162; Etkes, *Besht*, 272–288; Gries, "Historical Image," 418–421; Pedaya, "BeSHT's Holy Epistle," 311–354; Dauber, "Baal Shem Tov," 210–241; Moseson, "From Spoken Word," 35–117.

20. See Idel, *Kabbalah*, 74–111.

21. Translation based on Etkes, *Besht*, 276–277. See also Idel, "Models of Understanding Prayer," 23–26.

22. See Idel, *Hasidism*, 149–170; Elior, *Jewish Mysticism*, 41–58; and Dauber, "Baal Shem Tov," 232–236.

23. See Idel, *Hasidism*, 75–81. See also *In Praise*, no. 62, p. 82.

24. *Teivah* (word) and *teivah* (ark) are homonyms.

25. The BeSHT is interpreting the word "window" (*tsohar*) as "light," related to the word "noonday" (*tsahorayim*) in Isa. 16:3; Ps. 96:1.

26. *Degel Mahaneh Efrayim*, *noah*, 18–19.

27. The BeSHT is reading *be-tsidah* (at its side) in light of the Talmudic idiom for a question with a self-obvious answer (*teshuvato be-tsido*). See, for example, b. Sotah 29b.

28. *Degel Mahaneh Efrayim*, *noah*, 18–19. Cf. *Or ha-Me'ir*, *be-shalah*, 1:128. See also DHM, 55.

29. *Ben Porat Yosef*, vol. 1, *va-yetse*, p. 310, building on Zohar 2:124b; cf. *Toledot Ya'akov Yosef*, vol. 3,'*ekev*, 1183; and Zohar 1:184a, 2:146a–b.

30. See Idel, "Models of Understanding Prayer," 29 n. 59.

31. See *Degel Mahaneh Efrayim*, *likkutim*, 605.

32. b. Sukkah 21b.

33. *Divrei Moshe*, *va-yera*, 10b. See also ibid., *hayyei sarah*, 12b, on the listener trans-forming the ordinary words of another into sacred speech.

34. On the notion of *yihudim*, "unifications," of the various divine names and the *sefirot*, see Fine, "Contemplative Practice of Yihudim," 64–98.

35. *Tsofnat Pane'ah*, *yitro*, 1:405–406; and see also *Degel Mahaneh Efrayim*, *tazri'a*, 362.

36. See *Ketonet Passim*, *be-ha'alotekha*, 276; cf. *Tsofnat Pane'ah*, *va-era*, 1:131.

37. See Pedaya, "Outlines for a Religious Typology," 58–59, 66–69; and idem, "Two Types," 86–87.

38. *Toledot Ya'akov Yosef*, vol. 1, *hayye sarah*, 136. Cf. ibid., *shelah*, 910; ibid., *mattot*, 1115; *Ben Porat Yosef*, vol. 2, *derush le-shabbat tesuhvah* 1767, 672. See also *Kedushat Levi*, *eikhah*, 372.

39. See *Degel Mahaneh Efrayim, likkutim*, 595. See also *Toledot Ya'akov Yosef*, vol. 2, *va-yikra*, 507; *Degel Mahaneh Efrayim, va-yikra*, 319–320, 323; *Degel Mahaneh Efrayim, va-yikra*, 328; ibid., *kedoshim*, 388–389. This same teaching is found in ST, 29b, as something "heard from the BeSHT"; and MDL, no. 151, p. 251 without any attribution.

40. Aharon of Zhitomir, a disciple of Levi Yitshak of Barditshev, understood this connection between the Maggid and the BeSHT as well. See *Toledot Aharon, shelah*, 20c.

41. See also Bialik, "Revealment and Concealment in Language"; and the illuminating exploration of Wolfson, *Language, Eros, Being*, xi–xxxi.

42. See Idel, "*Tsadik* and His Soul's Sparks," 196–240; and Jacobs, "Uplifting of Sparks," 99–126.

43. Such transmutation is said to happen in the *sefirah binah*, among the uppermost spheres of the Godhead as well as a contemplative realm within the depths of the mystic's mind.

44. Buber, *Hasidism and Modern Man*, esp. 126–181; Scholem, "Buber's Interpretation of Hasidism," 228–250; and Brody, "Open to Me the Gates of Righteousness," 3–44.

45. This question has been a fundament of the philosophical tradition since Plato's *Cratylus*, in which two of the protagonists argue over the relationship between names and their referents.

46. See KTVK, 18b, and MDL, no. 68, pp. 114–115, on the oft-quoted division of creation into four categories: *domem* ("silent" or "inanimate,"), *tsomeah* ("plant"), *hayah* ("animal beings"), and *medabber* ("speakers").

47. LY, no. 264, fol. 81a.

48. See, more broadly, Ben-Sasson, *YHWH*.

49. See MDL, no. 112, p. 187.

50. The *tsaddik* here, as elsewhere in the Maggid's teachings, refers to a spiritually refined individual rather than a leader of a Hasidic community.

51. MDL, no. 60, pp. 94–95.

52. See Hollenback, *Mysticism*, 241–275; and Garb, *Manifestations of Power*, esp. 142–173.

53. b. Sanhedrin 39a.

54. SLA, 85; and MDL, no. 105, pp. 183–184.

55. See Sells, *Mystical Languages*, 63–89; Magid, *Hasidism Incarnate*, 70–90; and Nasr, "Heart of the Faithful," 32–45.

56. See also OT, *be-shalah*, no. 92, p. 128.

57. On such "arousal from below" in the Zohar, see Hellner-Eshed, *River Flows from Eden*, esp. 204–228.

58. See MDL, no. 119, p. 194; and *Or ha-Me'ir, pesah*, p. 255a. More broadly, see Patton, *Religion of the Gods*.

59. OHE, 12b. Cf. JER NLI MS HEB 8°5979, fol. 31a. See RaSHI's commentary to Proverbs ad loc. This seems to differ from the Zoharic interpretation of this verse, where it is taken as a reference to one who creates separation in the world of the *sefirot*; see Zohar 3:12a, 16b.

60. b. Sanhedrin 65b.

61. LY, no. 271, fol. 89b. See also 8°5307, fol. 117a-b.

62. See Hallamish, "Toward the Source," 211–223.

63. LY, no. 271, fol. 89b. See also JER NLI MS HEB 8°5307, fol. 117a-b, and DHM, 45–46.

64. See MDL, no. 146, p. 247.

65. Later Jewish exegetes, of course, sought to reinterpret key passages in light of their own linguistic theory; see esp. Gen. 1–2, 11; 2 Kings 18:26–37; Isa. 36:11–22; Zeph. 3:8–11; Ps. 33:6; Neh. 13:23–31.

66. See Schwartz, "Language, Power, and Identity," 3–47. See also Sanders, *Invention of Hebrew*; and Block, "Role of Language," 321–340.

67. Charles, *Book of Jubilees*, 12:25–27, pp. 95–96.

68. See Hollander and de Jonge, *Testaments of the Twelve Patriarchs*, 446–450; Eshel and Stone, "*Leshon haqodesh*," 169–177.

69. See, inter alia, *Bereshit Rabbah* 18:4; *Avot de-Rabbi Natan*, ch. 37; b. Shabbat 12b; b. Sotah 33a; *Sifrei Devarim*, 'ekev, piska 46; and m. Sotah 7:1–2; the sources in Bialik and Ravnitzki, *Book of Legends*, 7, 53, 59, 71, 87, 374–376, 449–451; and Rubin, "Language of Creation," 306–333.

70. y. Megillah 1:9.

71. See *Pirkei de-Rabbi Eli'ezer*, ch. 26.

72. See *Tanhuma, noah*, no. 19.

73. See Weiss, "*Sefer Yeṣirah*" and Its Contexts.

74. See Liebes, Ars Poetica in "*Sefer Yetsirah*," esp. 16–17, 53, 118–120.

75. See Dan, "Language of Creation and Its Grammar," 129–154.

76. See Roth, "Jewish Reactions to the *Arabiyya*," 63–84; and Frank, "Hearing and Saying," 611–618.

77. See esp. *Kuzari* 2:68, 4:25, and 3:53. More broadly, see the classic study of Bacher, "Views of Jehuda Halevi," 136–149; Pines, "On the Term *Ruhaniyyut*," 511–534; and Lobel, *Between Mysticism and Philosophy*.

78. See Maimonides, *Guide of the Perplexed*, 2:30, 3:8; and cf. *Commentary to the Mishnah, megillah* 2:1. See also Septimus, "Maimonides on Language," 35–54; Twersky, *Introduction to the Code*, 324; Kellner, "Maimonides on the 'Normality' of Hebrew," 413–444; and Brody, *Sa'adyah Gaon*, 79–96.

79. See his comments on Ex. 30:13, and the commentary of Bahye ben Asher ad loc. See also Sarfatti, "Language of the Patriarchs," 277–283. Yom Tov ben Avraham Asevilli (1235–1310), a follower of Nahmanides' school of Kabbalah, authored *Sefer ha-Zikaron*, a defense of Maimonides against the criticism of Nahmanides. When he reaches Maimonides' comments about the conventionality of Hebrew in *Guide*, 3:8, however, he vociferously refuses to defend them. See also the comments of Nissim of Gerona on b. Nedarim 2a.

80. See Dan, "Ashkenazi Hasidic Concept," 65–87; idem, "Language of the Mystics," 161–190; Wolfson, "Mystical Significance of Torah Study," 43–78; Scholem, *Major Trends*, 100–103; and Fishman, "Rhineland Pietist Approaches to Prayer," 313–331. See also *Ets Hayyim* 5; Magid, *From Metaphysics to Midrash*, 31–33; *Hesed le-Avraham*, 2:10–11, 2:24, 7:28; *Shenei Luhot ha-Berit, bayit ne'eman tinyana*; trans. in Krassen, *Isaiah Horowitz*, 148–163.

81. On the seventy languages, see m. Sotah 7:5; b. Megillah 13b; *Bereshit Rabbah* 49:2; and Idel, *Language, Torah, and Hermeneutics*, 9–10, 22–27, 102–110, 143–146. See also *Pardes Rimmonim* 22:1; *Hesed le-Avraham* 7:28.

82. See MDL, no. 188, pp. 287–288, commenting on Genesis 3:18–25; and *Bereshit Rabbah* 17:4. This story has long been a source of speculation regarding the beginnings of language; see the studies collected in Coudert, *Language of Adam*.

83. See also Shlomo of Lutsk's second introduction to MDL, 6.

84. See MDL, no. 85, pp. 147–148.

85. ST, fols. 9b–10a.

86. See Durkheim, *Elementary Forms*, 36–40, 227; Keane, "Religious Language," 47–71, esp. 50–51, 55; and Haeri, *Sacred Language*.

87. LY, no. 251, fol. 77a. See also *Me'or 'Einayim, va-yeshev*, 123; MDL, no. 29, p. 47; and *Dibrat Shlomo, balak*, 365.

88. See MDL, no. 130, p. 223, building on *Tikkunei Zohar, tikkun* 5, fol. 19b.

89. On this idea as a point of Hasidic innovation, see Avivi, *Kabbala Luriana*, 3:1464–1465.

90. b. Yoma 19b.

91. b. Sukkah 21b.

92. OT, *yitro*, no. 97, pp. 135–136.

93. See Chapter 4.

94. See OT, *pesukim*, no. 317, p. 365.

95. On this term, see Green, "*Da'at*."

96. This recalls Maimonides' remarks in *Guide*, 3:51, in which he refers to contemplating matters of the spirit even when engaged in mundane tasks.

97. m. Avot 5:6, listing the positive traits of the sage and their opposites in the ill-mannered person.

98. *Or ha-Me'ir*, vol. 1, *shir ha-shirim*, 283–284; cf. ibid.,vol. 1, *va-yera*, 33–34. See also *Orah le-Hayyim*, vol. 2, *ki tetse*, 362.

99. A plain-sense translation of the verse reads, "Behold, they may gather together, but not by Me."

100. MDL, no. 40, pp. 60–61.

101. This point recalls the legends in which the BeSHT shocks the Maggid by first greeting him with bizarre and mundane stories instead of inspiring homilies.

102. See Abrams, *Book of Bahir*, nos. 97–98, pp. 183–185.

103. MDL, no. 40, pp. 60–61; and see also *Kedushat Levi*, vol. 1, *hayyei sarah*, 62.

104. See LY, no. 213, fol. 63b; ibid., no. 253, fol. 77b. Cf. Rapoport-Albert, "God and Zaddik," 320; and Dresner, *Zaddik*, esp. 148–190; and Green, "Around the Maggid's Table," esp. 76–106.

105. See also *Dibrat Shlomo, be-ha'alotekha*, 312.

106. See Chapter 4; and OHE, 24b.

107. For example, see MDL, no. 90, pp. 155–157; ibid., no. 6, p. 19; OT, *bereshit*, no. 11a, p. 12; LY, no. 241, fol. 70a. See also Idel, "Your Word," 223–225.

108. See Kauffman, *In All Your Ways*, 426–466. She notes quite correctly that although Dov Ber generally does not cite the BeSHT, the Maggid frequently invokes his teacher's name regarding this subject, perhaps further revealing his own ambivalence; see ibid., 463.

109. OT, *tehillim*, no. 247, p. 300.

110. MDL, no. 70, pp. 118–120.

111. See MDL, no. 31, p. 50; *Ve-Tsivah ha-Kohen*, 84. See, more broadly, Hecker, *Mystical Bodies*.

112. See OT, *aggadot*, no. 455, p. 467; ibid., *aggadot*, no. 460, p. 473; and ibid., *tehillim*, no. 206, pp. 272–273.

113. See OT, *devarim*, no. 155, p. 206; and ibid., *aggadot*, no. 392, p. 416.

114. b. Hagigah 18b–19b, referring to stringent individuals who treat ordinary food (*hullin*) like the sanctified offerings consumed in the Temple by eating it only when they are ritually pure.

115. *Me'or 'Einayim*, vol. 1, *be-shalah*, 170.

116. Menahem Nahum's teachings evince a positive approach to the corporeal world. His own spiritual proclivities may have colored his understanding of the Maggid's words, but similar teachings appear elsewhere in Dov Ber's name.

117. See *Or ha-Me'ir*, vol. 1, *va-yera*, 28; LY, no. 265, fol. 83a.

118. See *Or ha-Me'ir*, vol. 1, *pesah*, 228–229.

119. MDL, no. 68, p. 114, translated in *Speaking Torah*, 1:148–149.

120. See Avivi, *Kabbala Luriana*, 3:1464–1465, and the important parallel in Yosef Gikatilla's *Sha'arei Orah*, *hakdamah*; and Huss, "Rabbi Joseph Gikatilia's Definition," 157–176.

121. Zohar 1:15a; cf. *Bereshit Rabbah* 21:5; *Pardes Rimmonim* 4:9, 16:3, 20:3; *Ets Hayyim*, *sha'ar ha-kellalim*, 1; ibid., 13:4, 41:3.

122. *Dibrat Shlomo*, *be-hukkotai*, 292–294.

123. Wolfson, "Body in the Text," 482.

124. My thanks to Dan Schifrin for helping me to formulate this point.

125. See Pachter, "Smallness and Greatness," 185–233; Scholem, "*Devekut*," 203–227. See also Mayse, "'Like a Moth," 364–406.

126. See the Maggid's formulation in OT, *'ekev*, no. 167, pp. 217–218.

127. See Sorkin, *Moses Mendelssohn*, 66–67; and the commentary to Gen. 11:1 in *Netivot ha-Shalom*. See also Altmann, *Moses Mendelssohn*, esp. 84–91 and 376–413.

128. Breuer and Sorkin, *Moses Mendelssohn's Hebrew Writings*, 246. See also Scorch, *Moses Mendelssohns Sprachpolitik*; and Sacks, *Moses Mendelssohn's Living Script*, esp. 14–28, 83–133, 171–223.

129. Breuer and Sorkin, *Moses Mendelssohn's Hebrew Writings*, 252.

130. Breuer and Sorkin, *Moses Mendelssohn's Hebrew Writings*, 56; and see also ibid., 66–76.

131. See also MDL, no. 146, p. 247.

132. It should be noted that the notion that Hasidism emerged from a "bilingual" rather than "polylingual" historical context is somewhat problematic, a reading that is shaped by a modern Jewish historiography that focused largely on Jewish language sources.

133. See Bartal, "From Traditional Bilingualism," 141–150; Kauffman, "Theological Aspects of Bilingualism," 131–156; and Mayse and Reiser, "Territories and Textures," 127–160.

134. On the development of this concept, see Mayse, "Expanding the Boundaries of the Holy."

CHAPTER 3

Note to epigraph: Wilson, *Origins of Creativity*, 26–27.

1. See Zohar 1: 65a and 246b; Tishby, *Mishnat ha-Zohar*, 1:153–154; Mopsik, "Pensée, voix et parole," 385–414.

2. See Pinker, *Stuff of Thought*, 30.

3. Here once more we find the Maggid's opinion regarding the uniqueness of Hebrew, at least on the oral level, to be quite complicated.

4. On the Hebrew letters described as "vessels" (*kelim*), "palaces" (*heikhalot*), and a "habitation" (*makhon*) for spiritual vitality in the teachings of Cordovero, see *Pardes Rimmonim* 27:2 and 30:3.

5. See LY, no. 118, fol. 25b. Following *Sefer Yetsirah* 4:12 and *Pardes Rimmonim* 30:1, the Hebrew letters are symbolically referred to as "stones." See MDL, no. 60, p. 94.

6. On the terms *heikhal, kelim,* and *makhon,* see above, page 265, note 15.

7. See Reddy, "Conduit Metaphor," 164–201.

8. See Abrams, *Book of Bahir,* no. 83, pp. 171–172; Scholem, *Origins of the Kabbalah,* 63–65, tracing the idea that "vowels of the Torah within the consonants are comparable to the soul of life in the body of man," which also appears in the Bahir, to Judah ha-Levi's *Kuzari* 4:3. See also Zohar 1:4a, 12b, 15b; *Pardes Rimmonim* 29:5; *Ets Hayyim* 5:1–5, 8:1. See Idel, *Language, Torah, and Hermeneutics,* 3, 7–8, 24, 42.

9. See LY, no. 238, p. 69a; and MDL, no. 130, p. 223. The association of *te'amim* with *hokhmah* is common in Lurianic Kabbalah.

10. See MDL, no. 87, pp. 150–151; ibid., no. 100, pp. 176–177. See also Wolfson, "Biblical Accentuation," 1–16; and idem, "Biblical Accentuation (Part Two)," 1–13.

11. See MDL, no. 158, p. 256; and cf. MDL, no. 189, pp. 292–293.

12. See MDL, no.130, p. 223; and ibid., no. 192, p. 302. Similar to an isolated letter, the individual *nekudah* includes no semantic content. But unlike the concrete and delimited consonantal letters, vowels are interpreted inchoate gestures that reach toward the ineffable realm beyond language.

13. See LY, no. 132, fols. 38b–39a. See *Tikkunei Zohar, tikkun* 18, fol. 34b; MDL, no. 158, p. 256.

14. See *Sefer Yetsirah* 2:6. LY, no. 264, fols. 81b–82a, gives only four true places of articulation, explaining that the fifth is the nearly silent *aleph,* which is present in all articulated words.

15. See *Tikkunei Zohar, hakdamah,* fols. 2a, 6b.

16. See *Tikkunei Zohar, hakdamah aheret,* fol. 17a; *Pardes Rimmonim* 23:7. This association is already suggested by the rabbinic locution *'al pi* or *mi-pi ha-dibbur*; b. Hullin 5a; *Tanhuma,* ed. Buber, *naso,* no. 22.

17. See TSVHR, no. 82, p. 34; and Scholem, *"Devekut,"* 217.

18. See Idel, *"Hitbodedut,"* 405–438.

19. See, more broadly, Goldreich, *Automatic Writing.* See also *'Emek ha-Melekh,* 16:37, pp. 867 and 870; and Wolfson, *Language, Eros, Being,* 278.

20. See Pedaya, "Outlines for a Religious Typology," 55–70.

21. According to MDL, ed. Kahn, no. 52, fol. 14a, in this case preferable to Schatz-Uffenheimer's text.

22. MDL, no. 29, p. 47. See also *Or ha-Me'ir,* vol. 2, *ve-zot ha-berakhah,* 320.

23. *Darkhei Tsedek,* no. 19, p. 4, amended according to the 1810 printing. See Gries, *Conduct Literature,* 314–316.

24. For example, see MDL, no. 60, pp. 89–96; and, more broadly, Idel, *Absorbing Perfections,* 46–56, 70.

25. See the bibliographic excursus in the appendix.

26. *Kedushat Levi,* vol. 2, *kedushah sheniyah,* 517–518.

27. Cf. *'Emek ha-Melekh* 1:3.

28. See MDL, no. 201, p. 326. For a story about the mystical significance of the shapes of the Hebrew letters and the "intentions" (*kavvanot*) needed to write the holy names in Torah scrolls, see *Kahal Hasidim ha-Hadash,* p. 11.

29. See Idel, "White Letters," 169–192.

30. See Zohar 1:74a. On the term *kol* in earlier Kabbalah, see Wolfson, "God, the Demiurge, and the Intellect," 77–111.

31. LY, no. 241, fols. 71b–72a. Cf. a significant variant in JER NLI MS HEB 8°5198, fol. 35a.

32. The Maggid alternately describes the process through which *kol* becomes manifest through *dibbur* as *tsimtsum* ("focusing" or "contraction") or *hakikah* ("hewing"). See MDL, no. 62, p. 102; and LY, no. 271, fol. 89b. See also *Sefer Yetsirah* 2:6; Zohar 2:66b.

33. See *Tikkunei Zohar, tikkun* 21, fol. 48a. Cf. LY, no. 269, fol. 88a.

34. See LY, no. 131, fol. 37a; OT, *aggadot*, no. 386, p. 411; and MDL, no. 59, p. 88. See also the warning against separating *kol* and *dibbur* in *Orah le-Hayyim*, vol. 1, *va-yetse*, 144.

35. See Schatz-Uffenheimer, *Hasidism as Mysticism*, 204–214. The phrase *'olam ha-dibbur* is exceedingly rare in Jewish literature. See Kuzari 4:25; *Zohar Hadash, yitro*, fol. 34a; Bahye ben Asher's comments on Ex. 25:9; and *Shenei Luhot ha-Berit, ta'anit, ner mitsvah*; ibid., *parashat terumah, or torah*.

36. See Idel, "Models of Understanding Prayer," 43 n. 111.

37. See MDL, no. 93, p. 161; and OT, *be-shalah*, no. 92, p. 128.

38. For example, see MDL, no. 50, pp. 70–71.

39. See MDL, no. 34, p. 53.

40. See Wolfson, *Language, Eros, Being*, 358–359; Pedaya, "Great Mother," 311–328.

41. See Fodor, *Language of Thought*; Searle, *Minds, Brains, and Science*; Pinker, *Stuff of Thought*, 1–24 and 89–152; and Katz, "Language, Epistemology, and Mysticism," 22–74. See also Rosenzweig, *Star of Redemption*, esp. 118–163; and Buber, "Word That Is Spoken," 353–360.

42. See also Werblowsky, "Mystical and Magical Contemplation," 9–36.

43. See Hurwitz, "Psychological Aspects," 171–173.

44. The claim that the five places of articulation are included as potential in thought is quite strange, as this would seem to be an essentially phonological concept.

45. LY, no. 264, fols. 80b–81a.

46. OT, *tehilim*, no. 245, p. 299.

47. See OHE, 62a.

48. LY, no. 221, fols. 65b–66a.

49. See also MDL, no. 50, p. 71.

50. See KTVK, 21b; and MDL, no. 171, pp. 269–270.

51. See the Maggid's account in LY, no. 271, 89b. As the divine mother, *binah* is described as the "parent" of *kol* and *dibbur*; see MDL no. 59, pp. 88–89.

52. See MDL, no. 47, p. 69; and OT, *aggadot*, no. 464, p. 475.

53. See MDL, no. 135, p. 236; and OT, *tehilim*, no. 245, p. 298.

54. See MDL, no. 49, p. 70.

55. See MDL, no. 1, pp. 11–12.

56. See MDL, no. 28, p. 46; ibid., no. 62, p. 99.

57. See MDL, no. 28, p. 46; ibid., no. 142, p. 240. See *Toledot Ya'akov Yosef*, vol. 1, *hayyei sarah*, 136; ibid., vol. 2, *shelah*, 910; and see also Maimonides, *Guide*, 3:51.

58. See MDL, no. 173, p. 273; ibid., no. 50, p. 72; ibid., no. 25, pp. 40–41.

59. See MDL, no. 29, p. 49.

60. See MDL, no. 56, p. 83; ibid., no. 59, p. 88.

61. See MDL, no. 60, p. 95.

62. See MDL, no. 28, p. 46.

63. See also Ettin, *Speaking Silences*.

64. See OT, *shir ha-shirim*, no. 97, pp. 256–257.

65. Weiss, "Great Maggid's Theory," 139–140, noted that whereas *Ayin* (Nothing) is associated with the *sefirah keter* in classical Kabbalah, with *Ein Sof* referring to the unlimited Divine beyond the *sefirot*, the Maggid's sermons generally connect *ayin* to the *sefirah hokhmah*. See his exegesis of Job 28:12 in MDL, no. 1, p. 9; and Scholem, *Origins of the Kabbalah*, 130–131, 265–289, 431–444; and Lorberbaum, "Attain the Attribute," 169–235.

66. See OT, *va-yehi*, no. 61, pp. 84–85; and MDL, no. 59, pp. 87–89.

67. See MDL, no. 131, p. 226; ibid., no. 97, p. 171; and ibid., no. 116, p. 189.

68. See MDL, no. 94, p. 162. See also Scholem, "Unconscious," 268–276; Hurwitz, "Psychological Aspects," 149–240; and Brill, *Thinking God*, 110–133 and 365–367.

69. See the comments of Hurwitz, "Psychological Aspects," 166.

70. See *Or ha-Me'ir*, vol. 2, *korah*, 109–110; cf. ibid., vol. 2, *rosh ha-shanah*, 257. See also Hurwitz, "Psychological Aspects," 229–239.

71. See MDL, no. 93, p. 161; and see Hurwitz, "Psychological Aspects," 175–176.

72. A similar formulation appears in Cordovero's *Tomer Devorah*, ch. 3.

73. OT, *va-yetse*, no. 43, p. 57. See Hurwitz, "Psychological Aspects," 196–198.

74. See MDL, no. 77, p. 132.

75. Cf. the formulation of Shneur Zalman of Liady in *Torah Or, megillat esther*, 91b; and *Likkutei Torah, be-hukkotai*, 46b; and ibid., *va-yikra*, 54a.

76. See Zori, *Not in the Hands of Heaven*, 72–74.

77. See Idel, "BeSHT as a Prophet," 124, 132–133; and Green, "Typologies of Leadership," 146–149. See also Garb, *Shamanic Trance*, 69–71, 101, and 210 n. 72.

78. For a disagreement over prophetic agency in the Maggid's school, see Schatz-Uffenheimer, *Hasidism and Mysticism*, 200–203; and Margolin, *Human Temple*, 315–318, 343–348. See also MDL, no. 87, p. 15; and Scholem, *Origins of the Kabbalah*, 239, 304–305, 419.

79. See MDL, no. 49, p. 70.

80. Ibid. Cf. OT, *tehillim*, no. 206, p. 274, on the transition from *histaklut* to prophecy.

81. LY, no. 48, fol. 9b.

82. See MDL, no. 85, p. 148, commenting on 2 Kings 22:11–20 and b. Megillah 14b.

83. See *Zohar* 1:15b; *Tikkunei Zohar, hakdamah*, fol. 12b.

84. LY, no. 238, fol. 69a.

85. This understanding of prophecy is linked to the Maggid's theory of revelation. See Chapter 5; and, inter alia, *Orah le-Hayyim*, vol. 1, *shemot*, 118–120; *Mevasser Tsedek, be-ha'alotekha*, 177; and MDL, no. 132, p. 228.

86. See also LY, no. 173, fol. 56a; and ST, 61a.

87. See OT, *pesukim*, no. 382, pp. 408–409.

88. m. Avot 3:13.

89. b. Hullin 8b.

90. OT, *aggadot*, no. 478, p. 481. See also TSVHR, no. 133, 25a.

91. b. Hullin 8b.

92. *Or ha-Me'ir*, vol. 2, *ruth*, 37. Cf. OHE, 5a. It is worth noting that Ze'ev Wolf continues by expressing his disagreement with the Maggid, arguing that one cannot live only in the World of Thought.

93. See Schatz-Uffenheimer, "Contemplative Prayer," 221–222.

94. See *'Avodat Yisra'el, likkutim*, 219; and cf. *'Avodat Yisra'el, noah*, 8.

95. See Pedaya, "Outlines for a Religious Typology," 25–73; and idem, "Two Types," 73–108.

96. See also LY, no. 13, fol. 3a.

97. Zohar 2:226b.

98. I.e., the mystic must not be like the horse whose movements can be directed against its will.

99. LY, no. 175, fols. 56a–56b. See also OT, *tehillim*, no. 224, pp. 283–284.

100. See the famous comments by Ishmael and 'Akiva in *Mekhilta* on Ex. 20:15; Savran, "Seeing Is Believing," 321–322; Wolfson, *Through a Speculum*, 13–51; Harvey, "Judah Halevi's Synesthetic Theory," 141–155. Beyond Judaism, see McGinn, "Language of Inner Experience," esp. 159–160.

101. See MDL, no. 73, pp. 124–127. See also OT, *pesukim*, no. 318, p. 366; MDL, no. 30, p. 49; ibid., no. 31, pp. 49–50; and ibid., no. 83, pp. 144–146, where the Maggid makes use of the homonym *'ayin* ("eye" or "appearance") and *ayin*.

102. See ST, 82a.

103. See MDL, no. 90, pp. 156–157; and OHE, 36a. Cf. Zohar 2:161a; also *Ets Hayyim* 4:3; and MDL, no. 59, p. 88.

104. See *Or ha-Me'ir*, vol. 1, *va-yera*, 25; and KTVK, 48b.

105. According to the Sephardic liturgy adapted by the Kabbalists and Hasidim, the *kedushah* prayer of the *mussaf* or "additional" service on Shabbat begins with the words *keter yitnu lekha* ("we shall adorn You with a crown").

106. LY, no. 224, fol. 66b; and see MDL, no. 118, p. 192. The notion that the commandments were given to fulfill a divine need is central to Jewish mysticism. See the comments of Nahmanides and Bahye ben Asher on Ex. 29:46; Gabbai, *'Avodat ha-Kodesh*, I:18, 28, and II:1; and *Shenei Luhot ha-Berit*, sha'ar ha-gadol; trans. in Krassen, *Isaiah Horowitz*, 298–351. More broadly, see Wolfson, "Mystical Rationalization," 223–235; Matt, "Mystic and the Mizwot," 367–404; and Green, "God's Need for Man," 247–261.

107. MDL, no. 118, pp. 191–192.

108. See the description in ST, 60a-b.

109. LY, no. 264, fol. 81a.

110. MDL, no. 146, p. 247.

111. Wolfson, *Giving Beyond the Gift*, esp. 1–33 and 154–200.

112. Based on *Bereshit Rabbah* 12:2.

113. A common term for *shekhinah*.

114. *Sefer Yetsirah* 2:6.

115. According to MDL, ed. Kahn, no. 152, fol. 48a.

116. MDL, no. 105, pp. 183–184.

117. MDL, no. 60, pp. 89–90.

118. See also *Or ha-Me'ir*, vol. 2, *ruth*, 39.

119. See *Kedushat Levi*, vol. 1, *parashat parah*, 258.

120. See MDL, no. 170, p. 267.

121. See Stern, *Wittgenstein on Mind and Language*; and Kripke, *Wittgenstein on Rules*. See also Liebes, "Nahman of Bratslav," 10–13, 134; and Rosenberg, "On Faith and Language," 173–206.

122. Wittgenstein, *Tractatus Logico-Philosophicus*, 89.

123. Perloff, *Wittgenstein's Ladder*, 12.

124. McGuinness, Nyberg, and von Wright, *ProtoTractatus*, 16.

125. MDL, no. 96, p. 167. See also OHE, 85a; and MDL, no. 65, p. 107.

126. See, for example, the passage translated in Matt, *Essential Kabbalah*, 121; Scholem, "*Sulam ha-'Aliyah*," 161–171; Fishbane, *As a Light Before Dawn*, 199–246; Idel, *Ascensions on*

High; and Brody, "Human Hands," 133–158. We should note the parallel between the Maggid's contemplative vision and that of the thirteenth-century Bonaventure presented in *Itinerarium Mentis in Deum* (The Mind's Journey into God), explored, inter alia, by Bowman, "Cosmic Exemplarism," 181–198.

127. OT, *noah*, no. 15, p. 20. See also KST, no. 145, p. 79; ibid., *hosafot*, no. 53, p. 312.

128. See Bialik, "Revealment and Concealment," 11–26; and Key, *Language Between God and the Poets*, 1–6, 110–151.

129. MDL, no. 62, 101–102; and Lorberbaum, "Attain the Attribute," n. 1.

CHAPTER 4

Notes to epigraphs: Scholem, "Neutralization," 200; Buber, "Dialogue Between Heaven and Earth," 221.

1. See Fishbane, "Speech of Being," 485–521.

2. See Scholem, *Major Trends*, 260–273; Idel, "On the Concept of *Zimzum*," 59–112; Lederberg, *Gateway*, 179–185; and Lorberbaum, "Attain the Attribute," 177–209.

3. See Boyarin, "Gospel of the *Memra*," 243–284; idem, *Border Lines*, 86–226; and Janowitz, "Re-creating Genesis," 393–405.

4. On Jewish teachings regarding the power of the letters in their broader cultural context, see Janowitz, *Icons of Power*, 19–32, 45–84; Weiss, *"Sefer Yeṣirah" and Its Contexts*, esp. 17–75; and Rubin, "Language of Creation or the Primordial Language," 308.

5. See Idel, "Reification of Language," 45–47. On creation in rabbinic literature, see Altmann, "Note on the Rabbinic Doctrine of Creation," 195–206; and Urbach, *Sages*, 184–213.

6. See m. Avot records 5:1; b. Rosh Hashanah 32b; and b. Megillah 21b. Cf. *Bereshit Rabbah* 17:1, ed. Albeck and Theodor, p. 151.

7. *Sifrei*, *'ekev*, no. 49.

8. See b. Berakhot 55a. For references to God's creative word that were incorporated into benedictions and liturgy, see b. Sanhedrin 42b and b. Berakhot 59a.

9. See *Bereshit Rabbah* 12:10, ed. Albeck and Theodor, pp. 107–109. See Fishbane, *Exegetical Imagination*, 14–18. Cf. y. Hagigah 2:1 and b. Menahot 29b. While the Hebrew Bible affords significant sanctity to the divine names, and Y-H-V-H in particular, no claims are made regarding their creative capacity; see Scholem, "Name of God," 68–72.

10. See *Bereshit Rabbah* 44:18, ed. Albeck and Theodor, 441–442.

11. See b. Kiddushin 71a. See Urbach, *Sages*, 130–131, 197. Rabbinic literature offers some conceptual and etymological explanations for the meanings of various divine names; see, inter alia, *Bereshit Rabbah* 5:7, ed. Albeck and Theodor, p. 37; 46:3, p. 460.

12. See b. Sanhedrin 65b. RaSHI connects the stories of Rabbah and the two sages to the tradition about Bezalel in b. Berakhot 55a, explaining that the quasi-magical activities of the former were accomplished by means of letter permutations. See Scholem, *Origins of the Kabbalah*, 31; idem, "Idea of the Golem," 158–204; and Idel, *Golem*, 4–22, 47–82, 262–265.

13. Cf. b. Sanhedrin 67b, in which the mysterious work studied by the two sages is called *Hilkhot Yetsirah*. Liebes, *Ars Poetica*, 67, 70, argues for an early dating of *Sefer Yetsirah* and suggests that the Talmudic sages were aware of it.

14. On the possible correlation between rabbinic traditions and Philo's notion of the divine *logos*, see Urbach, *Sages*, 197, 213; Boyarin, "Gospel of the Memra," 243–284; and, more

broadly, Wolfson, *Philo*, 1:230–240, 338; Winston, *Logos and Mystical Theology*, esp. 15, 21–25, and 49–50; and Calabi, *Language and the Law of God*, 3–30.

15. On this theme, see Urbach, *Sages*, 198–202; and Idel, *Absorbing Perfections*, 31–34, 40–53, 377–380. See also Holdrege, *Veda and Torah*, 131–223.

16. See *Bereshit Rabbah* 1:1.

17. m. Avot 3:14. See also the tradition quoted in *Sifre Devarim*, ed. Finkelstein, no. 48, p. 114.

18. See Scholem, "Name of God," 70–76; idem, *Origins of the Kabbalah*, 27–32; and Liebes, *Ars Poetica*, 105–107.

19. See Liebes, *Ars Poetica*, 57, 64–66, 73–75; and cf. Hayman, "Was God a Magician?" 233–234.

20. Scholem, *Jewish Gnosticism*, 78–79; Schäfer, *Hidden and Manifest God*, 133, 135; Janowitz, *Poetics of Ascent*, 25, 85, 87.

21. Abrams, "Some Phenomenological Considerations," 7–19. The rabbinic tradition of God's Creation by means of gazing into Torah is cited less frequently in these early kabbalistic works, but it does appear. See, for example, the end of Isaac the Blind's commentary on *Sefer Yetsirah*, ch. 2.

22. On the significant number of treatises explaining and interpreting the various divine names and their relationship to the emanated *sefirot*, see Porat, *Works of Iyyun*, 128–146, 153–155, 188–203; and Scholem, *Origins of the Kabbalah*, 99–102.

23. See Weiss, "Reception of *Sefer Yetsirah*," 26–46.

24. Perhaps more than any of the other early Kabbalists, Abulafia and Gikatilla explored the implications of these sacred creation myths for human language; see Idel, *Language, Torah, and Hermeneutics*, esp. 22–55, 109, 174.

25. For example, see Abrams, *Book of Bahir*, no. 53, p. 149; ibid., no. 60, p. 153.

26. See Scholem, *Origins of the Kabbalah*, 126–123, 270–289; idem, *Kabbalah*, 93–94; Liebes, "Pool," 131–138.

27. See Sendor, "Emergence of Provençal Kabbalah," 328, 343–344; Pedaya, *Name and Sanctuary*, 80, 97, 100–127; idem, *Vision and Speech*; Wolfson, *Language, Eros, Being*, 63–64; and Fishbane, "Speech of Being," 501–502.

28. Fishbane, "Speech of Being," 492.

29. On Creation in the Zohar, see Tishby, *Wisdom of the Zohar*, 2:549–560.

30. See Zohar 1:47b, 134a. The Zohar correlates the written Torah with *tif'eret,* which emerged from *hokhmah*, the abstract realm associated with the Torah that predated the world; see Zohar 3:160a. See below, Chapter 4.

31. For example, see Zohar 1:204a.

32. See Zohar 2:234a–234b. See also Zohar 2:180b, which refers to the "forty-two letters by which the world was created."

33. See Zohar 1:2b–3b. On this story, see Oron, "Narrative of the Letters," 97–110.

34. See Oron, "Narrative of the Letters," 99–100; and Dan, "*Ottiyyot de-Rabbi Akiva*," 5–30.

35. See *Pardes Rimmonim* 3:5; *Ets Hayyim* 5:1–6.

36. See Shatil, "Kabbalah of R. Israel Sarug," 158–187; *'Emek ha-Melekh* 1:2, pp. 117–118; ibid., 1:3–4, pp. 120–122. See *Likkutei Torah*, hosafot, fol. 51b, citing a tradition from Sarug— preserved in *'Emek ha-Melekh*—on the Hebrew letters being projected into the empty space left after the primoridal *tsimtsum*. My thanks to Amiel Vick for drawing my attention to this source.

37. On the divine utterances as mythic prototypes for the idea of the *sefirot*, see Idel, *Kabbalah*, 112–120.

38. b. Megillah 21b; b. Rosh ha-Shanah 32a, based on m. Avot 5:1.

39. The original transcriber may be speaking in the first person, citing an explanation he learned from the Maggid, or, alternatively, Dov Ber may be referring to a tradition he received from someone else.

40. See Targum Yerushalmi to Gen. 1:1, itself either a parallel to or reworking of the notion that the Torah predated the world as God's wisdom.

41. LY, no. 235, fol. 68b. Cf. OHE, 29a. See also the tradition recorded in *Benei Yissakhar*, vol. 2, *ma'amarei tishrei*, no. 2, p. 203.

42. The *bet* of *be-hokhmah* may be interpreted as one of instrument rather than location. Thus the phrase might be rendered "by means of Wisdom" instead of "in Wisdom," confirming the origin of the letters in *binah* rather than *hokhmah*.

43. See *Bereshit Rabbah* 1:14, paraphrased by RaSHI on Gen. 1:14.

44. For a similar formulation, see Zohar 1:256b. See also Zohar 1:16b.

45. This is an example of the Maggid using the word *lev* to refer to the mind and the seat of intellection, a common convention in medieval Hebrew.

46. MDL, no. 97, p. 172.

47. See Fishbane, "Speech of Being," 498–502; Pedaya, *Name and Sanctuary*, 80, 100–127; Green, *Keter*. On the theme of divine will, see Scholem's classic essay, "Iqvotav shel Gabirol ba-Kabbalah," 39–66.

48. See Sheveka, "Trace of the Tradition," 297–320.

49. This is Schatz-Uffenheimer's contention in her comments ad loc.

50. See Key, *Language Between God and the Poets*, 57–86.

51. *Areshet* is associated with the word *bereshit* by Bahye ben Asher in his comments on Gen. 1:2, but I have been unable to locate an earlier source.

52. b. Berakhot 55a. See also Zohar 2:152a.

53. See OT, *tetsaveh*, no. 102, pp. 142–143; translation based on Green et al., *Speaking Torah*, 1:222–223.

54. See Bahye ben Asher to Ex. 38:21; *Tanhuma, pekkudei*, no. 2; Zohar 2:59b, 127a, 149a; and Green, "Sabbath as Temple," 295–298.

55. See b. Berakhot 55a.

56. See Abrams, *Book of Bahir*, no. 116, p. 201. See Zohar 2:129b, 2:220b–221a.

57. See LY, no. 125, fols. 31b–32a, for a parallel in which the Maggid interprets Ex. 31:4 ("to contemplate the works, doing them," *la-hashov mahshavot, la-'asot*) as referring to Bezalel's ability to draw forth the correct thoughts and letter combinations from the precognitive realm of *hokhmah* or *keter*.

58. Here too we find a murmering echo of Benajamin's thinking on language and the infinite beyond; see his "Task of the Translator," esp. 258–259.

59. See also OT, *nitsavim*, no. 181, pp. 238–239.

60. See b. Berakhot 22a.

61. OT, *va-yehi*, no. 60, p. 82.

62. See also OT, *be-shalah*, no. 92, p. 128.

63. See Idel, "Your Word," 219–286.

64. See above.

65. The numerical value of *heh*, the definite article of *ha-shammayim*, is five.

66. MDL, no. 44, p. 66.

67. MDL, no. 209, p. 335; and see also MDL, no. 39, pp. 59–60.

68. OT, *ki tissa*, no. 105, p. 145.

69. *Dibbur* and *kol* correspond to the second *heh* and the *vav* (*malkhut* and *tif'eret*), and "breath" (*hevel*) seems to refer to *binah*. *Mahashavah* therefore corresponds to *hokhmah*, the first *heh* and *yod* of Y-H-V-H. See *Tikkunei Zohar, tikkun* 22, fol. 63b; ibid., *tikkun* 69, fol. 105b.

70. This enfolding of humanity into Israel (and the more-than-occasional exclusion of non-Jews) is deeply rooted in the discourse of power. See Lachter, *Kabbalistic Revolution*, esp. 15–44, 100–158.

71. See *Bereshit Rabbah* 1:4; and *Va-Yikra Rabbah* 36:4, paraphrased by RaSHI in his comments on Gen. 1:1. See also Swartz, *Signifying Creator*, 13–32. See also Zohar 1:24a. 2:20a, and 2:119a-b; *Tikkunei Zohar, tikkun* 40, fol. 80a. In the writings of Moshe Cordovero, the "thought" of this phrase is associated with the *sefirah hokhmah*; see *Pardes Rimmonim*, 6:9, 7:2, 23:10.

72. MDL, no. 55, p. 78. See also LY, no. 249, fols. 76b–77a; MDL, no. 62, pp. 99–100; OHE, 4b–5a; and cf. SLA, 89–90.

73. See OT, *pesukim*, no. 304, pp. 353–354; *Orah le-Hayyim*, vol. 1, *noah*, 70.

74. MDL, no. 1, pp. 9–10.

75. See Stern, "'First in Thought," 235–252; Scholem, *Major Trends*, pp. 208, 401 n. 41. See also *Pardes Rimmonim* 3:1, 3:5, 15:1; and *Sefer Yetsirah* 1:6.

76. See OT, *bereshit*, no. 11a, pp. 11–12.

77. LY, no. 264, fols. 80b–81a.

78. See MDL, no. 81, p. 140. Cf. ibid., no. 122, pp. 199–200; and Zohar 2:127a-b; Abrams, *Book of Bahir*, nos. 57–58, pp. 151–153.

79. The Maggid's sermons on the power of the human mind, which originates in the initial moment of creation. remind us that the Maggid does not necessarily extend this contemplative faculty beyond Israel. See MDL, no. 94, pp. 162–163; and ibid., no. 64, p. 105.

80. See b. Menahot 29b.

81. See MDL, no. 41, p. 63; and ibid., no. 22, p. 36. See also Sendor, "Emergence of Provençal Kabbalah," 186–187; Pedaya, *Name and Sanctuary*, 71–76; and Fishbane, *As Light Before Dawn*, 72, 238–239, 240 n. 168.

82. OHE, 33b.

83. See Wolfson, "Immanuel Frommann's Commentary on Luke," 194–196.

84. See MDL, no. 164, p. 263. For precedent in kabbalistic literature, see *Tikkunei Zohar, tikkun* 22, fol. 65b; and Wolfson, "Image of Jacob," 1–62. It is unclear if the Maggid is using the term *mahashavah* in reference to *keter, hokhmah*, or *binah*.

85. *Tikkunei Zohar, tikkun* 6, fol. 21a.

86. *Tanhuma, va-yakhel*, no. 7.

87. *Tikkunei Zohar, tikkun* 21, fol. 49b. *Shekhinah* is sometimes associated with the lungs when the *sefirot* are mapped onto the human structure and the divine anthropos.

88. MDL, no. 1, pp. 9–12. Based on Green et al., *Speaking Torah*, 1:136–137.

89. See Schatz-Uffenheimer, *Hasidism as Mysticism*, 207; and Margolin, *Human Temple*, 329–330, 383.

90. See Zohar 1:15a, 21a; 2:179b–180a; 3:10b; *Tikkunei Zohar, hakdamah*, fol. 5a. Describing the theology of the 'Iyyun work *Ma'ayan ha-Hokhmah*, perhaps one of the texts that Dov Ber studied with the BeSHT, Scholem wrote: "The Name of God . . . is the unity of movement of language branching out from the primordial root. . . . *Yod* is represented as the 'bubbling

source' of the movement of language, which after differentiation and ramification in the Infinite returns again to its center and origin"; see Scholem, *Origins of the Kabbalah*, 332. See also Wolfson, "Letter Symbolism," 203–205; idem, *Language, Eros, Being*, 282.

91. See Gikatilla, *Sha'arei Orah*, ch. 5, p. 182; Idel, "Kabbalistic Prayer," 278–279; Wolfson, *Language, Eros, Being*, 282–283; Septimus, "Isaac de Castellon," 53–80. The term "the tip of the *yod*" already appears in rabbinic literature, without any mystical significance; see b. Menahot 29a; *Bereshit Rabbah* 1:10; ibid., 12:10.

92. See MDL, no. 83, p. 144.

93. See b. Menahot 29b.

94. The numerical value of *yod* is ten, and that of *heh* is five.

95. LY, no. 241, fol. 70a-b.

96. Zohar 1:15b; *Tikkunei Zohar, hakdamah*, fol. 12b; ibid., *tikkun* 5, fol. 19a. This exegesis plays on the presence of the diacritical mark within the letter *bet*.

97. I have translated the verse as the Maggid interprets it.

98. b. Menahot 29b.

99. See b. Hullin 47a.

100. MDL, no. 192, pp. 301–304.

101. The letter *vav* is also associated with *ze'ir anpin*, the cluster of six *sefirot* that surround *malkhut*.

102. Gold is often associated with *gevurah*, whereas silver generally refers to *hesed*. See Abrams, *Book of Bahir*, no. 93, p. 179; Zohar 2:138b–139a. The order of the verse is thus the reverse of the typical schema of the *sefirot*.

103. Water is generally associated with *hesed*, whereas fire is associated with *gevurah*.

104. See b. Yoma 44b; and cf. Zohar 2:147a–148a, where gold represents *binah*, which encompasses the next seven *sefirot* before they emerge.

105. This refers to the seven days of creation, but also the emergence of the seven *sefirot* from *hesed* to *malkhut*. As mentioned above, the emanation of the *sefirot* and the formation of the physical world are intertwined processes.

106. See Lorberbaum, "Attain the Attribute," 202–207. *Hyle* (matter), a term adopted from Aristotelian philosophy, is mentioned by Nahmanides in the introduction to his commentary on the Torah as an initial sublime matter created by God from which all other creations were formed; see also Bahya ben Asher's comments on Gen. 1:1. See Dillon, "Solomon Ibn Gabirol's Doctrine," 3–60; and Idel, "Jewish Kabbalah," 328.

107. See Zohar 1:15b; *Tikkunei Zohar, hakdamah*, fol. 12b; ibid., *tikkun* 5, fol. 19a.

108. The final letter *mem* (ם), enclosed on all sides, is often associated with *binah*; see Zohar 2:127a-b.

109. This verse strangely includes a final *mem* in the middle of the word "to increase" (*le-marbeh*). See Zohar 1:34b. According to *Tikkunei Zohar, tikkun* 5, fol. 18a, the letter *bet* of *bereshit* was originally a final *mem*, but was then opened into a *bet* as the letter *vav* emerged forth. See also *Tikkunei Zohar, tikkun* 29, fol. 83a; cf. b. Sanhedrin 94a.

110. MDL, no. 180, pp. 280–281. See Hurwitz, "Psychological Aspects," 180.

111. See Zohar 2:119b; *Peri Ets Hayyim, derushei ha-pesah*, no. 11.

112. For an important example in addition to those discussed in detail below, see MDL, no. 193, pp. 306–310.

113. See MDL, no. 134, p. 234.

114. MDL, no. 122, p. 200; see above.

115. See MDL, no. 63, p. 103.

116. The Maggid later identifies these four stages of contraction as *hokhmah*, *binah*, *tif'eret*, and *malkhut*.

117. MDL, no. 122, p. 202.

118. Heb. *ro'eh*, according to OHE, 38d. Schatz-Uffenheimer's text and the first edition of MDL erroneously read "wants" (*rotseh*).

119. The student transcribing the teaching seems to be speaking in the first person.

120. MDL, no. 28, pp. 46–47.

121. See also Wolfson, "Hallevi and Maimonides," 60–119.

122. The Hebrew root NaGaD is often read in Hasidic and kabbalistic books in light of its Aramaic meaning of "to pull" or "to draw forth"; see also b. Shabbat 87a; *Ben Porat Yosef*, vol. 2, *derush le-shabbat ha-gadol*, 606.

123. LY, no. 282, fol. 101a. For a different version of this sermon, see MDL, no. 63, pp. 103–104.

CHAPTER 5

Note to epigraph: Heschel, *God in Search of Man*, 244.

1. See also Mayse, "Voices of Moses," 101–125.

2. See Halbertal, *People of the Book*, esp. 38–39.

3. See Holdrege, "Bride of Israel," 236–239; and *Ruth Zuta*, ed. Buber, 1:1.

4. See *Bereshit Rabbah* 1:1, 8:2. Cf. b. 'Eruvin 13a; *Midrash Tehillim*, ps. 3; and *Pirkei de-Rabbi Eliezer*, ch. 3, suggesting that the Torah has magical properties that may have been hidden from mankind to prevent their misuse. See also Fishbane, *Garments of Torah*, 33–48. On Philo's interpretation of Scripture and the *logos*, see Wolfson, *Philo*, 1:115–143.

5. See Scholem, "Meaning of the Torah," 32–86; Idel, *Absorbing Perspectives*, esp. 26–136; idem, "Infinities of Torah," 141–157; and Wolfson, *Language, Eros, Being*, 190–260, 513–545. Scholem, "Meaning of the Torah," 35, posed the question as to whether mystical conceptions of Scripture might not represent a point of commonality between Christian and Islamic theologians, wondering if there is any historical connection. For a comparison of Jewish and Hindu literatures, see Holdrege, *Veda and Torah*, esp. 131–223.

6. See Scholem, "Meaning of the Torah," 41–42; Idel, "Torah," 197–235; and Wolfson, "Iconicity of the Text," 215–242.

7. See Scholem, *Major Trends*, 45, and cf. Idel, "Concept of Torah," 23–84; Deutsch, *Gnostic Imagination*, 56–67.

8. See Dan, *Esoteric Theology*, 124; Wolfson, "Mystical Significance," 49; and Fishman, "Rhineland Pietists' Sacralization of Oral Torah," 9–16. On the text of the Torah as an incomplete revelation of the divine will, see Soloveitchik, "Three Themes," 312–325.

9. See Wolfson, "Hebraic and Hellenic Conceptions," 147–176.

10. See Pedaya, *Nahmanides*, 120–205; Halbertal, *By Way of Truth*, 315–318, 331–333; idem, *Concealment and Revelation*, 83–92. See also *Kitvei Ramban*, 2:167–168.

11. See Scholem, "Meaning of the Torah," 37–44; and cf. Dan, *Esoteric Theology*, 124. See also Idel, "Concept of Torah," 54; idem, *Absorbing Perfections*, 321.

12. Cf. b. 'Eruvin 13a.

13. See Scholem, "Meaning of the Torah," 32–86. See also Idel, *Absorbing Perfections*, esp. 96–110, 138–139; and Wolfson, *Through a Speculum*, 345–355; idem, "Mystical Significance," esp. 49; and Fishman, "Rhineland Pietists' Sacralization of Oral Torah," 9–16.

14. See Zohar 3:149a–149b. See also, inter alia, Zohar 2:95a, 98b; 3:79b. See also Tishby, *Wisdom of the Zohar*, 3:1077–1121; Hellner-Eshed, *River Flows from Eden*, esp. 155–228; and Wolfson, "Beautiful Maiden," 155–203.

15. See his comments on Num. 11:15; and Idel, *Kabbalah*, 213–214. On the idea of Torah and exegesis in the writings of Abulafia and Gikatilla, see Scholem, "Meaning of the Torah," 42; Idel, *Language, Torah, and Hermeneutics*, 29–124; and Morlok, *Rabbi Joseph Gikatilla's Hermeneutics*, 172–208.

16. See Zohar 3:71; cf. 2:124a.

17. See Zohar 2:60a. See Scholem, "Meaning of the Torah," 44–45.

18. See also *Perush ha-Aggadot le-Rabbi 'Azriel*, ed. Tishby, 2–3, 77, 81–82.

19. See Abrams, "'Text' in a Zoharic Parable," 7–54; and, more broadly, Harvey, "On Maimonides' Allegorical Readings of Scripture," 181–188; and Talmage, "Apples of Gold," 313–355.

20. See Zohar 3:152a.

21. On the revelatory power of the text vis-à-vis the visionary encounter with God in earlier mystical texts, see Scholem, "Meaning of the Torah," 41–42; Idel, "Torah," 197–235; Wolfson, "Iconicity of the Text," 215–242.

22. See the sixteenth-century Kabbalist Me'ir ibn Gabbai's *'Avodat ha-Kodesh*, I:21–22 and III:20–24; and the passage from Isaiah Horowitz's *Shenei Luhot ha-Berit*, cited in Scholem, "Revelation and Tradition," 300–303.

23. See Scholem, "Meaning of the Torah," 64–65; Liebes, "Myth vs. Symbol," 212–242; and Magid, *From Metaphysics to Midrash*, 1–15.

24. See Scholem, "Meaning of the Torah," 71–74.

25. See Scholem, *Sabbatai Sevi*, 11–12, 51–52, 319–324; Liebes, *On Sabbateanism*, 100, 164.

26. See *'Emek ha-Melekh*, 1:4, p. 127; *Hesed le-Avraham*, 2:10, p. 80.

27. See *'Emek ha-Melekh*, 6:47, pp. 241–244.

28. A commonly cited midrashic tradition suggests that Torah was created two thousand years before the world, but Maggid seems to have interpreted other rabbinic traditions as implying that Scripture was indeed coeternal: "The Holy One is preexistent (*kadmon*), and the Torah was preexistent (*mukdemet*)"; see OT, *tehilim*, no. 245, p. 285; and cf. *Bereshit Rabbah* 8:2; b. Avodah Zarah 9a.

29. MDL, no. 134, p. 234.

30. See LY, no. 122, fol. 28a-b; cf. MDL, no. 56, p. 83. This tension is already present in the Zohar. See Zohar 2:85a, 2:12a; and SLA, 8, 35, 135.

31. See *Or ha-Me'ir*, vol. 1, *pesah*, p. 244.

32. m. Avot 5:1.

33. Nahmanides on Gen. 1:3 explains that the word *amirah* refers to the divine "desire" (*hefets*) or "thought" (*mahashavah*), instructing the reader that God simply willed the world into existence without any sort of effort. Cf. Maimonides, *Guide*, 1:65. The word *amirah* is also associated with internal desire in Zohar 3:17b.

34. MDL, no. 202, p. 327. See also *Dibrat Shlomo, yitro*, 168; *Likkutei Torah, hukkat*, fol. 57c-d; *Or ha-Me'ir*, vol. 2, *sukkot*, 195.

35. See also MDL, no. 133, p. 232.

36. The Maggid is reading *'afa* as "folded" rather than the more conventional translation of "flying." This verse is interpreted by the Talmudic sages as referring to Torah; see b. 'Eruvin 21a, where this verse is used to claim that the size of the world is but a tiny fraction of Scripture; and RaSHI's commentary ad loc. Cf. MaHarSHA's interpretation ad loc.

37. MDL, no. 189, p. 292.

38. A medieval Hebrew *bon mot*, first attested in Bahye ben Asher. See his comments on Gen. 38:30 and his introduction to Num. 22.

39. OHE, 47b–48a. This appears to be a longer account of the following short conversation between Levi Yitshak and his teacher, the Maggid, in ST, 59. See also Lederberg, *Gateway*, 174–175.

40. See OT, *yitro*, no. 98, pp. 137–138; cf. SLA, 125–126.

41. In classical Kabbalah, the name Y-H-V-H is often associated with *tif'eret*, the written Torah, and the Tree of Life. See Zohar 1:27a, 2:117a, 3:271a (R.M.); *Sha'arei Orah*, ch. 5, pp. 252–256.

42. The numerical value of *GaN*, or "garden," is fifty-three.

43. See MDL, no. 192, pp. 300–306; LY, no. 264, fol. 81a.

44. See Zohar 3:152a.

45. MDL, no. 195, pp. 313–314. Based on Green et al., *Speaking Torah*, 1:104–105. Cf. MDL, no. 132, pp. 227–228.

46. MDL, no. 56, p. 83.

47. See his formulation in OT, *va-era*, no. 73, p. 101.

48. See MDL, no. 168, p. 266. Cf. OHE, 3b, for a different teaching about the ten names that cannot be erased.

49. MDL, no. 132, pp. 227–228.

50. LY, no. 46, fol. 9a. The different versions of this convoluted teaching vary widely; see OHE, 14b; SLA, 133; and Idel, *Absorbing Perfections*, 155–160 and 533 n. 98. See also *Likkutei Torah, massa'ei*, fol. 95b.

51. See Zohar 1:24a; 2:60a, 90b; Idel, "Concept of the Torah," 67; and Wolfson, "Beautiful Maiden," 167–168. The Maggid's disciples often use variations of the phrase "the blessed Holy One, Torah and Israel are all one," but this formulation appears rarely in the Maggid's sermons; see OHE, fol. 14b; *Or ha-Me'ir*, vol. 1, *pesah*, p. 244. On the origins and evolution of this formulation, see Tishby, "Holy One," 480–492. See also MDL, no. 12, p. 26; ibid., no. 24, p. 40; ibid., no. 86, pp. 149–150; ibid., no. 93, pp. 160–161; ibid., no. 97, p. 171; ibid., no. 122, p. 202; ibid., no. 173, p. 272; and the various parallels.

52. MDL, no. 132, p. 227. For "He and His causes . . . ," see *Tikkunei Zohar, hakdamah*, p. 3b. Cf. *Pardes Rimmonim* 16:2. See also *Ets Hayyim* 42:5, 47:2.

53. See also MDL, no. 126, p. 217; OT, *'ekev*, no. 162, pp. 212–213. Cf. MDL, no. 173, p. 272. See also *No'am Elimelekh*, vol. 1, *va-yera*, 40; translated in Green et al., *Speaking Torah*, 1:103–104.

54. See Wolfson, *Language, Eros, Being*, esp. 8, 31–59.

55. See MDL, no. 56, p. 83.

56. The original passage in the Zohar is also much less audacious than it would appear at first blush. The written Torah is associated with the *sefirah tif'eret*, to which the name "the blessed Holy One" (*kudsha berikh hu*) also corresponds. Hence, extending the logic of this symbol cluster, the written Torah and the blessed Holy One may be identified with one another.

57. MDL, no. 97, p. 171. Cf. *Peri ha-Arets, noah,* 14–16.

58. See *Or ha-Me'ir,* vol. 2, *'ekev,* 187. Cf. MDL, no. 134, p. 234; and OHE, 87b.

59. Ambivalence regarding the nonlegal sections of the Torah appears even in rabbinic literature. See b. Hullin 60b; and RaSHI's comments on Gen. 1:1. See Marcus, "Rashi's Historiosophy," 50–52.

60. For example, see LY, no. 288, fol. 108a.

61. The notion that a person is a "microcosm" (*'olam katan*) of the Divine is found several times in the Maggid's teachings; see LY, no. 285, fol. 106b; ibid., no. 129, fol. 35a. On the history of this phrase, see Idel, *New Perspectives,* 119–121, 150, 180, and 330 n. 37; Altmann "Delphic Maxim," 196–232.

62. See MDL, no. 193, pp. 206–208. See also *Toledot Ya'akov Yosef,* vol. 1, *be-shalah,* 377, commenting on Ex. 13:17.

63. Dov Ber reworks an older kabbalistic teaching that Israel descended to Egypt in order to lift up the divine sparks, described as the letters of idle speech trapped in the "husks," claiming that "The blessed Holy One wanted to redeem them, bringing these words and letters into the Torah and recombining them in a holy way [i.e., as a new permutation]." See LY, no. 251, fol. 77a; and cf. *Me'or 'Einayim,* vol. 1, *bo,* 162–163; and *Peri Ets Hayyim, sha'ar hag ha-matsot,* ch. 1. The Maggid interprets "that I may display these My signs (*otot*)," (Ex. 10:1) as a homiletical reference to the captive "letters" (*otiyyot*) in need of redemption.

64. See also Zornberg, *Bewilderments,* 263–285.

65. From *Va-Yikra Rabbah* 13:3, based on Isa. 51:4.

66. See LY, no. 250, fols. 76b–77a; and cf. the variant in MDL, no. 5, pp. 17–18.

67. Cf. *Imrei Tsaddikim,* 5b; Scholem, "Meaning of the Torah," 81–84; and the critique of Idel, "White Letters," esp. 183–187.

68. See also *Eikhah Rabbah, petihta,* 2; and *Me'or 'Einayim,* vol. 1, *tsav,* 219.

69. See MDL, no. 55, p. 79.

70. *Or ha-Me'ir,* vol. 1, *va-yetse,* 53. The Maggid assumes that Jacob was indentured to Laban in order to redeem the fallen letters—or sparks—in his possession, which then came together to shape the current text of the Torah. See also OHE, 3a.

71. This phrase may also be rendered "wholly Torah."

72. MDL, no. 24, pp. 39–40.

73. See Mayse, "Double-Take," 41–49; and below.

74. For a few versions of this tradition, see m. Kiddushin 4:14; b. Yoma 28a. See also Abrams, *Book of Bahir,* no. 132, p. 217; *Tanhuma, be-har,* no. 1. See also the rabbinic traditions about biblical characters studying Torah in the academies of Shem and 'Ever; *Bereshit Rabbah* 63:6, 84:8. Cf. *Shir ha-Shirim Rabbah* 6:6; Zohar 2:275b; *Zohar Hadash, noah,* fol. 38b.

75. See Green, *Devotion and Commandment;* idem, "Discovery and Retreat," 104–130; and Gellman, "Figure of Abraham," esp. 289–291.

76. Hasidic teachings rarely invoke the approach of Nahmanides, whose comments on Gen. 26:5 argue that Abraham grasped the Torah through a prophetic sense (*ruah ha-kodesh*) and fulfilled it voluntarily. The Hasidic masters seem to be interested in a fulfillment of the precepts of Torah that is achieved mystically without a legal rule-book.

77. The Maggid later identifies these four stages of contraction as *hokhmah, binah, tif'eret,* and *malkhut.*

78. *Bereshit Rabbah* 12:9.

79. See b. Bava Metsi'a 84a. The Maggid often cites this humorous Talmudic anecdote in explaining why *tsimtsum* is an expression of God's love.

80. That is, Abraham's love for the Divine inspired God to perform the *tsimtsum*, which the Maggid frequently refers to as an act of divine love and compassion.

81. MDL, no. 122, p. 202.

82. This phrase may refer to the mystical *kavvanot* ("intentions") accompanying the commandments rather than intent to fulfill the precepts of Scripture.

83. OHE, 36a.

84. See *Tif'eret 'Uziel, ki tavo*, p. 121, where this idea is attributed to Maimonides (based on Maimonides, *Commentary to the Mishnah, makkot* 3:17), and throughout Ya'akov Yosef of Polnoye's introduction to *Toledot Ya'akov Yosef*. See also *Toledot Ya'akov Yosef*, vol. 1, *yitro*, 351; *Ben Porat Yosef, hakdamah*, 28–29; ibid., *noah*, 108–109; *Mishneh Torah, hilkhot lulav*, 8:15; Joseph Albo, *Sefer ha-'Ikkarim*, 3:27, 29–30; and Hallamish, "Unification of 'Every One,'" 25–52.

85. See Wolfson, "Circumcision," 495–524.

86. See *Me'or 'Einayim*, vol. 1, *mi-kets*, 132–133; based on Arthur Green's forthcoming translation published by Stanford University Press. Cf. *Me'or 'Einayim, shemot*, 138.

87. b. 'Avodah Zarah 3b.

88. See *Tikkunei Zohar, tikkun* 69, 116a.

89. MDL, no. 134, p. 234.

90. See MDL, no. 77, pp. 132–133.

91. On this subject, see Kahana and Mayse, "Hasidic *Halakhah*," 375–408.

92. See Feldman, *Philo's Portrayal*, 258–279; and Hallamish, Kasher, and Ben Pazi, *Moses the Man*.

93. See Deut. 34:10–12; Malachi 3:22; Ezra 3:2, 7:6–10. In Jewish mystical literature, see Wolfson, *Through a Speculum*, 378–379, 388; idem, *Circle in the Square*, 3, 8–9, 14–15; Hellner-Eshed, *River Flows from Eden*, 75–76, 91–92. In Lurianic Kabbalah, see Fine, *Physician of the Soul*, 99–100, 314–320, 329–330; Idel, "Image of Man," 181–212. Cf. Abrams, *Book of Bahir*, no. 134, p. 219; and *Peri Ets Hayyim, sha'ar hag ha-matsot*, ch. 1.

94. See MDL, no. 92, p. 160; LY, no. 263, fol. 79b.

95. See MDL, no. 177, p. 275; ibid., no. 143, p. 242; OT, *va-yera*, no. 23, pp. 30–33; cf. LY, no. 1, fol. 1a.

96. See OT, *tetsaveh*, no. 103, pp. 143–144, interpreting a statement in b. Ta'anit 9a. Cf. MDL, no. 101, pp. 178–179.

97. See below.

98. MDL, no. 132, p. 228.

99. Ibid., 229.

100. Ibid.; and cf. OT, *aggadot*, no. 394, pp. 417–418.

101. MDL, no. 122, p. 203.

102. The "seven days of building" refer to the seven *sefirot* from *hesed* to *malkhut*. See, inter alia, Zohar 1:145a.

103. *Me'or 'Einayim*, vol.1, *shemot*, 155. My thanks to Arthur Green for sharing his translation. Menahem Nahum does not make clear how much of this passage belongs to the Maggid, but it is very much in the style of the Maggid and in keeping with his teachings. Cf. ibid., *shemot*, 138. See also ibid., vol. 1, *va-yera*, 51, where Menahem Nahum teaches that in its most abstract and pristine form, symbolized by the *yod* or *hokhmah*, the Torah is still unintelligible. Therefore, the Torah was given through Moses, who articulated Scripture by drawing through the *vav* or *tif'eret* and into the final *heh* (symbolizing *dibbur* and *malkhut*).

104. See SLA, 188.

105. Naftali of Ropshitz, *Zera' Kodesh*, vol. 2, *le-hag ha-shavu'ot*, 40a, suggests that revelation consisted only of the first *aleph* of *anokhi* ("I"), the initial word of the First Commandment. See also ibid., vol. 1, *yitro*, 72a; Scholem, "Religious Authority," 30–31, argued that, according to this theory, revelation was essentially silent. This reading was criticized by Idel, *Old Worlds*, 121–124. See also Harvey, "What Did the Rymanover Really Say . . . ?" 297–314; Sommer, "Revelation at Sinai," 422–451; and Gellman, "Wellhausen and the Hasidim," 193–207. For a possible source of the tradition in *Zera' Kodesh*, see *Menahem Tsiyon*, *be-shalah*, 47.

106. See OT, *tehilim*, no. 235, p. 292. Cf. SLA, 35, 184; LY, no. 287, fols. 107a–108a. Cf. OT, *balak*, no. 146, p. 198.

107. See SLA, 135–137. Cf. OT, *be-shalah*, no. 90, pp. 125–127; and Zohar 2:121a.

108. See KTVK, 37a-b.

109. See MDL, no. 62, p. 102. See also ibid., no. 133, p. 233.

110. See OT, *va-era*, no. 75, p. 106; and cf. ST, 50b.

111. See MDL, no. 133, p. 233.

112. Zohar 1:28b.

113. Lit. "the generation of the mouth," from Song 4:3.

114. MDL, no. 84, pp. 146–147. See also ibid., 92, p. 160.

115. See Green, "Around the Maggid's Table," 146–147.

116. *Iggerot ha-Kodesh*, pt. 2, 19–20; see above.

117. See Zohar 2:25b, building on the tradition of *shekhinah* accompanying the Jewish people into exile; see *Mekhilta*, *bo*, *mesekhta de-pisha* 14.

118. In the rabbinic version, the Israelites are described as a young warrior.

119. See b. Sotah 27b.

120. MDL, no. 164, pp. 263–264; cf. OT, *aggadot*, no. 402–403, pp. 424–425; LY, no. 130, fols. 36b–37a; and *Divrei Emet*, *va-ethanan*, 54b.

121. See also *Kedushat Levi*, vol. 1, *yitro*, 205.

122. Based on Habakkuk 2:11. See *Shemot Rabbah* 5:9; b. Zevahim 116a.

123. SLA, 188.

124. Paraphrasing *Shir ha-Shirim Rabbah* 1:2.

125. Cf. Ps. 78:37.

126. The editor notes that a similar teaching appears in "the writings of the BeSHT."

127. The origin of this watchword, often quoted by later Jewish exegetes in the name of the Talmudic sages, is unknown.

128. See Zohar 2:124b, reinterpreting Song of Songs 1:2; and cf. Zohar 1:184a, 2:146a-b. The phrase *ruha be-ruha* was important in Lurianic Kabbalah, where it describes the unification between a living mystic and a departed sage; see Fine, *Physician of the Soul*, 284–285; Garb, "Cult of the Saints," 203–229.

129. See b. Shabbat 88b.

130. ST, 21b–24a. See also Werthmann, "Spirit to Spirit," 586–609; and, more broadly, Penn, *Kissing Christians*.

131. See Michael Fishbane's magisterial commentary on the *Song of Songs*.

132. See Ezra of Gerona's commentary on Song of Songs 1:2, printed in *Kitvei Ramban*, ed. Chavel, 2:485; '*Avodat ha-Kodesh* 2:1; Kosman, "Breath, Kiss, and Speech," 96–124; Hellner-Eshed, *River Flows from Eden*, 296–300; Gordon, "Erotics of Negative Theology," 1–38; Hecker, "Kissing Kabbalists," 171–208; and Mayse, "Like a Moth," 364–406.

133. See ST, 83.

134. MDL, no. 134, p. 236.

135. See Sack, "Concept of Thought," 221–241.

136. See Mayse, "Voices of Moses," 101–125; Green, "Hasidic Homily," 237–265; and Polen, "Hasidic *Derashah*," 55–70.

137. On spiritual friendship, divine love and revelation, see Fine, "Mystical Fellowship," 210–214; and Fishbane, *Art of Mystical Narrative*, 54–127.

CHAPTER 6

Note to epigraph: Nasr, *Knowledge and the Sacred*, 149.

1. See Urbach, *Sages*, 286–314, 603–64; and Schremer, "[T]he[y] Did Not Read," 105–126.

2. More broadly, see Goldenberg, "Law and Spirit," 232–252.

3. See Boyarin, *Carnal Israel*, 134–166; and Biale, *Eros and the Jews*, 33–59.

4. See Chernus, *Mysticism*, esp. 38, 48–50, 93–94.

5. See Urbach, *Sages*, 184–213; Goshen-Gottstein, "*Ma'aseh Bereshit*," 185–201; and Liebes, "Account of the Chariot," 323–335.

6. Polen, "Derashah as Performative Exegesis," 123–153; and idem, "Spirit Among the Sages," 83–94.

7. For a few examples, see b. Pesahim 50b; Berakhot 17a.

8. See, for example, Abrams, *Book of Bahir*, no. 128, pp. 211–212; ibid., no. 137, p. 221; Zohar 1:142a, 168a. See also Maimonides, *Mishneh Torah*, *hilkhot talmud torah* 3:5; ibid., *hilkhot teshuvah* 10:5; idem, *Commentary to the Mishnah*, *Sanhedrin*, *hakdamah le-perek helek*; and, for an overview of differing conceptions of *Torah lishmah* before the eighteenth century, see Lamm, *Torah Lishmah*, 205–230.

9. See Kanarfogel, "Compensation for the Study of Torah," 135–147.

10. See Lamm, "Pukhovitzer's Concept," 149–156.

11. See ibn Pakuda, *Book of Direction*, 85–86, 91. More broadly, see Twersky, "Religion and Law," 69–82; idem, *Introduction to the Code*, 89–92, 196. On philosophy as the highest expression of knowing God, see Twersky, *Introduction to the Code*, 86–88; Davidson, "Study of Philosophy," 53–68.

12. See Katz, "Halakhah and Kabbalah," 56–87.

13. See Liebes, "Zohar and Eros," 67–119; and Hellner-Eshed, *River Flows from Eden*, 190–203.

14. See Fine, *Physician of the Soul*, 207–212, 230; idem, "Study of Torah," 29–40.

15. See *Peri Ets Hayyim*, *sha'ar hanhagat ha-limmud*, ch. 1.

16. See *Peri Ets Hayyim*, *sha'ar hanhagat ha-limmud*, passim. See Hayyim Vital's introduction to *Sha'ar ha-Hakdamot*; *'Emek ha-Melekh* 7:10, p. 341; ibid., 6:47, p. 244. For a different perspective, see *Hesed le-Avraham* 2:9, 2:28. See Fine, *Physician of the Soul*, 207–219. See, inter alia, *Shenei Luhot ha-Berit*, *massekhet shavu'ot*, *ner mitsvah*, nos. 63–69; ibid., *torah she-bi-ketav*, no. 4.

17. For a remarkable example, see Margoliot, *Sod Yakhin u-Vo'az*, 6–8. See also *Toledot Ya'akov Yosef*, vol. 1, *hakdamah*, 21; Scholem, "*Devekut*," 212–213. Cf. *Toledot Ya'akov Yosef*, vol. 1, *mishpatim*, 404. See Goetschel, "Torah Lishmah," 258–267.

18. LY, no. 264, fol. 81b; interpreting *Shir ha-Shirim Rabbah* 1.10.2; y. Hagigah 2:1.

19. See the summary in Wilensky, "Hasidic Mitnaggedic Polemics," 244–271.

20. See Weiss, "Torah Study," 66–67.

21. See Wilensky, "Hasidic Mitnaggedic Polemics," 261–266; Scholem, *"Devekut,"* 212–213; Schatz-Uffenheimer, *Hasidism as Mysticism,* 310–325; Lamm, *Torah Lishmah,* 230–324; and Nadler, *Faith of the Mithnagdim,* esp. 51–60, 151–153, 160–164.

22. The importance of Torah study is found in the earliest versions of the Maggid's *hanhagot.* See Gries, *Conduct Literature,* 114–121; and SLA, 54.

23. See OT, *aggadot,* no. 460, p. 473.

24. See OT, *tehilim,* no. 245, p. 298; MDL, no. 132, p. 227. Cf. ST, 83b–84a.

25. *Tikkunei Zohar, tikkun* 10, fol. 25b.

26. LY, no. 114, fol. 23a-b; translated in Green et al., *Speaking Torah,* 1:257–258. See also b. Menahot 110a; and b. Berakhot 35b, where this view is qualified by the Talmud.

27. See Margolin, *Human Temple,* esp. 127–138.

28. See LY, no. 337, fol. 69a. Cf. *Darkhei Tsedek,* 18.

29. LY, no. 29, fol. 5a-b. See also Schatz-Uffenheimer, *Hasidism as Mysticism,* 316–317; and SLA, 58–61.

30. Menahem Nahum of Chernobil claims: "My teacher [the Maggid] said that early on [in his path] he would turn his attention away from his studies and all other concerns, spending an hour or two meditating on one character trait until it had become perfectly clarified." See *Me'or Einayim,* vol. 1, *be-shalah,* 170; and Zohar 1:31a.

31. See LY, no. 216, fol. 64b, interpreting m. Avot 3:4, 7; cf. *Peri Hayyim,* ch. 2, fol. 22b; *Ahavat Dodim, shir ha-shirim,* fol. 46a.

32. See RaSHI's comment on Deut. 26:16, quoting *Tanhuma, ki tavo,* no. 1.

33. SLA, 22–23. See also LY, no. 264, fol. 81b; and Zohar 1:90a, 94b, 98b.

34. See Magid, *From Metaphysics to Midrash,* 43–46.

35. *Va-Yikra Rabbah,* 27:1.

36. *Yosher Divrei Emet,* no. 10, p. 114b; based on the translation in Green et al., *Speaking Torah,* 1:288–290.

37. Ibid.

38. Ibid. See also Krassen, *Uniter of Heaven and Earth,* 10. The word *'inbal* (clapper), when written in consonantal Hebrew, is quite similar to the word *'anavah* (humility), although this is harder to see in transliteration.

39. For just a few examples among the many, see MDL, no. 16, p. 3; OT, *aggadot,* no. 462, p. 474.

40. LY, no. 196, fol. 59b.

41. See OHE, fol. 15a; and cf. SLA, 137.

42. *Shekhinah,* the tenth of the *sefirot,* is associated with *heh* of the word *lishmah* and the final *heh* of Y-H-V-H.

43. See MDL, no. 97, p. 169. The notion that God "consumes" human devotion, i.e., that passionate devotion feeds, sustains, and gives pleasure to the Divine, is found frequently in the Maggid's name. For another example, see *Torei Zahav, pinhas,* 240.

44. See MDL, no. 63, p. 103. See also ibid., no. 28, p. 46; and Zohar 3:27b (R.M.)

45. See MDL, no. 31, pp. 49–51; ibid., no. 161, p. 261.

46. See *Or ha-Me'ir,* vol. 1, *pesah,* 244; and b. Shabbat 156a. This wordplay, which seems to carry with it strong antimagical associations, appears often in the Maggid's sermons and in the quotations attributed to him; see MDL, no. 100, p. 175; ibid., no. 127, pp. 119–120; ST, 54; *Kedushat Levi,* vol. 1, *eikha,* 372; *Zot Zikhron,* fol. 11b.

47. The Maggid seems to read *mazal* (constellation) as related to *nozel* (flowing).

48. For example, see Margoliot, *Sod Yakhin u-Vo'az*, 6–8; Etkes, *Besht*, 60–62, 273, 278–279; Rosman, *Founder*, 115, 129–130.

49. MDL, no. 86, pp. 149–150; and cf. OT, *va-ethanan*, no. 156, pp. 206–207.

50. See *'Eser Orot*, 14a. In one such story, which is found in various versions in many early Hasidic works, the Maggid is able to discern something about the maker of a vessel simply by examining the physical object; see *Ma'amarei Admor ha-Zaken 'al ha-Torah ve-ha-Mo'adim*, *re'eh*, 802. See also *Ner Mitsvah ve-Torah Or, sha'ar ha-emunah*, 48b. Other sources attribute a similar ability to the BeSHT. See KTVK, 32a; *Or ha-Me'ir*, vol. 2, *ha'azinu*, 289.

51. Either the Maggid or a transcriber of the sermon has combined Prov. 30:5, 2 Sam. 22:31, and Ps. 18:31.

52. The word *le-tsaref* is generally translated as "to combine" or "to permutate," but in this case the Maggid is using it in a slightly different sense.

53. OT, *pesukim*, no. 317, p. 365. This cryptic passage is one of the few teachings in OT with no parallel elsewhere in the Maggid's corpus.

54. See SLA, 22–23, where the Maggid claims: "A sage receives energy from the Torah (*hashpa'at ha-Torah*) in his eating; through such consumption, he attains Torah. His eating is immersion in Torah." See also MDL, no. 31, p. 50; and *Tanhuma*, *be-shalah*, no. 20. See Mekhilta, *be-shalah*, *hakdamah*; Zohar 2:60b.

55. See *Reshit Hokhmah, sha'ar ha-kedushah*, ch. 4.

56. MDL, no. 200, pp. 325–326. The teaching is quoted in *Mevasser Tsedek, be-shalah*, 53. See also ibid., *va-yakhel*, 88; ibid., *emor*, 156.

57. MDL, no. 181, pp. 281–282.

58. The Maggid is interpreting the word "find them" (*motseihem*) as "speak them aloud." See b. 'Eruvin 54a.

59. LY, no. 132, fol. 38b–39a.

60. OT, *'ekev*, no. 167, pp. 217–218, commenting on b. Sotah 14a.

61. On the kabbalistic background to these concepts, see Pachter, "Smallness and Greatness," 185–233.

62. See LY, no. 74, fol. 14a.

63. See *Tikkunei Zohar, tikkun* 19, fol. 38a. The word *gan* (garden) has a numerical value of fifty-three, the number of different portions in the Torah. See Hellner-Eshed, *River Flows from Eden*, 121–135; Idel, "Journey to Paradise," 7–16; and Yisraeli, "The Tree of Life and Its Roots," 269–289.

64. A manuscript preserves "jot" (*kots*) instead of "voice" (*kol*), perhaps referring to the tradition that the jot of the letter *yod* points to the highest realms of wisdom, the sefirah *keter*, which cannot be expressed in words.

65. See OT, *pinhas*, no. 151c, p. 202; MDL, no. 114, p. 187; and LY, no. 72, fol. 14a.

66. I have translated this citation from m. Avot 6:1 as the Maggid interprets it.

67. LY, no. 201, fol. 61a. Cf. ibid., no. 76, fol. 14b.

68. See MDL, no. 25, p. 41, on creative study as giving new *mohin* (cognitive vitality) to the words of Torah.

69. See SLA, 20–21.

70. The Maggid is interpreting the verse as "If you listen, *then* you will hear My voice."

71. *Dibrat Shlomo, yitro*, 170. Cf. OT, *be-shalah*, no. 92, p. 128; and OHE, 58c. For a disciple of the Maggid interpreting this verse as a mandate to hear God's voice in all human conversations, see *Or ha-Me'ir*, vol. 1, *yitro*, 141. See also SLA, 40.

72. See Mayse, "Voices of Moses," 101–125.

73. MDL, no. 180, p. 281.

74. Heb. *kshe-nofel le-adam sekhel kol de'hu*, perhaps a translation of the Yiddish verb *aynfallen* (to occur to). The Maggid uses similar terms in describing how "strange thoughts" (*mahshavot zarot*) spontaneously appear in the mind.

75. Cf. y. Hagigah 2:1; and, inter alia, Zohar 1:16b.

76. OHE, 24b; and cf. KTVK, 19a. On the kabbalistic background, see See *Ets Hayyim* 6:3; *Sefer ha-Derushim, derush 'olam ha-'akkudim*, 13–16; Avivi, *Kabbala Luriana*, 3:1351–1352; Fine, *Physician of the Soul*, 134–135; and Magid, *From Metaphysics to Midrash*, 23.

77. See OHE, 62b.

78. Cf. SLA, 20–21.

79. OHE, 58a.

80. This pause affords an opportunity to bring together speech and thought, uniting *dibbur* or *malkhut* with *mahashavah* and *binah*. See also *Hesed le-Avraham, va-yera*, p. 32.

81. Cf. Maimonides' introduction to the *Guide*.

82. OHE, 58a.

83. See MDL, no. 192, p. 302.

84. Lit. "opened an opening for him" (*patah leih pitha*).

85. LY, no. 266, fol. 85b; and cf. *Kedushat Levi*, vol. 1, *be-shalah*, 185.

86. *Va-Yikra Rabbah*, 22:1.

87. Zohar 3:7b.

88. LY, no. 283, fols. 102a–103b. Based, in part, on the translation in Green et al., *Speaking Torah*, 1:116–117. Cf. LY, no. 277, fols. 93b–94a.

89. See Mayse, "Time and Presence," 231–238.

90. See OHE, 62a.

91. See OHE, 58a; SLA, 20–21. See also Zohar 1:5a; *Ets Hayyim, sha'ar ha-kellalim*, ch. 10; *Peri Ets Hayyim, sha'ar ha-qaddishim*, ch. 2; Fine, *Physician of the Soul*, 139–140, 170, 176, 238–239; Magid, *From Metaphysics to Midrash*, 25–28, 127–136.

92. See OHE, 62a. See also *Kedushat Levi, purim*, p. 366; cf. b. Menahot 68b. On the concept of a *makif*, see *Pardes Rimmonim* 2:7, 6:3, 29:1; and inter alia, *Ets Hayyim, sha'ar ha-kelalim*, ch.1, 1:4; Avivi, *Kabbala Luriania*, 3:1420–1422, 1449; *Hesed le-Avraham*, 4:11, 5:31.

93. See OHE, fol. 66a.

94. SLA, 20. See m. Avot 6:2, based on Ex. 32:16. Cf. *Va-Yikra Rabbah*, 18:3.

95. See *Kedushat Levi*, vol. 1, *va-yiggash*, 119. This theme will reappear in our discussion of prayer in the following chapter.

96. See OT, *pesukim*, no. 384, p. 401; SLA, 85.

97. For example, see b. Berakhot 35b; b. Yoma 22b; and b. Bava Batra 25b.

98. The rest of the verse reads, "That I may have what to answer those who taunt me."

99. b. Mo'ed Katan 16b.

100. The verb *'osim* has the sense of both "perform" and "make," but the Maggid's interpretation is striking because he has chosen the one that is contextually unexpected.

101. MDL, no. 183, p. 284. This excerpt comes from a longer teaching about God's stipulation that all works of creation follow the will of the *tsaddikim*.

102. On the Maggid's understanding of miracles, see above.

103. See OT, *be-hukkotai*, no. 126, pp. 176–177. See also the tradition quoted in Yisra'el of Kozhenits's comments on Yehudah Leib of Prague, *Be'er ha-Golah*, 78a. My thanks to Benny Brown for pointing out this source.

104. See *Hesed le-Avraham* 2:1; and Hayyim ibn 'Attar's introduction to *Or ha-Hayyim*. See Scholem, "Revelation and Tradition," 300–303. The tension between creativity and the desire to conform to (primarily) oral traditions has been present in Kabbalah since its earliest days. For example, see Abrams, "Orality in the Kabbalistic School," 85–102; and Fishbane, *As Light Before Dawn*, 53–60, 84–90, 98–99, 114, 122.

105. See Mayse "Ever-Changing Path," 84–115; Kahana and Mayse, "Hasidic *Halakhah*," 375–408; and Lorberbaum, "Rethinking *Halakhah*," 232–259. See also MDL, no. 189, p. 291.

106. b. 'Eruvin 13b; b. Gittin 6b. See Sagi, *Open Canon*.

107. See MDL, no. 58, pp. 86–87. Cf. Hagigah 3b.

108. ST, 64a-b. Cf. OT, *bereshit*, no. 5, p. 7; and MDL, no. 188, pp. 287–288.

109. See b. 'Eruvin 13b. See *Bereshit Rabbah*, 20:12.

110. See b. Mo'ed Katan 16b.

111. See b. Bava Mets'ia 59b; b. Berakhot 52a. The Maggid's reading of Rabbi Joshua rejecting the heavenly voice because he wants to change the *halakhah* is a fascinating exegesis and not at all obvious.

112. See b. Niddah: "One who studies (*shoneh*) *halakhot* each day is assured a place in the World to Come, for it is written, 'eternal ways (*halikhot 'olam*) are His' (Hab. 3:6)—do not read *halikhot* ('ways') but *halakhot*."

113. LY, no. 277, fols. 94b–95a.

114. See also KTVK, 5b; and cf. *Kedushat Yisra'el*, 79. Such references, though rare, exist in tension alongside the wealth of teachings underscoring the virtually boundless nature of human creativity.

115. Cf. OT, *pesukim*, no. 312, p. 361; and KTVK, 5c.

116. See Green, "Hasidism and Its Response to Change," 319–336.

117. See *Or ha-Me'ir*, vol. 1, *terumah*, 140.

118. b. Berakhot 11b.

119. See Wiskind-Elper, *Hasidic Commentary*; Mayse and Reiser, "Territories and Textures," 127–160.

120. See Idel, *Absorbing Perfections*, 474; Green, "Hasidic Homily," 241–242; Wilensky, *Hasidim and Mitnaggedim*, 2:317–318.

121. Medieval kabbalistic literature generally attributes this prophetic state to Moses.

122. *Or ha-Me'ir*, vol. 1, *tsav*, 213.

123. *'Avodat Yisra'el*, *likkutim*, 219.

124. See OT, *aggadot*, no. 473, p. 479.

125. See OT, *korah*, no. 141, p. 190.

126. See OHE, 20d.

127. See *Or ha-Me'ir*, vol. 1, *va-yera*, 25.

128. See the fascinating tradition cited in *Orah le-Hayyim*, vol. 1, *noah*, 50–51. On the role of the "rebuker" (*mokhiah*) in eastern Europe, see Piekarz, *Beginning of Hasidism*, 100–104, 141–156.

129. See OT, *tetsaveh*, no. 103, p. 143.

130. This idea is found dozens of times in the Maggid's sermons, and often quoted by students in his name; see *Kedushat Levi*, vol. 1, *ki tissa*, p. 252; *Dibrat Shlomo*, *terumah*, 181.

131. b. Hullin 63b.

132. MDL, no. 101, p. 178. See also OT, *be-shalah*, no. 92, p. 128.

133. See Saperstein, *Jewish Preaching*, 93, 100–103.

134. See Stern, "Rhetoric and Midrash," 261–291; Boyarin, "History Becomes Parable," 54–71; Goshen-Gottstein, *God and Israel*.

135. See Weiss, "Four Parables," 111–126; Cohen, "Logic to Interpretation," 104–113.

136. See Wolfson, *Language, Eros, Being*, 158–164, 223–224, 276–278, 336; Sendor, "Emergence of Provençal Kabbalah," 205–223; and Shohat, "Vilna Gaon's Commentary," 265–301.

137. See Idel, "Parable of the Son," 87–116; and, more broadly, Wineman, *Hasidic Parable*.

138. See Wineman, "Parables and *Tsimtsum*," 293–300.

139. MDL, no. 131, p. 226. See also *Pirkei ha-Ne'ezar*, sec. 2, ch. 116, fol. 72a.

140. See ST, 47.

141. See *Ets Hayyim* 14:9, 37:4.

142. LY, no. 241, fol. 71a-b. Cf. ibid., no. 150, fol. 50b. See also MDL, no. 206, p. 331. For a more fully developed version of this teaching in the Maggid's name, see *Orah le-Hayyim*, vol. 2, *mattot*, pp. 240–241; and *Pirkei ha-Ne'ezar*, sec. 1, ch. 141, fol. 113b, referring to the "writings of the Maggid."

143. b. Berakhot 57b.

144. MDL, no. 205, pp. 329–330.

145. See OHE, 60b. Shlomo of Lutsk notes that at some point after the death of Yitshak Luria people misunderstood his teachings and interpreted them too literally; see MDL, 2. A similar concern with corporeal interpretations of Kabbalah appears in the teachings of the Maggid's son; see Stillman, "Transcendent God, Immanent Kabbalah," 310–330.

146. MDL, no. 126, pp. 217–218.

147. See Stern, *Parables in Midrash*; Donahue, *Gospel in Parable*; and Sells, *Mystical Languages*, pp. 6–9, 29–30, 39–44, 125–140, 159–164.

148. See Lakoff and Johnson, *Metaphors We Live By*, 3 and 6. See also ibid., 3–34, 77–86, 195–209. On metaphors, creativity, and language, see Ricoeur, *Rule of Metaphor*.

149. See the bibliographical excursus in the appendix.

150. Hamann, "Aesthetica in Nuce," 63.

151. OT, *ki tissa*, no. 105, p. 145; and the chapter on prayer.

152. Kirkwood, "Storytelling and Self-Confrontation," 59; and idem, "Parables as Metaphors," 422–440.

153. See Miura and Sasaki, *Zen Koan*; Heine and Wright, *Koan*; and Wolfson, *Eros, Language, Being*, 319–320.

154. Here we should note the Mahayana Buddhist concept of *upāya* or *upāyakauśalya*, often translated as "skillful means" and referring to a kind of pedagogy through specifically tailored means of education. See Harrison, "Mediums and Messages," 115–151.

155. See LY, no. 285, fol. 106b. See Loewenthal, *Communicating the Infinite*, 38.

156. The Maggid's point calls to mind the distinction between *Kenner* (connoisseurs) and *Liebhaber* (amateurs) often drawn by critics of literature and music. Excellent composers can write a piece that satisfies one or the other, but truly great composers can create works that electrify both types of people at the very same time; see Bernstein, "Pleyel's Emulation of Haydn," 1–24. My thanks to Nehemia Polen for drawing this analogy to my attention.

157. Maimon, *Autobiography*, 97.

158. Or *ha-Me'ir*, vol. 2, *kohelet*, 312. The final words are an adaptation of Ps. 19:4 and Isa. 40:3.

159. See SLA, 60. The BeSHT told stories with a self-referential element as well; see *Toledot Ya'akov Yosef*, vol. 2, *tsav*, 533.

160. b. Bava Kamma 60b. On the peregrinations of this tale, see Maciá, "Fable," 267–281; and Hartmann, "Parable of a Man," 189–199. My thanks to Paul Harrison for drawing my attention to these sources.

161. y. Sotah 8:3; *Tanhuma, bereshit,* no. 1.

162. See Zohar 1:11b.

163. On this term, see Tirosh-Samuelson, *Between Worlds,* 105–138.

164. *Or ha-Me'ir,* vol. 2, *devarim,* 160.

165. My thanks to Arthur Green for suggesting this reading, which had not otherwise crossed my mind.

166. *'Irin Kaddishin,* vol. 1, *shavu'ot,* 205.

167. See also Berger, *'Eser Orot,* fol. 12a.

168. See the accounts of the parable about the shofar and the king's children in the next chapter; and, more broadly, Mayse, "Double-Take," 41–49.

169. See also Loewenthal, *Communicating the Infinite,* 74, 90–97, who argues that conveying spiritual ideas to people of different intellectual rungs was a central concern of Shneur Zalman of Liady.

CHAPTER 7

Notes to epigraphs: Graham, *Beyond the Written Word,* 162–163; T. E. Brown, "Indwelling," *Old John and Other Poems* (London and New York: MacMillan, 1893) 151.

1. The issue of prayer is one in which the differences between the various collections of the Maggid's teachings are readily apparent. LY and TSVHR include many instructions regarding prayer, whereas the sermons in MDL, OT, and OHE are devoted more specifically to the theology behind such practices.

2. In one teaching the Maggid notes that; see *Ve-Tsiva ha-Kohen,* ch. 10, 84–85; cf. LY, no. 134, fol. 40b.

3. See MDL, no. 147, p. 248, a sermonic rereading of "I have wrestled divine wrestlings" (*naftulei Elohim niftalti,* Gen. 30:8) as connected to the word "prayer" (*tefillah*).

4. See esp. OT, *shir ha-shirim,* no. 198, p. 257.

5. See Greenberg, *Biblical Prose Prayer.*

6. See Fleischer, *Statutory Jewish Prayer;* Heinemann, *Prayer in the Talmud;* idem, "The Fixed and the Fluid," 45–52.

7. See m. Berakhot 4:5, 5:1; t. Berakhot 3:4, 14–16, 18. On these tensions, see m. Avot 2:13; b. Berakhot 33b; cf. b. Megillah 18a; and Goldenberg, "Law and Spirit," 232–252.

8. y. Berakhot 4:1 cites sages who prayed out loud at home; and cf. b. Berakhot 31a. See Ehrlich, *Nonverbal Language of Prayer.*

9. See Wolfson, *Through a Speculum,* 13–51.

10. See b. Shabbat 10a; and Elman, "Torah ve-Avodah," 61–124.

11. For an excellent overview, see Gottlieb, "Meaning of Prayer," 38–55.

12. See Scholem, *Major Trends,* 57–63; idem, *Jewish Gnosticism,* 20–30; Janowitz, *Poetics of Ascent,* esp. 6–10, 87, 92–93; Swartz, *Mystical Prayer,* 109–168. These liturgical traditions of the *heikhalot* mystics influenced the development of Jewish liturgy into the medieval period; see Bar-Ilan, *Mysteries of Jewish Prayer;* Boustan, *From Martyr to Mystic,* 41–45, 223–225.

13. See Scholem, *Major Trends*, 100–103; Dan, *Esoteric Theology*, 69–79, 140–141; Fishman, "Rhineland Pietist Approaches to Prayer," 313–331. See also Dan, "Emergence of Mystical Prayer," 221–257; idem, "Prayer as Text," 259–276.

14. See Fishman, *Becoming the People of the Talmud*, 182–217.

15. See Dan, "Emergence of Mystical Prayer," 229–231; Fishman, "Rhineland Pietist Approaches to Prayer," 318.

16. See Scholem, *Origins of the Kabbalah*, 243–248; Idel, "Kabbalistic Prayer in Provence," 165–186; Pedaya, *Name and Sanctuary*, 57–72, 161–186; Dan, "Emergence of Mystical Prayer," 248–257; and, more broadly, Afterman, *The Intention of Prayers*.

17. See Brody, "Human Hands," 133–158.

18. See Scholem, *Origins of the Kabbalah*, 419–421; idem, *"Devekut,"* 202–208.

19. See Scholem, *Origins of the Kabbalah*, 244–245; and idem, *Major Trends*, 5, 123. Scholem's argument that there is no true mystical union in Judaism been revised in recent years; see Idel, *Kabbalah: New Perspectives*, 59–73; Afterman, *"And They Shall be One Flesh,"* esp. 20–21, 37–38, 273–276, 330–332.

20. For a series of examples, see Ta-Shma, *Ha-Nigle She-Banistar*, 58–71.

21. See Tishby, "Prayer and Devotion," 341–399; and Benarroch, "Mystery of Unity," 231–256.

22. See Hellner-Eshed, *River Flows from Eden*, 66–67; and Mayse, "Like a Moth to the Flame," 364–406.

23. See Zohar 1:209b–210a, 3:210b (R.M.). This point is underscored by Isaac of Akko; see Fishbane, *As Light Before Dawn*, 132–133. Cf. Maimonides, *Guide*, 1:59; and cf. *Kuzari* IV:5, where Halevi underscores one must pray aloud in order to arouse the emotions.

24. See Kimelman, *Mystical Meaning*; and Green, "Some Aspects of Qabbalat Shabbat," 95–118.

25. See Sack, *Kabbalah of Rabbi Moses Cordovero*, 193–202; see also *'Emek ha-Melekh*, 13:24, 492.

26. See Ben-Shlomo, *Mystical Theology of Moses Cordovero*, 80–86; Brill, "Meditative Prayer," 45–60.

27. See Fine, *Physician of the Soul*, 220–258.

28. Of the various recensions of the Lurianic *kavvanot*, the collection *Peri Ets Hayyim* was a particular favorite of the early Hasidic masters. See Avivi, *Kabbala Luriania*, 1:635–649, 810–842.

29. Giller, Pinchas. *Shalom Shar'abi*, esp. 19–84 and 107–116.

30. On the *hanhagot* literature and its importance in the diffusion of Kabbalah, see Gries, "Fashioning of *Hanhagot* (Regimen Vitae)," 527–581.

31. See Green, "Early Hasidism," 445. On Hasidic approaches to prayer, see Jacobs, *Hasidic Prayer*; Idel, *Hasidism*, 149–170; idem, "Models of Understanding Prayer," 7–111; Schatz, "Contemplative Prayer," 209–226; and Margolin, *Human Temple*, esp. 202–204, 302–307.

32. See Gries, "Hasidic Prayer Stories," 219–235.

33. See Wilensky, "Hasidic Mitnaggedic Polemics," 248–253, 261–266; Nadler, *Faith of the Mithnagdim*, 50–55; Schatz-Uffenheimer, "Contemplative Prayer," 210; and Jacobs, *Hasidic Prayer*, 17–18.

34. See Etkes, *Besht*, 124–129. See *In Praise*, 50–53. Cf. LY, no. 28, fol. 5a. For a recent collection and translation of such teachings, see Kallus, *Pillar of Prayer*.

35. See, inter alia, *Toledot Ya'akov Yosef*, vol. 1, *va-yakhel*, 478; *Ben Porat Yosef*, vol. 1, *noah*, 121; *Degel Mahaneh Efrayim*, *toledot*, 71–72.

36. See BeSHT's letter to Ya'akov Yosef of Polnoye, cited in Rosman, *Founder*, 114–115; and cf. LY, no. 23, fol. 4b; ibid., no. 39, fol. 6b; ibid., no. 42, fol. 7a-b.

37. See Idel, *Hasidism*, 156–170; idem, "Models of Understanding Prayer," 23–49; idem, "Modes of Cleaving," 299–317; Etkes, *Besht*, 147–150.

38. See *Ben Porat Yosef, kuntres aharon*, 685; *Or ha-Me'ir*, vol. 1, *yitro*, 140. See also Schatz-Uffenheimer, *Hasidism as Mysticism*, 215–241; Idel, *Hasidism*, 160–170.

39. See *Ben Porat Yosef*, vol. 1, *toledot*, 276–277. See *'Avodat Yisra'el, terumah*, 70–71.

40. See MDL, no. 3, p. 16; and LY, no. 9, fol. 2a.

41. LY, no. 21, fol. 4a.

42. See LY, no. 2, fol. 1a.

43. See LY, no. 16, fol. 3a; ST, 54a; and Zohar 1:11b.

44. See LY, no. 41, fol. 6b. On the importance of *hitpashtut ha-gashmiyyut* for the Maggid and other early Hasidic thinkers, see Schatz-Uffenheimer, *Hasidism as Mysticism*, 67–79, 199–200; Piekarz, *Between Ideology and Reality*, 72–77; Idel, *Hasidism*, 64, 177–178; Margolin, *Human Temple*, 173–174, 189–193, 360–361; Kauffman, *In All Your Ways*, 426–466. See also *Arba'ah Turim, orah hayyim*, no. 98; and *Shulhan 'Arukh, orah hayyim*, no. 98:1; cf. Rabbenu Yonah's commentary on fol. 22b of Isaac Alfasi's summary of b. Berakhot, s.v. *tsarikh she-yiten*.

45. See ST, 54b.

46. See Schatz-Uffenheimer, *Hasidism as Mysticism*, 67–92; Piekarz, *Between Ideology and Reality*, esp. 69–70, 110–125; and Lorberbaum, "Attain the Attribute," 181–209. See also OHE, 9a.

47. MDL, no. 199, p. 324; see Margolin, *Human Temple*, 186.

48. See Idel, "Models of Understanding Prayer," 7–111. In one of the more extreme formulations, which likely dates back to the BeSHT, prayer is described as intercourse with *shekhinah*; see LY, no. 18, fol. 3b.

49. LY, no. 183, fol. 57b.

50. LY, no. 44, fol. 8a. See also *Orah le-Hayyim*, vol. 1, *va-yiggash*, 184.

51. See b. Berakhot 32a; b. Shabbat 10a; *Mishneh Torah, hilkhot tefillah* 1:2.

52. See Schatz-Uffenheimer, *Hasidism as Mysticism*, 144–167; Jacobs, *Hasidic Prayer*, 23–25; and Green, "Hasidic Homily," 251–253. See also Horwitz, "Abraham Joshua Heschel," 295–298.

53. m. Berakhot 5:1.

54. A reference to *keter*. See Zohar 3:10b–11a, 289b. Cf. *Tikkunei Zohar, tikkun* 21, fol. 44b.

55. OT, *va-yiggash*, no. 56, p. 76; and see also LY, no. 224, fol. 66b; MDL, no. 118, p. 192; *Torei Zahav, noah*, 9; *Peri Hayyim*, ch. 2, fols. 12a, 15b; *Divrei Emet, naso*, fol. 38b. Cf. *'Avodat Yisra'el, va-yiggash*, 51.

56. *Tikkunei Zohar, tikkun* 6, fol. 22a; and see Prov. 30:15.

57. OT, *pesukim*, no. 292, p. 346. See also LY, no. 45, fol. 8a.

58. MDL, no. 110, p. 186.

59. MDL, no. 106, p. 184. Cf. *Tif'eret 'Uziel, rosh ha-shanah*, 141. See also *Orah le-Hayyim*, vol. 2, *ha-azinu*, 393.

60. See LY, no. 18, fol. 3b; ibid., no. 33, fol. 6a; and cf. *In Praise*, 50–53.

61. Such is the argument in Weiss, "*Via Passiva*," 71–78; Schatz-Uffenheimer, *Hasidism as Mysticism*, 67–92, 144–167.

62. For a very different use of the image of the shofar, see LY, no. 147, fol. 49b. Cf. OT, *shemot*, no. 70, p. 96; OT, *berakhah*, no. 186, pp. 245–246. See also *Orah le-Hayyim*, vol. 1, *shemot*, 211; *Or ha-Me'ir*, vol. 2, *ruth*, 49.

63. See Margolin, *Human Temple*, 184–185, 346–352.

64. See Schatz-Uffenheimer, "Contemplative Prayer," 224. See also Nadler, *Faith of the Mithnagdim*, 68; *Toledot Ya'akov Yosef*, vol. 3, *va-ethanan*, 1150; and cf. *Or ha-Me'ir*, vol. 1, *shir ha-shirim*, 263.

65. m. Avot 3:13.

66. LY, no. 190, fol. 58a. See Zohar 2:20a. Cf. *Divrei Emet, noah*, fol. 2a.

67. See OT, *pesukim*, no. 285, pp. 342–343; b. Berakhot 31a, commenting on the events of 1 Sam. 1:9–19. Cf. MDL, no. 39, pp. 58–59. Cf. b. Ta'anit 25a. See *Dibrat Shlomo, be-shalah*, 152.

68. See LY, no. 27, fol. 5a. For an interesting parallel attributed to the BeSHT, see *Ketonet Passim, balak*, 326–327.

69. LY, no. 192, fol. 58a-b; cf. ibid., no. 6, fol. 1b; ibid., no. 211, fol 63a. A similar passage is found in the *hanhagot* based on the practices of Yitshak Luria; see *Toledoth ha-Ari*, ed. Benayahu, 324. The Maggid's bifurcation between inner and outer service in this teaching clearly recalls the distinction between *hovot ha-levavot* (inner duties) and *hovot ha-evarim* (physical duties) made by Bahye ibn Pakuda in his *Hovot ha-Levavot*.

70. See b. Berakhot 24b; and b. Sotah 32b; *Mishneh Torah, hilkhot tefillah* 5:9. Cf. b. Hagigah 14a, which describes teaching the secrets of Torah quietly (*be-lahash*), which obviously cannot mean silently. See also LY, no. 168, fol. 55a.

71. Together these two letters also spell *dam*, or "blood," referring to human physicality.

72. MDL, no. 24, pp. 38–40; based on the translation in Green et al., *Speaking Torah*, 2:18–19. See also Mayse, "Double-Take," 41–49.

73. Scholem, "*Devekut*," 226–227.

74. See Idel, *Kabbalah*, 64–69; Margolin, *Human Temple*, 181–186; and cf. Schatz-Uffenheimer, *Hasidism as Mysticism*, 72–74.

75. See MDL, no. 176, p. 275; ibid., no. 60, pp. 92–93; ibid., no. 48, pp. 69–70; *Orah le-Hayyim*, vol. 2, *'ekev*, 318; and cf. *'Avodat Yisra'el, va-yiggash*, 51. See also Green, "Zaddiq as Axis Mundi," 327–347.

76. *Peri Hayyim*, ch. 4, fol. 36a-b.

77. See OT, *aggadot*, no. 443, p. 460.

78. OT, *aggadot*, no. 418, pp. 435–436, commenting on b. Rosh Hashanah 16b. See also *Tif'eret 'Uziel, pesah*, 134.

79. See also Muffs, "Prayer of the Prophets," 204–210; and idem, "Who Will Stand in the Breach?," 9–48.

80. See MDL, no. 85, p. 148; LY, no. 238, p. 69; and above. *Kedushat Levi, pirkei avot*, 647 (commenting on b. Berakhot 32a), cites a similar tradition from Dov Ber, suggesting that *tsaddikim* control the course of God's vitality through the text of the liturgy without actually changing the divine will. This notion of prayer molding God's unformed will is intimately related to human language—both letters and words—shaping the infinite potential of divine energy; see *Kedushat Levi*, vol. 1, *bereshit*, 3; ibid., vol. 1, *balak*, 358–359.

81. b. Sukkah 14a.

82. b. Mo'ed Katan 16b.

83. See *Sefer Yetsirah* 4:12; and see above.

84. MDL, no. 60, pp. 90–91 and 94–95.

85. See *Orah le-Hayyim*, vol. 2, *'ekev*, 302–303.

86. See *Kedushat Levi, likkutim*, 481.

87. See *Kedushat Levi, kedushah shelishit—purim*, 542. See also *Kedushat Levi*, vol. 1, *va-yiggash*, 119. This accords with the biblical and Talmudic theology in which God *wants* the prophet to intercede for Israel.

88. Given the remarkable powers attributed to the *tsaddik* in Levi Yitshak's own theology, it is quite interesting that he portrays the Maggid's teachings in this way.

89. LY, no. 131, fol. 37a-b; based on the translation in Green et al., *Speaking Torah*, 1:230–232.

90. Rabbinic and medieval Jewish sources variously described the blowing of the shofar, the central event of Rosh Hashanah, as a call to repentance, an attempt to regale the Evil Inclination into submission, and a theurgic cry to evoke divine mercy; see, inter alia, t. Rosh ha-Shanah 1:11; *Va-Yikra Rabbah*, ch. 29; *Mishneh Torah, hilkhot shofar* 1:1; Zohar 3:99a-b, 232a, and 122a. See also *Peri Ets Hayyim, sha'ar rosh ha-shanah*, chs. 1–2; and *'Emek ha-Melekh* 6:62, p. 289; and Brown, "Of Sound and Vision," 83–113.

91. See Idel, "Parable of the Son," 87–116. See also ST, 76–78.

92. The overlap between the parables preserved by different students in the Maggid's name is remarkable, and it seems likely that they represent diverse textual witnesses of the same teaching. For an insightful discussion of these traditions, see Wineman, *Hasidic Parable*, 43–47. See also MDL, no. 38, pp. 57–58; and cf. the variant parallel in MOS RSL 182:353, fol. 14a.

93. See KTVK, fol. 21d; LY, no. 134, fols. 40b–41b; and the anonymous teachings in KST, nos. 330–331, pp. 205–207.

94. For a parable of this motif from the BeSHT, see *Toledot Ya'akov Yosef*, vol. 3, va-ethanan, 1165.

95. ST, 70; based on the translation in Green et al., *Speaking Torah*, 2:172.

96. Perhaps this is the source for Shneur Zalman of Liady's parable for the month of Elul, in which the king is described as being "in the field," namely, more accessible even through the physical world; see *Likkutei Torah, re'eh*, fol. 32a.

97. See also a shorter account of this parable, which notes that the Jewish people were sent into this world "exiled" in the physical realm in order to uplift the sparks, but along the way becoming too immersed in the corporeal world and thereby forgetting that their prayers embody the divine word. See OHE, 8a-b; LY, no. 289, fol. 108a-b; and Schatz, "Contemplative Prayer," 224–225.

98. The metaphor of being banished from their father's table has long been associated with the destruction of the Temple and subsequent exile; see b. Berakhot 3a.

99. *Or ha-Me'ir*, 2:260; based on the translation in Green et al., *Speaking Torah*, 2:173.

100. See *Toledot Ya'akov Yosef, kedoshim*, p. 636. Scholars continue to debate his relationship to specific Lurianic *kavvanot*: see Weiss, "Kavvanoth of Prayer," 99–105; Etkes, *Besht*, 129–131; and Kallus, "Relation of the Baal Shem Tov," 151–167.

101. See Wilensky, *Hasidim and Mitnaggedim*, 1:40–41, 45, 47–49, 67; idem, "Hasidic-Mitnaggedic Polemics," 248–253; Jacobs, *Hasidic Prayer*, 36–45. See also Schatz-Uffenheimer, *Hasidism as Mysticism*, 223–226; Hundert, *Jews in Poland-Lithuania*, 120, 197.

102. The struggle for control of Lurianic Kabbalah, which remained primarily in manuscripts during the Maggid's lifetime, may have been a factor in the conflict between the *mithnaggedim* and the early Hasidim; see Ettinger, "Hasidic Movement," 237–238.

103. See *Me'or 'Einayim*, vol. 1, *ki tissa*, 200. This notion is found dozens of times in the Maggid's sermons and is often connected to the following paraphrase of *Tikkunei Zohar, tikkun* 10, fol. 25b: "Words brought forth without love and awe cannot fly upward."

104. See LY, no. 134, fols. 40b–41b.

105. MDL, no. 13, p. 26. See the texts cited by Weiss, "Kavvanoth of Prayer," 106.

106. OHE, 64a, adds "since each and every letter is a world."

107. LY, no. 227, fol. 67a. See Weiss, "Kavvanoth of Prayer," 106–107.

108. See also *Ma'or va-Shemesh*, vol. 2, *nitsavim*, 646–647; and Krassen, *Uniter of Heaven and Earth*, 70–74.

109. See *Orah le-Hayyim*, vol. 1, *noah*, p. 66.

110. See MDL, no. 96, pp. 167–168. See also Hallamish, *Kabbalah*, 106–113; and Vick, "Through Which All of Israel Can Ascend," esp. 23–58.

111. See MDL, no. 199, pp. 323–324; b. Berakhot 33a-b; b. Megillah 18a; Zohar 1:21a. See also *Or ha-Me'ir, shir ha-shirim*, 255.

112. See *Yosher Divrei Emet*, no. 42, fol. 135a-b.

113. *Yosher Divrei Emet*, no. 17, fol. 118b, cites the practice of raising up "alien thoughts" as one of the elements of the Maggid's teachings that can be understood only by rare individuals. See Idel, "Prayer, Ecstasy, and 'Alien Thoughts,'" 57–120; Jacobs, *Hasidic Prayer*, 104–120; Yifrach, "Elevation of Foreign Thoughts."

114. See *Toledot Ya'akov Yosef*, vol. 3, *kuntres aharon*, 1375; *Tsofnat Pane'ah*, vol. 1, *be-shalah*, 267; *Ketonet Passim, balak*, 323.

115. See LY, no. 194, fols. 58b–59b.

116. See MDL, no. 25, pp. 40–41. See also *Or ha-Me'ir, shir ha-shirim*, 263; and Margolin, *Human Temple*, 185.

117. See ST, 54b.

118. See MDL, no. 112, p. 187.

119. See MDL, no. 50, pp. 70–72; and see OT, *aggadot*, no. 386, p. 411.

120. See MDL, no. 74, pp. 128–130. Cf. LY, no. 43, fols. 7b–8a; OHE, 7c; MDL, no. 50, p. 72; OT, *tehillim*, no. 208, pp. 275–276.

121. See MDL, no. 2, p. 15.

122. See MDL, no. 167, p. 265; and *Zot Zikhron*, 57.

123. The structure of Ya'akov Emden's influential commentary on the prayer book (*Siddur Ya'avets*) follows this notion of prayer as a journey through palaces.

124. See also OHE, 36d, for a teaching on uplifting the fallen forms of various emotions based on Lev. 27:33.

125. The Maggid's formulation in this case makes it unclear whether the new permutation is assembled by the worshipper, or somehow performed *for* him.

126. Zohar 2:245b, 1:234a. Cf. *Orah le-Hayyim*, vol. 1, *noah*, 65.

127. Elsewhere the Maggid compares prayer to Shabbat, likening one who thinks *mahshavot zarot* to someone who transgresses the Shabbat boundary; see MDL, no. 179, p. 279. Cf. Zohar 1:32a.

128. MDL, no. 55, pp. 80–81. Cf. LY, no. 194, fols. 58b–59b; OHE, 3b. See also MDL, no. 29, p. 48; and Margolin's insightful remarks in *Human Temple*, 189–191.

129. This journey recalls the notion of the "memory palace" found in many Italian Renaissance texts. See, for example, Spence, *Memory Palace*.

130. See Scholem, *Major Trends*, 49–54.

131. See Maimonides, *Mishneh Torah*, *hilkhot teshuvah* 1:1; and *Reshit Hokhmah, sha'ar ha-teshuvah*, ch. 5. See also Rapoport-Albert, "Confession," 161–198.

132. See OHE, 19b. See ST, 43; MDL, no. 127, p. 219; and cf. MDL, no. 102, p. 181.

133. *Tikkunei Zohar, tikkun* 10, fol. 25b.

134. *Dibrat Shlomo, devarim*, p. 381, based on Green et al., *Speaking Torah*, 2:182. See also *Ginzei Yosef*, vol. 1, *va-yeshev*, 150, on the necessary link between contemplative confession and spoken words.

135. See MDL, no. 147, p. 248, commenting on m. Megillah 4:8.

136. See Hallamish, *Kabbalah*, 474–485; Garb, *Shamanic Trance*, 31–35; see Tishby, "Prayer and Devotion," 381–383; Wolfson, "Weeping, Death, and Spiritual Ascent," 209–247; Fishbane, *Kiss of God*, 104–108, 110–120, 126–127.

137. b. Berakhot 14a.

138. LY, no. 146, fol. 45b. See also JER NLI MS HEB 8°5307, fols. 105b–106a.

139. The Maggid reads this verse as teaching that the physical world will endure as long as it is sustained by heaven, i.e., divine word within the corporeal realm.

140. On *Perek Shirah* in medieval Kabbalah and Hasidism, see Beit-Arie, "Perek Shira," 1:12–17, 24–35; Idel, "Your Word," 236 n. 74; *In Praise*, 242–245. See also SLA, 28, on the interconnectivity of every "element" (*perek*) of creation through God's language.

141. MDL, no. 209, pp. 334–445. It is worth noting that this homily, in which the Maggid was evidently asked to clarify an earlier teaching, appears as the final sermon of *Maggid Devarav le-Ya'akov* in many printings. Cf. MDL, no. 39, pp. 58–60.

142. See Maimon, *Autobiography*, 96; and Mazor, "Power of Song," 23–53; Goshen-Gottstein, "Speech, Silence, Song," 143–187; Smith, *Tuning the Soul*; and Polen, "*Niggun*."

143. See the gloss in MDL, no. 85, p. 148. This passage is clearly linked to the next teaching in the Korets editio princeps.

144. See MDL, no. 171, pp. 269–270.

145. *Dibrat Shlomo, be-ha'alotkha*, 312.

146. Ibid., invoking RaSHI's comment, based on b. Shabbat 21a, that the lamps of the menorah must be kindled such that the flame rises up of its own accord.

EPILOGUE

Note to epigraph: *Kerem Yisrael*, 11a; cf. Buber, *Tales of the Hasidim*, 111.

1. MDL, no. 9, p. 24.

2. See the tradition cited in *Peri Hayyim*, ch. 6, p. 142; and *Orah le-Hayyim*, vol. 1, *mishpatim*, 389.

3. None of Dov Ber's teachings are acutely messianic, and stories introducing such a note into his biography or sermons are later projections; see, for example, Buber, *Tales of the Hasidim*, 110–111.

4. See Scholem, "*Devekut*," 216–217; idem, "Neutralization," 176–202; Schatz-Uffenheimer, "Self-Redemption," 207–212; idem, "Messianic Element," 105–111; Faierstein, "Personal Redemption," 214–224; and Tishby, "Messianic Idea," 1–45.

5. Zohar 2:252a. This passage alludes to the verse in Zechariah, though only a tiny fragment of it is quoted explicitly and describes how human prayer redeems the divine vitality that is hidden in the earthly realm.

6. These attributes represent the seven lower *sefirot* from *hesed* to *malkhut*. Presumably the Maggid is referring to the "fallen," or negative, versions of these *middot*.

7. *Tikkunei Zohar*, tikkun 5, fol. 19b.

8. See b. Ketubot 64b.

9. MDL, no. 173, pp. 271–272.

10. See Schatz-Uffenheimer, *Hasidism and Mysticism*, 260, and, more broadly, 255–289. See also Weiss, "Mystical Hasidism," 277–285; and Etkes, *Ba'al ha-Tanya*, 196–199, for a discussion not included in the English edition of his book.

11. See Green, "Around the Maggid's Table," 73–106.

12. See Mayse, "Moving Mezritsh."

13. The disagreement between Avraham of Kalisk and Shneur Zalman is the best-known of these disputes. See Gries, "From Myth to Ethos," 117–146; Etkes, *Rabbi Shneur Zalman*, 201–258; Haran, "R. Abraham of Kalisk," 399–428.

14. OT, *balak*, no. 144, p. 196, commenting on Num. 24:2 and b. Bava Batra 60a. Based on Green et al., *Speaking Torah*, 2:54–55. Cf. Zohar 3:211b.

15. See also *Or ha-Me'ir*, vol. 2, *korah*, 104.

APPENDIX

Note to epigraph: Ginzberg, *Students, Scholars and Saints*, 132.

1. For a more detailed presentation, see Mayse, "Beyond the Letters," 40–95; and Moseson, "From Spoken Word," esp. 212–299.

2. On broader questions of orality, translation, and textual fluidity in Hasidic sources, see Mayse and Reiser, "Territories and Textures," 127–160, and the relevant literature cited therein.

3. See also Abrams, "Becoming of a Hasidic Book," 7–34.

4. See Mayse, "Double-Take," 37–93.

5. See Blair, "Note Taking," 85–107; Carter and Van Matre, "Note Taking Versus Note Having," 900–904.

6. Here we should recall *hypomnemata* (notes taken for private use) and *syngramma* (literary works intended to become an authoritative text), two different types of transcriptions found in Greek-influenced educational institutions.

7. See Zori, *Not in the Hands of Heaven*, esp. 8–12.

8. For a literary attempt to "back-translate" sermons into their original, see Mayse, "Who Amongst You," 364–381.

9. See, inter alia, Gries, "Hasidic Managing Editor," 141–155; idem, *Book in Early Hasidism*, 47–67; Green, "On Translating Hasidic Homilies," 63–72; idem, "Hasidic Homily," 237–265; Gellman, *Emergence of Hasidism*, 56–80; Idel, *Absorbing Perfections*, 470–481; and Heschel, *Kotsk*, 1:7–10. See also Saperstein, "Sermon as Oral Performance," 248–277.

10. See Ong, *Presence of the Word*; and Havelock, *Muse Learns to Write*.

11. See also Abrams, "Orality in the Kabbalistic School of Nahmanides," 85–102; Idel, *Kabbalah*, 20–22; Pedaya, *Name and Sanctuary*, 1–21; Wolfson, "Beyond the Spoken Word," 166–224; and Fishman, "Rhineland Pietists' Sacralization of Oral Torah," 9–16; Nahon, "Orality and Literacy," 145–168; and Fishman, *Becoming the People of the Talmud*, 121–217. Cf. MaHaRSHA to b. Bava Batra 10b.

12. See Chafe and Tannen, "Relation Between Written and Spoken Language," 383–407; Olson, "From Utterance to Text," 257–281; Ong, *Orality and Literacy*; and, for an instructive contemporary discussion, Tannen, "Commingling of Orality and Literacy," 34–43.

13. See Green, "Hasidic Homily," 240–244; Idel, *Hasidism*, 239–244; idem, *Absorbing Perfections*, 473–478; Etkes, *Rabbi Shneur Zalman*, 50–54; and Sagiv, *Dynasty*, 182–191, 249–250. See also Turniansky, "Oral and Written Sermons," 183–195.

14. For two early Hasidic texts that explicitly take up the question of why a disciple cannot simply absorb a master's ideas from a book, see *Me'or 'Einayim*, vol. 2, *likkutim*, 432–433; and *Likkutei Moharan*, 1:19.

15. See Gries, *Conduct Literature*, esp. 12–13. His work remains the most important work on the Hasidic *hanhagot*. On the earlier *hanhagot*, see Schechter, "Safed in the Sixteenth Century," 292–301; and *Toledoth ha-Ari*, ed. Benayahu, 315–334; translated in Fine, *Safed Spirituality*, 30–77; and Gries, *Conduct Literature*, 12–22 (introduction). See also Bar-Levav, "Ritualization of Jewish Life," 69–82.

16. See Schatz-Uffenheimer, *Hasidism as Mysticism*, 55; Gries, *Conduct Literature*, 23 n. 103.

17. See Gries, *Conduct Literature*, 23–26 (introduction), 150.

18. The Maggid wrote a short approbation to *Halakhah Pesukah*. This digest of the laws of ritual slaughter included approbations from several other prominent scholars from Mezritsh, Rovno, and Torchin, suggesting that the Maggid's name carried local cachet by the mid-1760s. On the letters, which touch on a local economic dispute involving Dov Ber's student Aharon of Karlin, see Ettinger, "Hasidism and the *Kahal*," 67; Wilensky, *Hasidim and Mitnaggedim*, 2:343–344; and Etkes, "Study of Hasidism," 449–450.

19. The title is based on the verse "He spoke (*maggid*) His words unto Jacob, His laws and decrees unto Israel" (Ps. 147:19), and a play on the word *maggid*. On the publication of MDL, see Gries, *Book in Early Hasidism*, 56–59; idem, "Hasidic Managing Editor," 150–152; Dynner, *Men of Silk*, 202–208. The number of times it was republished makes MDL one of the most frequently printed books before 1815, not far behind Shneur Zalman of Liady's *Likkutei Amarim-Tanya* (eleven printings) and tied with *Tsava'at ha-Ribash*.

20. Beginning with the Korets 1784 printing, most of the later editions of MDL divide the sermons differently.

21. On Shlomo of Lutsk as an editor and publisher, see Gries, "Hasidic Managing Editor," 146–154.

22. For a full translation, see Jacobs, *Hasidic Thought*, 66–74.

23. See *Maggid Devarav le-Ya'akov*, ed. Schatz-Uffenheimer.

24. See his trenchant remarks in Gries, "Hasidism: The Present State of Research," 196–200.

25. See also the more recent version published by the Habad Hasidic community; see *Maggid Devarav le-Ya'akov* (Brooklyn: Kehot Publication Society, 2012).

26. See *Or Torah ha-Shalem* (Brooklyn: Kehot Publication Society, 2011). This edition, published by the Habad Hasidic community, features very learned and useful notes as well as excellent indices.

27. See MDL, p. x.

28. See LY, no. 3, fol. 1a; ibid., no. 105, fols. 19b–20a; ibid., no. 165, fols. 54b–55a; ibid., no. 205, fol. 62a-b; and ibid., no. 274, p. 90b.

29. On this figure, a disciple of the Maggid and later of Yehiel Mikhel of Zlotshev, see Krassen, *Uniter of Heaven*, esp. 38. Other Hasidic masters whose teachings appear in *Likkutim Yekarim* include Menahem Mendel of Premishlan (Przemyślany) and Yehiel Mikhel of Yample (later of Zlotshev; Pol. Złoczów; mod. Ukr. Zolochiv).

30. The series of complicated teachings grounded in Lurianic Kabbalah is an interesting exception to this rule; see LY, nos. 137–159, fols. 46a–53b.

31. See Gries, *Conduct Literature*, 314–353; Weiss, "Authorship and Literary Unity," 170–182. See also the *hanhagot* in *Hayyim va-Hesed*, 1–8; SLA, 53–57; and ST, 4.

32. See Gries, "Editing of *Tsavat ha-Ribash*," 187–210; idem, *Conduct Literature*, esp. 149–230; Dynner, *Men of Silk*, 247.

33. See Gries, *Conduct Literature*, 179.

34. Ibid., 150.

35. See Nigal, "Primary Source for Hasidic Tales," 349–364; and Wilensky, *Hasidim and Mitnaggedim*, 2:328. Other books published by the editor, such as *Or ha-Ganuz le-Tsaddikim*, present teachings elsewhere attributed to other early Hasidic figures, such as those of the BeSHT.

36. For a few of the most important surviving manuscripts, see the bibliography.

37. See Loewenthal, "Rabbi Shneur Zalman," 89–137.

38. See LY, no. 256, fol. 78b, for a teaching that concludes with the words *nero ya'ir* ("may his light shine on"), a common honorific appended only to the name of a living sage.

39. See *Tsemah ha-Shem li-Tsevi, mattot*, 624.

40. *Be'erot ha-Mayim*, 150. See also ibid., 154, where the author quotes a teaching from the Maggid that he found in a manuscript belonging to Avraham Hayyim of Zlotshev.

41. See Gries, *Conduct Literature*, 157–158.

42. See the remarkable work of Moseson, "From Spoken Word," esp. 299–361; and Zucker, "Early Hasidic Manuscript," 223–235; Schatz-Uffenheimer's comments in MDL, 9–23 (introduction); Gries, "Editing of *Tsavat ha-Ribash*," 187–210; idem, *Conduct Literature*, 151–181; Abrams, *Kabbalistic Manuscripts*, esp. 626 n. 376; Nigal, "Analysis of an Early Hasidic Manuscript," 177–192.

43. Levi Yitshak gave an approbation to each book published in Barditshev during his lifetime. Perhaps such endorsements had become perfunctory, and he may never have examined this printing of MDL published shortly before his death.

44. Scholem MS RS 28, fol. 188b, mentions a teaching from the Maggid that Levi Yitshak received from Shlomo of Lutsk, but to my knowledge this incident is unique.

45. However, SLA must be used with some caution, Furthermore, a significant number of sermons in SLA also appear in *Me'or 'Einayim*, the collection of teachings by Menahem Nahum of Chernobil; see SLA, 166–170.

46. Cf. *Menorat Zahav* (Warsaw, 1902), attributed to Zusya of Hanipol; and *Butsina de-Nehora* (Lviv, 1879), attributed to Barukh of Mezhbizh. Ya'akov Yosef of Polnoye's *Ketonet Passim* (1866) was published many years after the author's death and long after his first three books were printed. See Weiss, "Is the Hasidic Book . . . ?," 81–83.

47. For example, see also JER SCHOC 17379, fols. 15a, 20b; and Montreal-Elberg 177, fols. 5a–6a, for five teachings from the Maggid. See also Bar Ilan 1030-Moussaief 114.

48. See Abrams, *Kabbalistic Manuscripts*, 625–628.

49. Ibid., 627.

50. In some cases, Klapholtz extends his net too widely, incorporating sources that are elsewhere attributed to Yehiel Mikhel, the "Maggid" of Zlotshev. See THM, 286, 403–404. See also Altshuler, *Messianic Secret*, esp. 52 n. 6, 358–360; and Piekarz's devastating review, "A Light That Does Not Illuminate."

51. See Blair, "Note Taking," 85–107.

52. See *Or ha-Me'ir*, vol. 1, *va-yera*, 34; *Likkutei Torah, masa'ei*, 96b-c; *Dibrat Shlomo, va-yeshev*, 58; ibid., *korah*, 339; ibid., *shoftim*, 401; *Zot Zikhron*, 43a; cf. OHE, 62a-b.

53. For example, see *Zikaron Zot, lekh lekha*, 10a.

54. See *Orah le-Hayyim*, vol. 1, *noah*, 49–51. Although this fascinating example of a student interpreting the Maggid's homily in light of the work of another disciple is an exception rather than the rule, it may point toward a closer relationship between the students than has been hitherto appreciated.

55. Dov Ber's students often quote traditions that they heard *be-shem* (in the name) of the Maggid, occasionally with the name of the disciple from whom they received the teach-

ing, confirming that Dov Ber's teachings were indeed being transmitted orally; see *Dibrat Shlomo, balak*, 363; *Ve-Tsivah ha-Kohen*, ch. 13, 105; *Bat 'Ayin, hukkat*, 367.

56. For examples of disciples citing from manuscripts, see *Yosher Divrei Emet*, no. 19, fol. 120a (referring to LY); no. 17, p. 118b (where he notes that only a few people had them). See also *Yosher Divrei Emet*, no. 15, fol. 117b; ibid., no. 19, fol. 120a; *Mevasser Tsedek, be-shalah*, 53–54; ibid., *be-har*, 164; and *Ginzei Yosef*, vol. 2, *nitsavim*, 193.

57. See Rosman, "Hebrew Sources,"163–166. See also idem, *Founder*, xlii–xliv and 137–142; Etkes, "Historical BESHT," 432–433.

58. For example, *Mevasser Tsedek, va-yikra*, 102; and *Or ha-Me'ir*, vol. 1, *va-yera*, 34; and ibid., vol. 2, *ruth*, 39. On occasion, Ya'akov Yosef of Polnoye cites traditions from the BeSHT even when his master's words run counter to the thrust of his own sermon. See *Toledot Ya'akov Yosef*, vol. 1, *bo*, 308. My thanks to Nehemia Polen for drawing my attention to this interesting phenomenon.

59. An earlier version of these remarks appeared in Reiser and Mayse, *Sefat Emet be-Sefat ha-Em*.

60. Allon, *Style and Function*; idem, "Oral Composition and Transmission," 39–61; and Schopen, "On the Absence of Urtexts," 189–219.

61. Kelber, *Oral and the Written Gospel*, 18.

62. See, for example, Crone and Cook, *Hagarism*; Wansbrough, *Quranic Studies*; Crone, *Meccan Trade and the Rise of Islam*; Donner, *Muhammad and the Believers*, 54–57.

63. For reflections on the literatures and orality of Hasidism in light of those of other mystical movements, see Buber, "Interpreting Hasidism," 218–225.

64. Graham, *Beyond the Written Word*, 6.

65. Ibid.

66. See Graham, *Beyond the Written Word*, 31–32; and Eisenstein, *Printing Revolution*; and Clancy, *From Memory to Written Record*.

67. Mendelssohn, *Jerusalem*, 103.

68. See *Ma'or va-Shemesh, rimzei shabbat hol ha-mo'ed sukkot*.

69. See Manguel, *History of Reading*; and Darnton, "First Steps," 152–177.

70. See Balogh, "Voces Paginarum," 84–109.

71. Polanyi, *Personal Knowledge*, 92.

72. See Green, "Translating Hasidic Homilies," 67–68.

73. Gries, "Between Literature and History," 153.

74. Seidman, *Faithful Renderings*, 18–19.

75. Ibid., 9.

76. Ibid., 26–27.

77. See Turniansky, "Oral and Written Sermons," 183–186; idem, "Languages of the Jews," 61–76; and idem, "Bi-Lingual Writings," 85–99.

78. Johns, *Nature of the Book*, 88.

79. Abrams, *Kabbalistic Manuscripts*, 7. It is here worth recalling the much-debated arguments of Michel Foucault, "Authorship," 16: "Assuming that we are dealing with an author, is everything he wrote and said, everything he left behind, to be included in his work? . . . These practical considerations are endless once we consider how a work can be extracted from the millions of traces left by an individual after his death."

80. At least one teaching preserved in a manuscript concludes with the phrase "from the writing of my master himself" (*mi-ketivat mori 'atsmo*), perhaps implying that it was copied from the Maggid's own writings. I have been unable to find other evidence supporting

this notion. We should not rule out the possibility that such private writings did exist, but, as noted by Elly Moseson, other parallels to this passage end with "from the master's mouth." See Scholem MS RS 28, fol. 136a; and ST, 62a.

81. See Prov. 24:7; Job 28:18.

82. See Zohar 2:23a.

83. The word *mazkeret* is of biblical origin (Num. 5:15). Though it appears rarely in rabbinic literature, a strikingly similar tradition is found in the hagiographical collection *Toledoth ha-Ari*, ed. Benayahu, 164.

84. See b. Bekhorot 31b; cf. Yevamot 96b. It is interesting to note that the Talmud is *not* discussing the act of writing down teachings, but rather their oral transmission from master to disciple.

85. MDL, 3. See Gries, *Book in Early Hasidism*, 57–58; and Dynner, *Men of Silk*, 201.

86. See Gries, *Book in Early Hasidism*, 58–59.

87. See Loewenthal, *Communicating the Infinite*, 66–68; Etkes, *Rabbi Shneur Zalman*, 52–54.

88. The word *mazkeret* may be intended to invoke Maimonides' formulation *zikaron ba-shemu'ot*, found in the introduction to his *Mishneh Torah*, describing the written records of oral traditions transcribed by rabbinic sages for personal use even during the classical period of the oral Torah.

89. See y. Shekalim 2:5; cf. b. Yevamot 97a; and b. Megillah 15a.

90. See LY, no. 91, fol. 16b; MDL, no. 28, p. 46; and OHE, 16a. Cf. *Likkutei Moharan*, I:12.

91. See Scholem, *Major Trends*, 333–334, 340–341.

Bibliography

MANUSCRIPTS CONSULTED

Bar Ilan 1030-Moussaief 114, Mousaieff Manuscripts Collection, Wurzweiler Central Library, Bar-Ilan University. http://moussaieff.biu.ac.il/he/?item=%2FMoussaieff_1030.

Chabad MS 187, Library of Agudas Chassidei Chabad, Brooklyn, New York.

Chabad MS 1821, Library of Agudas Chassidei Chabad, Brooklyn, New York.

Chabad MS 2220, Library of Agudas Chassidei Chabad, Brooklyn, New York.

JER NLI MS HEB 8°5198, The National Library of Israel, Department of Manuscripts and Institute of Microfilmed Hebrew Manuscripts, Jerusalem. https://web.nli.org.il/sites/NLI/Hebrew/digitallibrary/pages/viewer.aspx?presentorid=MANUSCRIPTS&docid=PNX_MANUSCRIPTS000046029-2.

JER NLI MS HEB 8°5307, The National Library of Israel, Department of Manuscripts and Institute of Microfilmed Hebrew Manuscripts, Jerusalem. https://web.nli.org.il/sites/NLI/Hebrew/digitallibrary/pages/viewer.aspx?presentorid=MANUSCRIPTS&docid=PNX_MANUSCRIPTS000042917-1.

JER NLI MS HEB 8°5979, The National Library of Israel, Department of Manuscripts and Institute of Microfilmed Hebrew Manuscripts, Jerusalem. https://web.nli.org.il/sites/NLI/Hebrew/digitallibrary/pages/viewer.aspx?presentorid=MANUSCRIPTS&docid=PNX_MANUSCRIPTS002570082-1#|FL44433014.

JER NLI MS HEB 8°1467, The National Library of Israel, Department of Manuscripts and Institute of Microfilmed Hebrew Manuscripts, Jerusalem.

JER NLI MS HEB 8°3282, The National Library of Israel, Department of Manuscripts and Institute of Microfilmed Hebrew Manuscripts, Jerusalem.

JER SCHOC 17379, The Schocken Institute for Jewish Research, Jerusalem, Israel.

Montreal-Elberg 177, The National Library of Israel, Department of Manuscripts and Institute of Microfilmed Hebrew Manuscripts, Jerusalem.

MOS RSL 182:353, The Russian State Library in Moscow. https://dlib.rsl.ru/viewer/01006581355.

Scholem MS RS 28, The National Library of Israel, Scholem Collection, Jerusalem.

PUBLISHED WORKS OF THE MAGGID

Dibberot ha-Maggid. Jerusalem: Mechon Genuzim, 2018.

Keter Shem Tov. Zolkiev, 1794. Expanded reprint: *Keter Shem Tov ha-Shalem.* Brooklyn: Kehot Publication Society, 2004. All citations refer to this version.

Kitvei Kodesh. Lemberg, 1862.

Likkutim Yekarim. Lemberg, 1792. Expanded reprint: *Likkutim Yekarim.* Ed. Avraham
   Yitshak Kahn. Jerusalem: Yeshivat Toledot Aharon, 1973. All citations refer to this
   version.

Maggid Devarav le-Ya'akov. Korets, 1781. Reprinted as a critical edition: *Maggid Devarav le-
   Ya'akov.* Ed. Rivka Schatz-Uffenheimer. Jerusalem: Magnes Press, 1976. All citations
   refer to this version.

Or ha-Emet. Husyatin, 1899.

Or Torah. Korets, 1804. Expanded reprint: *Or Torah ha-Shalem.* Brooklyn: Kehot Publication
   Society, 2011.

Sefer Likkutei Amarim. Lemberg: Bukhdr St. Kübler, 1911. Expanded reprint: *Sefer Likkutei
   Amarim.* Jerusalem: Shuvi Nafshi, 2009.

Shemu'ah Tovah. Warsaw: M. Lifshits, 1938.

Torat ha-Maggid. Ed. Yisra'el Klapholtz. Tel Aviv, 1969.

Tsava'at ha-RiBaSH. Zolkiev, 1793. Expanded reprint: *Tsava'at ha-RiBaSH.* Brooklyn: Kehot
   Publication Society, 1998.

EDITIONS OF CLASSICAL, HASIDIC, AND KABBALISTIC
BOOKS AND COLLECTIONS OF HASIDIC TALES

Abrams, Daniel, ed. *The Book Bahir: An Edition Based on the Earliest Manuscripts.* 2 vols. Los
   Angeles: Cherub Press, 1994.

Aharon of Zhitomir. *Toledot Aharon.* Lemberg, 1864.

Albeck, Hanokh, and Julius Theodor, eds. *Bereshit Rabbah.* 3 vols. Jerusalem: Shalem,
   1965.

Avraham ben Dov Ber. *Bat 'Ayin.* Ashdod: Merkaz Prager, 1999.

Avraham of Trisk. *Magen Avraham.* Lublin, 1887.

Avraham Hayyim of Zlotshev. *Orah le-Hayyim.* 2 vols. Montreal: Refa'el Hertsog, 2009.

———. *Peri Hayyim.* Jerusalem: Keren Zikhron Yesha'yahu, 1987.

Azulai, Abraham. *Hesed le-Avraham.* Jerusalem: Yosef ben Yitshak ha-Kohen, 2012.

Bachrach, Naftali.*'Emek ha-Melekh.* 2 vols. Jerusalem: Yerid ha-Sefarim, 2003.

Barnai, Ya'akov, ed. *Hasidic Letters from Eretz-Israel.* Jerusalem: Yad Yitshak Ben-Tsevi, 1980.

Berger, Israel. *'Eser Orot.* Piotrków: 1907.

Bi-leshon Hasidim Titkadesh. Zurich: Mekhon Zikhron Barukh, 2012.

Binyamin of Zalocze. *Torei Zahav.* Jerusalem: Yonatan Ze'ev Landau, 1989.

Blokh, Joseph. *Ginzei Yosef.* 2 vols. Jerusalem: H. Grinfeld v-M.D. Blum, 1960.

Bodek, Menahem Mendel. *Seder ha-Dorot ha-Hadash.* Lemberg, 1865. Reprint, Jerusalem:
   2000.

Buber, Shlomo, ed. Midrash Tanhuma. Vilna, 1885.

Buber, Shlomo, ed. *Ruth Zuta.* Berlin, 1894.

Butsina de-Nehora. Lviv, 1879.

Charles, R. H., ed. *Book of Jubilees.* London: Adam and Charles Black, 1902.

Cordovero, Moshe. *Or Ne'erav.* Jerusalem: Kol Yehudah, 1965.

———. *Pardes Rimmonim,* Jerusalem: Hotsa'at Yosef Hasid, 1998.

Darkhei Tsedek. Lemberg, 1796.

Darkhei Tsiyyon. Polnoye, 1797.

Divrei David. Husyatin: 1904.

Divrei Moshe. Polnoye, 1801.

Emden, Ya'akov. *Siddur Ya'avets.* Altona, 1745–1748.

Epstein, Kalonymous Kalman. *Ma'or va-Shemesh.* 2 vols. Jerusalem: Mekhon Even Yisra'el, 1992.

Finkelstein, Louis, ed. *Sifrei Devarim.* New York: Jewish Theological Seminary of America, 2001.

Friedman, Ya'akov. *Ohalei Ya'akov.* Tel Aviv: Beit ha-Kenesset ha-Admorei Husyatin, 2006.

Gabbai, Meir Ibn. *'Avodat ha-Kodesh.* Jerusalem: Yerid ha-Sefarim, 2004.

Gikatilla, Yosef. *Sha'arei Orah.* Jerusalem: M. Borenstein, 2005.

Halakhah Pesukah. Turka, 1765.

Halperin, David ben Israel. *Darkhei Tsiyyon.* Polnoye, 1797.

Hayyim Haykl of Amdur. *Hayyim va-Hesed.* Jerusalem: Ha-Mossad le-Hotsa'at Sifrei Mussar ve-Hasidut, 1954.

Heilman, Hayyim Meir. *Beit Rabbi.* Jerusalem: Torat Habad, 2013.

Heller, Meshullam Feibush. *Yosher Divrei Emet.* Ed. Avraham Yitshak Kahn. Jerusalem: Yeshivat Toledot Aharon, 1981.

Heschel, Avraham Yehoshua. *Ohev Yisra'el.* Jerusalem: 1998.

Hesed le-Avraham. Jerusalem: Mekhot Siftei Tsaddikim, 2013.

Hillel, Y. M., ed. *Shivhei ha-Ari.* Jerusalem: Ahavat Shalom, 1991.

Hillman, David Tsevi. *Iggerot Ba'al ha-Tanya u-Venei Doro.* Jerusalem: 1953.

Hollander, H. W., and M. de Jonge. *The Testaments of the Twelve Patriarchs: A Commentary.* Leiden: E.J. Brill, 1985.

Hapstein, Yisra'el. *'Avodat Yisrael.* Jerusalem: 1996.

Horowitz, Yeshayah. *Shenei Luhot ha-Berit ha-Shalem.* 4 vols. Haifa: 1992.

Horowitz, Ya'akov Yitshak. *Divrei Emet.* Munkacs: 1943.

———. *Zikaron Zot.* Warsaw, 1869.

———. *Zot Zikaron.* Lemberg, 1851.

Horowitz, Shmu'el Shmelke. *Divrei Shmu'el.* Jerusalem: Mosdot Boston, 1988.

ibn Pakuda, Bahya. *The Book of Direction to the Duties of the Heart.* Trans. Menahem Mansoor. London: Routledge & K. Paul, 1973.

In Praise of the Baal Shem Tov [Shivhei ha-Besht]: The Earliest Collection of Legends About the Founder of Hasidism. Trans. Dan Ben-Amos and Jerome R. Mintz. Northvale, NJ: Jason Aronson, 1993.

'Irin Kaddishin, 2 vols. Jerusalem: Mekhon Siftei Tsaddikim, 2009.

Isaiah Horowitz: The Generations of Adam [Shenei Luhot ha-Berit, toledot adam]. Trans. Miles Krassen. New York: Paulist Press, 1996.

Katz, Ya'akov Yosef. *Ben Porat Yosef.* 2 vols. Jerusalem: Yitshak Aizik Eichen, 2011.

———. *Ketonet Passim.* Jerusalem: Yitshak Aizik Eichen, 2011.

———. *Toledot Ya'aqov Yosef.* 3 vols. Jerusalem: Yitshak Aizik Eichen, 2011.

———. *Tsofnat Pane'ah.* 2 vols. Jerusalem: Yitshak Aizik Eichen, 2011.

Kedushat Yisra'el. Jerusalem: 1955/1956.

Kerem Yisrael. Lublin: 1930.

Kitvei Ramban. Ed. C. D. Chavel. Jerusalem: Mossad Ha-Rav Kook, 1961.

Kitvei Yoshiya Shub. Jerusalem: n.d.

ha-Kohen, Aharon. *Or ha-Ganuz le-Tsaddikim*. Zolkiev, 1800.

———. *Ve-Tsivah ha-Kohen*. Jerusalem: Ha-Mossad le-Hotsa'at Sifrei Mussar ve-Hasidut, 1953.

Levi Yitshak of Barditshev. *Kedushat Levi*. Ed. Michael Darbarmediger. 2 vols. Monsey: 1995.

Limmudei Atsilut. Munkatsh, 1897.

Maimonides, Moses. *The Guide of the Perplexed*. Trans. Shlomo Pines. 2 vols. Chicago: University of Chicago Press, 1963.

Margoliot, Meir. *Sod Yakhin u-Vo'az*. London: 1956.

Meisels, 'Uziel. *Tif'eret 'Uziel*. Jerusalem: 1962.

Menahem Mendel of Vitebsk. *Peri ha-Arets*. 2 vols. Jerusalem: Mekhon Peri ha-Arets, 2014.

Menahem Tsiyon. Benei Brak: Mekhon Benei Shileshim, 2004.

Menorat Zahav. Warsaw: 1902.

Mondshine, Yehoshua, ed. *Shivhei ha-Besht: A Manuscript*. [In Hebrew and Yiddish.] Jerusalem: 1982.

Moshe Ephraim Hayyim of Sudlikow. *Degel Mahaneh Efrayim*. Benei Brak: 2013.

Naftali of Ropshitz. *Zera' Kodesh*. Jerusalem: 1971.

Nahman of Bratslav. *Likkutei Moharan*. Ostre, 1821.

Ner Yisra'el. 6 vols. Benei Berak: 1994.

Pirkei ha-Ne'ezar. Lublin, 1886.

Poppers, Meir. *Peri Ets Hayyim*. Jerusalem: n.d.

Rabinowitz, Gedaliyah. *Teshu'ot Hen*. Ashdod: 2012.

Sefer ha-Zohar. Ed. Reuven Margoliot. 3 vols. Jerusalem: Mossad ha-Rav Kook, 1999.

Shapira, Pinhas. 2 vols. *Imrei Pinhas ha-Shalem*. Benei Berak: Yehezkel Sheraga Frankel 2003.

Shapira, Tsevi Elimelekh of Dinov. *Benei Yissakhar*. 3 vols. Benei Berak: Mekhon Benei Shileshim, 2005.

———. *Igra de-Kalla*. Lemberg, 1868.

———. *Igra de-Pirka*. Jerusalem: S. Ayzikowitsh, 1973.

Shlomo of Lutsk. *Dibrat Shlomo*. Jerusalem: Ya'akov Yitshak Weiss, 2011.

Shneur Zalman of Liady. *Iggerot Kodesh—Admor ha-Zaken*. Brooklyn: Kehot Publication Society, 1987.

———. *Likkutei Amarim-Sefer ha-Tanya*. Brooklyn: Kehot Publication Society, 1998.

———. *Likkutei Torah*. Brooklyn: Kehot Publication Society, 2012.———. *Ma'amarei Admor ha-Zaken 'al ha-Parashiyot ve-ha-Mo'adim*. 2 vols. Brooklyn: Kehot Publication Society, 1983.

———. *Tefillot mi-kol ha-Shanah*. Brooklyn: Kehot Publication Society, 2008.

———. *Torah Or*. Brooklyn: Kehot Publication Society, 2012.

Tikkunei Zohar. Ed. Reuven Margoliot. Jerusalem: Mossad Ha-Rav Kook, 1978.

Tishby, Isaiah, ed. *Perush ha-Aggadot le-Rabbi 'Azriel*. Jerusalem: Mekitsei Nirdamim, 1945.

Toledoth ha-Ari. Ed. Meir Benayahu. Jerusalem: 1967.

Tsevi Hirsch of Nadvorna. *Tsemah ha-Shem li-Tsevi*. 2 vols. Benei Berak: Ha-Mekhon le-Hotsa'at Sifrei ha-Maggid mi-Nadvorna, 2007.

Twersky, Menahem Nahum. *Me'or 'Einayim*. 2 vols. Jerusalem: Mekhon Or ha-Torah, 2002.

Vidas, Elijah de. *Reshit Hokhmah*. 3 vols. Jerusalem: Or Ha-Mussar,1984.

Vital, Hayyim. *Ets Hayyim*. Korets, 1784.

Walden, Aharon. *Shem ha-Gedolim ha-Hadash*. Warsaw, 1864.

Weisblum, Elimelekh. *No'am Elimelekh*. Ed. Gedaliah Nigal. 2 vols. Jerusalem: Mossad Ha-Rav Kook, 1978.

Yehudah Aryeh Leib ben Betsalel. *Be'er ha-Golah.* Piotrków: 1910.
Yesod Yosef. Minkovits, 1803.
Yissakhar Dov Baer of Zlotshev. *Mevasser Tsedeq.* Safed: Yisra'el Meir Mendelowitz, 2010.
Yitshak Dov Baer ben Tsevi Hirsh. *Kahal Hasidim ha-Hadash.* Lemberg: 1902.
Ze'ev Wolf of Zhitomir. *Or ha-Me'ir.* 2 vols. Jerusalem: 2000.

SECONDARY SOURCES

Abrams, Daniel. "'The Becoming of a Hasidic Book': An Unpublished Article by Joseph Weiss; Study, Edition, and English Translation." *Kabbalah* 28 (2012): 7–34.
———. *Kabbalistic Manuscripts and Textual Theory: Methodologies of Textual Scholarship and Editorial Practice in the Study of Jewish Mysticism.* 2nd rev. ed. Jerusalem: Cherub Press, 2013.
———. "Orality in the Kabbalistic School of Nahmanides: Preserving and Interpreting Esoteric Traditions and Texts." *Jewish Studies Quarterly* 3, no. 3 (1996): 85–102.
———. "Some Phenomenological Considerations on the 'Account of Creation' in Jewish Mystical Literature." *Kabbalah* 10 (2004): 7–19.
———. "'Text' in a Zoharic Parable: A Chapter in the History of Kabbalistic Textuality." *Kabbalah* 25 (2001): 7–54.
Afterman, Adam. *"And They Shall be One Flesh": On the Language of Mystical Union in Judaism.* Leiden: Brill, 2016.
———. *The Intention of Prayers in Early Ecstatic Kabbalah: A Study and Critical Edition of an Anonymous Commentary to the Prayers.* [In Hebrew.] Los Angeles: Cherub Press, 2004.
Alfasi, Yitzhak. *he-Hasidut: mi-Dor la-Dor.* 2 vols. Jerusalem: 1995.
Allon, Mark. "The Oral Composition and Transmission of Early Buddhist Texts." In *Indian Insights: Buddhism, Brahmanism, and Bhakti: Papers from the Annual Spalding Symposium on Indian Religions,* ed. Peter Connolly and Sue Hamilton, 39–61. London: Luzac Oriental, 1997.
———. *Style and Function: A Study of the Dominant Stylistic Features of the Prose Portions of Pāli Canonical Sutta Texts and Their Mnemonic Function.* Tokyo: The International Institute for Buddhist Studies of the International College for Advanced Buddhist Studies, 1997.
Altmann, Alexander. "The Delphic Maxim in Medieval Islam and Judaism." In *Biblical and Other Studies,* 196–232. Cambridge, MA: Harvard University Press, 1963.
———. *Moses Mendelssohn: A Biographical Study.* Philadelphia: Jewish Publication Society, 1973.
———. "A Note on the Rabbinic Doctrine of Creation." *Journal of Jewish Studies* 7, no. 3/4 (1956): 195–206.
Altshuler, Mor. *The Messianic Secret of Hasidism.* Leiden: Brill, 2006.
Amshalem, Jeffrey G. "'Why Do You Not Tell Stories in My Praise Also?' The Image of Dov Ber, the Maggid of Mezritsh, in the Earliest Hasidic Tales." *Kabbalah* 31 (2014): 27–64.
Assaf, David. *The Regal Way: The Life and Times of Rabbi Israel of Ruzhin.* Stanford: Stanford University Press, 2002.
———. "The Teachings of Dov Ber the Maggid of Mezritch in Solomon Maimon's Autobiography." [In Hebrew.] *Zion* 71 (2006): 99–101.
Avivi, Joseph. *Kabbala Luriana.* [In Hebrew.] 3 vols. Jerusalem: Mekhon Ben-Tsevi, 2008.
Bacher, W. "The Views of Jehuda Halevi Concerning the Hebrew Language." *Hebraica* 8, no. 3/4 (1892): 136–149.

Balogh, Josef. "Voces Paginarum." *Philologus* 82, no. 1-4 (1927): 84–109.

Bar-Ilan, Meir. *The Mysteries of Jewish Prayer and Hekhalot.* [In Hebrew.] Ramat-Gan: Bar-Ilan University Press, 1987.

Bar-Levav, Avriel. "Ritualization of Jewish Life and Death in the Early Modern Period." *Leo Baeck Institute Yearbook* 47, no. 1 (2002): 69–82.

Bartal, Israel. "From Traditional Bilingualism to National Monolingualism." In *Hebrew in Ashkenaz: A Language in Exile,* ed. Lewis Glinert, 141–150. New York: Oxford University Press, 1993.

Beit-Arie, Malachi. "Perek Shira: Introductions and Critical Edition." 2 vols. [In Hebrew.] PhD diss., Hebrew University, 1966.

Benarroch, Jonatan. "'The Mystery of Unity': Poetic and Mystical Aspects of a Unique Zoharic *Shema* Mystery." *AJS Review* 37, no. 2 (2013): 231–256.

Benjamin, Walter. "On Language as Such and on the Language of Man." In *Walter Benjamin: Selected Writings,* vol. 1, *1913–1926,* ed. Marcus Bullock and Michael W. Jennings, 62–74. Cambridge, MA: Harvard University Press, 1996.

———. "The Task of the Translator." In Bullock and Jennings, *Walter Benjamin,* 1:253–263. Cambridge, MA: Harvard University Press, 1996.

Ben-Sasson, Haim Hillel. "'The Name of God and the Linguistic Theory of the Kabbalah' Revisited." *Journal of Religion* 98, no. 1 (2018): 1–28.

———. *YHWH: Its Meanings in Biblical, Rabbinic, and Medieval Jewish Thought.* [In Hebrew.] Jerusalem: Magnes, 2019.

Ben-Shlomo, Joseph. *The Mystical Theology of Moses Cordovero.* [In Hebrew.] Jerusalem: Bialik Institute, 1965.

Berger, Peter L. *The Sacred Canopy: Elements of a Sociological Theory of Religion.* Garden City, NY: Doubleday Books, 1967.

Bernstein, Lawrence F. "Pleyel's Emulation of Haydn: 'Easy' Symphonies and the Intended Audience." In *Musical Implications: Essays in Honor of Eugene Narmour,* ed. Lawrence F. Bernstein and Alexander Rozin, 1–24. Hillsdale, NY: Pendragon Press, 2013.

Biale, David. *Eros and the Jews: From Biblical Israel to Contemporary America.* New York: BasicBooks, 1992.

———. *Gershom Scholem: Kabbalah and Counter-History.* 2nd ed. Cambridge, MA: Harvard University Press, 1982.

Biale, David, et al. *Hasidism: A New History.* Princeton: Princeton University Press, 2018.

Bialik, Haim Nahman. "Revealment and Concealment in Language." In *Revealment and Concealment,* 11–26. Jerusalem: Ibis Editions, 2000.

Bialik, Hayyim Nahman, and Yehoshua Ravnitzki, eds. *The Book of Legends.* Trans. William Gordon Braude. New York: Schocken Books, 1992.

Blair, Ann. "Note Taking as an Art of Transmission." *Critical Inquiry* 31, no. 1 (2004): 85–107.

Block, Daniel I. "The Role of Language in Ancient Israelite Perceptions of National Identity." *Journal of Biblical Literature* 103, no. 3 (1984): 321–340.

Bloom, Harold. *Kabbalah and Criticism.* New York: Continuum, 1975.

Bono, James J. *The Word of God and the Languages of Man: Interpreting Nature in Early Modern Science and Medicine.* Vol. 1, *Ficino to Descartes.* Madison: University of Wisconsin Press, 1995.

Boustan, Ra'anan S. *From Martyr to Mystic.* Tübingen: Mohr Siebeck, 2005.

Bowman, Leonard J. "The Cosmic Exemplarism of Bonaventure." *Journal of Religion* 55, no. 2 (1975): 181–198.

Boyarin, Daniel. *Border Lines: The Partition of Judaeo-Christianity.* Philadelphia: University of Pennsylvania Press, 2006.

———. *Carnal Israel: Reading Sex in Talmudic Culture.* Berkeley: University of California Press, 1995.

———. "The Gospel of the *Memra*: Jewish Binitarianism and the Prologue to John." *Harvard Theological Review* 94, no. 3 (2001): 243–284.

———. "History Becomes Parable: A Reading of the Midrashic *Mashal*." In *Mappings of the Biblical Terrain: The Bible as Text*, ed. Vincent L. Tollers and John Maier, 54–71. Lewisburg: Bucknell University Press, 1990.

Breuer, Edward, and David Sorkin, eds. *Moses Mendelssohn's Hebrew Writings.* Trans. Edward Breuer. New Haven: Yale University Press, 2018.

Brill, Alan. "Meditative Prayer in Moshe Cordovero's Kabbalah." In *Meditation in Judaism, Christianity, and Islam: Cultural Histories*, ed. Halvor Eifring, 45–60. London: Bloomsbury Academic, 2013.

———. *Thinking God: The Mysticism of Rabbi Zadok of Lublin.* Jersey City: KTAV Publishing House, 2002.

Brody, Robert. *Sa'adyah Gaon.* Trans. Betsy Rosenberg. Oxford: Littman Library of Jewish Civilization, 2013.

Brody, Seth. "Human Hands Dwell in Heavenly Heights: Contemplative Ascent and Theurgic Power in Thirteenth-Century Kabbalah." In *Mystics of the Book: Themes, Topics, and Typologies*, ed. Robert A. Herrera, 133–58. New York: P. Lang, 1993.

———. "'Open to Me the Gates of Righteousness': The Pursuit of Holiness and Non-Duality in Early Hasidic Teaching." *Jewish Quarterly Review* 89, no. 1/2 (1998): 3–44.

Brown, Jeremy Philip. "Of Sound and Vision: The Ram's Horn in Medieval Kabbalistic Rituology." In *Qol Tamid: The Shofar in Ritual, History, and Culture*, ed. Jonathan Friedman and Joel Gereboff, 83–113. Claremont, CA: Claremont Press, 2017.

Buber, Martin. "Dialogue Between Heaven and Earth." In *On Judaism*, ed. Nahum N. Glatzer, 214–225. New York: Schocken Books, 1996.

———. *Ecstatic Confessions: The Heart of Mysticism.* Ed. Paul Mendes-Flohr. Trans. Esther Cameron. Syracuse: Syracuse University Press, 1996.

———. *Hasidism and Modern Man.* Trans. and ed. Maurice Friedman. New York: Horizon Press, 1958.

———. *I and Thou.* Trans. Walter Kaufmann. New York: Touchstone, 1996.

———. "Interpreting Hasidism." *Commentary* 36 (September 1963): 218–225.

———. *Tales of the Hasidim.* Vol. 1, *The Early Masters.* Trans. Olga Marx. New York: Schocken Books, 1978.

———. "The Word That Is Spoken." *Modern Age* 5, no. 4 (1961): 353–360.

Calabi, Francesca. *The Language and the Law of God: Interpretation and Politics in Philo of Alexandria.* Atlanta: Scholars Press, 1998.

Carter, F., and Nicholas H. Van Matre. "Note Taking Versus Note Having." *Journal of Educational Psychology* 67, no. 6 (1975): 900–904.

de Certeau, Michel. *The Mystic Fable.* Vol. 1, *The Sixteenth and Seventeenth Centuries.* Trans. Michael B. Smith. Chicago: University of Chicago Press, 1992.

Chafe, Wallace, and Deborah Tannen. "The Relation Between Written and Spoken Language." *Annual Review of Anthropology* 16 (1987): 383–407.

Chernus, Ira. *Mysticism in Rabbinic Judaism.* Berlin: Walter de Gruyter, 1982.

Clancy, M. T. *From Memory to Written Record.* 3rd ed. Malden, MA: Wiley-Blackwell, 2013.

Cohen, Mordechai Z. "Logic to Interpretation: Maimonides' Use of al-Fârâbî's Model of Metaphor." *Zutot* 2 (2002): 104–113.

Cooper, Levi. "'But I Will Tell of Their Deeds': Retelling a Hasidic Tale About the Power of Storytelling." *Journal of Jewish Thought and Philosophy* 22, no. 2 (2014): 127–163.

Coudert, Allison P., ed. *The Language of Adam [= Die Sprache Adams].* [In English and German.] Wiesbaden: Harrassowitz, 1999.

Crescas, Hasdai. *Light of the Lord (Or Hashem).* Trans. Roslyn Weiss. Oxford: Oxford University Press, 2018.

Crone, Patricia. *Meccan Trade and the Rise of Islam.* Princeton: Princeton University Press, 1987.

Crone, Patricia, and Michael Cook. *Hagarism: The Making of the Islamic World.* Cambridge: Cambridge University Press, 1977.

Dan, Joseph. "The Ashkenazi Hasidic Concept of Language." In *Jewish Mysticism*, vol. 2, *The Middle Ages*, 65–87. Northvale, NJ: Jason Aronson, 1998.

———. "A Bow to Frumkinian Hasidism." *Modern Judaism* 11, no. 2 (1991): 175–193.

———. "The Emergence of Mystical Prayer." In *Jewish Mysticism*, vol. 2, *The Middle Ages*, 221–257. Northvale, NJ: Jason Aronson, 1998.

———. *The Esoteric Theology of Ashkenazi Hasidism.* [In Hebrew.] Jerusalem: Bialik Institute, 1968.

———. "Gershom Scholem: Between Mysticism and Scholarship." *Germanic Review* 72 (1997): 4–22.

———. "The Language of Creation and Its Grammar." In *Jewish Mysticism*, vol. 1, *Late Antiquity*, 129–154. Northvale, NJ: Jason Aronson, 1998.

———. "The Language of the Mystics in Medieval Germany." In *Jewish Mysticism*, vol. 4, *General Characteristics and Comparative Studies*, 161–190. Northvale, NJ: Jason Aronson, 1999.

———. "The Name of God, the Name of the Rose, and the Concept of Language in Jewish Mysticism." *Medieval Encounters* 2, no. 3 (1996): 228–248.

———. "*Ottiyyot de-Rabbi Akiva* and Its Concept of Language." [In Hebrew.] *Daat* 55 (2005): 5–30.

———. "Prayer as Text and Prayer as Mystical Experience." In *Jewish Mysticism*, vol. 2, *The Middle Ages*, 259–276. Northvale, NJ: Jason Aronson, 1998.

Darnton, Robert. "First Steps Toward a History of Reading." *Australian Journal of French Studies* 51, no. 2-3 (2014): 152–177.

Dauber, Jonathan. "The Baal Shem Tov and the Messiah: A Reappraisal of the Baal Shem Tov's Letter to Gershon of Kutov." *Jewish Studies Quarterly* 15, no. 2 (2008): 210–241.

Davidson, Herbert A. "The Study of Philosophy as a Religious Obligation." In *Religion in a Religious Age*, ed. S. D. Goitein, 53–68. Cambridge: Association for Jewish Studies, 1974.

Deutsch, Nathaniel. *The Gnostic Imagination: Gnosticism, Mandaeism, and Merkabah Mysticism.* Leiden: Brill, 1995.

Dillon, John M. "Solomon Ibn Gabirol's Doctrine of Intelligible Matter." In *Neoplatonism and Jewish Thought*, ed. Lenn E. Goodman, 43–60. Albany: State University of New York, 1992.

Dinur, Benzion. "The Origins of Hasidism and Its Social and Messianic Foundations." In *Essential Papers on Hasidism: Origins to Present*, ed. Gershon D. Hundert, 86–208. New York: New York University Press, 1991.

Donahue, John R. *The Gospel in Parable: Metaphor, Narrative, and Theology in the Synoptic Gospels.* Minneapolis: Fortress Press, 1988.

Donner, Fred M. *Muhammad and the Believers: At the Origins of Islam*. Cambridge: Belknap Press of Harvard University Press, 2010.

Dresner, Samuel H. *The Zaddik: The Doctrine of the Zaddik According to the Writings of Rabbi Yaakov Yosef of Polnoy*. London: Abelard-Schuman, 1960.

Dubnow, Simon. "The Maggid of Miedzyrzecz, His Associates, and the Center in Volhynia (1760–1772)." In *Essential Papers on Hasidism*, ed. Gershon D. Hundert, 58–85. New York: New York University Press, 1991.

———. *Toledot ha-Hasidut*. Tel Aviv: Devir, 1959.

Dunn, James. *Unity and Diversity in the New Testament: An Inquiry into the Character of Christianity*. 3rd ed. London: SCM Press, 2006.

Dupré, Louis. "Spiritual Life in a Secular Age." *Daedalus* 111, no. 1 (1982): 21–31.

Durkheim, Émile. *The Elementary Forms of Religious Life*. Trans. Carol Cosman. Oxford: Oxford University Press, 2001.

Dynner, Glenn. "The Hasidic Tale as a Historical Source: Historiography and Methodology." *Religion Compass* 3/4 (2009): 655–675.

———. *Men of Silk: The Hasidic Conquest of Polish Jewish Society*. Oxford: Oxford University Press, 2006.

———. *Yankel's Tavern: Jews, Liquor, and Life in the Kingdom of Poland*. Oxford: Oxford University Press, 2014.

Ehrlich, Uri. *The Nonverbal Language of Prayer: A New Approach to Jewish Liturgy*. Trans. Dena Ordan. Tübingen: Mohr Siebeck, 2004.

Ehrman, Bart D. *Lost Christianities: The Battles for Scripture and the Faiths We Never Knew*. New York: Oxford University Press, 2003.

Elman, Yaakov. "Torah ve-Avodah: Prayer and Torah Study as Competing Values in the Time of Hazal." In *Jewish Spirituality and Divine Law*, ed. Adam Mintz and Lawrence Schiffman, 61–124. Jersey City: KTAV Publishing House, 2005.

Eisenstadt, Shmuel N. *Comparative Civilizations and Multiple Modernities*. Leiden: Brill, 2003.

Eisenstein, Elizabeth L. *The Printing Revolution in Early Modern Europe*. Cambridge: Cambridge University Press, 2005.

Eliade, Mircea. *The Sacred and the Profane: The Nature of Religion*. Trans. Willard Trask. New York: Harcourt, Brace Jovanovich, 1959.

Elias, Norbert. *The Court Society*. Trans. Edmund Jephcott. New York: Pantheon Books, 1983.

Elior, Rachel. *The Mystical Origins of Hasidism*. Trans. Shalom Carmy. Oxford: Littman Library of Jewish Civilization, 2006.

———. "The Paradigms of *Yesh* and *Ayin* in Hasidic Thought." In *Hasidism Reappraised*, ed. Ada Rapoport-Albert, 168–179. London: Littman Library of Jewish Civilization, 1997.

———. *The Paradoxical Ascent to God: The Kabbalistic Theosophy of Habad Hasidism*. Trans. Jeffrey M. Green. Albany: State University of New York Press, 1993.

Eshel, Esther, and Michael Stone. "*Leshon haqodesh* in the End of Days in the Light of a Fragment from Qumran." [In Hebrew.] *Tarbiz* 62 (1993): 169–177.

Etkes, Immanuel. *Ba'al ha-Tanya: Rabbi Shneur Zalman of Liady and the Origins of Habad Hasidism*. [In Hebrew.] Jerusalem: The Zalman Shazar Center for Jewish History, 2011.

———. *The Besht: Magician, Mystic, and Leader*. Trans. Saadya Sternberg. Waltham: Brandeis University Press, 2005.

———. "The Early Hasidic 'Court.'" In *Text and Context: Essays in Modern Jewish History and Historiography in Honor of Ismar Schorsch*, ed. Eli Lederhendler and Jack Wertheimer, 157–169. New York: Jewish Theological Seminary, 2005.

———. "The Historical BESHT: Between Reconstruction and Deconstruction." [In Hebrew.] *Tarbiz* 66 (1997): 432–433.

———. *Rabbi Shneur Zalman of Liady: The Origins of Habad Hasidism.* Trans. Jeffrey M. Green. Waltham: Brandeis University Press, 2005.

———. "The Study of Hasidism: Past Trends and New Directions." In *Hasidism Reappraised,* ed. Ada Rapoport-Albert, 447–464. London: Littman Library of Jewish Civilization, 1997.

———. "The Zaddik: The Interrelationship Between Religious Doctrine and Social Organization." In Rapoport-Albert, *Hasidism Reappraised,* 159–167.

Ettin, Andrew Vogel. *Speaking Silences: Stillness and Voice in Modern Thought and Jewish Tradition.* Charlottesville: University of Virginia Press, 1994.

Ettinger, Shmuel. "The Hasidic Movement—Reality and Ideals." In *Essential Papers on Hasidism,* ed. Gershon D. Hundert, 237–238. New York: New York University Press, 1991.

———. "Hasidism and the *Kahal.*" In *Hasidism Reappraised,* ed. Ada Rapoport-Albert, 63–75. London: Littman Library of Jewish Civilization, 1997.

Faierstein, Morris M. "Personal Redemption in Hasidism." In *Hasidism Reappraised,* ed. Ada Rapoport-Albert, 214–224. London: Littman Library of Jewish Civilization, 1997.

Feiner, Shmuel. *The Origins of Jewish Secularization in Eighteenth-Century Europe.* Philadelphia: University of Pennsylvania Press, 2011.

Feldman, Louis H. *Philo's Portrayal of Moses in the Context of Ancient Judaism.* Notre Dame: University of Notre Dame Press, 2007.

Fine, Lawrence. "The Contemplative Practice of Yihudim in Lurianic Kabbalah." In *Jewish Spirituality,* vol. 2, *From the Sixteenth-Century Revival to the Present,* ed. Arthur Green, 64–98. New York: Crossroad, 1986.

———. "A Mystical Fellowship in Jerusalem." In *Judaism in Practice: From the Middle Ages through the Early Modern Period,* ed. Lawrence Fine, 210–214. Princeton: Princeton University Press, 2001.

———. *Physician of the Soul, Healer of the Cosmos: Isaac Luria and His Kabbalistic Fellowship.* Stanford: Stanford University Press, 2003.

———. *Safed Spirituality: Rules of Mystical Piety, the Beginning of Wisdom.* New York: Paulist Press, 1984.

———. "The Study of Torah as a Rite of Theurgical Contemplation in Lurianic Kabbalah." In *Approaches to Judaism in Medieval Times,* ed. David R. Blumenthal, 3:29–40. Chico, CA: Scholars Press, 1988.

Fishbane, Eitan P. *The Art of Mystical Narrative: A Poetics of the Zohar.* Oxford: Oxford University Press, 2018.

———. *As a Light Before Dawn: The Inner World of a Medieval Kabbalist.* Stanford: Stanford University Press, 2009.

———. "Mystical Contemplation and the Limits of the Mind: The Case of *Sheqel ha-Qodesh.*" *Jewish Quarterly Review,* n.s., 93, no. 1/2 (2002): 1–27.

———. "Perceptions of Greatness: Constructions of the Holy Man in *Shivhei ha-Ari.*" *Kabbalah* 27 (2012): 195221.

———. "The Speech of Being, the Voice of God: Phonetic Mysticism in the Kabbalah of Asher ben David and His Contemporaries." *Jewish Quarterly Review* 98, no. 4 (2008): 485–521.

Fishbane, Michael. *The Exegetical Imagination: On Jewish Thought and Theology.* Cambridge, MA: Harvard University Press, 1998.

———. *The Garments of Torah: Essays in Biblical Hermeneutics.* Bloomington: Indiana University Press, 1989.

———. *The Kiss of God: Spiritual and Mystical Death in Judaism.* Seattle: University of Washington Press, 1994.

———. *Song of Songs: The Traditional Hebrew Text with the New JPS Translation.* Philadelphia: Jewish Publication Society, 2015.

Fishman, Talya. *Becoming the People of the Talmud: Oral Torah as Written Tradition in Medieval Jewish Cultures.* Philadelphia: University of Pennsylvania Press, 2011.

———. "Rhineland Pietist Approaches to Prayer and the Textualization of Rabbinic Culture." *Jewish Studies Quarterly* 11, no. 4 (2004): 313–331.

———. "The Rhineland Pietists' Sacralization of Oral Torah." *Jewish Quarterly Review* 96, no. 1 (2006): 9–16.

Fleischer, Ezra. *Statutory Jewish Prayer: Their Emergence and Development.* [In Hebrew.] Ed. Shulamit Elizur and Tova Beeri. 2 vols. Jerusalem: Magnes Press, 2012.

Fodor, A. *The Language of Thought.* Cambridge, MA: Harvard University Press, 1975.

Forman, Robert K. C. *The Problem of Pure Consciousness: Mysticism and Philosophy.* New York: Oxford University Press, 1990.

Forster, Michael N. "Herder's Philosophy of Language, Interpretation, and Translation: Three Fundamental Principles." *Review of Metaphysics* 56, no. 2 (2002): 323–356.

Foucault, Michel. "Authorship: What Is an Author?" *Screen* 20, no. 1 (1979): 13–34.

Frank, Richard M. "Hearing and Saying What Was Said." *Journal of the American Oriental Society* 116, no. 4 (1996): 611–618.

Franke, William, ed. *On What Cannot Be Said: Apophatic Discourses in Philosophy, Religion, Literature, and the Arts.* Notre Dame: University of Notre Dame, 2007.

Garb, Jonathan. "The Cult of the Saints in Lurianic Kabbalah." *Jewish Quarterly Review* 98, no. 2 (2008): 203–229.

———. *Manifestations of Power in Jewish Mysticism.* [In Hebrew.] Jerusalem: Magnes Press, 2005.

———. *Shamanic Trance in Modern Kabbalah.* Chicago: University of Chicago Press, 2011.

———. *Yearnings of the Soul: Psychological Thought in Modern Kabbalah.* Chicago: University of Chicago Press, 2015.

Gellman, Jerome. "The Figure of Abraham in Hasidic Literature." *Harvard Theological Review* 91, no. 3 (1998): 279–300.

———. "Wellhausen and the Hasidim." *Modern Judaism* 26, no. 2 (2006): 193–207.

Gellman, Uriel. *The Emergence of Hasidism in Poland.* [In Hebrew.] Jerusalem: Zalman Shazar Center, 2018.

German, Terence J. *Hamann on Language and Religion.* Oxford: Oxford University Press, 1981.

Germano, David Francis. "Poetic Thought, the Intelligent Universe, and the Mystery of Self: The Tantric Synthesis of Rdzogs Chen in Fourteenth-Century Tibet." PhD diss., University of Wisconsin-Madison, 1992.

Giller, Pinchas. *Shalom Shar'abi and the Kabbalists of Beit El.* Oxford: Oxford University Press, 2008.

Ginzberg, Louis. *Students, Scholars, and Saints.* Philadelphia: Jewish Publication Society, 1945.

Girón-Negrón, Luis M. "Dionysian Thought in Sixteenth-Century Spanish Mystical Theology." *Modern Theology* 24 (2008): 693–706.

Goetschel, Roland. "Torah Lishmah as a Central Concept in the Degel Mahaneh Efrayim of Moses Hayyim Ephraim of Sudylkow." In *Hasidism Reappraised*, ed. Ada Rapoport-Albert, 258–267. London: Littman Library of Jewish Civilization, 1997.

Goldenberg, Robert. "Law and Spirit in Talmudic Religion." In *Jewish Spirituality*, vol. 1, *From the Bible Through the Middle Ages*, ed. Arthur Green, 232–252. New York: Crossroad, 1986.

Goldreich, Amos. *Automatic Writing in Zoharic Literature and Modernism*. [In Hebrew.] Los Angeles: Cherub Press, 2010.

Goody, Jack. "Religion and Ritual: The Definitional Problem." *British Journal of Sociology* 12, no. 2 (1961): 142–164.

Gordon, Peter Eli. "The Erotics of Negative Theology: Maimonides on Apprehension." *Jewish Studies Quarterly* 2, no. 1 (1995): 1–38.

Goshen-Gottstein, Alon. "God and Israel as Father and Son in Tannaitic Literature." [In Hebrew.] PhD diss., Hebrew University, 1987.

———. "Is Ma'aseh Bereshit Part of Ancient Jewish Mysticism." *Journal of Jewish Thought and Philosophy* 4 (1995): 185–201.

———. "Speech, Silence, Song: Epistemology and Theodicy in a Teaching of R. Nahman of Breslav." *Philosophia* 30, no. 1 (2003): 143–187.

Gottlieb, Efraim. "The Meaning of Prayer in Kabbalah." [In Hebrew.] In *Studies in the Kabbala Literature*, ed. Joseph Hacker, 38–55. Tel Aviv: Tel Aviv University Press, 1976.

Graetz, Heinrich. *History of the Jews*. Ed. and trans. Bella Lowy. Vol. 5. London, 1892.

Graham, William. *Beyond the Written Word: Oral Aspects of Scripture in the History of Religion*. Cambridge: Cambridge University Press, 1987.

de Grazia, Margreta. "The Secularization of Language in the Seventeenth Century." *Journal of the History of Ideas* 41, no. 2 (1980): 319–329.

Green, Arthur. "Around the Maggid's Table: *Tsaddik*, Leadership, and Popularization in the Circle of Dov Ber of Miedzyrzec." [In Hebrew.] *Zion* 78 (2013): 73–106.

———. "Buber, Scholem, and the *Me'or Eynayim*: Another Perspective on a Great Controversy." In *Swimming against the Current: Reimagining Jewish Tradition in the Twenty-First Century: Essays in Honor of Rabbi Chaim Seidler-Feller*, ed. David N. Myers and Shaul Seidler-Feller. Boston: Academic Studies Press, forthcoming.

———. "*Da'at*: Spiritual Awareness in a Hasidic Classic." In *Religious Truth: Essays in Jewish Theology of Religions*, ed. Alon Goshen-Gottstein. New York: Lexington Books, forthcoming.

———. *Devotion and Commandment: The Faith of Abraham in the Hasidic Imagination*. Cincinnati: Hebrew Union College Press, 1989.

———. "Early Hasidism: Some Old/New Questions." In *Hasidism Reappraised*, ed. Ada Rapoport-Albert, 441–446. London: Littman Library of Jewish Civilization, 1997.

———. "God's Need for Man: A Unitive Approach to the Writings of Abraham Joshua Heschel." *Modern Judaism* 35, no. 3 (2015): 247–261.

———. *A Guide to the Zohar*. Stanford: Stanford University Press, 2004.

———. "The Hasidic Homily: Mystical Performance and Hermeneutical Process." In *As a Perennial Spring: A Festschrift Honoring Rabbi Dr. Norman Lamm*, ed. Benzi Cohen, 237–265. New York: Downhill Publishing, 2013.

———. "The Hasidic Tsaddik and the Charisma of Relationship." In *A Festschrift for Moshe Idel*, ed. Ron Margolin and Avriel Bar-Levav, forthcoming.

———. "Hasidism: Discovery and Retreat." In *The Other Side of God: A Polarity in World Religions*, ed. Peter L. Berger, 104–130. Garden City, NY: Anchor Press, 1981.

———. "Hasidism and Its Response to Change." *Jewish History* 27, no. 2–4 (2013): 319–336.

———. *Keter: The Crown of God in Early Jewish Mysticism.* Princeton: Princeton University Press, 1997.

———. "Levi Yizhak of Berdichev on Miracles." In *The Heart of the Matter: Studies in Jewish Mysticism and Theology,* 254–268. Philadelphia: Jewish Publication Society, 2015.

———. "On Translating Hasidic Homilies." *Prooftexts* 3 (1983): 63–72.

———. "Sabbath as Temple: Some Thoughts on Space and Time in Judaism." In *Go and Study: Essays and Studies in Honor of Alfred Jospe,* ed. Raphael Jospe and Samuel Z. Fishman, 287–305. Washington, DC: B'nai B'rith Hillel Foundations, 1980.

———. "Some Aspects of Qabbalat Shabbat." In *Sabbath—Idea, History, Reality,* ed. Gerald J. Blidstein, 95–118. Beer Sheva: Ben Gurion University of the Negev Press, 2004.

———. "Typologies of Leadership and the Hasidic Zaddiq." In *Jewish Spirituality,* vol. 2, *From the Sixteenth-Century Revival to the Present,* ed. Arthur Green, 127–156. New York: Crossroad, 1987.

———. "The Zaddiq as Axis Mundi in Later Judaism." *Journal of the American Academy of Religion* 45, no. 3 (1977): 327–347.

Green, Arthur, with Ebn Leader, Ariel Evan Mayse, and Or N. Rose. *Speaking Torah: Spiritual Teachings from Around the Maggid's Table.* 2 vols. Woodstock: Jewish Lights, 2013.

Greenberg, Moshe. *Biblical Prose Prayer as a Window to the Popular Religion of Ancient Israel.* Berkeley: University of California Press, 1983.

Gries, Zeev. "Between Literature and History." [In Hebrew.] *Tura* 3 (1994): 153–181.

———. *The Book in Early Hasidism: Genres, Authors, Scribes, Managing Editors, and Its Review by Their Contemporaries and Scholars.* [In Hebrew.] Tel Aviv: Ha-Kibbutz ha-Me'uhad, 1992.

———. *The Conduct Literature (Regimen Vitae): Its History and Place in the Life of Beshtian Hasidism.* [In Hebrew.] Jerusalem: Bialik Institute, 1989.

———. "The Editing of *Tsavat ha-Ribash.*" [In Hebrew.] *Kirjat Sefer* 52 (1977): 187–210.

———. "The Fashioning of *Hanhagot* (Regimen Vitae) Literature at the End of the Sixteenth Century and During the Seventeenth Century and Its Historical Significance." [In Hebrew.] *Tarbiz* 56 (1986–1987): 527–581.

———. "From Myth to Ethos—Outlines for the History of Rabbi Avraham of Kalisk." [In Hebrew.] In *Nation and History,* ed. Shmuel Ettinger, 2:117–146. Jerusalem: Zalman Shazar Center, 1983.

———. "The Hasidic Conduct Literature from the Mid-18th Century to the '30s of the 19th Century." [In Hebrew.] *Zion* 46, nos. 3–4 (1981): 198–236 and 278–305.

———. "The Hasidic Managing Editor as an Agent of Culture." In *Hasidism Reappraised,* ed. Ada Rapoport-Albert, 141–155. London: Littman Library of Jewish Civilization, 1997.

———. "Hasidic Prayer Stories as a Source for the Hasidic Weltanschauung." [In Hebrew.] In *Shefa Tal: Studies in Jewish Thought in Honor of Bracha Sack,* ed. Zeev Gries, 219–235. Beer-Sheva: Ben Gurion University of the Negev Press, 2004.

———. "Hasidism: The Present State of Research and Some Desirable Priorities (Sequel)." *Numen* 34 (1987): 196–200.

———. *The Hebrew Book: An Outline of Its History.* [In Hebrew.] Jerusalem: Bialik Institute, 2015.

———. "The Historical Image of the Besht—Between the Scalpel of the Historian to the Paint Brush of the Literature Researcher." [In Hebrew.] *Kabbalah* 5 (2000): 418–421.

Grözinger, Karl Erich. "The Source Value of the Basic Recensions of *Shivhei haBesht*." In *Hasidism Reappraised*, ed. Ada Rapoport-Albert, 354–363. London: Littman Library of Jewish Civilization, 1997.

Haeri, Niloofar. *Sacred Language, Ordinary People: Dilemmas of Culture and Politics in Egypt*. New York: Palgrave Macmillan, 2003.

Halbertal, Moshe. *By Way of Truth: Nahmanides and the Creation of Tradition*. [In Hebrew.] Jerusalem: Shalom Hartman, 2006.

———. *Concealment and Revelation: Esotericism in Jewish Thought and Its Philosophical Implications*. Trans. Jackie Feldman. Princeton: Princeton University Press, 2007.

———. *People of the Book: Canon, Meaning, and Authority*, Cambridge, MA: Harvard University Press, 1997.

Hallamish, Moshe. *Kabbalah: In Liturgy, Halakhah, and Customs*. [In Hebrew.] Ramat-Gan: Bar-Ilan University Press, 2000.

———. "On Silence in Kabbalah." [In Hebrew.] In *Religion and Language: Philosophical Essays*, ed. Moshe Hallamish and Asa Kasher, 79–89. Tel Aviv: Mif'alim Universati'iyim, 1981.

———. "Toward the Source of the Kabbalistic Expression: 'One Who Blows—Blows from Within Himself.'" [In Hebrew.] *Bar-Ilan* 13 (1976): 211–223.

———. "The Unification of 'Every One': One Commandment and One Letter." [In Hebrew.] *Daat* 71 (2011): 25–52.

Hallamish, Moshe, Hannah Kasher, and Hanokh Ben Pazi, eds. *Moses the Man: Master of Prophets*. [In Hebrew.] Ramat-Gan: Bar-Ilan University Press, 2010.

Hamann, Johann Georg. "Aesthetica in Nuce: A Rhapsody in Cabbalistic Prose." In *Hamann: Writings on Philosophy and Language*, ed. Kenneth Haynes, 60–95. Cambridge: Cambridge University Press, 2007.

———. "The Last Will and Testament of the Knight of the Rose-Cross." In Haynes, *Hamann*, 96–110. Cambridge: Cambridge University Press, 2007.

Haran, Raya. "R. Abraham of Kalisk and Shneur Zalman of Ladi—A Friendship Cut Off." [In Hebrew.] In *Kolot Rabbim: Rivka Schatz-Uffenheimer Memorial Volume,* ed. Rachel Elior and Joseph Dan, 2:399–428. Jerusalem: Hebrew University, 1996.

Harrison, Paul. "Mediums and Messages: Reflections on the Production of Mahayana Sutra." *Eastern Buddhist* 35 (2003): 115–151.

Hartmann, Jens-Uwe. "The Parable of a Man and His Two Ladies: A Fragment from an Unknown Story Collection." In *Festschrift for Prof. Xu Wenkan on the Occasion of His 70th Birthday*, ed. Xu Quansheng and Liu Zhen, 189–199. Lanzhou University Press, 2015.

Harvey, Warren Zev. "Judah Halevi's Synesthetic Theory of Prophecy and a Note on the *Zohar*." [In Hebrew.] *Jerusalem Studies in Jewish Thought* 12 (1996): 141–155.

———. "On Maimonides' Allegorical Readings of Scripture." In *Interpretation and Allegory: Antiquity to the Modern Period*, ed. Jon Whitman, 181–188. Leiden: Brill, 2000.

———. "What Did the Rymanover Really Say About the Aleph of *Anokhi*?" [In Hebrew.] *Kabbalah* 34 (2016): 297–314.

Havelock, Eric Alfred. *The Muse Learns to Write: Reflections on Orality and Literacy from Antiquity to the Present*. New Haven: Yale University Press, 1986.

Hayman, Peter. "Was God a Magician? Sefer Yesira and Jewish Magic." *Journal of Jewish Studies* 40 (1989): 233–234. Hecker, Joel. "Kissing Kabbalists: Hierarchy, Reciprocity, and Equality." *Studies in Jewish Civilization* 18 (2008): 171–208.

———. *Mystical Bodies, Mystical Meals: Eating and Embodiment in Medieval Kabbalah.* Detroit: Wayne State University Press, 2005.

Heine, Steven, and Dale S. Wright, eds. *The Koan: Texts and Contexts in Zen Buddhism.* Oxford: Oxford University Press, 2000.

Heinemann, Joseph. "The Fixed and the Fluid in Jewish Prayer." In *Prayer in Judaism: Continuity and Change,* ed. Gabriel Cohn and Harold Fisch, 45–52. Northvale, NJ: Jason Aronson, 1996.

———. *Prayer in the Talmud: Forms and Patterns.* Berlin: De Gruyter, 1977.Hellner-Eshed, Melila. *A River Flows from Eden: The Language of Mystical Experience in the Zohar.* Trans. Nathan Wolski. Stanford: Stanford University Press, 2009.

Herzfeld, Smadar. *Trail of Miracles.* Trans. Aloma Halter. Seattle: AmazonCrossing, 2017.

Heschel, Abraham Joshua. *The Circle of the Baal Shem Tov: Studies in Hasidism.* Chicago: University of Chicago Press, 1985.

———. *God in Search of Man: A Philosophy of Judaism.* New York: Farrar, Straus and Giroux, 1976.

———. "The God of Israel and Christian Renewal." In *Moral Grandeur and Spiritual Audacity: Essays,* ed. Susannah Heschel, 268–285. New York: Farrar, Straus and Giroux, 1996.

———. *Kotsk: A Struggle for Integrity.* [In Yiddish.] 2 vols. Tel Aviv: Ha-Menorah, 1973.

Holdrege, Barbara A. "The Bride of Israel: The Ontological Status of Scripture in the Rabbinic and Kabbalistic Traditions." In *Rethinking Scripture: Essays from a Comparative Perspective,* ed. Miriam Levering, 236–239. Albany: State University of New York Press, 1989.

———. *Veda and Torah: Transcending the Textuality of Scripture.* Albany: State University of New York Press, 1996.

Hollenback, Jess Byron. *Mysticism: Experience, Response, and Empowerment.* University Park: Pennsylvania State University Press, 1996.

Horwitz, Rivka. "Abraham Joshua Heschel on Prayer and His Hasidic Sources." *Modern Judaism* 19, no. 3 (1999): 295–298.

———. "Hamman and Rosenzweig on Language—The Revival of Myth." *Daat* 38 (1997): v–xxviii.

Hundert, Gershon D. *Jews in Poland-Lithuania in the Eighteenth Century.* Berkeley: University of California Press, 2004.

Hurwitz, Siegmund. "Psychological Aspects in Early Hasidic Literature." In *Timeless Documents of the Soul,* trans. Hildegard Nagel, 149–240. Evanston: Northwestern University Press, 1968.

Huss, Boaz. "Rabbi Joseph Gikatilia's Definition of Symbolism and Its Influence on Kabbalistic Literature." [In Hebrew.] In *Kolot Rabbim: Essays in Memory of Rivka Schatz-Uffenheimer,* ed. Rachel Elior and Joseph Dan, 1:57–176. Jerusalem: Magnes Press, 1996.

Idel, Moshe. *Absorbing Perfections: Kabbalah and Interpretation.* New Haven: Yale University Press, 2002.

———. *"Adonay Sefatay Tiftah*: Models of Understanding Prayer in Early Hasidism." *Kabbalah* 18 (2008): 7–111.

———. *Ascensions on High in Jewish Mysticism: Pillars, Lines, Ladders.* Budapest: Central European University Press, 2005.

———. *Ben: Sonship and Jewish Mysticism.* London: Continuum, 2007.

———. "The BeSHT as a Prophet and Talismanic Magician." [In Hebrew.] In *Studies in Jewish Narrative: Ma'aseh Sippur Presented to Yoav Elstein,* ed. Avidov Lipsker and Rella Kushelevsky, 21–145. Ramat-Gan: Bar-Ilan University Press, 2006.

———. "'The Besht Passed His Hand over His Face': On the Besht's Influence on His Followers—Some Remarks." In *After Spirituality: Studies in Mystical Traditions*, ed. Philip Wexler and Jonathan Garb, 79–106. New York: Peter Lang, 2012.

———. "The Concept of Torah in *Heikhalot* Literature and Its Metamorphoses in Kabbalah." [In Hebrew.] *Jerusalem Studies in Jewish Thought* 1 (1981): 23–84.

———. *Golem: Jewish Magical and Mystical Traditions on the Artificial Anthropoid*. Albany: State University of New York Press, 1990.

———. *Hasidism: Between Ecstasy and Magic*. Albany: State University of New York Press, 1995.

———. "*Hitbodedut* as Concentration in Ecstatic Kabbalah." In *Jewish Spirituality*, vol. 1, *From the Bible Through the Middle Ages*, ed. Arthur Green, 405–438. New York: Crossroad, 1986.

———. "The Image of Man Above the *Sefirot*: David ben Yehuda he-Hasid's Theosophy of Ten Supernal *Sahsahot* and Its Reverberations." *Kabbalah* 20 (2009): 181–212.

———. "Infinities of Torah in Kabbalah." In *Midrash and Literature*, ed. Geoffrey H. Hartman and Sanford Budick, 141–157. New Haven: Yale University Press, 1986.

———. "Jewish Kabbalah and Platonism in the Middle Ages and Renaissance." In *Neoplatonism and Jewish Thought*, ed. Lenn E. Goodman, 319–351. Albany: State University of New York, 1992.

———. "The Journey to Paradise: The Jewish Transformations of a Greek Mythological Motif." [In Hebrew.] *Jerusalem Studies in Jewish Folklore* 2 (1982): 7–16.

———. *Kabbalah: New Perspectives*. New Haven: Yale University Press, 1988.

———. "Kabbalistic Prayer in Provence." [In Hebrew.] *Tarbiz* 62 (1993): 278–279.

———. *Language, Torah, and Hermeneutics in Abraham Abulafia*. Trans. Menahem Kallus. Albany: State University of New York Press, 1989.

———. "Martin Buber and Gershom Scholem on Hasidism: A Critical Appraisal." In *Hasidism Reappraised*, ed. Ada Rapoport-Albert, 389–403. London: Littman Library of Jewish Civilization, 1997.

———. "Modes of Cleaving to the Letters in the Teachings of Israel Baal Shem Tov: A Sample Analysis." *Jewish History* 27, no. 2-4 (2013): 299–317.

———. "Multiple Forms of Redemption in Kabbalah and Hasidism." *Jewish Quarterly Review* 101, no. 1 (2011): 27–70.

———. *The Mystical Experience in Abraham Abulafia*. Trans. Jonathan Chipman. Albany: State University of New York Press, 1989.

———. *Old Worlds, New Mirrors: On Jewish Mysticism and Twentieth-Century Thought*. Philadelphia: University of Pennsylvania Press, 2010.

———. "On the Concept of *Zimzum* in Kabbalah and Its Research." [In Hebrew.] *Jerusalem Studies in Jewish Thought* 10 (1992): 59–112.

———. "'One from a Town, Two from a Clan': The Diffusion of Lurianic Kabbala and Sabbateanism: A Reexamination." *Jewish History* 7, no. 2 (1993): 79–104.

———. "The Parable of the Son of the King and the Imaginary Walls in Early Hasidism." In *Judaism—Topics, Fragments, Faces, Identities*, ed. Haviva Pedaya and Ephraim Meir, 87–116. Beer Sheva: Ben Gurion University of the Negev Press, 2007.

———. "Prayer, Ecstasy, and 'Alien Thoughts' in the Religious Experience of the Besht." In *Let the Old Make Way for the New: Studies in the Social and Cultural History of Eastern European Jewry Presented to Immanuel Etkes*, vol. 1, *Hasidism and the Musar Movement*, ed. David Assaf and Ada Rapoport-Albert, 57–120. Jerusalem: Zalman Shazar Center, 2009.

———. "Reification of Language in Jewish Mysticism." In *Mysticism and Language*, ed. Steven T. Katz, 42–79. New York: Oxford University Press, 1992.

———. "Torah: Between Presence and Representation of the Divine in Jewish Mysticism." In *Representation in Religion: Studies in Honor of Moshe Barasch*, ed. Jan Assmann and Albert I. Baumgarten, 197–235. Leiden: Brill, 2001.

———. "The *Tsadik* and His Soul's Sparks: From Kabbalah to Hasidism." *Jewish Quarterly Review* 103, no. 2 (2013): 196–240.

———. "White Letters: From R. Levi Isaac of Berditchev's Views to Postmodern Hermeneutics." *Modern Judaism* 26, no. 2 (2006): 169–192.

———. "'Your Word Stands Firm in Heaven'—An Inquiry into the Early Traditions of Israel Baal Shem Tov and Their Reverberations in Hasidism." [In Hebrew.] *Kabbalah* 20 (2009): 219–286.

Inge, William Ralph. *Christian Mysticism: Considered in Eight Lectures Delivered Before the University of Oxford*. London: Methuen, 1899.

Izmirlieva, Valentina. *All the Names of the Lord: Lists, Mysticism, and Magic*. Chicago: University of Chicago Press, 2008.

Jacobs, Louis. *Hasidic Prayer*. Oxford: Littman Library of Jewish Civilization, 2001.

———. *Hasidic Thought*. New York: Behrman House, 1976.

———. "The Uplifting of Sparks in Later Jewish Mysticism." In *Jewish Spirituality*, vol. 2, *From the Sixteenth-Century Revival to the Present*, ed. Arthur Green, 99–126. New York: Crossroad, 1987.

James, William. *The Varieties of Religious Experience: A Study in Human Nature*. New York: Longmans, Green, 1904.

Janowitz, Naomi. *Icons of Power: Ritual Practices in Late Antiquity*. University Park: Pennsylvania State University Press, 2002.

———. *The Poetics of Ascent: Theories of Language in a Rabbinic Ascent Text*. Albany: State University of New York Press, 2012.

———. "Re-creating Genesis: The Metapragmatics of Divine Speech." In *Reflexive Language: Reported Speech and Metapragmatics*, ed. John A. Lucy, 393–405. Cambridge: Cambridge University Press, 1993.

Jay, Nancy. "Gender and Dichotomy." *Feminist Studies* 7, no. 1 (1981): 38–56.

Johns, Adrian. *The Nature of the Book: Print and Knowledge in the Making*. Chicago: University of Chicago Press, 1998.

Juynboll, Gautier H. A. *Studies on the Origins and Uses of Islamic Hadith*. Brookfield, VT: Variorum Publishing, 1996.

Kahana, Maoz. "Changing the World's Measures—Rabbi Zeev Olesker and the Revolutionary Scholars Circle in Brody Kloyz." [In Hebrew.] *AJS Review* 37, no. 1 (2013): 29–53.

Kahana, Maoz, and Ariel Evan Mayse. "Hasidic *Halakhah*: Reappraising the Interface of Spirit and Law." *AJS Review* 41, no. 2 (2017): 375–408.

Kallus, Menachem. *The Pillar of Prayer: Teachings of Contemplative Guidance in Prayer, Sacred Study, and the Spiritual Life from the Ba'al Shem Tov and His Circle*. Louisville: Fons Vitae, 2011.

———. "The Relation of the Baal Shem Tov to the Practice of Lurianic *Kavvanot* in Light of His Comments on the Siddur Rashkov." *Kabbalah* 2 (1997): 151–167. Kanarfogel, Ephraim. "Compensation for the Study of Torah in Medieval Rabbinic Thought." In *Of Scholars, Savants, and Their Texts: Studies in Philosophy and Religious Thought; Essays in Honor of Arthur Hyman*, ed. Ruth Link-Salinger, 135–147. New York: Lang, 1989.

Karlinsky, Nahum. "The Dawn of Hasidic—Haredi Historiography." *Modern Judaism* 27, no. 1 (2007): 20–46.

Katz, Jacob. "Halakhah and Kabbalah and Competing Disciplines of Study." In *Divine Law in Human Hands: Case Studies in Halakhic Flexibility*, 56–87. Jerusalem: Magnes Press, 1998.

———. *Tradition and Crisis: Jewish Society at the End of the Middle Ages*. Trans. Bernard Dov Cooperman. Syracuse: Syracuse University Press, 2000.

Katz, Steven T. "The 'Conservative' Character of Mystical Experience." In *Mysticism and Religious Traditions*, ed. Steven T. Katz, 3–60. New York: Oxford University Press, 1983.

———. "Language, Epistemology, and Mysticism." In *Mysticism and Philosophical Analysis*, ed. Steven T. Katz, 22–74. New York: Oxford University Press, 1978.

Kauffman, Tsippi. "The Hasidic Story: A Call for Narrative Religiosity." *Journal of Jewish Thought and Philosophy* 22, no. 2 (2014): 101–126.

———. "Hasidic Women: Beyond Egalitarianist Discourse." In *Be-Ron Yahad: Studies in Jewish Thought and Theology in Honor of Nehemia Polen*, ed. Ariel Evan Mayse and Arthur Green, 223–257. Boston: Academic Studies Press, 2019.

———. *In All Your Ways Know Him: The Concept of God and Avodah be-Gashmiyut in the Early Stages of Hasidism*. [In Hebrew.] Ramat-Gan: Bar-Ilan University Press, 2009.

———. "Theological Aspects of Bilingualism in Hasidic Society." [In Hebrew.] *Gal-Ed* 23 (2013): 131–156.

———. "Typology of the Tsaddik in the Teachings of Abraham the Angel." *Kabbalah* 33 (2015): 239–272.

Keane, Webb. "Religious Language." *Annual Review of Anthropology* 26, no. 1 (1997): 47–71.

Kelber, Werner H. *The Oral and the Written Gospel: The Hermeneutics of Speaking and Writing in the Synoptic Tradition, Mark, Paul, and Q*. Bloomington: Indiana University Press, 1997.

Kellner, Menachem. "Maimonides on the 'Normality' of Hebrew." In *Judaism and Modernity: The Religious Philosophy of David Hartman*, ed. Jonathan W. Malino, 413–444. Burlington, VT: Ashgate, 2004.

Key, Alexander. *Language Between God and the Poets: Ma'na in the Eleventh Century*. Berkeley: University of California Press, 2018.

Kimelman, Reuven. *Mystical Meaning of Lekhah Dodi and Kabbalat Shabbat*. [In Hebrew.] Jerusalem: Magnes Press, 2003.

Kirkwood, William G. "Parables as Metaphors and Examples." *Quarterly Journal of Speech* 71, no. 4 (1985): 422–440.

———. "Storytelling and Self-Confrontation: Parables as Communication Strategies." *Quarterly Journal of Speech* 69, no. 1 (1983): 58–74.

Kosman, Admiel. "Breath, Kiss, and Speech as the Source of the Animation of Life: Ancient Foundations of Rabbinic Homilies on the Giving of the Torah as the Kiss of God." In *Self, Soul, and Body in Religious Experience*, ed. Albert I. Baumgarten, Jan Assmann, and Guy G. Stroumsa, 96–124. Leiden: Brill, 1998.

Krassen, Miles. *Uniter of Heaven and Earth: Rabbi Meshullam Feibush Heller of Zbarazh and the Rise of Hasidism in Eastern Galicia*. Albany: State University of New York Press, 1998.

Kripke, Saul A. *Wittgenstein on Rules and Private Language: An Elementary Exposition*. Cambridge, MA: Harvard University Press, 1982.

Lachter, Hartley. *Kabbalistic Revolution: Reimagining Judaism in Medieval Spain*. New Brunswick: Rutgers University Press, 2014.

Lakoff, George, and Mark Johnson. *Metaphors We Live By*. Chicago: University of Chicago Press, 1980.

Lamm, Norman. "Pukhovitzer's Concept of *Torah Lishmah.*" *Jewish Social Studies* 30, no. 3 (1968): 149–156.

———. *Torah Lishmah: Torah for Torah's Sake in the Works of Rabbi Hayyim of Volozhin and His Contemporaries*. New York: Ktav Publication House, 1989.

Lederberg, Netanel. *The Gateway to Infinity: Rabbi Dov Ber, the Maggid Meisharim of Mezhirich*. [In Hebrew.] Jerusalem: Rubin Mass, 2011.

Levy, Ze'ev. "Johann Georg Hamann's Concept of Judaism and Controversy with Mendelssohn's *Jerusalem.*" *Leo Baeck Institute Yearbook* 29, no. 1 (1984): 295–329.

Liebes, Yehuda. "The Account of the Chariot and the Account of Creation as Mystical Teachings in Philo of Alexandria." [In Hebrew.] *Kabbalah* 19 (2009): 323–335.

———. *Ars Poetica in "Sefer Yetsirah."* [In Hebrew.] Jerusalem: Schocken Books, 2000.

———. "Myth vs. Symbol in the Zohar and in Lurianic Kabbalah." In *Essential Papers on Kabbalah*, ed. Lawrence Fine, 212–244. New York: New York University Press, 1995.

———. "Nahman of Bratslav and Ludwig Wittgenstein." [In Hebrew.] *Dimui* 19 (2001): 10–13, 134.

———. *On Sabbateanism and Its Kabbalah: Collected Essays*. [In Hebrew.] Jerusalem: Bialik Institute, 1995.

———. "The Pool, the Daughter, and the *Male* in the Book Bahir." [In Hebrew.] *Kabbalah* 21 (2010): 131–138.

———. "Zohar and Eros." [In Hebrew.] *Alpayyim* 9 (1994): 67–119.

Lifschitz, Avi. *Language and Enlightenment: The Berlin Debates of the Eighteenth Century*. Oxford: Oxford University Press, 2016.

Lobel, Diana. *Between Mysticism and Philosophy: Sufi Language of Religious Experience in Judah Ha-Levi's "Kuzari."* Albany: State University of New York, 2000.

Loewenthal, Naftali. *Communicating the Infinite: The Emergence of the Habad School*. Chicago: University of Chicago Press, 1990.

———. "Rabbi Shneur Zalman of Liadi's *Kitzur Likkutei Amarim* British Library Or 10456." In *Studies in Jewish Manuscripts*, ed. Joseph Dan and K. Hermann, 89–137. Tübingen: Mohr Siebeck, 1999.

Lorberbaum, Menachem. "'Attain the Attribute of *'Ayyin*': The Mystical Religiosity of *Maggid Devarav Le-Ya'aqov.*" [In Hebrew.] *Kabbalah* 31 (2014): 169–235.

———. "Rethinking *Halakhah* in Modern Eastern Europe: Mysticism, Antinomianism, Positivism." In *The Cambridge Companion to Judaism and Law*, ed. Christine Hayes, 232–259. Cambridge: Cambridge University Press, 2017.

Maciá, Lorena Miralles. "The Fable of 'The Middle-Aged Man with Two Wives': From the Aesopian Motif to the Babylonian Talmud Version in b. B. Qam. 60b." *Journal for the Study of Judaism* 39, no. 2 (2008): 267–281.

Magid, Shaul. *From Metaphysics to Midrash: Myth, History, and the Interpretation of Scripture in Lurianic Kabbala*. Bloomington: Indiana University Press, 2008.

———. *Hasidism Incarnate: Hasidism, Christianity, and the Construction of Modern Judaism*. Stanford: Stanford University Press, 2015.

Maimon, Solomon. *The Autobiography of Solomon Maimon: The Complete Translation*. Trans. Paul Reitter. Ed. Yitzhak Y. Melamed and Abraham Socher. Princeton: Princeton University Press, 2018.

Manguel, Alberto. *A History of Reading*. New York: Viking, 1996.

Marcus, Ivan. "Rashi's Historiosophy in the Introductions to His Bible Commentaries." *Revue des études juives* 157, no. 1-2 (1998): 47–55.

Margolin, Ron. *The Human Temple: Religious Interiorization and the Structuring of Inner Life in Early Hasidism*. [In Hebrew.] Jerusalem: Magnes Press, 2005.

Marmur, Michael. "God of Language." In *Imagining the Jewish God*, ed. Leonard Kaplan and Ken Koltun-Fromm, 267–292. Lanham, MD: Lexington Books, 2016.

Matt, Daniel C. "*Ayin*: The Concept of Nothingness in Jewish Mysticism." In *Essential Papers on Kabbalah*, ed. Lawrence Fine, 67–108. New York: New York University Press, 1995.

———. *The Essential Kabbalah: The Heart of Jewish Mysticism*. San Francisco: HarperCollins, 1996.

———. "The Mystic and the Mizwot." In *Jewish Spirituality*, vol. 1, *From the Bible Through the Middle Ages*, ed. Arthur Green, 367–404. New York: Crossroad, 1988.

Mayse, Ariel Evan. "Beyond the Letters: The Question of Language in the Teachings of R. Dov Baer of Mezritch." PhD diss., Harvard University, 2015.

———. "Double-Take: Textual Artifacts and the Memory of Hasidic Teachings." *Kabbalah* 37 (2017): 37–93.

———. "The Ever-Changing Path: Visions of Legal Diversity in Hasidic Literature." *Conversations* 23 (2015): 84–115.

———. "Expanding the Boundaries of the Holy: Hasidic Devotion, Sacred Speech, and Early Modern Jewish Thought." *Jewish Social Studies* n.s., 25, no. 1 (2019): 45–101.

———. "'Like a Moth to the Flame': The Death of Nadav and Avihu in Hasidic Literature." In *Be-Ron Yahad: Studies in Jewish Thought and Theology in Honor of Nehemia Polen*, ed. Ariel Evan Mayse and Arthur Green, 364–406. Boston: Academic Studies Press, 2019.

———. "'Moving Mezritsh': The Legacy of the Maggid and the Hasidic Community in the Land of Israel." *Jewish History* (forthcoming).

———. "Time and Presence: Eternity in Hasidism." In *Eternity: A History*, ed. Yitzhak Melamed, 231–238. Oxford: Oxford University Press, 2016.

———. "The Voices of Moses: Theologies of Revelation in an Early Hasidic Circle." *Harvard Theological Review* 112, no. 1 (2019): 101–125.

———. "Who Amongst You Is Transcribing my Teachings?': Orality and Vitality in Written Hasidic Homilies." [In Yiddish.] *Yerusholaymer Almanakh* 29 (2012): 364–381.

Mayse, Ariel Evan, and Daniel Reiser. "Territories and Textures: The Hasidic Sermon as the Crossroads of Language and Culture." *Jewish Social Studies*, n.s., 24, no. 1 (2018): 127–160.

Mazor, Yaakov. "The Power of Song in Hasidic Thought and Its Role in Religious and Social Life." [In Hebrew.] *Yuval: Studies of the Jewish Music Research Centre* 7 (2002): 23–53.

McGinn, Bernard, ed. *The Essential Writings of Christian Mysticism*. New York: Random House, 2006.

———. "The Language of Inner Experience in Christian Mysticism." *Spiritus: A Journal of Christian Spirituality* 1, no. 2 (2001): 156–171.

———. "Theoretical Foundations: The Modern Study of Mysticism." In *The Foundations of Mysticism*, 265–343. New York: Crossroad, 1991.

McGuinness, B. F., T. Nyberg, G. H. von Wright, eds. *ProtoTractatus—An Early Version of "Tractatus Logico- Philosophicus."* Trans. D. F. Pears and B. F. McGuinness. Ithaca: Cornell University Press, 1971.

Meir, Jonatan. "Hasidism: Unknown Lectures by Gershom Scholem from 1945." [In Hebrew.] *Kabbalah* 43 (2019): 93–120.

———. *Literary Hasidism: The Life and Words of Michael Levi Rodkinson*. Trans. Jeffrey G. Amshalem. Syracuse: Syracuse University Press, 2016.

Melamed, Yitzhak Y. "Spinozism, Acosmism, and Hassidism: A Closed Circle." In *The Concept of Judaism in German Idealism*, ed. Amit Kravitz and Jörg Noller, 75–85. Berlin: Suhrkamp Verlag, 2018.

Mendelssohn, Moses. *Jerusalem: Or on Religious Power and Judaism*. Trans. Allan Arkush. Hanover: Brandeis University Press, 1986.

Miura, Isshū, and Ruth Fuller Sasaki. *The Zen Koan: Its History and Use in Rinzai Zen*. New York: Harcourt Brace, 1965.

Mondshine, Yehoshua. *Migdal 'Oz*. Kefar Habad: Mekhon Lubavitch, 1980.

Mopsik, Charles. "Pensée, voix et parole dans le Zohar." *Revue de l'histoire des religions* 213, no. 4 (1996): 385–414.

Moseson, Chaim Elly. "From Spoken Word to the Discourse of the Academy: Reading the Sources for the Teachings of the BeSHT." PhD diss., Boston University, 2017.

Muffs, Yochanan. "The Prayer of the Prophets." [In Hebrew.] *Molad* 7 (1975): 204–210.

———. "Who Will Stand in the Breach? A Study of Prophetic Intercession." In *Love and Joy: Law, Language, and Religion in Ancient Israel*, 9–48. New York: Jewish Theological Seminary of America, 1992.

Nadler, Allan. *The Faith of the Mithnagdim: Rabbinic Responses to Hasidic Rapture*. Baltimore: Johns Hopkins University Press, 1997.

Nahon, Gérard. "Orality and Literacy: The French Tosaphists." In *Studies in Medieval Jewish Intellectual and Social History: Festschrift in Honor of Robert Chazan*, ed. David Engel, Lawrence H. Schiffman, and Elliot R. Wolfson, 145–168. Leiden: Brill, 2012.

Nasr, Seyyed Hossein. "The Heart of the Faithful Is the Throne of the All-Merciful." In *Paths to the Heart: Sufism and the Christian East*, ed. James S. Cutsinger, 32–45. Bloomington: World Wisdom, 2002.

———. *Knowledge and the Sacred*. Albany: State University of New York, 1989.

Nigal, Gedalyah. "Analysis of an Early Hasidic Manuscript." [In Hebrew.] In *Heker ve-'Iyyun be-Mada'ei ha-Yahadut*, ed. Yaacov Bahat, Mordechai Ben-Asher, and Terry Fenton, 177–192. Haifa: Haifa University, 1976.

———. *The Hasidic Tale*. Trans. Edward Levin. Oxford: Littman Library of Jewish Civilization, 2008.

———. "A Primary Source for Hasidic Tales: On the Book *Keter Shem Tov* and Its Sources." [In Hebrew.] In *Studies in Hasidism*, 2:349–364. Jerusalem: Ha-makhon le-Heker ha-Sifrut ha-Hasidit, 1999.

Olson, David R. "From Utterance to Text: The Bias of Language in Speech and Writing." *Harvard Educational Review* 47, no. 3 (1977): 257–281.

Ong, Walter J. *Orality and Literacy: The Technologizing of the Word*. London: Methuen, 1982.

———. *The Presence of the Word: Some Prolegomena for Cultural and Religious History*. New Haven: Yale University Press, 1967.

Oron, Michal. "The Narrative of the Letters and Its Source: A Study of a Zoharic Midrash on the Letters of the Alphabet." [In Hebrew.] In *Studies in Jewish Mysticism, Philosophy, and Ethical Literature Presented to Isaiah Tishby on His Seventy-Fifth Birthday*, ed. Joseph Dan and Joseph Hacker, 97–110. Jerusalem: Magnes Press, 1986.

Otto, Rudolf. *The Idea of the Holy: An Inquiry into the Non-Rational Factor in the Idea of the Divine and Its Relation to the Rational*. Trans. John W. Harvey. London: Oxford University Press, 1958.

Pachter, Mordechai. "Smallness and Greatness." In *Roots of Faith and Devequt: Studies in the History of Kabbalistic Ideas*, 185–233. Los Angeles: Cherub Press, 2004.

Papo, Eliezer. "From Messianic Apologetics to Missionary Counterattack in the Sabbatian Sacred Romancero." *Jewish Quarterly Review* 107, no. 4 (2017): 476–505.

Patton, Kimberley C. "Juggling Torches: Why We Still Need Comparative Religion." In *A Magic Still Dwells: Comparative Religion in the Postmodern Age*, ed. Kimberly C. Patton and B. C. Ray, 153–171. Berkeley: University of California Press, 2000.

———. *Religion of the Gods: Ritual, Paradox, and Reflexivity*. Oxford: Oxford University Press, 2009.

Pedaya, Haviva. "The Baal Shem Tov, R. Jacob Joseph of Polonnoye, and the Maggid of Mezhirech: Outlines for a Religious Typology." [In Hebrew.] *Daat* 45 (2000): 25–73.

———. "The BeSHT's Holy Epistle." [In Hebrew.] *Zion* 70 (2005): 311–354.

———. "The Great Mother: The Struggle Between Nahmanides and the Zohar Circle." In *Temps i espais de la Girona jueva*, ed. Silvia Planas i Marcé, 311–328. Girona: Patronat del Call de Girona, 2011.

———. *Nahmanides: Cyclical Time and Holy Text*. [In Hebrew.] Tel Aviv: Am Oved, 2003.

———. *Name and Sanctuary in the Teaching of R. Isaac the Blind: A Comparative Study in the Writings of the Earliest Kabbalists*. [In Hebrew.] Jerusalem: Magnes Press, 2001.

———. "On the Development of the Social-Religious-Economic Model of Hasidism: The *Pidyon*, the *Havurah*, and the Pilgrimage." [In Hebrew.] In *Zaddik and Devotees: Historical and Sociological Aspects of Hasidism*, ed. David Assaf, 343–397. Jerusalem: Zalman Shazar Center, 2001.

———. "Two Types of Ecstatic Experience in Hasidism." [In Hebrew.] *Daat* 55 (2005): 73–108.

———. *Vision and Speech: Models of Revelatory Experience in Jewish Mysticism*. [In Hebrew.] Los Angeles: Cherub Press, 2002.

Penn, Michael Philip. *Kissing Christians: Ritual and Community in the Late Ancient Church*. Philadelphia: University of Pennsylvania Press, 2005.

Perloff, Marjorie. *Wittgenstein's Ladder: Poetic Language and the Strangeness of the Ordinary*. Chicago: University of Chicago Press, 1999.

Petrovsky-Shtern, Yohanan. *The Golden Age Shtetl: A New History of Jewish Life in East Europe*. Princeton: Princeton University Press, 2014.

———. "The Master of an Evil Name: Hillel Ba'al Shem and His *Sefer ha-Heshek*." *AJS Review* 28, no. (2004): 217–248.

———. "'You Will Find It in the Pharmacy': Practical Kabbalah and Natural Medicine in the Polish-Lithuanian Commonwealth, 1690–1750." In *Holy Dissent: Jewish and Christian Mystics in Eastern Europe*, ed. Glenn Dynner, 13–54. Detroit: Wayne State University Press, 2011.

Piekarz, Mendel. *The Beginning of Hasidism: Ideological Trends in Derush and Musar Literature*. Jerusalem: Bialik Institute, 1978.

———. *Between Ideology and Reality: Humility, Ayin, Self-Negation, and Devekut in Hasidic Thought*. [In Hebrew.] Jerusalem: Bialik Institute, 1994.

———. *Hasidic Leadership*. [In Hebrew.] Jerusalem: Bialik Institute, 1999.

———. "A Light That Does Not Illuminate." *Haaretz*, July 18, 2003.

Pines, Shlomo. "On the Term *Ruhaniyyut* and Its Origin, and on Judah Ha-Levi's Doctrine." [In Hebrew.] *Tarbiz* 57 (1988): 511–534.

Pinker, Steven. *The Stuff of Thought: Language as a Window into Human Nature*. New York: Viking, 2007.

Polanyi, Michael. *Personal Knowledge: Towards a Post-Critical Philosophy*. Chicago: University of Chicago Press, 1974.

Polen, Nehemia. "Derashah as Performative Exegesis." In *Midrash and the Exegetical Mind*, ed. Lieve Tuegels and Rivka Ulmer, 123–153. Piscataway, NJ: Gorgias Press, 2010.

———. "Hasidic *Derashah* as Illuminated Exegesis." In *The Value of the Particular: Lessons from Judaism and the Modern Jewish Experience; Festschrift for Steven T. Katz on the Occasion of His Seventieth Birthday*, ed. Michael Zank and Ingrid Anderson, 55–70. Leiden: Brill, 2015.

———. "*Niggun* as Spiritual Practice, with Special Focus on the Writings of Rabbi Kalonymos Shapiro, the Rebbe of Piaseczna." In *The Contemporary Uses of Hasidism*, ed. Shlomo Zuckier. New York and Jerusalem: Urim Press, forthcoming.

———. "Rebbetzins, Wonder-Children, and the Emergence of the Dynastic Principle in Hasidism." In *The Shtetl: New Evaluations*, ed. Steven T. Katz, 53–84. New York: New York University Press, 2007.

———. "The Spirit Among the Sages: *Seder Olam*, the End of Prophecy." In *It's Better to Hear the Rebuke of the Wise Than the Song of Fools*, ed. W. David Nelson and Rivka Ulmer, 83–94. Piscataway, NJ: Gorgias Press, 2015.

Porat, Oded. *The Works of Iyyun: Critical Editions*. [In Hebrew.] Los Angeles: Cherub Press, 2013.

Proudfoot, Wayne. *Religious Experience*. Berkeley: University of California Press, 1985.

Putnam, Hilary. "On Negative Theology." *Faith and Philosophy* 14, no. 4 (1997): 407–422.

Rapoport-Albert, Ada. "Confession in the Circle of Rabbi Nahman mi-Braslav." In *Hasidic Studies: Essays in History and Gender*, 161–198. Liverpool: Littman Library of Jewish Civilization, 2018.

———. "God and the Zaddik as the Two Focal Points of Hasidic Worship." *History of Religions* 18, no. 4 (1979): 296–325.

———. "Hagiography with Footnotes: Edifying Tales and the Writing of History in Hasidism." *History and Theory* 27, no. 4 (1988): 119–159.

———. "Hasidism After 1772: Structural Continuity and Change." In *Hasidism Reappraised*, ed. Ada Rapoport-Albert, 76–140. London: Littman Library of Jewish Civilization, 1997.

Reddy, Michael J. "The Conduit Metaphor: A Case of Frame Conflict in Our Language About Language." *Metaphor and Thought* 2 (1979): 164–201.

Reiner, Elhanan. "Wealth, Social Position, and the Study of Torah: The Status of the Kloyz in Eastern European Jewish Society in the Early Modern Period." [In Hebrew.] *Zion* 58, no. 3 (1993): 287–328.

Reiser, Daniel, and Ariel Evan Mayse. *Sefat Emet be-Sefat ha-Em*. [In Hebrew.] Jerusalem: Magnes Press, forthcoming.

Ricoeur, Paul. *The Rule of Metaphor: Multi-Disicplinary Studies in the Creation of Meaning in Language*. Toronto: Univeristy of Toronto Press, 1977.

Robinson, Chase F. "The Study of Islamic Historiography: A Progress Report." *Journal of the Royal Asiatic Society* 7, no. 2 (1997): 199–227.

Rosenberg, Shimon Gershon. "On Faith and Language According to the *Alter Rebbe* of Habad from the Perspective of Wittgenstein's Philosophy of Language." [In Hebrew.] In *Nehalekh be-Regesh*, ed. Zohar Maor and Shim'on Deitsh, 173–206. Efratah: Mekhon Kitvei ha-Rav Shagar, 2007.

Rosenzweig, Franz. *The Star of Redemption*. Trans. Barbara E. Galli. Madison: University of Wisconsin Press, 2005.

Rosman, Moshe. *Founder of Hasidism: A Quest for the Historical Baal Shem Tov.* 2nd rev. ed. Oxford: Littman Library of Jewish Civilization, 2013.

———. "Hebrew Sources on the Baal Shem Tov: Usability vs. Reliability." *Jewish History* 27 (2013): 153–169.

Roth, Norman. "Jewish Reactions to the *Arabiyya* and the Renaissance of Hebrew in Spain." *Journal of Semitic Studies* 28, no. 1 (1983): 63–84.

Rubin, Milka. "The Language of Creation or the Primordial Language: A Case of Cultural Polemics in Antiquity." *Journal of Jewish Studies* 49, no. 2 (1998): 306–333.

Ruderman, David. *Kabbalah, Magic, and Science: The Cultural Universe of a Sixteenth-Century Jewish Physician.* Cambridge, MA: Harvard University Press, 1988.

Sack, Bracha. "The Concept of Thought, Speech, and Action." [In Hebrew.] *Daat* 50–52 (2003): 221–241.

———. "The Influence of *Reshit Hokhmah* on the Teachings of the Maggid of Mezhirech." In *Hasidism Reappraised,* ed. Ada Rapoport-Albert, 251–257. London: Littman Library of Jewish Civilization, 1997.

———. *The Kabbalah of Rabbi Moses Cordovero.* [In Hebrew.] Jerusalem: Bialik Institute, 1995.

Sacks, Elias. *Moses Mendelssohn's Living Script: Philosophy, Practice, History, Judaism.* Bloomington: Indiana University Press, 2016.

Sagi, Abraham. *The Open Canon: On the Meaning of Halakhic Discourse.* London: Continuum, 2007.

Sagiv, Gadi. *Dynasty: The Chernobyl Hasidic Dynasty and Its Place in the History of Hasidism.* [In Hebrew.] Jerusalem: Zalman Shazar Center, 2014.

Sanders, Seth L. *The Invention of Hebrew.* Urbana: University of Illinois Press, 2009.

Saperstein, Marc. *Jewish Preaching, 1200–1800 (An Anthology).* New Haven: Yale University Press, 1989.

———. "The Sermon as Oral Performance." In *Transmitting Jewish Traditions: Orality, Textuality, and Cultural Diffusion,* ed. Yaakov Elman and Israel Gershoni, 248–277. New Haven: Yale University Press, 2000.

Sarfatti, Gad B. "The Language of the Patriarchs According to Nachmanides." [In Hebrew.] In *Studies in Ancient and Modern Hebrew in Honour of M. Z. Kaddari,* ed. Shimon Sharvit, 277–283. Ramat-Gan: Bar-Ilan University Press, 1999.

Savran, George. "Seeing Is Believing: On the Relative Priority of Visual and Verbal Perception of the Divine." *Biblical Interpretation* 17, no. 3 (2009): 320–361.

Schäfer, Peter. *The Hidden and Manifest God: Some Major Themes in Early Jewish Mysticism.* Trans. Aubrey Pomerance. Albany: State University of New York Press, 1992.

Schatz-Uffenheimer, Rivka. "Contemplative Prayer in Hasidism." In *Studies in Mysticism and Religion Presented to Gershom G. Scholem,* ed. Ephraim E. Urbach, R. J. Zwi Werblowsky, and Chaim Wirszubsk, 209–226. Jerusalem: Magnes Press, 1967.

———. *Ha-Hasidut ke-Mistikah.* Jerusalem: Magnes Press, 1968.

———. *Hasidism as Mysticism.* Trans. Jonathan Chipman. Princeton and Jerusalem: Princeton University Press and Magnes Press, 1993.

———. "The Messianic Element in Hasidic Thought: Is There an Historical Messianic Tone in the Hasidic Idea of Redemption?" [In Hebrew.] *Molad* 1 (1967): 105–111.

———. "Self-Redemption in Hasidic Thought." In *Types of Redemption: Contributions to the Themes of the Study-Conference Held at Jerusalem 14th to 19th July,* ed. R. J. Zwi Werblowsky and C. Jouco Bleeker, 207–212. Leiden: Brill, 1970.

Schechter, Solomon. "Safed in the Sixteenth Century: Appendix A." In *Studies in Judaism*, 2:292–301. Philadelphia: Jewish Publication Society, 1908.

Schleiermacher, Friedrich. *Hermeneutics: The Handwritten Manuscripts*. Trans. James Duke and Jack Forstman. Missoula, MT: Scholars Press and American Academy of Religion, 1978.

Schmidt, Leigh Eric. "The Making of Modern 'Mysticism.'" *Journal of the American Academy of Religion* 71, no. 2 (2003): 273–302.

Scholem, Gershom. "Chapters from the Work *Sulam ha-'Aliyah* by Rabbi Yehudah Albotini." *Kirjat Sepher* 22 (1945): 161–171 (Hebrew)

———. "*Devekut*, or Communion with God." In *The Messianic Idea in Judaism and Other Essays on Jewish Spirituality*, 214–222. New York: Schocken Books, 1995.

———. "The Idea of the Golem." In *On the Kabbalah and Its Symbolism*, trans. Ralph Manheim, 158–204. New York: Schocken Books, 1996.

———. "Iqvotav shel Gabirol ba-Kabbalah." In *Studies in Kabbalah*, ed. Joseph Ben-Shlomo and Moshe Idel, 39–66. Tel Aviv: Am Oved, 1998.

———. *Jewish Gnosticism, Merkabah Mysticism, and Talmudic Tradition*. New York: Jewish Theological Seminary of America, 1965.

———. *Major Trends in Jewish Mysticism*. New York: Schocken Books, 1995.

———. "Martin Buber's Interpretation of Hasidism." In *The Messianic Idea in Judaism and Other Essays on Jewish Spirituality*, 228–250. New York: Schocken Books, 1995.

———. "The Meaning of the Torah in Jewish Mysticism." In *On the Kabbalah and Its Symbolism*, trans. Ralph Manheim, 32–86. New York: Schocken Books, 1996.

———. "The Name of God and the Linguistic Theory of the Kabbala." *Diogenes* 79 (1972): 59–80.

———. "The Name of God and the Linguistic Theory of the Kabbala (Part 2)." *Diogenes* 80 (1972): 164–194.

———. "The Neutralization of the Messianic Element in Early Hasidism." In *The Messianic Idea in Judaism and Other Essays on Jewish Spirituality*, 176–202. New York: Schocken Books, 1995.

———. *Origins of the Kabbalah*. Ed. R. J. Zwi Werblowsky. Trans. Allan Arkush. Philadelphia: Jewish Publication Society, 1987.

———. "Religious Authority and Mysticism." In *On the Kabbalah and Its Symbolism*, trans. Ralph Manheim, 5–31. New York: Schocken Books, 1996.

———. "Revelation and Tradition as Religious Categories in Judaism." In *The Messianic Idea in Judaism and Other Essays on Jewish Spirituality*, 300–303. New York: Schocken Books, 1995.

———. *Sabbatai Sevi: The Mystical Messiah, 1626–1676*. Princeton: Princeton University Press, 1973.

———. "Thoughts About Our Language." In *On the Possibility of Jewish Mysticism in Our Time and Other Essays*, ed. Avraham Shapira, trans. Jonathan Chipman, 27–29. Philadelphia: Jewish Publication Society, 1997.

———. "Tradition and New Creation in the Ritual of the Kabbalists." In *On the Kabbalah and Its Symbolism*, trans. Ralph Manheim, 118–157. New York: Schocken Books, 1996.

———. "The Unconscious and the Concept *Kadmut ha-Sekhel* in Hasidic Literature." [In Hebrew.] In *The Latest Phase: Essays on Hasidism*, ed. David Assaf and Esther Liebes, 268–276. Jerusalem: Magnes Press, 2008.

Schopen, Gregory. "On the Absence of Urtexts and Otiose Ācāryas: Buildings, Books, and Lay Buddhist Ritual at Gilgit." *Écrire et transmettre en Inde classique* 23 (2009): 189–219.

Schremer, Adiel. "'[T]he[y] Did Not Read in the Sealed Book': Qumran Halakhic Revolution and the Emergence of Torah Study in Second Temple Judaism." In *Historical Perspectives: From the Hasmoneans to Bar Kokhba in Light of the Dead Sea Scrolls*, ed. David Goodlblatt, Avital Pinnick, and Daniel R. Schwartz, 105–126. Leiden: Brill, 2001.

Schwartz, Seth. "Language, Power, and Identity in Ancient Palestine." *Past and Present: A Journal of Historical Studies* 148 (1995): 3–47.

Scorch, Grit. *Moses Mendelssohns Sprachpolitik*. Berlin: De Gruyter, 2012.

Searle, John. *Minds, Brains, and Science*, Cambridge, MA: Harvard University Press, 1984.

Seidman, Naomi. *Faithful Renderings: Jewish-Christian Difference and the Politics of Translation*. Chicago: University of Chicago Press, 2006.

Seligman, Adam B., Robert, P. Weller, Michael J. Puett, and Bennett Simon. *Ritual and Its Consequences: An Essay on the Limits of Sincerity*. Oxford: Oxford University Press, 2008.

Sells, Michael. *Mystical Languages of Unsaying*. Chicago: University of Chicago Press, 1994.

Sendor, Mark Brian. "The Emergence of Provençal Kabbalah: Rabbi Isaac the Blind's Commentary on Sefer Yezirah." PhD diss., Harvard University, 1994.

Septimus, Bernard. "Isaac de Castellon: Poet, Kabbalist, Communal Combatant." *Jewish History* 22, no. 1-2 (2008): 53–80.

———. "Maimonides on Language." In *The Heritage of the Jews of Spain*, ed. Avivah Doron, 35–54. Tel Aviv: Ha-Mikhlalah, 1994.

Shatil, Sharron. "The Kabbalah of R. Israel Sarug: A Lurianic-Cordoverian Encounter." *Review of Rabbinic Judaism* 14, no. 2 (2011): 158–187.

Sheveka, Avi. "A Trace of the Tradition of Diplomatic Correspondence in Royal Psalms." *Journal of Semitic Studies* 50, no. 2 (2005): 297–320.

Shmeruk, Chone. "The Hasidic Movement and the 'Arendars.'" [In Hebrew.] *Zion* 35 (1970): 182–192.

Shohat, Raphael. "The Vilna Gaon's Commentary to *Mishnat Hasidim*: The *Mashal* and the *Nimshal* in Lurianic Works." [In Hebrew.] *Kabbalah* 3 (1998): 265–301.

Shonkoff, Sam Berrin. "Sacramental Existence: Embodiment in Martin Buber's Philosophical and Hasidic Writings." PhD diss., University of Chicago, 2018.

Shor, Avraham Avish. *Ketavim: Pirkei Toledah ve-Iyyun be-Mishnat Karlin-Stolin*. Jerusalem: 2018.

Sisman, Cengiz. *The Burden of Silence: Sabbatai Sevi and the Evolution of the Ottoman-Turkish Donmes*. New York: Oxford University Press, 2015.

Smith, Chani Haran. *Tuning the Soul: Music as a Spiritual Process in the Teachings of Rabbi Nahman of Bratzlav*. Boston: Brill, 2010.

Smith, Jonathan Z. *Imagining Religion: From Babylon to Jonestown*. Chicago: University of Chicago Press, 1982.

Socher, Abraham. *The Radical Enlightenment of Solomon Maimon: Judaism, Heresy, and Philosophy*. Stanford: Stanford University Press, 2006.

Soloveitchik, Haym. "Three Themes in the *Sefer Hasidim*." *AJS Review* 1 (1976): 312–325.

Sommer, Benjamin D. "Revelation at Sinai in the Hebrew Bible and in Jewish Theology." *Journal of Religion* 79, no. 3 (1999): 422–451.

Sorkin, David. *Moses Mendelssohn and the Religious Enlightenment*. Berkeley: University of California Press, 1996.

Sparling, Robert Alan. *Johann Georg Hamann and the Enlightenment Project*. Toronto: University of Toronto Press, 2011.

Spence, Jonathan. *The Memory Palace of Mateo Ricci*. New York: Viking, 1984.

Stampfer, Shaul. *Families, Rabbis, and Education: Traditional Jewish Society in Nineteenth-Century Eastern Europe.* Oxford: Littman Library of Jewish Civilization, 2010.

———. "How and Why Hasidism Spread." *Jewish History* 27, no. 2-4 (2013): 201–219.

Stern, David. *Parables in Midrash: Narrative and Exegesis in Rabbinic Literature.* Cambridge. MA: Harvard University Press, 1994.

———. "Rhetoric and Midrash: The Case of the Mashal." *Prooftexts* 1, no. 3 (1981): 261–291.

Stern, David G. *Wittgenstein on Mind and Language.* Oxford: Oxford University Press, 1996.

Stern, Eliyahu. *The Genius: Elijah of Vilna and the Making of Modern Judaism.* New Haven: Yale University Press, 2013.

Stern, S. M. "'The First in Thought Is the Last in Action': The History of a Saying Attributed to Aristotle." *Journal of Semitic Studies* 7, no. 2 (1962): 235–252.

Stillman, Avinoam J. "Transcendent God, Immanent Kabbalah: Avraham ha-Malakh's Theory of Hasidism." In *Be-Ron Yahad: Studies in Jewish Thought and Theology in Honor of Nehemia Polen,* ed. Ariel Evan Mayse and Arthur Green, 310–330. Boston: Academic Studies Press, 2019.

Swartz, Michael D. *Mystical Prayer in Ancient Judaism: An Analysis of Ma'aseh Merkavah.* Tübingen: J.C.B. Mohr, 1992.

———. *The Signifying Creator: Non-Textual Sources of Meaning in Ancient Judaism.* New York: New York University Press, 2012.

Talmage, Frank. "Apples of Gold: The Inner Meaning of Sacred Texts in Medieval Judaism." In *Jewish Spirituality,* vol. 1, *From the Bible Through the Middle Ages,* ed. Arthur Green, 313–355. New York: Crossroad, 1986.

Tannen, Deborah. "The Commingling of Orality and Literacy in Giving a Paper at a Scholarly Conference." *American Speech* 63, no. 1 (1998): 34–43.

Ta-Shma, Israel M. *Ha-Nigle She-Banistar: The Halachic Residue in the Zohar.* [In Hebrew.] Tel Aviv: Ha-Kibbutz ha-Me'uhad, 2001.

Taylor, Charles. *The Language Animal: The Full Shape of the Human Linguistic Capacity.* Cambridge, MA: Harvard University Press, 2016.

Terazakis, Katie. *The Immanent Word: The Turn to Language in German Philosophy, 1759–1801.* New York: Routledge, 2007.

Thomas, Rosalind. *Literacy and Orality in Ancient Greece.* Cambridge: Cambridge University Press, 1992.

Tirosh-Samuelson, Hava. *Between Worlds: The Life and Thought of Rabbi David ben Judah Messer Leon.* Albany: State University of New York, 1991.

Tishby, Isaiah. "The Holy One, Blessed Be He, Torah, and Israel Are All One: The Source of This Aphorism in Ramhal's Commentary to the *Idra Rabba.*" [In Hebrew.] *Kirjat Sepher* 50 (1974–1975): 480–492.

———. "The Messianic Idea and Messianic Trends in the Growth of Hasidism." [In Hebrew.] *Zion* 32 (1967): 1–45.

———. *Mishnat ha-Zohar.* 2 vols. Jerusalem: Mossad Bialik, 1949.

———. "Prayer and Devotion in the Zohar." In *Essential Papers on Kabbalah,* ed. Lawrence Fine, 341–399. New York: New York University Press, 1995.

———. *The Wisdom of the Zohar: An Anthology of Texts.* Trans. David Goldstein. 3 vols. Oxford: Littman Library of Jewish Civilization, 1989.

Turner, Denys. *The Darkness of God: Negativity in Christian Mysticism.* Cambridge: Cambridge University Press, 2011.

Turniansky, Chava. "Bi-Lingual Writings in Jewish Ashkenazic Society: Its Character." [In Hebrew.] *Proceedings of the World Congress of Jewish Studies* 4 (1980): 85–99.

———. "The Languages of the Jews of Eastern Europe: Hebrew and Yiddish." [In Hebrew.] *Polin* 7 (1994): 61–76.

———. "Oral and Written Sermons as Mediating between Canonical Culture and the Public." [In Hebrew.] In *Studies in the History of Popular Culture*, ed. B. Z. Kedar, 183–195. Jerusalem: Zalman Shazar Center, 1996.

Twersky, Isadore. *Introduction to the Code of Maimonides (Mishneh Torah)*. New Haven: Yale University Press, 1980.

———. "Religion and Law." In *Religion in a Religious Age*, ed. S. D. Goitein, 69–82. Cambridge: Association for Jewish Studies, 1974.

Underhill, Evelyn. *Mysticism: A Study in the Nature and Development of Man's Spiritual Consciousness*. London: Methuen, 1912.

Urbach, E. E. *The Sages—Their Concepts and Beliefs*. Trans. Israel Abrahams. Cambridge, MA: Harvard University Press, 1987.

Verman, Mark. *Books of Contemplation: Medieval Jewish Mystical Sources*. Albany: State University of New York Press, 1992.

Vick, Amiel. "Through Which All of Israel Can Ascend: On R. Shneur Zalman of Lyady's Composition of Nusah haAri." [In Hebrew.] Master's thesis, Hebrew University, 2012.

Wacks, Ron. "The *Yihud* in Speech in Hasidism." [In Hebrew.] *Daat* 57–59 (2006): 143–163.

Wansbrough, John E. *Quranic Studies: Sources and Methods of Scriptural Interpretation*. Oxford: Oxford University Press, 1977.

Wasserstrom, Steven M. *Religion After Religion: Gershom Scholem, Mircea Eliade, and Henry Corbin at Eranos*. Princeton: Princeton University Press, 1999.

Weiss, Joseph G. "The Authorship and Literary Unity of the *Darkhei Yesharim*." In *Studies in East European Jewish Mysticism and Hasidism*, ed. David Goldstein, 170–182. London: Littman Library of Jewish Civilization, 1997.

———. "The Beginnings of Hasidism." [In Hebrew.] In *Studies in Hasidism*, ed. Avraham Rubinstein, 122–181. Jerusalem: Zalman Shazar Center, 1977.

———. "The Great Maggid's Theory of Contemplative Magic." *Hebrew Union College Annual* 31 (1960): 137–147.

———. "Is the Hasidic Book *Kethoneth Passim* a Literary Forgery?" *Journal of Jewish Studies* 9 (1958): 81–83.

———. "The Kavvanoth of Prayer in Early Hasidism." In *Studies in East European Jewish Mysticism and Hasidism*, ed. David Goldstein, 99–105. London: Littman Library of Jewish Civilization, 1997.

———. "Mystical Hasidism and the Hasidism of Faith: A Typological Analysis." In *God's Voice from the Void: Old and New Studies in Bratslav Hasidism*, ed. Shaul Magid, 277–285. Albany: State University of New York Press, 2002.

———. "One of the Sayings of the Great Maggid." [In Hebrew.] *Zion* 20 (1955): 107–109.

———. *Studies in Braslav Hasidism*. [In Hebrew.] Jerusalem: Bialik Institute, 1974.

———. "Torah Study in Early Hasidism." In *Studies in East European Jewish Mysticism and Hasidism*, ed. David Goldstein, 56–68. London: Littman Library of Jewish Civilization, 1997.

———. "The *Via Passiva* in Early Hasidism." In *Studies in Eastern European Jewish Mysticism*, ed. David Goldstein, 69–94. London: Littman Library of Jewish Civilization, 1997.

Weiss, Roslyn. "Four Parables About *Peshat* as Parable." In *The Legacy of Maimonides: Religion, Reason, and Community*, ed. Yamin Levy and Shalom Carmy, 111–126. Brooklyn: Yashar Books, 2006.

Weiss, Tzahi. "The Reception of *Sefer Yetsirah* and Jewish Mysticism in the Early Middle Ages." *Jewish Quarterly Review* 103 (2013): 26–46.

———. *"Sefer Yeṣirah" and Its Contexts: Other Jewish Voices*. Philadelphia: University of Pennsylvania Press, 2018.

Werblowsky, R. J. Zwi. *Joseph Karo: Lawyer and Mystic*. Philadelphia: Jewish Publication Society, 1977.

———. "Mystical and Magical Contemplation: The Kabbalists in Sixteenth-Century Safed." *History of Religions* 1, no. 1 (1961): 9–36.

Werthmann, Tanja. "'Spirit to Spirit': The Imagery of the Kiss in the Zohar and Its Possible Sources." *Harvard Theological Review* 111, no. 4 (2018): 586–609.

Wilensky, Mordecai. "Hasidic Mitnaggedic Polemics in the Jewish Communities of Eastern Europe: The Hostile Phase." In *Essential Papers on Hasidism*, edited by Gershon D. Hundert, 244–271. New York: New York University Press, 1991.

———. *Hasidim and Mitnaggedim*. [In Hebrew.] 2 vols. Jerusalem: Bialik Institute, 1970.

Wilson, Edward O. *The Origins of Creativity*. New York: Liveright, 2017.

Wineman, Aryeh. *The Hasidic Parable*. Philadelphia: Jewish Publication Society, 2001.

———. "Parables and *Tsimtsum*." *Prooftexts* 16, no. 3 (1996): 293–300.

Winston, David. *Logos and Mystical Theology in Philo of Alexandria*. Cincinnati: Hebrew Union College Press, 1985.

Wiskind-Elper, Ora. *Hasidic Commentary on the Torah*. London: Littman Library of Jewish Civilization, 2018.

Wittgenstein, Ludwig. *Tractatus Logico-Philosophicus*. Trans. D. F. Pears and B. F. McGuinness. New York: Humanities Press, 1961.Wodziński, Marcin. *Haskalah and Hasidism in the Kingdom of Poland: A History of Conflict*. Trans. Sarah Cozens and Agnieszka Mirowska. Oxford: Littman Library of Jewish Civilization, 2005.

Wolfson, Elliot R. "Beautiful Maiden Without Eyes: *Peshat* and *Sod* in Zoharic Hermeneutics." In *The Midrashic Imagination: Jewish Exegesis, Thought, and History*, ed. Michael Fishbane, 155–203. Albany: State University of New York, 1993.

———. "Beyond the Spoken Word: Oral Tradition and Written Transmission in Medieval Jewish Mysticism." In *Transmitting Jewish Traditions: Orality, Textuality, and Cultural Diffusion*, ed. Yaakov Elman and Israel Gershoni, 166–224. New Haven: Yale University Press, 2000.

———. "Biblical Accentuation in a Mystical Key: Kabbalistic Interpretations of the *Te'amim*." *Journal of Jewish Music and Liturgy* 11 (1988–1989): 1–16.

———. "Biblical Accentuation in a Mystical Key: Kabbalistic Interpretations of the *Te'amim* (Part Two)." *Journal of Jewish Music and Liturgy* 12 (1989–1990): 1–13.

———. "The Body in the Text: A Kabbalistic Theory of Embodiment." *Jewish Quarterly Review* 95, no. 3 (2005): 479–500.

———. *Circle in the Square: Studies in the Use of Gender in Kabbalistic Symbolism*. Albany: State University of New York Press, 1995.

———. "Circumcision, Vision of God, and Textual Interpretation." In *Essential Papers on Kabbalah*, ed. Lawrence Fine, 495–524. New York: New York University Press, 1995.

———. *Giving Beyond the Gift: Apophasis and Overcoming Theomania*. New York: Fordham University Press, 2014.

———. "God, the Demiurge and the Intellect: On the Usage of the Word 'Kol' in Abraham Ibn Ezra." *Revue des études juives* 149, no. 1-3 (1990): 77–111.

———. "Hebraic and Hellenic Conceptions of Wisdom in Sefer ha-Bahir." *Poetics Today* 19, no. 1 (1998): 147–176.

———. "Iconicity of the Text: Reification of Torah and the Idolatrous Impulse of Zoharic Kabbalah." *Jewish Studies Quarterly* 11, no. 3 (2004): 215–242.

———. "The Image of Jacob Engraved upon the Throne: Further Reflection on the Esoteric Doctrine of the German Pietists." In *Along the Path: Studies in Kabbalistic Myth, Symbolism, and Hermeneutics*, 1–62. Albany: State University of New York Press, 1995.

———. "Immanuel Frommann's Commentary on Luke and the Christianizing of Kabbalah." In *Holy Dissent: Jewish and Christian Mystics in Eastern Europe*, ed. Glenn Dynner, 171–222. Detroit: Wayne State University Press, 2011.

———. *Language, Eros, Being: Kabbalistic Hermeneutics and Poetic Imagination*. New York: Fordham University Press, 2005.

———. "Letter Symbolism and Merkavah Imagery in the Zohar." In *Alei Shefer: Studies in the Literature of Jewish Thought Presented to Rabbi Dr. Alexandre Safran*, ed. Moshe Hallamish, 195–236. Ramat-Gan: Bar-Ilan University Press, 1990.

———. "Mystical Rationalization of the Commandments in *Sefer ha-Rimmon.*" *Hebrew Union College Annual* 58 (1988): 223–235.

———. "The Mystical Significance of Torah Study in German Pietism." *Jewish Quarterly Review* 84, no. 1 (1993): 43–78.

———. "Negative Theology and Positive Assertion in the Early Kabbalah." *Daat* 32–33 (1994): v-xxii.

———. *Through a Speculum That Shines: Vision and Imagination in Medieval Jewish Mysticism.* Princeton: Princeton Univeristy Press, 1994.

———. "*Via Negativa* in Maimonides and Its Impact on Thirteenth-Century Kabbalah." *Maimonidean Studies* 5 (2008): 393–442.

———. "Walking as a Sacred Duty: Theological Transformation of Social Reality in Early Hasidism." In *Hasidism Reappraised*, ed. Ada Rapoport-Albert, 180–207. London: Littman Library of Jewish Civilization, 1997.

———. "Weeping, Death, and Spiritual Ascent in Sixteenth-Century Jewish Mysticism." In *Death, Ecstasy, and Other Worldly Journeys*, ed. John J. Collins and Michael Fishbane, 209–247. Albany: State University of New York Press, 1995.

Wolfson, Harry Austryn. "Hallevi and Maimonides on Prophecy." *Jewish Quarterly Review* 32, no. 4 (1942): 60–119.

———. *Philo: Foundations of Religious Philosophy.* 2 vols. Cambridge, MA: Harvard University Press, 1947.

Yadin, Azzan. "The Hammer on the Rock: Polysemy and the School of Rabbi Ishmael." *Jewish Studies Quarterly* 10 (2003): 1–17.

Yifrach, Yehudah. "The Elevation of Foreign Thoughts in the Traditions of Israel Baal Shem Tov as Transmitted in the Works of His Students." [In Hebrew.] Master's thesis, Bar-Ilan University, 2007.

Yisraeli, Oded. "The Tree of Life and Its Roots—A History of a Kabalistic Symbol." In *A Garden Eastward in Eden: Traditions of Paradise; Changing Jewish Perspectives and Comparative Dimensions of Culture*, ed. Rachel Elior, 269–289. [In Hebrew.] Jerusalem: Magnes, 2010.

Zori, David. *Not in the Hands of Heaven: The Limits of Human Action in the Teachings of Early Hassidic Masters*. [In Hebrew.] Jerusalem: Magnes Press, 2016.

Zornberg, Avivah Gottlieb. *Bewilderments: Reflections on the Book of Numbers*. New York: Schocken Books, 2015.

Zucker, Shlomo. "An Early Hasidic Manuscript." [In Hebrew.] *Kirjat Sefer* 49 (1973–1974): 223–235.

Zwiep, Irene E. *Mother of Reason and Revelation: A Short History of Medieval Jewish Linguistic Thought*. Amsterdam: Brill, 1997.

Index

Acknowledgments

This project is driven by the power of language to speak infinities. It is with this in mind that I offer my gratitude, with the trust that the recipients hear the untold thankfulness and appreciation that hovers within these words.

Thanks begin with the faculty and staff of the Department of Near Eastern Languages and Civilizations at Harvard University, who shepherded me from the early moments of coursework to the advanced stages of writing. The majority of my research was carried out at the Scholem Collection of the National Library of Israel, and I thank its staff and patrons for their forbearance of my daily presence. My colleagues in the Department of Religious Studies at Stanford University, whose faculty I joined in 2017, have left an indelible mark of wisdom on this book. They continuously pushed me to examine my project with new eyes, getting at bigger questions and exploring the deeper issues driving it forward.

An earlier draft of *Speaking Infinities* was read by David Biale, Shaul Magid, Steven Zipperstein, Jane Shaw, Alexander Key, and Kelda Jamison as part of a manuscript review workshop sponsored by the Stanford Humanities Center. Their critical remarks fundamentally changed the trajectory of this book and improved it immeasurably. At the University of Pennsylvania Press, Jerome Singerman, and series editors Shaul Magid, Francesca Trivellato, and Steven Weitzman, have been encouraging and supportive. The learned and insightful comments of Eitan P. Fishbane and Jonathan Garb, who served as readers for the Press, greatly improved and deepened the argument of this book.

Across the years I have benefited enormously from conversations with friends and colleagues, both in Israel and the United States, including Elliot Wolfson, Michael Marmur, Daniel Abrams, Glenn Dynner, Daniel Reiser, Ebn Leader, Or N. Rose, Jonatan Meir, Benjamin Brown, Zvi Leshem, Elly Moseson, Amiel Vick, Uriel Gellman, Gadi Sagiv, Edward Breuer, Maoz

Kahana, Levi Cooper, Elli Stern, Tsippi Kauffman, Herzl Hefter, Dena Weiss, Joshua Ladon, and David Broniatowski. Tanya Luhrmann, Daniel Schifrin, and Rachel Bickel read the manuscript in part or in full, helping me polish the prose and uncover what I was really trying to say.

My wonderful students at Yeshivat Orayta, Hebrew College, and Stanford were a captive audience for many of the questions and texts central to this book; their questions and comments helped me to clarify my thinking and translate these ideas into more accessible terms. The Shalom Hartman Institute of Jerusalem was my intellectual residence for three important years, and I wish to thank this remarkable institution for its commitment to supporting the next generation of scholars. Menachem Lorberbaum, Melila Hellner-Eshed, and Yair Furstenburg, my teachers at the Institute, challenged and broadened my intellectual vision. I thank my friends from the *beit midrash* programs, many of whom have been my fellow travelers in this journey into the world of scholarship.

David Biale, my first guide in the world of Jewish studies, my undergraduate mentor, and eventually my friend, nurtured my interest in these issues and gave me a base of textual and analytical skills that laid the groundwork for this project. Bernard Septimus guided my education with a hand that is at once warm and rigorous, showing me how to bring together precise textual interpretation, scholarly creativity, and felicitous writing. Luis M. Girón-Negrón shared with me his expansive vision of mystical literature, and I have benefited much from his graduate seminars, his incisive comments, and the many delightful conversations we have shared over the years.

It was the opportunity to work with Arthur Green that brought me to Boston, and from our very first conversations it was clear that we shared an intuitive language of the spirit in addition to our love of Hasidism. Over the past decade he has raised me up by challenging, encouraging, and stretching me, and reading and rereading this work (and so many others) countless times, until we were both satisfied with the result. I look forward to many, many more years of working, writing, and thinking together.

It seems as if no words at all can express my gratitude toward the family who has made this journey possible. Together with the memory of my father, my mother has been a constant font of inspiration, friendship, and occasionally solace. She has carefully given me so much that was necessary for success in my quest, and has always done so in her own quiet and sublime way. Her voice was joined by that of my stepfather, Robert Bernstein, whose energy and attentiveness to my development have known no measure. My in-laws,

Nehemia Polen and Lauri Wolff, have been truly indefatigable in their encouragement, and at every stage of this project they have showered me with their wisdom and their interminable support. Their incredible warmth and generosity of spirit have carried me in moments of great frustration and darkness.

And to you Adina, my dearest friend and love of my life, I cannot even begin to offer thanks. Your patience, critical thinking, and insight have left their mark on this work in countless ways. I am no less grateful for the endless hours you spent ensuring that I was free to work on this project. I hope that our project of heart and soul is one that will bring joy and light to our beloved children, Ezra Elimelech Meir, Menahem Nahum Eliyahu, and Daniel Ohr Yisrael. Our family is the heart of all that I know and hold dear, and it brings me unspeakable joy to know that so many of our wondrous journeys have yet to unfold.